T0332774

Machine Learning for Societal Improvement, Modernization, and Progress

Vishnu S. Pendyala
San Jose State University, USA

A volume in the Advances in Human and Social Aspects of Technology (AHSAT) Book Series

Published in the United States of America by
    IGI Global
    Engineering Science Reference (an imprint of IGI Global)
    701 E. Chocolate Avenue
    Hershey PA, USA 17033
    Tel: 717-533-8845
    Fax: 717-533-8661
    E-mail: cust@igi-global.com
    Web site: http://www.igi-global.com

                      Library of Congress Cataloging-in-Publication Data

Names: Pendyala, Vishnu, 1968- editor.
Title: Machine learning for societal improvement, modernization, and
    progress / Vishnu Pendyala, editor.
Description: Hershey, PA : Engineering Science Reference, [2023] | Includes
    bibliographical references and index. | Summary: "'Machine learning for
    societal improvement, modernization, and progress' portrays the
    application of Machine Learning that is playing a prominent role in
    improving the quality of life and the progress of civilization. It
    focuses on not just Machine Learning, but its application to specific
    domains that are resulting in substantial global progress"-- Provided by
    publisher.
Identifiers: LCCN 2022008798 (print) | LCCN 2022008799 (ebook) | ISBN
    9781668440452 (h/c) | ISBN 9781668440469 (s/c) | ISBN 9781668440476
    (ebook)
Subjects: LCSH: Machine learning.
Classification: LCC Q325.5 .M32225 2023 (print) | LCC Q325.5 (ebook) |
    DDC 006.3/1--dc23/eng20220503
LC record available at https://lccn.loc.gov/2022008798
LC ebook record available at https://lccn.loc.gov/2022008799

This book is published in the IGI Global book series Advances in Human and Social Aspects of Technology (AHSAT)
(ISSN: 2328-1316; eISSN: 2328-1324)

British Cataloguing in Publication Data
A Cataloguing in Publication record for this book is available from the British Library.

All work contributed to this book is new, previously-unpublished material. The views expressed in this book are those of the
authors, but not necessarily of the publisher.

For electronic access to this publication, please contact: eresources@igi-global.com.

Advances in Human and Social Aspects of Technology (AHSAT) Book Series

Mehdi Khosrow-Pour, D.B.A.
Information Resources Management Association, USA

ISSN:2328-1316
EISSN:2328-1324

MISSION

In recent years, the societal impact of technology has been noted as we become increasingly more connected and are presented with more digital tools and devices. With the popularity of digital devices such as cell phones and tablets, it is crucial to consider the implications of our digital dependence and the presence of technology in our everyday lives.

The **Advances in Human and Social Aspects of Technology (AHSAT) Book Series** seeks to explore the ways in which society and human beings have been affected by technology and how the technological revolution has changed the way we conduct our lives as well as our behavior. The AHSAT book series aims to publish the most cutting-edge research on human behavior and interaction with technology and the ways in which the digital age is changing society.

COVERAGE

- Digital Identity
- Technology Adoption
- Cyber Behavior
- Computer-Mediated Communication
- Gender and Technology
- Technoself
- Human-Computer Interaction
- Cultural Influence of ICTs
- Information ethics
- Human Development and Technology

IGI Global is currently accepting manuscripts for publication within this series. To submit a proposal for a volume in this series, please contact our Acquisition Editors at Acquisitions@igi-global.com or visit: http://www.igi-global.com/publish/.

Titles in this Series

For a list of additional titles in this series, please visit: www.igi-global.com/book-series

701 East Chocolate Avenue, Hershey, PA 17033, USA
Tel: 717-533-8845 x100 • Fax: 717-533-8661
E-Mail: cust@igi-global.com • www.igi-global.com

To my mother, Smt. P. Vijaya Srinivas, who taught me ABCs and laid the foundations of learning in me for societal improvement, modernization, and progress.

Table of Contents

Detailed Table of Contents

    Vishnu S. Pendyala, San Jose State University, USA
    Saritha Podali, San Jose State University, USA

Among the most pressing issues in the world today is the impact of globalization and energy consumption on the environment. Despite the growing regulatory framework to prevent ecological degradation, sustainability continues to be a problem. Machine learning can help with the transition toward a net-zero carbon society. Substantial work has been done in this direction. Changing electrical systems, transportation, buildings, industry, and land use are all necessary to reduce greenhouse gas emissions. Considering the carbon footprint aspect of sustainability, this chapter provides a detailed overview of how machine learning can be applied to forge a path to ecological sustainability in each of these areas. The chapter highlights how various machine learning algorithms are used to increase the use of renewable energy, efficient transportation, and waste management systems to reduce the carbon footprint. The authors summarize the findings from the current research literature and conclude by providing a few future directions.

    Veysel Gökhan Aydin, Ondokuz Mayis University, Turkey
    Elif Bulut, Faculty of Economics and Administrative Sciences, Ondokuz Mayis University, Turkey

Average life expectancy may change among different regions within the same society as well as among countries. In this study, a multiple linear regression model and a support vector regression model were established by addressing some economic and social variables of the countries. The data of 32 countries for the years 2017 and 2018 was compiled within the scope of the study, and it was attempted to determine which model was better. The aim of this study is to compare the prediction performances of support vector regression and multiple linear regression analyses. Support vector regression analysis was applied by the use of radial basis functions, linear, polynomial, and sigmoid kernel functions. In addition, the multiple linear regression analysis method was also applied using the least squares method, and the results were compared. For the comparison of the results, error bound accuracy rates were calculated, and the comparison was made according to these rates. The predictions were also examined through graphical methods, and it was attempted to determine the best model.

Chapter 3

Savitesh Kushwaha, Postgraduate Institute of Medical Education and Research, Chandigarh, India
Rachana Srivastava, Postgraduate Institute of Medical Education and Research, Chandigarh, India
Harsh Vats, University of Delhi, India
Poonam Khanna, Postgraduate Institute of Medical Education and Research, Chandigarh, India

Machine learning approaches are utilized in healthcare for computational decision-making in cases where critical medical data analysis is required to identify hidden linkages or anomalies that are not evident to humans. Artificial intelligence (AI) tools can assess a wide range of health data; patient data from multi-omics methods; clinical, behavioural, environmental, pharmacological data; and data from the biomedical literature to respond to research issues that necessitate a big sample size on a difficult-to-reach population. In healthcare, digitising health data has eased the development of computational models and AI systems to extract insights from the data. This chapter initially addressed the prospectus of machine learning in public health with significant focus areas. The medical devices and equipment section contain device-based modelling approaches to various diseases. The chapter also includes brief details on chatbots, wearable technologies, drug distribution systems, vending machines, and text recognition from prescriptions and medicine boxes are addressed.

Chapter 4

Manaswini Pradhan, Fakir Mohan University, India
Ranjit Kumar Sahu, AIIMS, Bhubaneswar, India

Determining lung tumor level and reducing patient mortality is a challenging task. So, the identification of benign or malignant lung nodules requires efficient and accurate methods of lung nodule diagnosis. For achieving this aim, in this paper, an adaptive radial basis neural network (RBNN) is proposed. Initially, the texture features are extracted and the extracted features are fed to the classifier to classify a nodule as benign or malignant nodule. In addition, the radial basis neural network is enhanced by using red deer optimization algorithm, which is used for optimal parameter selection. The effectiveness of the proposed approach is calculated by using different evaluation metrics. The effectiveness of the classification performance is compared with existing algorithms.

Chapter 5

Jayesh Soni, Florida International University, USA

Cybersecurity attacks are rising both in rate and complexity over time. More development and constant improvement in defensive approaches are needed to secure the operational systems against such attacks. Several malicious attacks pose severe security threats to organizations and users in today's internet age. It is vital to train enhanced malware classification systems to capture the variation in the malware type that belongs to the same family type. In this chapter, the author addresses the malware detection issue using a learning-based approach. First, the author explains various machine learning and deep learning algorithms to solve the problem. Next, the author provides practical implementation by proposing a deep learning-based framework on the open-source benchmark dataset on API calls. The dataset contains API calls during normal and malware-infected processes. The proposed framework trains a hybrid model of convolution neural network followed by long short-term memory to have a high malware detection rate.

Chapter 6
Hammad Khawar, Baqai Medical University, Pakistan
Tariq Rahim Soomro, Institute of Business Management (IoBM), Karachi, Pakistan
Muhammad Ayoub Kamal, Institute of Business Management (IoBM), Karachi, Pakistan

The world's population is expanding, and people want to live in cities, making city administration a difficult task. Traditional cities, with their shared characteristics, will be unable to provide human demands. Machine learning (ML) techniques are being used to increase an application's understanding and capabilities as the volume of data received rises. Smart transportation is defined as an umbrella concept that describes route optimization, parking, street lighting, and infrastructure applications in this evaluation. The purpose of this research is to present a self-contained assessment of machine learning techniques and internet of things applications in intelligent transportation to provide a clear picture of the current state of circumstances. In this chapter, the authors attempt to explain several features of smart transportation in greater depth.

Chapter 7
Parul Saxena, Madhav Institute of Technology and Science, Gwalior, India
R. S. Jadon, Madhav Institute of Technology and Science, Gwalior, India

This chapter describes the semantic tagging of events in videos using an effective combination of machine learning and neural network. Hybrid neural network architecture is proposed to consider the object features generated for each video and combine them with the LSTM model running over the label. The entire system is highly efficient for training and learning as the training dataset is optimized by applying multiple machine learning techniques. Experiments were done on the KTH dataset. Results show that the approach used gives 97% accuracy for the KTH dataset.

Chapter 8
Basak Buluz Komecoglu, Gebze Technical University, Turkey
Burcu Yilmaz, Gebze Technical University, Turkey

It is a known fact that all of the events that people in the society are exposed to while continuing their lives have important effects on their quality of life. Events that have significant effects on a large part of the society are shared with the public through news texts. With a perspective that keeps up with the digital age, the problem of automatic detection and tracking of events in the news with natural language processing methods is discussed. An event-based news clustering approach is presented for data regimentation, which is necessary to extract meaningful information from news in the form of heaps in online environments. In this approach, it is aimed to increase clustering performance and speed by making use of named entities. Additionally, an event-based text clustering dataset was created by the researchers and brought to the literature. By using the B-cubed evaluation metric on this test dataset, which consists of 930 different event groups and has a total of 19,848 news, a solution to the event-based text clustering problem was provided with an F-score of over 85%.

Chapter 9

Yavuz Kömeçoğlu, Kodiks Bilişim, Turkey
Serdar Akyol, Kodiks Bilisim, Turkey
Fethi Su, Kodiks Bilisim, Turkey
Başak Buluz Kömeçoğlu, Gebze Technical University, Turkey

Print-oriented PDF documents are excellent at preserving the position of text and other objects but have difficulties in processing. Processable PDF documents will provide solutions to the unique needs of different sectors by paving the way for many innovations such as searching within documents, linking with different documents, or restructuring in a format that will increase the reading experience. In this chapter, a deep learning-based system design is presented that aims to export clean text content, separate all visual elements, and extract rich information from the content without losing the integrated structure of content types. While the F-RCNN model using the Detectron2 library was used to extract the layout, the cosine similarities between the wod2vec representations of the texts were used to identify the related clips, and the transformer language models were used to classify the clip type. The performance values on the 200-sample data set created by the researchers were determined as 1.87 WER and 2.11 CER in the headings and 0.22 WER and 0.21 CER in the paragraphs.

Chapter 10

Anupama Kumari, Indian Institute of Technology, Roorkee, India
Mukund Madhaw, Independent Researcher, India
Vishnu S. Pendyala, San Jose State University, USA

The formation of gas hydrates in the pipelines of oil, gas, chemical, and other industries has been a significant problem for many years because the formation of gas hydrates may block the pipelines. Hence, the knowledge of the phase equilibrium conditions of gas hydrate became necessary for the economic and safe working of oil, gas, chemical industries. Various thermodynamic approaches with various mathematical techniques are available for the prediction of formation conditions of gas hydrates. In this chapter, the authors have discussed the least square support vector machine and artificial neural network models for the prediction of stability conditions of gas hydrates and the use of genetic programming (GP) and genetic algorithm (GA) to develop a generalized correlation for predicting equilibrium conditions of gas hydrates.

Chapter 11

Ali Ayci, Ankara Yıldırım Beyazıt Universtiy, Turkey
Shivam Tyagi, Amazon, USA

Technological and commercial developments in the 21st century have increased the demands and expectations of consumers. Big data analysis and machine learning can play a critical role in establishing healthy communication. The insights obtained from big data analysis and ML models can help in making marketing communication more personalized and useful to customers. In this chapter, the authors present an exploratory analysis of the role of big data and ML in the marketing communication of enterprises. For this, Amazon, which provides big data analysis infrastructures to other businesses which are big data users, is being researched as a case study. This study is one of the first studies in the literature to examine the significance of big data and ML in marketing communication and investigate the obstacles encountered when using them. The insights presented in this chapter will help professionals in the marketing communication domain to better understand how they can utilize big data and ML models to make a significant impact on their customers and sales.

Preface

Machine Learning continues to be the mortar of modernization, driving innovation and progress of civilization. The prospects of Artificial Intelligence (AI) and its branch, Machine Learning (ML) that is increasingly becoming synonymous with it, are huge. Human intelligence and learning have millions of years of evolution behind it. Many human learning paradigms have not yet been considered in the 50 or 60 years that artificial intelligence has been in existence and that includes the long "AI winter". It can be said with some confidence that we have hardly scraped the full potential of artificial intelligence and its branch, machine learning. For many years to come, machine learning will continue to be a key economic driver and push the envelope of human civilization to unprecedented levels. Investments in research in AI/ML are bound to fetch amazing results for us, humans, the environment, and the universe in general.

A book showcasing the myriad applications of machine learning in diverse aspects of our lives and driving the progress of the civilization has been the need of the hour in the literature. This book helps fill that gap. In a language and notation that is not too difficult to follow, the chapters in this book explain the various applications in assorted areas ranging from the most essential environmental sustainability and healthcare to the esoteric gas hydrates formation and marketing communications. The book brings out varying perspectives from several authors on how machine learning is changing our lives directly or indirectly. The book can be appreciated by anyone with some knowledge of machine learning and technology in general. The book can serve as a recommended reading to graduate and undergraduate students of machine learning. The first chapter should serve as an inspiration to the students as it is jointly authored by my student, Saritha Podali and I and addresses an important problem.

We want to live. We want to live longer, healthier, safer, and enjoy the quality of our lives. Ecological sustainability is imperative for this. The book chapters start with this theme. The first chapter summarizes interesting and innovative ways machine learning has been used for the cause of ecological sustainability. The chapter answers five important research questions in this direction. It identifies the predominant areas of this problem domain where machine learning has and potentially can play an important role. The chapter describes some interesting predictions, correlations, and findings with respect to ecological sustainability as determined by applying machine learning. For instance, in 2018, researchers determined that Beijing's Ecological Footprint doubled between 1996 and 2015 and further predicted that it would triple by 2020.

How long are we going to live? The next chapter uses machine learning to address this question. Lifespan prediction is essentially a regression problem. Two important algorithms used for regression are support vector machines and linear models. The chapter briefly explains the theory underlying these algorithms and uses support vector regression and multiple linear regression to estimate lifespan using the data from 32 different countries collected over two years. The dataset includes ten features such as air pollution, per capita income, and number of hospital beds per 1000 residents. These are the independent variables and lifespan is the dependent variable. Using several evaluation metrics, the chapter concludes the superior performance of support vector regression in making this important prediction.

An important parameter that determines lifespan is healthcare. In the third chapter, researchers from Postgraduate Institute of Medical Education and Research (PGIMER), which is ranked second in India among the medical universities, along with another researcher from University of Delhi discuss how chatbots, wearables, and other implements in the healthcare domain are used in the context of machine learning to improve public health. The chapter details how machine learning is used for diverse aspects of healthcare such as disease surveillance, health promotion, nutritional epidemiology, and drug distribution. The chapter includes a focused discussion on COVID-19 stating how machine learning algorithms help in categorizing patients based on their risk for the disease and predict a patient's trajectory through the disease progression and recession.

The fourth chapter continues the journey into healthcare. Early detection of lung cancer is important for the recovery of the patient. Professors from Fakir Mohan University and the highest ranked medical institution in India, AIIMS detail how an adaptive radial basis neural network using the red deer optimization algorithm can be used for lung cancer tumour classification. The unique contributions are clearly brought out in the chapter and the performance, evaluated by multiple metrics is claimed to be superior to other approaches in the literature. When accepting the chapter proposal, I alerted the authors that a literature review shows that solutions to the problem already exist, therefore they should clearly bring out how their work is different and the value-add it brings. The authors were kind enough to oblige.

Cybercrime is a growing international problem threatening multiple entities including governments, corporate giants, and the common man. Malware, like other software, typically uses API calls to do its thing. The fifth chapter details an effective system to prevent cyberattacks. The system extracts relevant features from API call sequences using convolution neural networks (CNN). The features are then passed to Long Short-term Memory (LSTM) and dense layers to classify the API call sequence as malicious or benign. The topology used involves one million parameters that are determined in the process of training the model. The chapter also gives insights into the underlying machine learning concepts in case the reader is uninitiated or needs a refresher.

The transportation of the future will be smart and based on Internet of Things (IoT). The next chapter, titled "Machine Learning for Internet of Things-Based Smart Transportation Networks," surveys the landscape, presenting unique and interesting aspects of the use of Ant Colony Optimization algorithm, Genetic algorithm, and various commonly used machine learning algorithms in the multitude aspects of smart transportation based on IoT. Read inside about creating groups of routes using Markov Decision Process (MDP) over Vehicle-to-Vehicle (V2V) communication, finding car parking using Support vector Machines (SVM) and Markov Random Field (MRF), and smart traffic lighting system using LSTM (Long Short Term Memory).

In the chapter titled "Semantic Tagging of Events in Video Using HNN," the authors use Principal Component Analysis (PCA), a linear method to determine the important latent features of semantic objects in videos and feed them to a series of CNN and LSTM layers to identify the activity in the video frames, such as "running," "walking," and "boxing," with superlative accuracy. The authors also provide a link to their code. The next chapter transitions into detecting topics and tracking them across various news sources. This is done using several machine learning techniques and algorithms. Language models such as BERT are used for Named Entity Recognition and subsequent clustering using well-known density-based clustering algorithms like DBSCAN and OPTICS.

We all feel the need to get a quick summary from a long pdf file without having to go through the entire text word-by-word, picture-by-picture. Authors of "Deep Learning for Information Extraction From Digital Documents: An Innovative Approach to Automatic Parsing and Rich Text Extraction From PDF Files" use Faster-RCNN, Support Vector Machines, and BERT to do this summarized extraction for us. With the help of several figures and illustrations, they explain the process and present the impressive results. The next chapter explains how machine learning algorithms and genetic programming have been used in the prediction of the conditions for formation of gas hydrates. The chapter starts with the motivation and explains how the algorithms are used for the purpose, providing the underlying math.

The book concludes with a powerful analysis of the use of machine learning for marketing communications. The authors from Ankara Yıldırım Beyazıt University and Amazon use a case study of Amazon for their analysis. The chapter explains the intricate details of data collection, preprocessing, and analysis of text, image, and video data with illustrations. The case study includes details of Amazon Personalize (AP) as a marketing communications tool. The authors get the information for their analysis and case study by also interviewing experts from Amazon.

The 11 chapters are carefully chosen from a pool of 40 chapter proposals and 20 full chapters submitted from all over the world. The suggestions and comments from the reviews helped strengthen the manuscripts further. Some chapters had to go through multiple rounds of reviews, so much as to annoy the authors. I sincerely thank the authors for their patience and cooperation during the year-long exercise. This is my second edited book with the publisher, IGI Global and I look forward to a third. The entire team has been respectful and supportive all through the process. I gratefully acknowledge all their help. I am also happy to note that this book is already indexed by libraries of some top universities and in other countries as well, months before its release.

My two middle-schooler daughters, Kriti and Mahadyuti showed great interest in machine learning concepts that I used to teach them during the weekends, which motivated me to inspire them better through these scholarly activities. Thanks is due to my employer, San Jose State University for the encouragement they give to faculty authors like me – one of the reasons why I switched over to academia from the well-paying industry. My sister, Krishna Pendyala who is a professor has been a great advisor in matters relating to the academia. My father wished that both his children attain the highest level of education and become professors, something that served as a motivation to both of us. He died when both of us were teenagers, much before his dream came true. Finally, thanks to you, all the readers who are the main reason for me to continue to contribute to the growing literature.

Vishnu S. Pendyala
San Jose State University, USA

Acknowledgment

The book has been in the works for more than a year. The accomplishment would not have been possible without the excellent cooperation of all involved. The editor specifically thanks the following subject matter experts for their timely reviews of the chapters. Special shoutout to Dr. Weiwei Jiang, Assistant Professor, Beijing University of Posts and Telecommunications, China for his particularly prompt and helpful reviews.

Reviewers (in alphabetical order)

Ahmed Marouf, (PhD), University of Calgary, Alberta, Canada
https://www.linkedin.com/in/ahmed-al-marouf/

Hari Mohan Rai, PhD, Dronacharya Group of Institutions, India
https://scholar.google.co.in/citations?user=yhHryvEAAAAJ&hl=en

Hasna Njah, PhD, University of Gabes, Gabes, Tunisia
https://orcid.org/0000-0002-0050-7173

Hemlata Goyal, PhD, Manipal University, Jaipur, India
https://scholar.google.com/citations?user=E7gGCM4AAAAJ&hl=en

Jayesh Soni, (PhD), Florida International University, USA
https://scholar.google.com/citations?user=vQbpsiMAAAAJ&hl=en

Kanaka Durga A, PhD, Stanley College of Engineering and Technology for Women, India
https://in.linkedin.com/in/dr-a-kanaka-durga-b2275b128

Kumar Abhishek, Expedia Group, USA
https://www.linkedin.com/in/kumarabhisheknitt/

Parul Saxena, PhD, Madhav Institute of Technology & Science, India
https://in.linkedin.com/in/parul-saxena-30641b171

Parvathi C, PhD, Don Bosco Institute of Technology, Bangalore

Acknowledgment

Priti Sajja, PhD, Sardar Patel University, India
http://pritisajja.info/

Shivam Tyagi, MTech, MS, Amazon, USA
https://www.linkedin.com/in/shivamtyagi18

Srinath Ravindran, PhD, Yahoo
https://research.yahoo.com/researchers/rsrinath

Varun Vala, Moody's Analytics
https://www.linkedin.com/in/varun-vala

Veysel Gökhan Aydin, (PhD), Ondokuz Mayıs University, Turkey
https://tr.linkedin.com/in/vgokhanaydin

Vinay Perni, University of Illinois at Urbana-Champaign, USA
https://www.linkedin.com/in/vinayperni

Weiwei Jiang, PhD, Beijing University of Posts and Telecommunications, China

Chapter 1
Machine Learning for Ecological Sustainability:
An Overview of Carbon Footprint Mitigation Strategies

Vishnu S. Pendyala

https://orcid.org/0000-0001-6494-7832
San Jose State University, USA

Saritha Podali
San Jose State University, USA

ABSTRACT

Among the most pressing issues in the world today is the impact of globalization and energy consumption on the environment. Despite the growing regulatory framework to prevent ecological degradation, sustainability continues to be a problem. Machine learning can help with the transition toward a net-zero carbon society. Substantial work has been done in this direction. Changing electrical systems, transportation, buildings, industry, and land use are all necessary to reduce greenhouse gas emissions. Considering the carbon footprint aspect of sustainability, this chapter provides a detailed overview of how machine learning can be applied to forge a path to ecological sustainability in each of these areas. The chapter highlights how various machine learning algorithms are used to increase the use of renewable energy, efficient transportation, and waste management systems to reduce the carbon footprint. The authors summarize the findings from the current research literature and conclude by providing a few future directions.

DOI: 10.4018/978-1-6684-4045-2.ch001

INTRODUCTION

Human existence is inextricably intertwined with nature. Ecology by its inherent trait supplies humanity with vast natural resources. It aids in the sustenance of the huge living population and compensates for the ecological imbalances that surface repeatedly. Due to the rising global population, the consumption of nature's wealth is ever-increasing. The surge in production of energy, food, goods, services, etc., to meet the demand and supply gaps has led to a colossal depletion of raw materials worldwide over the years. Overexploitation of the flora and fauna has endangered numerous species while putting several others in the high-risk category threatening the ecosystem's equilibrium.

A sustainability metric for measuring human impact on Earth's ecosystems called the *"Ecological Footprint"* was proposed in the early 1990s by two Ph.D. researchers at the University of British Columbia (Wackernagel & Rees, 1996). Considering the dependency of humanity on the biosphere, Ecological Footprint (EF) is defined as a measure of the area necessary to sustain any given population. In its broadest sense, it is a measure that incorporates all forms of water and energy use, infrastructure, forest management, and other material inputs required by humans to flourish day in and day out, as well as accounting for the land devoted to waste assimilation. Ecological Footprint per capita is one of the most widely recognized indicators of environmental sustainability. Human society becomes unsustainable when its Ecological Footprint surpasses its biocapacity. Considering the sustainability of natural resources becomes essential due to the burgeoning demands of the growing population. Ecological Footprint and sustainability are emerging research areas that have grabbed the attention of contemporary researchers and policymakers.

The carbon component of the Ecological Footprint, highlighted in red in Figure 1, is also an indication of the amount of forest land that will be required to absorb the Greenhouse Gas (GHG) emissions from the burning of fossil fuels. The carbon footprint measures the amount of greenhouse gas released due to the consumption of fossil fuels excluding the fraction absorbed by the oceans. The amount of greenhouse gas emitted into the atmosphere when fossil fuels are burned contributes directly to an ecological footprint. As more greenhouse gases are released into the atmosphere, there will be a need for more sea and forest areas to remove them. Lacking the requisite sea and forest areas will increase the carbon footprint. A larger carbon footprint implies a more substantial ecological footprint. In this chapter, we examine the use of Machine Learning to address the problem of increasing carbon footprint in the context of ecological footprints and sustainability.

Machine Learning (ML) is a progressive technology that has the potential to offer practical solutions for environmental sustainability. Machine Learning has much to offer in terms of monitoring, analyzing, and resolving sustainability issues. Even with exceptional advancements in the field, the area continues to have a lot of scope for improvement. The discipline's ever-expanding horizons still hold plenty of opportunities for solving challenging real-world problems. Artificial Intelligence (AI) and ML handle complex data, enabling data scientists to make accurate forecasts. These technologies can recommend comprehensive rational solutions that help in achieving sustainable development across the globe.

Prior research on Machine Learning applications in the sustainability domain is promising, and we believe that Machine Learning can support the development of culturally tailored organizational processes and individual responsibilities to cut down natural resources and energy consumption. We believe that ecological sustainability is the key to balancing the rising Ecological Footprint. Eventually, AI/ML will be highly valuable in contributing to environmental governance and not just limited to minimizing society's energy, water, and land usage intensities. In this survey, we study the applications of Machine Learning to analyze and predict the impact of the Ecological Footprint and to strategize carbon footprint reduction.

Figure 1. Components of Ecological Footprint

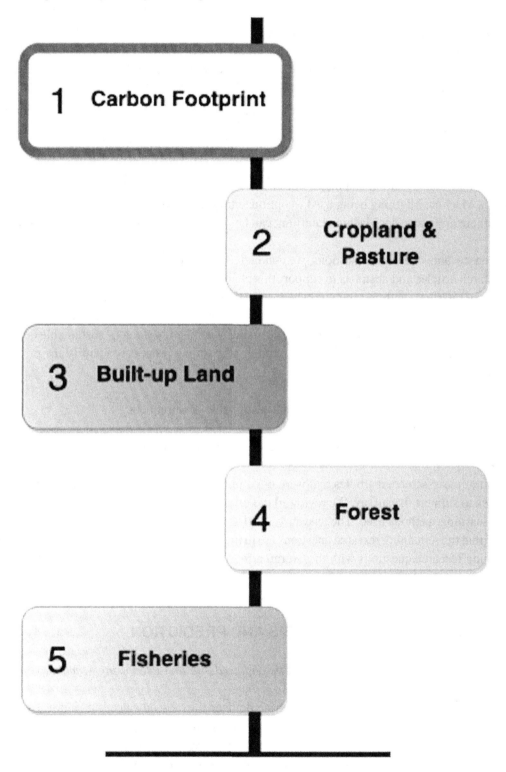

METHODOLOGY

We started by framing the following research questions:

RQ1: What are the important areas of ecological sustainability and social innovation that can take advantage of Machine Learning and related algorithms?

RQ2: Can the carbon or ecological footprint be analyzed and predicted using Machine Learning and statistical models?

RQ3: How can Machine Learning help at the production end, given that renewable energy is critical to sustainable progress?

RQ4: Given that transportation is a major domain at the ecological consumption end of the spectrum, how is Machine Learning being used to optimize transportation logistics?

RQ5: Are there any ways that Machine Learning can help with waste management to aid sustainability?

Based on the above research questions, we conducted a keyword-based search on Google Scholar to gather research articles and abstracts to support this chapter. Google Scholar can rank articles based on the number of citations, authors, and publishers and allows filtering by published year which allows us to find the latest research articles in this domain. Search terms include "ecological footprint using Machine Learning", "energy consumption forecasting using Machine Learning", "sustainable development using Machine Learning", etc. We then went through a screening process to identify the most relevant articles satisfying the criteria below:

- The theme of the paper must be directed at sustainable development
- The approach must be data-driven
- The approach to solving the sustainability problem must employ Machine Learning methods

Furthermore, we screened articles that were cited in the articles selected above as additional candidate articles to support the survey. We reviewed the articles to understand the problem domain and the Machine Learning methods used. The answer to RQ1 is too extensive to be detailed in this chapter but confirmed that the remaining research questions are in the right direction. Therefore, we are set to answer the remaining research questions with the overall aim to provide an overview of the usage of Machine Learning for sustainable development.

ECOLOGICAL FOOTPRINT ANALYSIS AND PREDICTION

RQ2: *Can the carbon or ecological footprint be analyzed and predicted using Machine Learning and statistical models?*

Environmental degradation and the climate crisis demand the most advanced and innovative strategies in an increasingly complex world. AI/ML will truly succeed when it can promote and facilitate environmental governance, not simply reduce energy, water, and land consumption (Nishant et al., 2020). **Table 1** shows a general review of Machine Learning models and statistical methods employed in analyzing and forecasting Ecological Footprint.

Table 1. Summary of Machine Learning/Statistical methods for ecological footprint

Application	Area Under Study	Years	Data	Machine Learning/ Statistical methods	Key Contributors	References
Ecological Footprint Prediction	Beijing, China	1996-2015	Data concerning retail sales, coal consumption, energy consumption, urbanization rate, population, GDP, the proportion of industries, total foreign trade	SVM BPNN	Construction Land	(Liu & Lei, 2018)
Ecological Footprint Analysis and Prediction	Tianjin, China	1994-2014	Data concerning energy consumption, urbanization rate, population, GDP, proportion of industries	ARIMA–BPNN	Population, Industrial Infrastructure	(Wu et al., 2019)
Ecological Footprint Analysis and Prediction	41 countries	1971-2014	Energy consumption data, Ecological Footprint data, and population data + Synthetic data using SMOGN algorithm	Correlation K-Nearest Neighbor regression Random Forest regression ANNs (ReLU, SPOCU)	Fossil Fuels	(Jankovic et al., 2021)
Environmental Performance and Global Convergence Analysis	188 countries and territories	1961-2016	cross-sectional time-series data on ecological indicators and socio-economic indicators	Panel Kernel Regularized Least Squares, Dynamic Bootstrap-corrected fixed-effects panel	Carbon Footprint, Population Density, Global Economic Development, International Trade, Economic Growth and Income Levels	(Sarkodie, 2021)

An urban Ecological Footprint prediction may emphasize the interdependency between the urban social economy and the natural environment, and serve as a data source for urban planning. The Ecological Footprint can exhibit dynamic and nonlinear characteristics depending on a combination of economic development, energy use, and population. Therefore, it is necessary to consider Machine Learning models that can handle non-linearity. Machine Learning has wide applicability in such complex nonlinear problems, providing deep insights, and high prediction accuracies that significantly reduce the labor, and mitigate the need for repetitive experimentation that may often result in unnecessary resource consumption (Roohi et al., 2020).

To determine the most suitable prediction model for Beijing's Ecological Footprint, researchers (Liu & Lei, 2018) compared two nonlinear models, Back Propagation Neural Network (BPNN) and Support Vector Machine (SVM). Their experiments concluded that the SVM performed better than BPNN. Support Vector Machines offer the potential to avoid not only the limitations of linear models but also the need to determine the nodes in backpropagation neural networks. Human involvement in the prediction process is thereby further reduced. Furthermore, SVM trains faster than BPNN over a shorter learning period. BPNN has the disadvantage of getting trapped in local minimums, which significantly slows the convergence rate.

Beijing's ecological footprint between 1996 and 2015 was calculated using Partial Least Squares (PLS) to identify 6 major indicators of ecological footprint changes – Gross domestic product (GDP), population, retail sales of consumer goods, industrial production, foreign trade, and energy consumption. PLS provides an evaluation metric called Variable Importance for Projection (VIP) that allows one to determine which variable between multiple independent variables with multicollinearity is most meaningful. Six of the indicators mentioned earlier had VIPs > 1. The BPNN's predictive accuracy has been compared with that of the SVM using six indicators as inputs and ecological footprint as output. Using this model, an ecological footprint forecast for Beijing in 2020 was established. In 2014, the relative error of the prediction and the actual value was 2% and 1%, and in 2015 it was 3% and 0.53%, respectively. The fact that the standard deviation of the SVM is close to zero indicates its higher stability and accuracy than that of the BPNN. According to the results, Beijing's Ecological Footprint doubled between 1996 and 2015. Additionally, the model predicted that Beijing's Ecological Footprint would triple by 2020 (Liu & Lei, 2018).

Societies rely heavily on energy as it aids in human sustainability. Carbon footprints make up a large part of the ecological footprint primarily because of energy consumption. Energy consumption and associated CO_2 emissions around the world have increased rapidly in the past few decades due to the rising population and living standards. As a result of a growing dependence on energy, there are significant costs to be considered. The processes involved in the generation, consumption, and disposal of energy have an enormous impact on the environment. According to data collected from multiple sources representing 41 countries from 1971 to 2014, the total Ecological Footprint of each country's energy consumption and the availability of fossil fuels correlated strongly (Jankovic et al., 2021).

To predict the Ecological Footprint of energy consumption, researchers (Jankovic et al., 2021) evaluated four hybrid Machine Learning models based on Bayesian parameter estimation. Among the models developed are K-nearest neighbor regression, Random Forest Regression (RFR), and two artificial neural networks (ANN) with different activation functions in hidden layers. The parameters of the model are crucial to how well it performs. In modeling Artificial Neural Networks, for example, selecting an appropriate number of hidden layers and hidden nodes is critical. This is because the incorrect choice of hidden layers or nodes will impact the model's generalization capability, resulting in overfitting or underfitting. Bayesian optimization can be used to achieve the best set of hyperparameters faster and better generalization performance on test sets. When choosing what hyperparameter is set to test next, it considers the combinations it has seen so far. **Table 2** shows the model parameters suggested by the parameter optimization technique and the resulting model performances. Among the three models, K-Nearest Neighbor regression had the lowest errors and fastest computation time. A further test with the Synthetic Minority Over-Sampling Technique for Regression with Gaussian Noise (SMOGN) generated data established that the model is effective (Jankovic et al., 2021).

Large portions of the global economy depend on conventional energy sources to fuel their productivity, so countries with limited fossil fuel reserves must import fuel from countries with abundant supplies. Consequently, environmental degradation is transferrable both directly and indirectly based on economic status. Upon closer examination, a study confirmed that the degree of environmental degradation is the same across nations under similar conditions regardless of income level.

According to their 56-year mean trends of biocapacity, ecological status, ecological and carbon footprint measurements compared with the worldwide average, China, India, Japan, Russia, and the United States have been identified as global Ecological Footprint hotspots. Global partnership is crucial for the achievement of environmental sustainability, as shown by this fact. Using Ecological Footprint and biocapacity as indicators, an empirical study (Sarkodie, 2021) analyzed the ecological performance of countries. Two estimation approaches derived from machine learning and econometrics were used for estimating environmental performance, Ecological Footprint, and carbon footprint.

Table 2. Hyper parameter optimization recommendations by Jankovic et al. using Bayesian Optimization algorithm and resulting model performance

Model	K-Nearest Neighbor regression	Random Forest regression	ANN ReLU	ANN SPOCU
Parameters	Number of neighbors = 2 Type of algorithm = brute p=1 Leaf size = 69	Number of estimators = 93 Bootstrap = False Minimum samples split = 2 Maximum depth = 33 Maximum features = sqrt	Batch Size = 256 Number of neurons = (120, 136) Number of hidden layers = 2 Dropout = 0.3	Batch Size = 32 Number of neurons = (14, 168) Number of hidden layers = 2 Dropout = 0.3
Results	MASE = 0.029 NRMSE = 0.006 MAPE = 5.136 SMAPE = 5.214 Training Time = 0.129s Validation Time = 1.878s	MASE = 0.032 NRMSE = 0.007 MAPE = 5.688 SMAPE = 5.520 Training Time = 0.319s Validation Time = 3.322s	MASE = 0.064 NRMSE = 0.015 MAPE = 13.3794 SMAPE = 13.428 Training Time = 1.743s Validation Time = 7.767s	MASE = 0.089 NRMSE = 0.011 MAPE = 22.454 SMAPE = 18.311 Training Time = 5.743s Validation Time = 18.009s

Panel kernel regularized least squares and a dynamic bootstrap-corrected fixed-effects panel are the approaches. These were used to account for omitted variable bias, heterogeneous effects across countries, and misspecification errors. As a result of resource exploitation, environmental degradation is caused by economic development, as outlined in the scale effects hypothesis. Internationally, fossil fuels are transportable and are traded. Renewable energy sources, however, are localized, so there is no between-nation emission flow. Therefore, it may have policy implications for understanding how natural resources are depleted and how it contributes to environmental degradation. Technologies that harness renewable energy must be embraced at a global level. Their efficiency must also be improved to compete with fossil fuels, and clean and modern energy investments must be made (Sarkodie, 2021).

Using an Ecological Footprint approach to study Tianjin in China provides theoretical support and scientific evidence for sustainable urban growth. To forecast the state of sustainability and varying trends in the ecological parameters of Tianjin, the Autoregressive Integrated Moving Average – Back Propagation Neural Network (ARIMA–BPNN) model was used, resulting in solid policy recommendations. As the population increases, Ecological Footprint becomes an imperative issue. Hence, a population policy was recommended to promote population migration from primary and secondary industrial areas to the tertiary sector. Further, the introduction of regulations to control the expansion of energy-intensive industries was suggested to popularize the use of modern technology, and renewable energy, and reduce energy consumption. It is possible to influence the overall energy efficiency by optimizing the industrial structure and influencing the energy consumption structure (Wu et al., 2019).

Time series datasets tend to have both linear and nonlinear attributes. When ARIMA or BPNN are used exclusively, they do not adequately capture the attributes of time series, which can lead to biased results (Zhang, 2003). ARIMA, for example, assumes a linear time series, i.e., the future value of a variable is a linear function of the past observations and random errors. Therefore, it performs poorly with non-linear data. Although BPNN does a good job setting data with non-linearity, its forecasting performance is inferior to linear data (Marugán et al., 2018). In a hybrid ARIMA-BPNN model, the limitations of each method are overcome by the other, resulting in robust forecasts. Despite the ARIMA, BPNN, and hybrid models' ability to replicate real-world data's trajectory, the comparison of hybrid model results to ARIMA and BPNN showed a better fit to historical data. ARIMA-BPNN's RMSE and MAPE values were distinctly lower than those of ARIMA. The hybrid model showed a significant improvement in prediction performance compared to ARIMA or BPNN models alone (Wu et al., 2019).

SUSTAINABILITY

It is the consumers who demand and burn fossil fuels that drive the energy companies' production and supply. Consumption patterns in society are driven by lifestyle choices such as those that shape food, housing, mobility, consumer goods, and communication. All of these have interplay with each other causing unsustainable trends. Lifestyles need to change to ensure the transition to a low-carbon footprint. There is a need to understand the underlying lifestyle factors that contribute to carbon-intensive consumption patterns. While creating awareness among the population helps, the use of technology can aid in accomplishing sustainability goals more efficiently. Technology empowers humanity to maximize productivity while resulting in huge savings. The gains are many including optimal usage of resources, reduced operational costs, minimal waste production, reuse-reduce-recycle of waste generated, supervising, and tracking progress. AI/ML in particular can address sustainability effectively.

The raison d'être of the concept of sustainability is that the naturally available resources are limited in quantity. Therefore, resources must be used conservatively to satisfy the present requirements and as much as possible, preserved for future consumption. A society thrives when all parties that make up the community work toward the common goals of sustenance. The population must utilize resources judiciously, be socially accountable, and focus on the protection of the ecosystems through calculated expanding and implementing strategies for replenishing the used-up raw materials whenever possible. Taking the above steps becomes vital to restore ecological stability and save nature's assets for upcoming times. Understanding the short- and long-term benefits of adopting sustainable development practices becomes easier when humanity realizes the price they will need to pay for non-compliance. The world will exhaust fossil fuel reserves due to excessive usage, once abundant animal species may need to be classified as rare or extinct due to a decline in their number, food/water/air i.e., environmental toxicity are some adverse effects (not limited to) humans may have to deal with. The following sections examine various aspects of sustainability and how Machine Learning can help with each.

Renewable Energy

RQ3: *At the production end, given that renewable energy is critical to sustainable progress, how can Machine Learning help in this domain?*

For better sustainability, green energy must become the norm in the future. A growing number of developed countries are focusing on generating renewable energy. The energy industry has made enormous progress in the field of renewable energy. Nevertheless, the industry still faces a few challenges since we rely on sources that are out of our control. As depicted in Figure 2, AI and ML have the potential to turn the renewable energy industry into an industry of the future. Power companies can more effectively forecast, manage power grids, and schedule maintenance using AI.

Since 2013, IBM has been working with the US Department of Energy on ways to leverage Watson, its AI engine, for cleaner energy. Data about the weather and the atmosphere were gathered from about 1,600 locations across the United States to build the Machine Learning model. This model became more accurate over time at predicting power output. Today, over 150 companies use IBM's forecasting

Figure 2. Machine Learning applications in building smart energy, smart grids, and vehicle-to-grid technologies

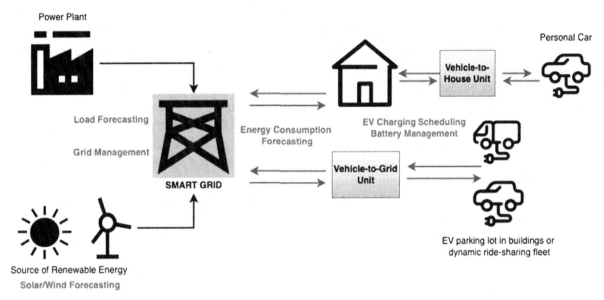

technology to predict solar and wind conditions for 15 mins to 30 days in advance (Environment - Solutions for Environmental Sustainability - 2013 IBM Corporate Responsibility Report, n.d.). Likewise, in 2018, DeepMind started applying Machine Learning algorithms to 700 MW of Google's wind power capacity in the central US. To give the readers an idea, 700 MW can power a medium-sized city. The neural network used historical turbine data and weather forecasts to predict wind power output 36 hours in advance (Machine Learning Can Boost the Value of Wind Energy, 2019).

Renewable energy is, without a doubt, the way of the future, but are they reliable? Resources like sunlight, wind, and water are crucial to the production of renewable energy. Resources such as these are dependent on the weather, which is out of human control. The predictive capabilities that Machine Learning offers can prove to be invaluable in this field. **Table 3** shows a review of Machine Learning models applied in this area. Existing literature suggests that given the stochastic nature of wind speed and solar irradiance, it is irrational to compare the superiority of one model over the other. Instead, it is crucial to evaluate what Machine Learning model is most appropriate under concerning conditions for forecasting energy generation.

Additionally, it is extremely important to evaluate a model's performance based on how well it can generalize for different climatic zones and times of the year. If the forecast is evaluated over only a few months with clear skies and low illuminance variability, it will not be clear how the algorithm performs in other highly variable months. The top-performing models for solar forecasting differ for clear- and all-sky conditions, making it more challenging to prescribe one model. The best approach is therefore to consider a family of models.

Research (Yagli et al., 2019) recommends the tree-based method family – Cubist (CUB), Extremely Randomized Trees (ERT), and Random Forest (RF) as a less risky choice because these algorithms consistently performed well in all climates and for all-sky scenarios. Under clear sky conditions, Multi-Layer Perceptron (MLP) and Support Vector Regression (SVR) families performed better than others. Besides model performance, it is also crucial to choose a model based on its training time because, in a real-time scenario, where there is a need to forecast on an hourly basis if the training time of the model exceeds an hour, the model becomes useless irrespective of its high prediction capabilities. Several methods such as Quantile Regression with ANN (ANNqr), ERT, Tree Models using Genetic Algorithms (EVTREE), and Gaussian Process with Polynomial Kernel (GPPoly) require more time than the one-hour limit making them inappropriate for one-hour-ahead forecasting under hourly rolling training (Yagli et al., 2019).

A wide range of Machine Learning models is constantly being revamped using hybridization and ensembles to improve computation complexity, functionality, robustness, and accuracy. Ensemble models have long been popular in classification and regression problems because of the ability to retain the bias of their learners while reducing their variance. In simple terms, in an ensemble learning process, even if one learning model predicts incorrectly, another learning model can rectify the mistake and offer a stable conclusion. Further, integrating the models with data processing approaches and optimization algorithms to develop several hybrid algorithms can aid in improving the forecasting models.

In wind energy forecasting, Support Vector Regression and Multilayer Perceptron are the most frequently used Machine Learning techniques. The emphasis is, however, on ensemble methods for forecasting wind and solar energy due to their variability. The input patterns for a study (Torres-Barrán et al., 2019) to predict wind energy were taken from the European Center for Medium Weather Forecasts (ECMWF) numerical weather prediction system (NWP). NWP forecasts are given for several weather variables at each point of a rectangular grid covering the study areas. Due to their large grids and a potentially substantial number of features at each grid point, these problems apply to Big Data research. Due to the hourly nature of renewable energy forecasts, an ML perspective will see a small sample size: even if a year has 8760 hours, NWP forecasts are produced every three hours, which results in 2920 patterns. This suggests that the pattern dimension becomes extremely large despite the modest sample size. These large dimensions become particularly relevant when working with regression trees. In practice, the splitting features are picked at random from a fraction of the dimensions. These are combinations between a grid point and a weather variable, and some combinations are more significant than others. Even though random feature selection is unaware of such properties, it can nonetheless produce subsets with disparate feature relevance.

Random Forest Regression, Gradient Boosting Regression (GBR), and Extreme Gradient Boosting (XGB) ensemble methods were compared with Support Vector Regression and Multi-Layer Perceptron models in this context and there was no clear winner. In predicting wind energy at the farm level, Random Forest regression and Extreme Gradient Boosting outperformed Support Vector Regression whereas Gradient Boosting Regression and Extreme Gradient Boosting were no better than Support Vector Regression for predicting wind energy in peninsular regions. Moreover, Gradient Boosting Regression and Extreme Gradient Boosting performed better for solar radiation predictions compared to Support Vector Regression and Random Forest regression. Multi-Layer Perceptron fell behind for all the use cases. This further emphasizes that several predictive approaches may need to be employed for forecasting purposes and to keep a close eye on their performances (Torres-Barrán et al., 2019).

EnsemLSTM employs a nonlinear learning ensemble technique using Long Short-Term Memory (LSTM), Support Vector Regression Machine, and External Optimization (EO) for the prediction of wind speed, which is vital for obtaining the most power from wind turbines. Compared to other extremely popular prediction models, such as ARIMA, Support Vector Regression, Artificial Neural Network, KNN, and Gradient Boosting Regression Trees, the EnsemLSTM achieved better forecasting results with minimal values for evaluation metrics, MAE, RMSE, and MAPE and maximum R (Correlation coefficient) values. In addition, the external optimization of the nonlinear-learning top-layer of the Support Vector Regression Machine is superior when compared to ANNLSTM, MeanLSTM, and single LSTMs (Chen et al., 2018).

Machine Learning has also been used to predict energy load patterns by understanding consumer behavior for efficient and effective grid management. Sustainable energy systems must manage their grids effectively. Anticipating the amount of energy that may be needed soon ranging from the next hour to the upcoming weeks is crucial for power companies. Keeping track of this can help them manage their grids effectively to minimize outages. Increasing energy production will be necessary if consumption is predicted to be high. Alternatively, they may choose to reduce production during periods of low energy demand. For gathering data, energy providers install smart meters that periodically send usage information. Individuals and communities consume in diverse ways, so gathering the necessary data is essential to predicting and managing loads.

With data-driven predictive capabilities integrated into smart grids, countries will be able to rely more effectively on renewable energy and avoid dealing with solar and wind energy irregularities. For real-time energy consumption data, hybrid models are recommended. Normally, these models offer much higher precision than single models or even ensembles. This is because they can incorporate the advantages of and compensate for the deficiencies of individual models and optimize algorithms to improve prediction accuracy. Hybrid models, however, require a deep understanding of individual models and techniques to optimize them for the desired outcome (Chou & Tran, 2018). A summary of the use of Machine Learning models for renewable energy applications is presented in Table 3. As can be seen, Machine Learning models played a significant role in this domain.

Table 3. Summary of Machine Learning Models used in literature for Renewable Energy applications

Application	Area Under Study	Years	Data	Machine Learning models	References
Solar Irradiance Forecasting	7 stations in 5 different climate zones in the continental United States	2013–2016	satellite-derived irradiance data	68 models evaluated, tree-based methods - CUB, ERT, and Random Forest found superior	(Yagli et al., 2019)
Solar Irradiance Forecasting	Sotaventos, Peninsular Spain	2011 - 2013	Numerical Weather Predictions	GBR and XGB	(Torres-Barrán et al., 2019)
Wind Energy Forecasting	Sotaventos, Peninsular Spain	2011 - 2013	Numerical Weather Predictions	SVR, MLP RFR, GBR, and XGB	(Torres-Barrán et al., 2019)
Wind Speed Forecasting	Wind farm in China	*10 min ahead forecasting:* Nov 23, 2012 - Nov 28, 2012 *1-hour ahead forecasting:* April 1, 2013, to April 30, 2013	*Short-term forecasting* - every 10 min wind speed data *1-hour ahead forecasting* - mean one-hour wind speed data	EnsemLSTM	(Chen et al., 2018)
Load Forecasting and Grid Management	Not specified	Four weeklong sliding windows	Real-time energy consumption data collected from the smart grid network	SARIMA-MetaFA-LSSVR and SARIMA-PSO-LSSVR (Hybrid Models)	(Chou & Tran, 2018)

Smart Transportation

RQ4: *Transportation being a major domain at the ecological consumption end of the spectrum, how is Machine Learning being used to optimize transportation logistics?*

Transport systems make up a web of interconnected systems that is crucial for the development and expansion of any society. Globally, a large amount of transportation occurs daily, but a lot of it is inefficient, causing unnecessary greenhouse gas emissions. Transportation sector emissions represent about a quarter of total CO_2 emissions (Global Warming of 1.5 °C, n.d.). Given a wide variety of vehicles on the road today, many require high fuel density which limits switching to low-carbon alternatives, making transportation an area that is exceedingly difficult to decarbonize. Reducing transportation and its frequency, improving vehicle efficiency, using alternative fuels, or switching to low-carbon modes of commute may contribute to mitigating greenhouse gas emissions from transportation.

Fortunately, as can be seen from Figure 3, Machine Learning has much to offer in each of these mitigation options. Machine Learning can enable intelligent infrastructure to build Smart Transportation Systems in cities. As Machine Learning solutions become more prevalent, they tend to recommend changes in planning, maintenance, and operations of transportation systems, and therefore, results become apparent over time. **Table 4** shows a few applications discussed for enabling Smart Transportation.

In smart transportation systems, traffic prediction is essential. Planning routes, directing dispatching, and alleviating traffic congestion is made easier with accurate traffic predictions. It can be challenging to solve this problem due to the complex and dynamic spatial-temporal relationships between different regions within the road network. There have been several traditional Machine Learning methods proposed for traffic prediction, including Support Vector Regression, Random Forest regression, and Multi-Layer Perceptron. In addition to processing high-dimensional data, these methods can capture non-linear relationships, both of which are complex. The Random Forest and Linear Regression models were effective when traffic patterns were almost linear; however, they had large RMSE values when traffic patterns abruptly changed.

In contrast, Support Vector Regression, and Artificial Neural Network (ANN) models such as Multi-Layer Perceptron were able to adapt to abrupt changes in speed. It was found that Linear Regression (LR) and Random Forest models are less accurate when speeds vary widely than Neural Network and Support Vector Regression models. For larger changes in the traffic flow, the Neural Network model had better predictability, while the Support Vector Regression model had better accuracy during shorter changes. As compared to the other three models, the Neural Network model had the most near-zero errors in its predictions. Both linear and non-linear patterns were handled by the Neural Network and Support Vector Regression models (Bratsas et al., 2019). Research efforts have advanced traffic prediction capabilities in recent years, particularly using deep learning methods. Deep Learning algorithms are a specific set of Machine Learning algorithms involving Artificial Neural Networks. A variety of architectures have been developed for handling large-scale, Spatio-temporal data (Yin et al., 2021).

Combining small shipments into vehicle loads is an efficient and frequent method of shipping since it concentrates large volumes onto a small number of transportation routes. This is commonly known as freight or shipment consolidation. As a result of freight consolidation, the number of trips is dramatically reduced resulting in decreased greenhouse gas emissions. Logistics providers and freight forwarders often decide how freight is consolidated and routed. This complex interaction of shipments, modes, origin-destination pairs and service requirements can be optimized using Machine Learning. For

Figure 3. A few strategies to reduce the carbon footprint from transportation using Machine Learning

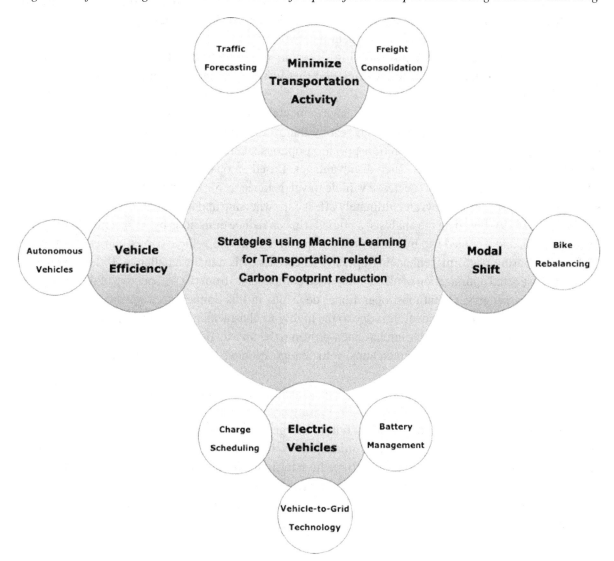

example, clustering algorithms can be used to group suppliers that are geographically close and ship to the same production sites.

Often, regenerative problems arise in shipping consolidation, where one decides how to strike a balance between shipping cost and delay. Upon arriving in a warehouse, orders are shipped sequentially to customers, so it is critical to keep track of all orders that need to be delivered to one location. In response to a new order, the warehouse decides whether to consolidate all incoming orders and ship them together or wait for additional orders. Research suggests that by learning the optimal actions directly from the input data without constructing explicit predictions of future inputs, it is possible to adapt to changes in the input distribution more effectively.

Using a model-based approach to solve the Markov Decision Process (MDP) exhibits high run-time complexity since every time a prediction is updated, a new MDP must be solved. Meanwhile, it should be noted that deep learning models such as Deep Reinforcement Learning (DRL) and Imitation Learning (IL) can adapt automatically to changes in input distribution as they learn policies directly from historical data and merely require an inference by neural networks at run-time (Jothimurugan et al., 2021). In contrast to DRL, imitation learning is useful in situations where it is easier to demonstrate the desired behavior rather than specifying a reward function that would generate the same behavior or directly learning the policy.

Ride-sharing companies can reduce their environmental impact dramatically by leveraging Machine Learning. Despite contradictory studies suggesting that ride-hailing services contribute to traffic congestion and air pollution, low-carbon transportation options such as pooled trips and electric vehicles can minimize - or even eliminate - such disadvantages. Based on observations from Hangzhou, China, pooled trips have the potential to decrease vehicle travel distance by 58,124 km per day, decrease vehicle usage by 3,061 vehicles per day, and ultimately affect car ownership and travel habits (Chen et al., 2021; Zheng et al., 2019). Based on the analysis, a pooled trip can reduce emissions by 33%, a ride-hailing trip by about 53%, and a pooled trip by about 68% compared to a private vehicle trip (Anair et al., 2020).

For ridesharing platforms, enhancing operational efficiency is a major challenge. Rider sharing requires sophisticated optimization of all the integrated components, from the perspective of the platforms, drivers, and passengers. Oftentimes, operational decisions in this domain are sequential and strongly spatially and temporally dependent. It is due to the highly stochastic nature of demand and supply in the domain. The use of RL in ridesharing has been proven to be an excellent method for solving optimization problems such as ride-sharing matchups, vehicle repositioning, ride-pooling, routing, and dynamic pricing (Qin et al., 2021).

These optimization procedures aim to resolve sequential decision-making problems in a stochastic environment with a long-term objective. A ride-sharing platform's decision system must make decisions for assigning available drivers to passengers within a large spatial decision-making region as well as for repositioning drivers who do not have any orders nearby. It is critical to note that these decisions affect revenue and driver availability in the short to medium term. In addition, they also affect the distribution of available drivers in the city over the long term. To guarantee that future orders are met efficiently, these distributions are crucial. Consequently, the problem has characteristics unique to reinforcement learning due to the exploration-exploitation dilemma and the delayed effects of assignment actions.

Table 4. Summary of Machine Learning Models used in literature for carbon footprint reduction from transportation

Application	Machine Learning models	References
Shared Mobility Optimization	Reinforcement Learning	(Qin et al., 2021)
Bike Rebalancing	GBM, LSTM, GRU, RF	(Regue & Recker, 2014, Wang & Kim, 2018)
Traffic Forecasting	ANN, SVR, RFR, MLP	(Bratsas et al., 2019, Yin et al., 2021)
Freight Consolidation	MDP, DRL, IL	(Jothimurugan et al., 2021)
EV Routing and Battery Management	MLR + NN	(Cauwer et al., 2017)
EV Energy Consumption Charge Scheduling	MLR, Transfer Learning	(Fukushima et al., 2018)
Vehicle-to-Grid Technology	Reinforcement Learning	(Vázquez-Canteli & Nagy, 2019)
Autonomous Vehicles	Reinforcement Learning	(Lee et al., 2020, Li & Görges, 2019)

Thanks to Machine Learning, self-driving cars are becoming a reality. Despite a great deal of uncertainty surrounding autonomous driving, the development of self-driving cars is currently one of the top trends in the world of AI and ML. There is evidence that energy emissions would be substantially lower in the future when shared autonomous vehicles (AV) are preferred to personal vehicles. Introducing fully automated self-driving cars may attract new customers, which could lead to more trips and vehicle miles traveled, resulting in higher energy consumption. Shared autonomous vehicles provide both a means of reducing traffic congestion and energy consumption while still maintaining the benefits of driverless driving and convenient point-to-point mobility (Ross & Guhathakurta, 2017). It is reasonable to say that autonomous vehicles are considered the future of transportation and most vehicle manufacturers and ride-sharing companies are invested in this direction.

Considering the advent of autonomous vehicles, eco-driving research has become increasingly relevant. Optimization of the speed profile of the vehicle is a challenging problem. This requires consideration of a variety of factors, including the vehicle's energy consumption, the slope of the road, and the traffic and other drivers on the road. Optimizing the vehicle speed profile can be extremely helpful, as vehicle efficiency can be increased without requiring any changes to the vehicle hardware and the technology can be applied to any vehicle. As more vehicles can be operated without human drivers soon, devising an eco-driving strategy that optimizes the vehicle speed profile is of importance. Machine Learning algorithms in the self-driving car need to render the surrounding environment continuously and predict potential changes to that environment.

Reinforcement learning can be applied as a real-time controller by adapting to the environment as it learns through the interaction between the agent and the environment. Considering this fact, reinforcement learning is an excellent way to approach the eco-driving control problem, since it is based on the probabilistic approach to finding the optimum solution when faced with a variety of complex environments. There has been research on the effect of reinforcement learning on eco-driving. To improve eco-driving, researchers developed a model-based reinforcement learning algorithm. This algorithm separates vehicle energy consumption estimation from driving environment estimation. Reinforcement learning involves domain knowledge of vehicle dynamics and powertrain systems while retaining model-free properties by updating the approximation model through experience replay.

To compare the proposed algorithm with dynamic programming (DP) and conventional cruise control, the researchers performed a vehicle simulation. Simulation results showed that the speed profile optimized using model-based reinforcement learning had similar performance characteristics to the global solution which was obtained via dynamic programming and was more energy-efficient than cruise control, which proved the strength and feasibility of this approach. As compared to cruise control, the proposed algorithm saved 1.2% - 3.0% in terms of energy (Lee et al., 2020). A multi-objective deep Q-learning approach was used in another study to arrive at the best route to minimize fuel consumption and traveling time for the eco-routing problem (Li & Görges, 2019).

Electric Vehicles (EVs) are thought to be the primary aid to decarbonizing transportation, whether using batteries or hydrogen fuel cells or by electrifying roads and railways. In general, electric vehicles emit little greenhouse gas, depending however on the carbon intensity of the electricity they run on. EVs will become more popular as more people drive them, so it will be important to understand how they are used. Since EVs have a limited drive range, it is important to suggest rest areas along highways so that the vehicle does not run out of battery power.

In-vehicle sensors and communication data now exist and offer a way to learn about the charging behavior of EV owners and to place charging stations more efficiently. An evaluation of EVs' energy consumption is imperative when determining the most suitable rest areas. Multiple Linear Regression (MLR) was applied to predict the energy consumption of EVs which resulted in high accuracy for existing EV models. It is difficult to forecast EV energy consumption accurately due to a lack of data. The study outlined a method for building a transfer learning model based on previous research to fill that gap (Fukushima et al., 2018).

Alternative solutions to the problem of the limited range are energy-efficient routes. To optimize EV routing, an energy consumption prediction method was developed based on a data-driven methodology. Using real-world measurement data, weather data, and geographical data from EVs, the proposed method combines Machine Learning and statistical methods. Global Positioning System (GPS) coordinates are used to link real-world driving, energy, weather, and geographical data to individual road segments by location. Multiple Linear Regression over the underlying physical attributes such as speed and acceleration, and an artificial neural network to account for external disturbances such as weather conditions and road characteristics on the speed profile are used for the estimation of energy consumption.

The regression model forecasts the energy consumption based on the predicted values for the microscopic driving parameters from the Neural Network, besides the measurable road and external parameters in addition to being computationally simple, the Multiple Linear Regression method allows for enhanced interpretability of the model due to the causal relationships embedded in the model. To assess the influence of individual parameters on energy consumption, trips were further segmented into shorter trips, to ensure the variances are captured in the data. It is necessary to allocate a cost for energy utilization to each segment of the road network to implement energy-efficient routing. Given the complex interactions between road characteristics, traffic situations, and drivers that are likely to have non-linear and interdependent relationships with speed and acceleration, Neural Networks were used. Neural Networks are powerful algorithms capable of predicting nonlinear, complex relationships through black-box function approximation (Cauwer et al., 2017).

Another topic of interest when considering EVs is Vehicle-to-Grid (V2G) technology which is shown in Figure 2. It allows plug-in electric vehicles to communicate with power grids and serve as power reserves for grids to draw from. Battery-powered electric vehicles can be used as energy storage during natural disasters or other emergencies when not in use. It is crucial to incorporate user feedback and consumption patterns into the demand response control loop in the future. It is possible to achieve this through reinforcement learning. Utilizing EVs in vehicle-to-grid technology has been explored using this approach (Vázquez-Canteli & Nagy, 2019).

Bike-sharing is an environmental-friendly and sustainable form of urban transportation. One of the biggest challenges in bike-sharing is the bike-rebalancing problem. By improving forecasts of bike demand and inventory, Machine Learning can assist bike-sharing companies with the rebalancing problem, where shared bikes accumulate in one area while being lacking in other areas. When Gradient Boosting Machine was applied to the Hubway Bike Sharing system in Boston for demand forecasting, it produced higher prediction accuracy when compared to Neural Network and Linear Regression. For the 20, 40, and 60-min predictions, GBM models without calibration performed 1.33%, 8.7%, and 13.27% better than the equivalent Neural Network models. Moreover, the results show that the same parameters - algorithmic and others, can be applied for every station, resulting in a faster computation process. While the Gradient Boosting Machine model has limited application in the transportation sector, it has been successfully used for forecasting traffic under abnormal conditions and enhancing the accuracy of real-time risk assessment (Regue & Recker, 2014).

Among the principal advantages of the Gradient Boosting Machine are that it is unlikely to be influenced by outliers and is robust to transformations in the explanatory variables. The decision tree internally selects the variables, making the algorithm robust enough to process irrelevant input variables, and it does not rely on imputed missing values. To counter overfitting in Gradient Boosting Machine, a variety of constraints or regularization methods can be utilized. In addition, when new data are acquired, Gradient Boosting Machine does not have to be retrained since the boosting process can be carried over from the previous model (Friedman, 2001). Also, recurrent neural networks (RNN) such as Long Short-Term Memory (LSTM) and Gated Recurrent Unit (GRU), and tree-based methods such as Random Forest have shown effectiveness in forecasting station-level availability of bike-sharing. Random Forest performed better for short-term forecasting, that is, when the time intervals were shorter (Wang & Kim, 2018).

Waste Management

RQ5: *Are there any ways that Machine Learning can help with waste management to aid sustainability?*

In addition to the amount of land and water resources required for the sustenance of an individual, the ecological footprint measures the ability of these resources to absorb waste products generated by their consumption. Carbon footprint is an important indicator of Greenhouse Gas (greenhouse gas) emissions (Wiedmann & Minx, 2008). Globally, landfills and waste are the biggest sources of greenhouse gas emissions. The decomposition of organic materials/waste releases greenhouse gas such as carbon dioxide and methane.

Additionally, the production of inorganic products and management of inorganic waste such as plastic consume enormous amounts of natural resources such as natural gas, oil, and coal. It leads to the emission of many pollutants and greenhouse gases. Waste management activities such as incineration and transportation add to the emission of greenhouse gas thus increasing the ecological footprint. As a result, more forest cover and natural water resources will be needed to absorb these toxic greenhouse gases. Consequently, more countries are embracing waste disposal, prevention, and recycling technology to improve waste management.

Waste management has been an ongoing research topic and there are multifarious publications on the usage of AI/ML in this area of research. AI/ML can be used to solve many Solid Waste Management (SWM) problems, such as forecasting waste characteristics, detecting of waste in bins, setting up process parameters, rerouting vehicles, and overall planning of waste management. Further, it has found its application in many areas of waste management. One such application scenario is the introduction of autonomous robots for sorting distinct types of waste using visual recognition capabilities. The other is to use Machine Learning for the prediction of waste generation to assess the availability of dust bins or dumping grounds. Yet another is to avoid food waste using dynamic pricing methodologies for about-to-expire products encouraging customers to buy them at discounted prices (Wasteless, n.d.). **Table 5** is a review of some of the Machine Learning methodologies used in literature for waste management applications.

Waste generation has been estimated by several Machine Learning Models on a national and municipal level. For instance, using 10-year daily collection data from the New York City Department of Sanitation, a research study was conducted with the objective of route optimization for waste collection trucks in dense urban environments besides waste generation predictions. The Machine Learning model, Gradient Boosting Regression Trees (GBRT) was applied to estimate weekly and daily waste generation at the building scale for over 750,000 residential properties in the City. Gradient Boosting Regression

Table 5. Summary of Machine Learning Models used in literature for Waste Management Applications

Application	Area Under Study	Years	Data	Machine Learning models	References
Waste Generation Estimation and Collection Truck Route Optimization	New York City	Over 10 years	individual building attributes, neighborhood socioeconomic characteristics, weather, and daily waste collection data	GBRT	(Kontokosta et al., 2018)
Plastic Waste Generation Estimation	Dhanbad, India	One week	Survey Questionnaire followed by waste sampling bags to sample households	ANN, SVM, and RF	(Kumar et al., 2018)
Waste Classification	Not specified	Not specified	TrashNet image dataset	ResNet-50 (CNN) (Transfer Learning)	(Adedeji & Wang, 2019
Recyclable Waste Classification	Not specified	Not specified	TrashNet image dataset	MobileNetV2 (CNN) (Transfer Learning)	(Ziouzios et al., 2020)
Compostable Waste Classification	Not specified	Not specified	TrashNet image dataset augmented with the addition of photos of food waste and landfill waste	CompostNet (CNN) (Transfer Learning)	(Frost et al., 2019)

Tree minimizes overfitting through hyperparameter tuning, and it can compensate for complex, nonlinear relationships between variables, which is a significant improvement over a simple linear model.

Additionally, Gradient Boosting Regression Trees are robust to outliers in the data and collinearity within features, unlike linear models. Gradient Boosting Regression Trees resulted in an R-squared value of 0.87 for waste generation prediction and the truck route validation use cases, the model resulted in 99.8% and 93.9% prediction accuracy, respectively (Kontokosta et al., 2018). In recent years, non-linear Machine Learning models have gained popularity due to their high prediction capabilities for complex problems, ability to work on non-linear data, and are free from any assumptions to be made. For instance, in linear models, a linear relationship is assumed between the dependent variable and the independent variables. On the contrary, as opposed to making assumptions, a non-linear model such as an artificial neural network learns the interactions between the independent variables through iteration.

Massive amounts of plastic are disposed of in landfills and in the ocean, where they take centuries to decompose. Hence, recycling all recyclable plastic is necessary to reduce landfills, preserve energy and conserve the environment. To make informed decisions, it is imperative to understand the sources of plastic waste generation, the rate at which it is generated, and how it can be recycled. Researchers at the Indian Institute of Technology used three non-linear methods - Artificial Neural Network, Support Vector Machine, and Random Forest to forecast different types of plastic waste generation. In this study, income, education, occupation, and type of house were used as independent variables, while the plastic waste generation rate was regarded as a dependent variable. Artificial Neural Network ($R^2 = 0.75$) was better than the Support Vector Machine ($R^2 = 0.74$) and Random Forest model ($R^2 = 0.66$) in predicting the outcome (Kumar et al., 2018).

Recycling is vital for a sustainable future. The process plays a significant role in our planet's economic and environmental wellbeing. Municipal Solid Waste (MSW) needs to be managed using sustainable recycling and waste reusing methods, according to researchers (Demirbas et al., 2016). As observed in (Krizhevsky et al., 2012), ever since the convolutional neural network (CNN) algorithm was successfully used to win the 2012 ImageNet large-scale visual recognition challenge (ILSVRC), many different CNN architectures have been developed in recent years, solving a variety of image classification problems. To separate different components of waste, ResNet-50, a CNN that is 50 layers deep, combined with Support Vector Machine was employed achieving an accuracy of 87% (Adedeji & Wang, 2019). This Machine Learning application has enormous potential to achieve a faster waste separation process and reduction of manual labor. Features extracted from a pre-trained ResNet-50 model were input to a multi-Class Support Vector Machine model. The SoftMax layer of the pre-trained model was replaced with Support Vector Machine as there is evidence of better performance with classification tasks (Tang, 2013).

Another study extended the waste classification problem to separate the recyclable contents from the waste using the MobileNet model, a convolutional neural network (CNN) that is 53 layers deep, and the model was trained on a TrashNet dataset created by researchers at Stanford University (Yang & Thung, 2016). MobileNetV2 is a recommendation by the Google Research team (Sandler et al., 2018). Data augmentation and hyperparameter tuning were applied to improve classification accuracy. Consequently, the model achieved an accuracy of 96.57%. The model confused glass for plastic and metal. The authors concluded that without the knowledge of weight and properties, humans would find it hard to distinguish them too (Ziouzios et al., 2020). Students at the University of California, Santa Cruz, developed an iPhone application to help users identify if their waste is recyclable. To maximize the efficiency of recycling, they designed and implemented CompostNet, CNN, which is believed to be the first of a kind as it can classify compostable waste as well. This study further emphasizes how transfer learning yields reliable results when there is not much data availability (Frost et al., 2019).

FUTURE RESEARCH DIRECTIONS

The purpose of the present research is to contribute to the literature on how to promote sustainability by reducing the ecological footprint and in particular, the carbon footprint. The following are some of the research directions that can be further pursued.

- A social and economic lockdown unprecedented in history occurred globally in the year 2020, owing to the COVID-19 outbreak. A comprehensive study of greenhouse gas emissions associated with energy consumption in the industrial, agricultural, tertiary, and residential sectors of the Italian economy and in the provinces of Italy has shown that a considerable reduction in carbon footprint has occurred from 2015-2019 by around 20%. The cause is believed to be the drastic reduction in natural gas, oil, and petroleum product consumption (Rugani & Caro, 2020). By extending these studies to assess the impact of COVID-19-related lockdown on greenhouse gas emissions worldwide, relevant information might be gained regarding potential climate implications. This could be a key to future opportunities to mitigate greenhouse gas emissions. In addition, the pandemic situation has also presented a unique chance to evaluate and calibrate energy production and consumption models to help countries meet their sustainability goals, which may be pursued as a future research topic.
- We focused solely on the carbon part of the ecological footprint in this chapter. The carbon footprint was surveyed in the areas of renewable energy, transportation, and waste management. Food

consumption is another major driver of carbon footprints (Ivanova et al., 2016), and Machine Learning can be used to advance sustainability in agriculture. Besides carbon footprint, food consumption could also have a large impact on other components of the ecosystem footprint - cropland, grazing land, fisheries, built-up land, and forested areas. It is reasonable to state that a future survey of the research literature should be in the direction of providing a more comprehensive overview of other mitigation strategies not covered in this chapter to aid ecological sustainability.

- The United Nations 2030 Sustainable Development Goals have become the subject of more research studies in recent years. Studies continue to use statistical methods for modeling Ecological Footprint from various perspectives to study how it is affected in different countries. Research that relates to Machine Learning applications for ecological footprints is limited. As researched in this paper, Deep Learning and Reinforcement Learning methods are being widely used due to their ability to handle complex, high-dimensional data that are highly dynamic and nonlinear in spatial-temporal environments. Factors affecting ecological footprint are a fitting example to which such methods can be applied with a certain degree of reliability. Future research in this direction may yield good results.

- Machine Learning models are energy-intensive and leave a large carbon footprint due to their computational demands. Despite efficiency improvements, GPUs are more power-demanding than their CPU predecessors and, as such, they consume more power resulting in a much higher environmental impact. Machine Learning, as a technology, can contribute to sustainable ecological development. However, we must set up Machine Learning procedures in ways that minimize the carbon footprint of the process. Otherwise, it may negate the benefits of Machine Learning for sustainable development. Research is already underway on model reusability, data collection and filtering, multi-objective optimization of hyperparameters, and other approaches that can potentially reduce the footprint of Machine Learning (Shterionov & Vanmassenhove, 2022). There is still quite some potential in this direction.

Akin to the way our brains work, Machine Learning can draw rapid inferences and solve problems using deep neural networks. Machine Learning algorithms, like human beings, learn from experience. Each new data point allows a Machine Learning algorithm to refine its inferences and predictions. For certain tasks, it is, however, much faster than humans at performing this process. Having the ability to predict needs and wants is a dream of every business owner and policymaker. Machine Learning models and appropriate data can help make this a reality. The ability to find patterns within patterns in data is the hallmark of deep learning which will help them make sense of complex consumption patterns. Today, it is imperative that the latest developments in AI and Machine Learning be leveraged to make confident predictions about their behavior. Researchers should continue to build on existing research in this area to fight ecological sustainability problems.

CONCLUSION

Environmental sustainability is far from assured, and societal decisions will play a significant role in determining it. The world is on a never-ending quest for energy and natural resources, and Machine Learning can help create a sustainable future. An integrated portfolio of approaches will be needed across policy, industry, and academia to encourage the application of Machine Learning to reduce footprints while also being aware of the impact of such applications that might contradict sustainability goals. With the rapid spread of Machine Learning and the increasing urgency of environmental degradation, society today is faced with a critical window of opportunity to shape Machine Learning's impact for decades to come.

As one of the most relevant indicators of sustainable development, studies on reducing ecological footprints have evolved over the years with technological innovations, research, and development planning. Sustainable development calls for low carbon emissions. Low carbon emissions are achieved through energy conservation and emissions reduction. Applying AI/ML to promote ecological sustainability by adopting low-carbon solutions will benefit society at large and help with making further advances in the field of AI/ML. Machine Learning has been critical in helping develop strategies across different domains to mitigate the carbon footprint problem. The greatest power of Machine Learning lies in its ability to learn from experience, compiling gigantic amounts of data from its environment, intuiting connections that humans miss, and recommending appropriate actions based on that knowledge. The world may not always become a better place because of Machine Learning and ethical issues will persist. But it can, if the technology is used properly, as we demonstrated in this chapter.

REFERENCES

Adedeji, O., & Wang, Z. (2019). intelligent Waste Classification System Using Deep Learning Convolutional Neural Network. *Procedia Manufacturing*, *35*, 607–612. doi:10.1016/j.promfg.2019.05.086

Anair, D., Martin, J., Pinto, M. C., & Goldman, J. (2020, February 25). *Ride-Hailing Climate Risks*. Union of Concerned Scientists. https://www.ucsusa.org/resources/ride-hailing-climate-risks

Bratsas, C., Grau, J. M. S., Koupidis, K., Giannakopoulos, K., Kaloudis, A., & Aifadopoulou, G. (2019, December). A Comparison of Machine Learning Methods for the Prediction of Traffic Speed in Urban Places. *Sustainability*, *12*(1), 142. doi:10.3390u12010142

Cauwer, C. D., Coosemans, T., Verbeke, W., Faid, S., & Mierlo, J. V. (2017). A Data-Driven Method for Energy Consumption Prediction and Energy-Efficient Routing of Electric Vehicles in Real-World Conditions. *Energies*, *10*(5), 608. doi:10.3390/en10050608

Chen, J., Zeng, G.-Q., Zhou, W., Du, W., & Lu, K.-D. (2018, June). Wind speed forecasting using nonlinear-learning ensemble of deep learning time series prediction and extremal optimization. *Energy Conversion and Management*, *165*, 681–695. doi:10.1016/j.enconman.2018.03.098

Chen, X., Zheng, H., Chen, X., & Wang, Z. (2021). Exploring impacts of on-demand ridesplitting on mobility via real-world ridesourcing data and questionnaires. *Transportation*, *48*(4), 1541–1561. doi:10.100711116-018-9916-1

Chou, J. S., & Tran, D.-S. (2018, December 5). Forecasting energy consumption time series using Machine Learning techniques based on usage patterns of residential householders. *Energy, 165*(B), 709-726. doi:10.1016/j.energy.2018.09.144

Demirbas, A., Alamoudı, R. H., Ahmad, W., & Sheıkh, M. H. (2016). Optimization of municipal solid waste (MSW) disposal in Saudi Arabia. *Energy Sources. Part A, Recovery, Utilization, and Environmental Effects*, *38*(13), 1929–1937. doi:10.1080/15567036.2015.1034385

Environment - Solutions for Environmental Sustainability - 2013 IBM Corporate Responsibility Report. (n.d.). *IBM*. Retrieved February 19, 2022, from https://www.ibm.com/ibm/responsibility/2013/environ-ment/solutions-for-environmental-sustainability.html

Friedman, J. H. (2001). Greedy Function Approximation: A Gradient Boosting Machine. *Annals of Statistics*, *29*(5), 1189–1232. doi:10.1214/aos/1013203451

Frost, S., Tor, B., Agrawal, R., & Forbes, G., A. (2019, October). CompostNet: An Image Classi-fier for Meal Waste. *IEEE Global Humanitarian Technology Conference (GHTC)*, 1-4. 10.1109/GHTC46095.2019.9033130

Fukushima, A., Yano, T., Imahara, S., Aisu, H., Shimokawa, Y., & Shibata, Y. (2018, August). Prediction of energy consumption for new electric vehicle models by Machine Learning. *IET Intelligent Transport Systems*, *12*(9), 1751–956X. doi:10.1049/iet-its.2018.5169

Global Warming of 1.5 °C. (n.d.). *IPCC*. Retrieved February 21, 2022, from https://www.ipcc.ch/sr15/

Ivanova, D., Konstantin, S., Kjartan, S., Wood, R., Vita, G., Tukker, A., & Hertwich, G. (2016). Envi-ronmental impact assessment of household consumption. *Journal of Industrial Ecology*, *20*(3), 26–536. doi:10.1111/jiec.12371

Jankovic, R., Štrbac, N., Mihajlović, I. N., & Amelio, A. (2021). Machine learning models for ecological footprint prediction based on energy parameters. *Neural Computing & Applications*, *33*(12), 7073–7087. Advance online publication. doi:10.100700521-020-05476-4

Jothimurugan, K., Andrews, M., Lee, J., & Maggi, L. (2021). *Learning Algorithms for Regenerative Stop-ping Problems with Applications to Shipping Consolidation in Logistics*. arXiv preprint. arXiv:2105.02318

Kontokosta, C. E., Hong, B., Johnson, N. E., & Starobin, D. (2018). Using Machine Learning and small area estimation to predict building-level municipal solid waste generation in cities. *Computers, Environ-ment and Urban Systems, 70*, 151-162. . doi:10.1016/j.compenvurbsys.2018.03.004

Krizhevsky, A., Sutskever, I., & Hinton, G. E. (2012). ImageNet Classification with Deep Convolutional Neural Networks. *ImageNet Classif. with Deep Convolutional Neural Networks*, 1097–1105. https://proceedings.neurips.cc/paper/2012/file/c399862d3b9d6b76c8436e924a68c45b-Paper.pdf

Kumar, A., Samadder, S. R., Kumar, N., & Singh, C. (2018, September). Estimation of the generation rate of different types of plastic wastes and possible revenue recovery from informal recycling. *Waste Management (New York, N.Y.)*, *79*, 781–790. doi:10.1016/j.wasman.2018.08.045 PMID:30343811

Lee, H., Kim, N., & Cha, S. W. (2020). Model-Based Reinforcement Learning for Eco-Driving Control of Electric Vehicles. *IEEE Access: Practical Innovations, Open Solutions*, *8*, 202886–202896. doi:10.1109/ACCESS.2020.3036719

Li, G., & Görges, D. (2019). Ecological adaptive cruise control for vehicles with step-gear transmission based on reinforcement learning. *IEEE Transactions on Intelligent Transportation Systems*, *21*(11), 4895–4905. doi:10.1109/TITS.2019.2947756

Liu, L., & Lei, Y. (2018). An accurate ecological footprint analysis and prediction for Beijing based onSVM model. *Ecological Informatics*, *44*, 33–42. doi:10.1016/j.ecoinf.2018.01.003

Machine learning can boost the value of wind energy. (2019, February 26). *DeepMind*. Retrieved February 19, 2022, from https://deepmind.com/blog/article/machine-learning-can-boost-value-wind-energy

Marugán, A. P., Márquez, F. P. G., Perez, J. M. P., & Ruiz-Hernández, D. (2018, October). A survey of artificial neural networks in wind energy systems. *Applied Energy*, *228*, 1822–1836. Advance online publication. doi:10.1016/j.apenergy.2018.07.084

Nishant, R., Kennedy, M., & Corbett, J. (2020, August). Artificial intelligence for sustainability: Challenges, opportunities, and a research agenda. *International Journal of Information Management*, *53*(102104), 102104. Advance online publication. doi:10.1016/j.ijinfomgt.2020.102104

Qin, Z. T., Zhu, H., & Ye, J. (2021). Reinforcement Learning for Ridesharing: A Survey. *2021 IEEE International Intelligent Transportation Systems Conference (ITSC)*, 2447-2454. 10.1109/ITSC48978.2021.9564924

Regue, R., & Recker, W. (2014, November). Proactive vehicle routing with inferred demand to solve the bikesharing rebalancing problem. *Transportation Research Part E, Logistics and Transportation Review*, *72*, 192–209. doi:10.1016/j.tre.2014.10.005

Roohi, R., Jafari, M., Jahantab, E., Aman, M. S., Moameri, M., & Zare, S. (2020). Application of artificial neural network model for the identification of the effect of municipal waste compost and biochar on phytoremediation of contaminated soils. *Journal of Geochemical Exploration*, *208*(106399), 106399. Advance online publication. doi:10.1016/j.gexplo.2019.106399

Ross, C., & Guhathakurta, S. (2017). Autonomous Vehicles and Energy Impacts: A Scenario Analysis. *Energy Procedia*, *143*, 47–52. doi:10.1016/j.egypro.2017.12.646

Rugani, B., & Caro, D. (2020). Impact of COVID-19 outbreak measures of lockdown on the Italian Carbon Footprint. *The Science of the Total Environment*, *737*(139806), 139806. Advance online publication. doi:10.1016/j.scitotenv.2020.139806 PMID:32492608

Sandler, M., Howard, A., Zhu, M., Zhmoginov, A., & Chen, L.-C. (2018). MobileNetV2: Inverted Residuals and Linear Bottlenecks. *The IEEE Conference on Computer Vision and Pattern Recognition (CVPR)*, 4510-4520. https://arxiv.org/abs/1801.04381

Sarkodie, S. A. (2021). Environmental performance, biocapacity, carbon & ecological footprint of nations: Drivers, trends and mitigation options. *Science of The Total Environment, 751*. doi:10.1016/j.scitotenv.2020.141912

Shterionov, D., & Vanmassenhove, E. (2022). *The Ecological Footprint of Neural Machine Translation Systems*. arXiv preprint. arXiv:2202.02170

Tang, Y. (2013). *Deep Learning using Linear Support Vector Machines*. arXiv preprint arXiv:1306.0239

Torres-Barrán, A., Alonso, Á., & Dorronsoro, J. R. (2019, January). Regression tree ensembles for wind energy and solar radiation prediction. *Neurocomputing, 326-327*, 151–160. doi:10.1016/j.neucom.2017.05.104

Vázquez-Canteli, J. R., & Nagy, Z. (2019, February). Reinforcement learning for demand response: A review of algorithms and modeling techniques. *Applied Energy, 235*(1), 1072–1089. doi:10.1016/j.apenergy.2018.11.002

Wackernagel, M., & Rees, W. (1996). *Our Ecological Footprint: Reducing Human Impact on the Earth.* New Society Publishers.

Wang, B., & Kim, I. (2018). Short-term prediction for bike-sharing service using Machine Learning. *Transportation Research Procedia, 34*, 171–178. doi:10.1016/j.trpro.2018.11.029

Wasteless. (n.d.). Retrieved February 6, 2022, from https://www.wasteless.com

Wu, M., Wei, Y., Lam, P. T. I., Liu, F., & Li, Y. (2019, November). Is urban development ecologically sustainable? Ecological footprint analysis and prediction based on a modified artificial neural network model: A case study of Tianjin in China. *Journal of Cleaner Production, 237*(117795), 117795. Advance online publication. doi:10.1016/j.jclepro.2019.117795

Yagli, G. M., Yang, D., & Srinivasan, D. (2019, May). Automatic hourly solar forecasting using Machine Learning models. *Renewable & Sustainable Energy Reviews, 105*, 487–498. doi:10.1016/j.rser.2019.02.006

Yang, M., & Thung, G. (2016). *Classification of Trash for Recyclability Status.* CS229 Project Report.

Yin, X., Wu, G., Wei, J., Shen, Y., Qi, H., & Yin, B. (2021). Deep learning on traffic prediction: Methods, analysis and future directions. *IEEE Transactions on Intelligent Transportation Systems.* https://arxiv.org/pdf/2004.08555.pdf

Zhang, P. G. (2003, January). Time series forecasting using a hybrid ARIMA and neural network model. *Neurocomputing, 50*, 159–175. doi:10.1016/S0925-2312(01)00702-0

Zheng, H., Chen, X., & Chen, X. M. (2019). How Does On-Demand Ridesplitting Influence Vehicle Use and Purchase Willingness? A Case Study in Hangzhou, China. *IEEE Intelligent Transportation Systems Magazine, 11*(3), 143–157. doi:10.1109/MITS.2019.2919503

Ziouzios, D., Tsiktsiris, D., Baras, N., & Dasygenis, M. (2020). A Distributed Architecture for Smart Recycling Using Machine Learning. *Future Internet, 12*(9), 141. doi:10.3390/fi12090141

LIST OF ABBREVIATIONS

AI/ML: - Artificial Intelligence/Machine Learning
ANN: - Artificial Neural Network
ANNqr: - Quantile Regression with ANN
ANN ReLU: - ANN Rectified Linear Unit
ANN SPOCU: - ANN Scaled Polynomial Constant Unit

ARIMA–BPNN: - Autoregressive Integrated Moving Average - Back Propagation Neural Network
AV: - Autonomous Vehicle
BPNN: - Back Propagation Neural Network
CNN: - Convolutional Neural Network
CUB: - Cubist
DP: - Dynamic Programming
DRL: - Deep Reinforcement Learning
ECMWF: - European Center for Medium Weather Forecasts
EF: - Ecological Footprint
ERT: - Extremely Randomized Trees
EV: - Electric Vehicle
EVTREE: - Tree Models using Genetic Algorithms
GBR: - Gradient Boosting Regression
GBRT: - Gradient Boosting Regression Tree
GDP: - Gross Domestic Product
GHG: - Green House Gas
GPPoly: - Gaussian Process with Polynomial Kernel
GPS: - Global Positioning System
GRU: - Gated Recurrent Unit
IL: - Imitation Learning
ILSVRC: - Image-Net Large-Scale Visual Recognition Challenge
KNN: - K-nearest neighbors
KNNReg: - K-nearest neighbors Regression
LR: - Logistic Regression
MASE: - Mean Absolute Scaled Error
MAPE: - Mean Absolute Percentage Error
MetaFA: - Metaheuristic Firefly Algorithm
MetaFA-LSSVR: - Metaheuristic Firefly Algorithm-based Least Squares Support Vector Regression
MDP: - Markov Decision Process
MLP: - Multi-Layer Perceptron
MLR: - Multiple Linear Regression
MSW: - Municipal Solid Waste
NRMSE: - Normalized Root-mean-squared Error
NWP: - Numerical Weather Prediction system
PLS: - Partial Least Squares
PSO: - Particle Swarm Optimization
NN: - Neural Network
RF: - Random Forest
RFR: - Random Forest Regression
RL: - Reinforcement Learning
RNN: - Recurrent Neural Network
SARIMA: - Seasonal Autoregressive Integrated Moving Average
SMAPE: - Symmetric Mean Absolute Percentage Error
SMOGN: - Synthetic Minority Over-Sampling Technique for Regression with Gaussian Noise

SVM: - Support Vector Machine
SVR: - Support Vector Regression
SWM: - Solid Waste Management
VIP: - Variable Importance for Projection
XGB: - Extreme Gradient Boosting

Chapter 2
Lifespan Prediction Using Socio-Economic Data Using Machine Learning

Veysel Gökhan Aydin

https://orcid.org/0000-0002-8121-745X

Ondokuz Mayis University, Turkey

Elif Bulut

https://orcid.org/0000-0001-8278-1821

Faculty of Economics and Administrative Sciences, Ondokuz Mayis University, Turkey

ABSTRACT

Average life expectancy may change among different regions within the same society as well as among countries. In this study, a multiple linear regression model and a support vector regression model were established by addressing some economic and social variables of the countries. The data of 32 countries for the years 2017 and 2018 was compiled within the scope of the study, and it was attempted to determine which model was better. The aim of this study is to compare the prediction performances of support vector regression and multiple linear regression analyses. Support vector regression analysis was applied by the use of radial basis functions, linear, polynomial, and sigmoid kernel functions. In addition, the multiple linear regression analysis method was also applied using the least squares method, and the results were compared. For the comparison of the results, error bound accuracy rates were calculated, and the comparison was made according to these rates. The predictions were also examined through graphical methods, and it was attempted to determine the best model.

DOI: 10.4018/978-1-6684-4045-2.ch002

INTRODUCTION

Regression analysis, in its most basic form, is a type of analysis used to determine whether or not there is a relationship between the dependent variable(s) and the independent variable(s), as well as the direction and strength of the relationship. Thus, the relationships among the variables are defined, and prediction is therefore able to be performed (Özdamar, 2013).

In the literature, there are numerous types of regression analysis. Regression analysis is able to get different names depending on the number of dependent and independent variables or on the structure of the data (Özdamar, 2013).

Today, there are different regression models using the more developed machine learning methods etc. as well as regression models using classical statistical methods. Along with the development of technology, new regression techniques that can perform much better predictions than the classic regression models have been developed and are continuing to be developed today.

Average life expectancy differs as per the countries' economic and social development levels. In general, while developed countries have a longer average life expectancy, less developed countries have a relatively shorter average life expectancy (Jetter, Laudage & Stadelmann, 2019). In particular, when it is accepted that economic growth directly affects the average life expectancy, the average life lengthens as economic growth increases. Similarly, economic growth means an increase in income level and an increase in development through investments in the domain of health. Variables such as the natural conditions of the geography in which people live, and their habits as well as economic growth can all have an impact on average life. It is known that air pollution and habits like consumption of tobacco products, alcohol etc. also have a negative effect on human health.

Average life expectancy may change among different regions within the same society as well as among countries. In this study, a multiple linear regression model and a support vector regression model were established by addressing some economic and social variables of the countries. The data of 32 countries for the years 2017 and 2018 was compiled within the scope of the study, and it was attempted to determine which model was better. There are similar studies with respect to average life, and examination was performed often by the use of a multiple linear regression model and less independent variables. The said studies were generally applied to smaller datasets.

A significant change in the average life expectancy of the countries is not expected within a year. On the other hand, some of the independent variables may cause significant change year after year. In this study, it was intended for the model to be more sensitive due to very small changes in the dependent variables in the face of the average change in independent variables in the models established by the compilation of the data over two years.

The main purpose of this study is to compare the prediction performances of support vector regression and multiple linear regression analyses. For this purpose, average life and socio-economic data for 2 years were compiled from the databases of The Organisation for Economic Co-operation and Development (OECD) and the World Bank. Support vector regression analysis was applied by the use of radial basis functions, linear, polynomial, and sigmoid kernel functions. In addition, the multiple linear regression analysis method was also applied using the least squares method, and the results were compared. For the comparison of the results, error bound accuracy rates were calculated, and the comparison was made according to these rates. The predictions were also examined through graphical methods, and it was attempted to determine the best model.

In the methods section, the mathematical backgrounds of the methods used in the research are explained. Support vector regression was studied using four different kernel structures. Eight different methods were used to compare the methods. The formulas of the comparison methods are stated in the relevant section. The source of the data, the number of observations and information about the variables are explained in the data description section. Afterwards, the findings obtained as a result of the research were examined. Descriptive statistics about the data set were shared and the analysis results were examined comparatively. The findings obtained in the conclusion and recommendations section were evaluated and suggestions were made for similar studies.

As a result of the research, it was seen that the support vector regression achieved more successful results than the multiple linear regression. The right statistical methods used in the right data structure, of course, give successful results. However, with the developing technology, machine learning methods give more successful results. When the results of the support vector regression in different kernel structures are examined, it is seen that choosing the method suitable for the data structure is extremely important in machine learning methods. In the data structure used in the research, the support vector regression in the "radial basis function" kernel structure gave the best result. Different kernel structures can achieve more successful results in a different data structure.

BACKGROUND

In the literature, it is possible to find similar studies in which both the support vector regression analysis and the average life expectancy variable were used. In the study, Parveen, Zaidi, and Danish (2017) used support vector machines, multiple linear regression, and artificial neural networks to predict the effects of input parameters on the adsorption capacity of CR (VI). When the comparative results were examined, they determined that support vector regression (SVR) was providing prediction with a lower error rate than artificial neural network (ANN) and multiple linear regression (MLR).

Mirowsky et al. (2000) tested the hypothesis about expecting of longer lives with higher socio-economics status on American adults. T test and ordinary least squares regression were chosen as statistical analysis. They found that achieved socio-economic status influence subjective life expectancy.

In their study, Shaw, Horrace, and Vogel (2005) examined the effect of medication consumption on life expectancy at middle and older ages. In the study performed using multiple linear regression analysis, independent variables relevant to lifestyle such as tobacco usage, medication consumption, and vegetable and fruit consumption were also used. It was determined that medication consumption had a positive effect on life expectancy at middle and older ages.

In their research, Guo, Lucas, and Ponsonby (2013) attempted to predict the vitamin-D status of participants using a model based on parameters derived from survey data. In their research, support vector regression and multiple linear regression analyses were used as methods. And as a result of the research, it was determined that the results of support vector regression analysis showed a higher correlation with real data compared to the results of multiple linear regression analysis applied using the radial basis function kernel.

Kavitha, Varuna, and Ramya (2016) separated the evaluation data of students compiled from the UCI data repository into education and testing and applied multiple linear regression analysis and support vector regression analysis. And from the results obtained, they observed that the support vector regression model operated faster and with a lower error rate.

In their study, Jiang, Luo, Xu, and Wang (2018) examined the effect of social development on life expectancy. A geographical weighted regression analysis method was used, and it was worked on 10 years of data. In the research, nine independent variables were used under the headings of health, education, environment, and social cohesion. As a result of the research, it was determined that developments in the domains of health and education may significantly improve life expectancy.

Ceylan (2019) evaluated in his study the potential of machine learning tools such as multiple linear regression, support vector regression, and Gaussian process regression for predicting the agricultural energy consumption of Turkey. Ceylan, who addressed the dataset as training and test data, determined that Gaussian process regression outperformed multiple linear regression and support vector regression in terms of prediction capacity.

In their study, Daş et al. (2019) formed wind power density prediction model of the regions using the data based on the measurements of Turkish State Meteorological Service with regard to wind energy potential in different regions of Turkey. In the formation of the model, they used the polynomial, normalized polynomial, radial basis function, and Pearson VII function kernel models of support vector regression, and determined that the best model among them belonged to the polynomial kernel.

Karacan et al. (2020) defined the variables influence the life expectancy at birth by using a decision tree analysis. They collected data from 166 countries for the year 2013 from the database of World Bank. The study findings showed that some of environmental, economic and demographic variables have significant effect in life expectancy.

In his article on life expectancy, Miladinov (2020) investigated the effects of socio-economic development on life expectancy in five EU accession candidate countries. He used regression model for the pooled cross-sectional time series. The study showed that the life expectancy at birth was largely affected by the population health and socio-economic development in the country.

In the study named "Machine Learning Techniques for Life Expectancy Prediction", Vydehi et al. (2020) proposed a machine learning model to predict the life expectancy of a person. They used a data set from Kaggle and applied various regression algorithms to predict life expectancy. They noticed that random forest regression gave the exact outcomes in prediction.

Bali et al. (2021) studied life expectancy according to educational, health, economic and social welfare services. Authors applied different machine learning algorithms and tried to obtain better accuracy to the features of the dataset. Random forest performed the best solution in their study.

Faisel et al. (2021) used World Health Organization (WHO) life expectancy dataset to determine which factors are statistically significant by evaluating multiple machine learning models. Random forest regression was noticed as the best model in prediction.

Socio-economic variation in life expectancy according to demographic variables was described by Ingleby and his friends (2021). They referred Poisson regression in the analysis of sample which was included the people living in England and Wales.

In his study, Kabir (2021) attempted to determine the socio-economic determinants of life expectancy for 91 developing countries by using multiple linear regression and probit regression. As a result of the research, it was determined that socio-economic variables such as per capita income, education, health expenditure, access to clean water, and urbanization cannot always be deemed effective in the determination of life expectancy.

In their study, Makridis et al. (2021) examined the contribution of demographic, socio-economic and geographic characteristics to guide the public health policies. They used machine learning to build predictive models. They noticed that socio-economic characteristics explain large differences in physical and overall well-being.

METHODS

Multiple Linear Regression Analysis

In the presence of two or more independent variables in the dataset discussed in the research, the mathematical notation of the relationship between the independent variables and the dependent variable is established using multiple linear regression analysis (Timm, 2002).

In the multiple linear regression analysis, there was one dependent variable (Y) and at least two independent variables ($X_1, X_2, X_3, ..., X_n$). The regression analysis examined the linear relationship between these independent variables and the dependent variable (Özdamar, 2013).

The matrix representation of the multiple linear regression analysis was as follows (Weisberg, 2005):

$$\begin{bmatrix} Y_1 \\ Y_2 \\ \vdots \\ Y_n \end{bmatrix} = \begin{bmatrix} 1 & X_{11} & \cdots & X_{p1} \\ 1 & X_{12} & \cdots & X_{p2} \\ \vdots & \vdots & \cdots & \vdots \\ 1 & X_{1n} & \cdots & X_{pn} \end{bmatrix} \begin{bmatrix} \beta_0 \\ \beta_1 \\ \vdots \\ \beta_p \end{bmatrix} + \begin{bmatrix} \varepsilon_1 \\ \varepsilon_2 \\ \vdots \\ \varepsilon_n \end{bmatrix}$$

In the multiple linear regression analysis, the linear model established for p units of explanatory/independent variables and n units of observations was expressed as follows:

$$Y_i = \beta_0 + \beta_1 X_{1i} + \beta_2 X_{2i} + ... + \beta_p X_{pi} + \varepsilon_i; \quad i=1,2,3,...,n$$

In this statement, β_ps are defined as regression coefficients, and ε is expressed as the error term in the model.

Nonlinear models are also frequently found in real-world data. In this case, linear models are able to be obtained by using appropriate conversions for nonlinear models. Cases such as being unable to obtain linear models as a result of the conversion are also possible. In such cases, nonlinear regression models should be preferred instead of multiple linear regression models (Parmaksız, 2019).

The least squares method is extensively used in multiple linear regression analysis. By the least squares method, it is attempted to minimize the sum of squares of the distances of real values to the least squares plane. The multiple linear regression equation for two independent variables and one dependent variable is expressed as follows (Rencher and Schaalje, 2007):

$$Y = \beta_0 + \beta_1 X_1 + \beta_2 X_2 + \varepsilon$$

For this equation, it is expected for the following expression of least squares plane to be minimum:

$$\sum \left(\varepsilon \right)^2 = \sum (Y - \Delta)^2 = \sum \left(Y - \hat{\beta}_0 - \hat{\beta}_1 X_1 - \hat{\beta}_2 X_2 \right)^2$$

For this reason, the value of the expression is made minimum by equalizing the equation to zero:

$$\sum \left(\varepsilon \right)^2 = \sum \left(Y - \hat{\beta}_0 - \hat{\beta}_1 X_1 - \hat{\beta}_2 X_2 \right)^2 = 0$$

Multiple linear regression analysis is used to obtain the equation of the relationship between the dependent variable and the independent variables. The correct definition of the relationship between the variables and the provision of consistent results by this equation depend on the obtainment of the assumptions of multiple linear regression analysis.

Assumptions of Multiple Linear Regression Analysis

The provision of consistent results, the correct definition of the relationship, and the provision of correct prospective predictions by the multiple linear regression analysis depend on the obtainment of the following assumptions (Franzo and Farmer, 2014);

- Normality assumption;
  Regression analysis assumes that the variables are normally distributed. Highly skewed or outliers can disrupt relationships and tests of significance.
- Linearity assumption;
  Standard multiple linear regression predicts the relationship between dependent variable and independent variables linearly due to the nature of the relationships. If the relationship between the independent variables and the dependent variable is not linear, the results of the regression analysis will not reflect the truth.
- Reliability assumption;
  An unreliable measurement in simple regression analysis increases the risk of Type II error. In the multiple linear regression analysis, the effect sizes of the variables can be overestimated.
- Homoscedasticity assumption;
  Homoscedasticity means that the variance of the unit values of the dependent variable remains constant while the unit values of the independent variables change. In case of heteroscedasticity, the findings can be severely impaired.

Support Vector Machines

Support vector machines (SVM) were initially introduced by Vapnik and Cortes in 1995. SVM are extensively used in many different domains. Face detection, text and hyperlink text classification, image classification, bioinformatics, protein crossing, remote homology determination, handwriting recognition, geology and environmental sciences, and generalized predictive control applications are some of these domains. Support vector machines were initially used extensively for the solution of classification problems, and then they have been developed as support vector regression for regression and time series prediction problems (Ceylan, 2019).

SVR, when compared with conventional learning methods, doesn't just minimize the empirical measurement error, but also uses the principle of structural risk minimization, which intends to minimize the upper limit of generalization error. By minimizing the structural risk, the SVR method shows successful generalization performance in test data by using the input and output relationships learned in the training process (Karal, 2018).

The advantages of the support vector machine approach may be expressed as follows (Tolun, 2008):

Support vector machines use the principle of structural risk minimization. For this reason, they attempt to establish a balance between empirical measurement error and the prevention of overfit.

It is a convex quadratic programming problem. Thus, there is no non-global minimum, and the problem may be solved by using quadratic programming techniques.

The classifiers obtained by the support vector machines may completely be determined by their own support vector types and kernel function types.

The learning method performs good generalizations even with relatively few data points in the training dataset, and the boundaries on the generalization error may be directly predicted in the training dataset.

Figure 1. Geometry of support vector machines

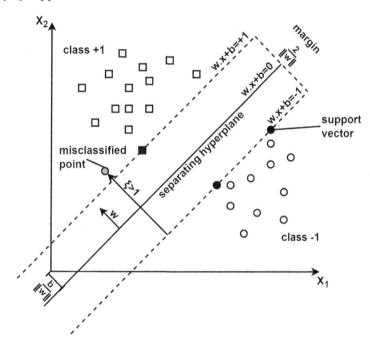

There are many possible linear separators for a separable training dataset with two classes as in Figure 1. While some machine learning methods, such as perceptron algorithm, find any linear separator, methods such as Naive Bayes seek the best linear separator as per some criteria. In particular, the support vector machines seek a decision surface at a maximum distance from any data point. As also seen in Figure 1, the margin area is determined by the distance to the data point closest to the decision surface. The data points defining this decision surface, namely the position of the separator, are called the support vectors. Other data points play no role in the determination of separator hyperplane.

In the prediction, the data points will fall on the bottom or top side of the hyperplane. For this reason, the decision function of the classifier of a linear SVM may be defined as follows:

$$f\left(\vec{x}\right) = sign\left(\vec{w}^{T}\vec{x} + b\right)$$

Class labels are +1 or -1. The closest points to the separator hyperplane are called the support vectors. The margin of a classifier is the maximum width that may be drawn by separating the support vectors of the two classes (Nachev and Teodosiev, 2018).

Here; w expresses the weight vector, x expresses the input vector, and b expresses the deviation. If the result obtained for a new value to be added to the model is smaller than 0, it will be close to white points and will be classified as white. If the result is equal to or greater than 0, it will be close to black points and will be classified as black. These may be expressed as follows (Yang, Awan, and Vall-Llosera, 2019):

$$\hat{y} = \begin{cases} 0 & if \quad w^{T}.x + b < 0, \\ 1 & if \quad w^{T}.x + b \geq 0 \end{cases}$$

In real-world data, the margin may not always separate the data as clearly as in Figure 1. In this case, some observations will fall within the margin area. When Figure 2 is examined, "hard margin" and "soft margin" are observed. Some observations may be present in the margin area. In real-world data, it may be necessary to prefer soft margin in some cases (Yukihiro, Yasunori, and Sadaaki, 2008).

Figure 2. Hard margin and Soft margin

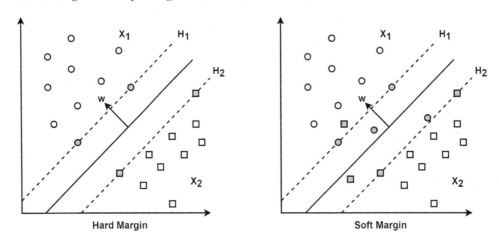

When the status in the above Figure 2 is examined, if it is $\xi_{k}=0$, then the data points are on or within the correct margin border. If it is $0<\xi_{k}\leq1$, then the data points are either on the edge or correct side of the decision boundary. And if it is $\xi_{k}>1$, it means that the data points are classified incorrectly (Yukihiro, Yasunori, and Sadaaki, 2008).

The balance between the hard margin and soft margin is able to be controlled by the parameter "c" in the support vector machines. As "c" gets bigger, the margin becomes narrow.

Figure 3. The effect of parameter "c" on the margin in SVM

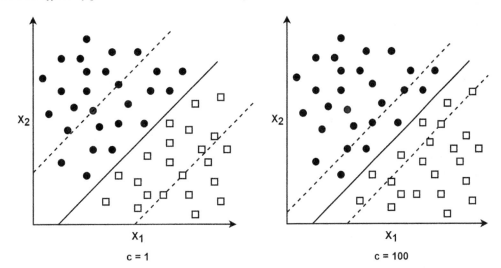

In the model, as the parameter "c" gets bigger, the model will become overfit and will begin to memorize. And a model becoming overfit may give extremely successful results in training data, but its prediction power will be very low for a subsequent new observation. For this reason, it is necessary to ensure the balance and to select an appropriate parameter "c" for the model not to be overfit.

In real-world data, the data may not always be able to be separated by a straight line. In a case like the one in Figure 4, it is not possible to separate the data with a straight line. It is required to separate this type of data in a different manner. At this point, kernel concept of the support vector machines gets involved in the process. The cause lying under the support vector machines' success in the literature is the ability to use the kernel methods (Metlek and Kayaalp, 2020).

Kernel function is one of the principal components of support vector machines. Support vector machines are actually mathematical methods that allow the two-dimensional classification performance of a one-dimensional dataset. In general, a kernel function maps the data by reflecting it from low-dimensional space to high-dimensional space (Patle and Chouhan, 2013).

The extensively used kernel functions are shown in the below Table 1 (Ceylan, 2019).

Support Vector Regression

The use of support vector machines in the prediction side is extensive, as well as in the classification. In the prediction process, the method is named "support vector regression" (Ceylan, 2019).

In support vector regression, complexity appears as a term defining how many parameters are present in the regression function. Even if a learning machine exhibits very good learning capability in a very high complexity state, its prediction capability may not be very good. Similarly, it may not have a

Figure 4. Data that cannot be separated with straight line

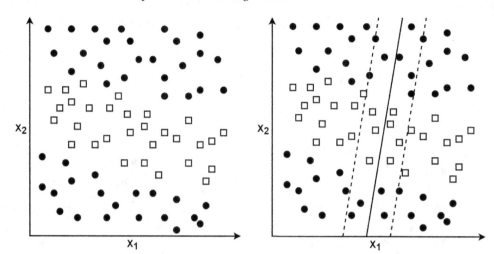

Table 1. Extensively used kernel functions

Kernel Function	Formula
Linear	$k(x_i, x_j) = x_i . x_j$
Polynomial	$k(x_i, x_j) = (\gamma x_i + x_j + c)d$
Sigmoid	$k(x_i, x_j) = \tanh(\gamma x_i + x_j + c)d$
Radial Basis Function (RBF)	$k\left(x_i, x_j\right) = e^{\gamma x_i - x_j}$

good learning capability also in the case of very low complexity. In regression, "approximation error" is used instead of margin between an optimal separator hyperplane and support vectors (Tolun, 2008).

Structural risk in support vector regression arises from the empirical risk of the function and from a complexity term. The general SVR (support vector regression) prediction function is expressed as follows:

$$f(x) = (w.\Phi(x)) + b$$

Here, $w \in R^n$, $b \in R$ and Φ expresses a non-linear transformation from R^n to high-dimensional space. The purpose is to find the values of w and b in a manner by which the values of x may be determined by minimizing the regression risk.

$$R_{reg}\left(f\right) = C\sum_{i=1}^{l}\Gamma\left(f\left(x_i\right) - y_i\right) + \frac{w^2}{2}$$

$x_i \in R^n$, $y_i \in R^n$, $w \in R^n$

Here, Γ expresses the sum of error between prediction data and real data, and it is defined as the cost function. This also appears as an empirical risk, defined as training error. In the model, C is the regularization parameter, and w vector may be expressed as follows in terms of data points:

$$w = \sum_{i=i}^{l} \left(\alpha_i - \alpha_i^* \right) \Phi \left(x_i \right)$$

If we combine the general SVR prediction function and the w function, the formula may be written as follows:

$$f(x) = \sum_{i=1}^{l} \left(\alpha_i - \alpha_i^* \right) \left(\Phi(x_i) . \Phi(x) \right) + b = \sum_{i=1}^{l} \left(\alpha_i - \alpha_i^* \right) k \left(x_i, x \right) + b$$

In the above formula, the dot product may be replaced with $k(x_i, x)$ known as kernel function. Kernel functions ensure the actualization of the dot product in high-dimensional feature space by the use of low-dimensional space data input without knowing the Φ transformation. All the kernel functions should meet the condition of Mercer corresponding to the dot product of some feature spaces. In support vector regression, the RBF kernel function is extensively used. The RBF kernel function may be expressed as follows (Wu, Ho, and Lee, 2004):

$$k(x_i, x) = exp\{-y \mid x - x_i \mid^2\}$$

Figure 5. SVR in different kernel structures

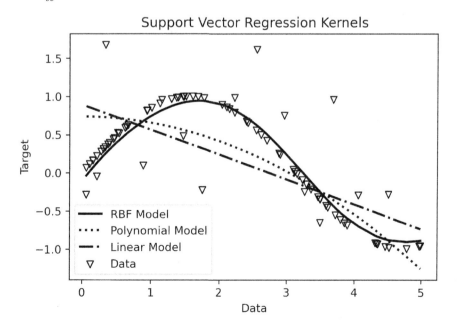

The support vector regression has models that may be established in different kernel structures. A graphical presentation of some of these kernels is expressed in Figure 5.

In support vector regression, there are linear models and non-linear models, as in the classification.

Linear Support Vector Regression

In linear support vector regression, it is intended to find the flattest possible $f(x)$ function, having maximum ε deviation, from yi being the real response variable for all the training data. In a linear state, $f(x)$ may be expressed as follows (Daş et al., 2019):

$$f(x) = w.x + b \quad w \in R^D, b \in R$$

In this equation, the linearity of the given function means the smallness of w. A way of ensuring this is minimizing the w^2 norm (Daş et al., 2019):

$$min \frac{1}{2} w^2$$

Such that;

$$y_i - (w.x_i + b) \leq \varepsilon$$

$$(w.x_i + b) - y_i \leq \varepsilon$$

Non-Linear Support Vector Regression

Non-linear regression problems are often discovered in real-world data. The solution to these problems is harder compared to linear problems, but the support vector regression is able to be extended easily in order to overcome the non-linear regression problems. In principle, support vector regression is a method developed for the solution of these non-linear regression problems. In the simplest form, the prediction model may be expressed as follows:

$$f\left(x\right) = w.x = \sum_{i=1}^{n} \left(\alpha_i^- - \alpha_i^+\right) x_i, x$$

When non-linear ϕ mapping is given to the high-dimensional space, the corresponding kernel function is defined as follows:

$$k(x,z) = \phi(x), \phi(z)$$

When the k dot product is given, the calculation may be performed as follows through the extensively used Gaussian (RBF) kernel function:

$$k(x,z) = \exp\left(-\gamma x - z_2^2\right)$$

The RBF kernel function corresponds to an infinite dimensional space, and gives successful results as being used frequently. Besides, for the use of a RBF kernel function and SVRs, a regularization parameter necessitates the adjustment of the parameter c. Here, the task of c is to ensure the balance between empirical error and overfit of the model to the training data (Frenay and Verleysen, 2011).

Comparison Methods

In regression analyses, the extensively used method for model comparison is comparing the error rates. In these indicators, the prediction powers of the models are compared. The lowest error amount between the predicted data and real data ensures the determination of the model showing the best performance. In the research, 8 different indicators were used. The techniques and calculation methods used are given in the below Table 2.

Table 2. Comparison methods

Method	Abbreviation	Formula
R^2	-	$1 - \dfrac{RSS}{TSS}$
R^2_{adj}	-	$1 - \left[\dfrac{\left(1-R^2\right)\left(n-1\right)}{n-k-1}\right]$
Mean Square Error	MSE	$\dfrac{1}{n}\sum_{i=1}^{n}\left(Y_i - Y_i'\right)^2$
Root Mean Square Error	RMSE	$\sqrt{\dfrac{1}{n}\sum_{i=1}^{n}\left(Y_i - Y_i'\right)^2}$
Mean Absolute Error	MAE	$\dfrac{1}{n}\sum_{i=1}^{n}\left|Y_i - Y_i'\right|$
Median Absolute Error	MAE2	$median\left(\left|Y_1 - Y_1'\right|,\ldots,\left|Y_i - Y_i'\right|\right)$
Mean Absolute Percentage Error	MAPE	$\dfrac{1}{n}\sum_{i=1}^{n}\left|\dfrac{Y_i - Y_i'}{Y_i}\right|$
Relative Absolute Error	RAE	$\dfrac{\sum_{i=1}^{n}\left|Y_i - Y_i'\right|}{\sum_{i=1}^{n}\left|Y_i - \bar{Y}\right|}$

DATA DESCRIPTION

The countries included in the databases of the World Bank and OECD constituted the universe of the study. Due to the high number of countries, and the inability to access values of all the variables for all the countries for the years 2017 and 2018, the study was carried out with a smaller number of countries. The data of 32 different countries was compiled as the sample of the research. Due to the compilation of 2 years of data, it was included as N = 64 in the analysis results.

All the data used in the study was obtained from the databases of the World Bank and the OECD. Thus, 2 years of data of 32 different countries were included in the study. In the research, there were 1 dependent variable, and 10 independent variables. The main reason for the low number of countries is the inability to access the values of each country for the independent variables used. The most up-to-date data for the variables discussed in the research could be determined for the year 2018. For this reason, research was conducted on the observations for the years 2017 and 2018.

In the following table, the dependent variable and independent variables, and the abbreviations included in the study are provided.

Table 3. Variables included in the study

Variable	Unit of Measurement	Abbreviation
Average Life	Year	Y
Alcohol Consumption per Person	Liter	X_1
Rate of Forestland	Percentage	X_2
Rate of Elderly Population (65+)	Percentage	X_3
Air Pollution (exposure to PM2.5)	Microgram per m^3	X_4
CO_2 Emission per Person	Ton	X_5
Health Expenditure	Dollar	X_6
Employment Rate of Population	Percentage	X_7
Per Capita Income	Dollar	X_8
Rate of Medication Expenditure	Percentage	X_9
Bed Number of Hospitals (per 1,000 Persons)	Unit	X_{10}

Descriptive statistics of all the variables are given in the below Table 4.

World Bank and OECD databases links are given in the references to access the data. When the link given for the World Bank is entered, the "World Development Indicators (WDI)" database must be selected from the listed databases. The data can be accessed when the variables given in Table 3 are written in the "Series" section of the WDI databases. Similarly, when the link given for OECD is entered, the data can be accessed by typing the names of the variables given in Table 3 into the search section. Since not all variables are included in a single database, some of the data were compiled from the OECD database and some from the World Bank database.

For the dataset discussed in the research, multiple linear regression analysis and support vector regression analysis methods were used. Least squares method was preferred for multiple linear regression analysis, and linear, polynomial, radial basis, and sigmoid kernels were used for the support vector regression analysis. The models were established using independent variables that were determined to have a positive or negative effect on the average life expectancy through a literature review. And for the determination of which analysis methods were performing calculations with the lowest error rate, R^2, R^2_{adj}, MSE, RMSE, MAE, MAE2, MAPE, and RAE values were calculated and compared.

Table 4. Descriptive statistics of all the variables

Variable	N	Mean	St. Deviation	Minimum	Quantile 1	Median	Quantile 3	Maximum
Y	64	80.543	2.820	72.450	78.725	81.545	82.575	84.210
X_1	64	10.099	2.146	3.200	8.908	10.350	11.675	14.450
X_2	64	37.95	18.22	0.49	30.41	34.84	53.49	73.73
X_3	64	18.282	3.478	7.880	16.188	18.930	19.830	28.140
X_4	64	12.139	5.014	5.330	7.988	11.595	15.550	27.450
X_5	64	7.398	3.392	1.500	4.975	6.650	8.875	15.300
X_6	64	4078	1906	1445	2309	4175	5246	10528
X_7	64	70.297	6.410	53.500	66.615	70.555	74.795	86.100
X_8	64	47351	18332	20368	33797	43771	55290	116481
X_9	64	15.832	5.708	6.330	11.955	15.115	18.398	27.730
X_{10}	64	5.009	2.692	1.110	2.970	4.505	6.555	13.050

RESULTS

In the study, support vector regression (SVR) and multiple linear regression (MLR) models were established by using the social and economic independent variables and the average life expectancy terms of the countries for the years 2017 and 2018. The dataset, consisting of 64 observations, was divided in such a manner that 1/3 of it would be test data and 2/3 of it would be training data. It was attempted to predict the test data through the models formed by the training data. The Spyder 5.0.5 (Python 3.8) program was used for the analyses.

A dataset was formed by the compilation of data in Table 3 for the years 2017 and 2018. Due to the differences among the measurement units of the data, standardization operation was performed on the data before the analysis. The correlation values and distribution of independent variables are provided in the following Figure 6 and Table 5.

When the Table 5 and Figure 6 are examined, it is observed that the correlations among the independent variables are smaller than 0.80. It was determined that all the VIF values were in the range of $1,33 < VIF_{X_k} < 3,00\ (k=1,2,...,10)$ in the regression models established in a similar manner. Accordingly, it cannot be referred to multicollinearity problem among the independent variables.

When the multiple linear regression model established is examined, it is observed from Table 6 that the regression model for the training data was significant (p<0.05).

Eight different comparison criteria were calculated for the comparison of the models established, and the calculated values are expressed in the below Table 7.

Table 5. Correlation matrix of independent variables

	X_1	X_2	X_3	X_4	X_5	X_6	X_7	X_8	X_9
X_2	-0.165								
X_3	0.176	0.162							
X_4	0.018	0.150	-0.138						
X_5	0.080	0.062	-0.116	-0.067					
X_6	-0.063	-0.227	0.063	-0.469	0.347				
X_7	0.088	-0.108	0.080	-0.424	0.124	0.365			
X_8	0.131	-0.297	-0.153	-0.416	0.384	0.671	0.280		
X_9	0.152	0.260	0.083	0.536	-0.149	-0.698	-0.434	-0.640	
X_{10}	0.237	0.332	0.293	0.538	0.215	-0.191	0.049	-0.184	0.380

Figure 6. Correlation graph of independent variables

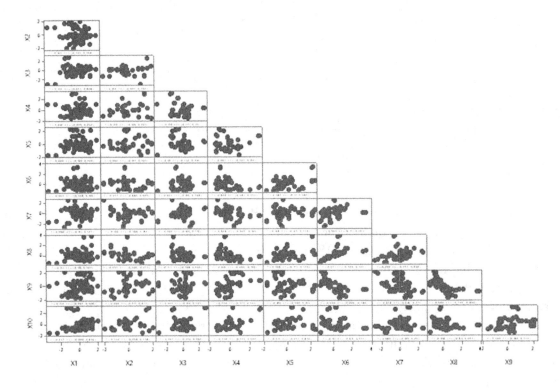

Table 6. Results of ANOVA for training data

Source	DF	Adj SS	Adj MS	F-Value	P-Value
Regression	10	30.5070	3.05070	6.96	0.000
Error	31	13.5854	0.43824		
Total	41	44.0924			

All the comparison criteria in Table 7 were used for model preference operation in models being more complex than the regression analysis methods in which ordinary least squares method is used. In the models established, the smallest MSE, RMSE, MAE, MAE2, MAPE, and RAE values, and the largest R^2 and R^2_{adj} values were accepted as the model best explaining the dataset. Because R^2, R^2_{adj}, MSE, RMSE, MAE, MAE2, MAPE, and RAE are the indicators that show the model's error rates.

Table 7. Comparison of models

	MLR	SVR (linear)	SVR (polynomial, degree=3)	SVR (radial basis)	SVR (sigmoid)
Test Data					
R^2	0.5192	0.4000	0.7673	0.9261	-0.0766
R^2_{adj}	0.0822	-0.1454	0.5558	0.8589	-1.0554
MSE	0.4209	0.5253	0.2037	0.0647	0.9426
RMSE	0.6488	0.7248	0.4513	0.2544	0.9709
MAE	0.5594	0.5633	0.3429	0.1972	0.7026
MAE2	0.5504	0.5185	0.2851	0.1513	0.5247
MAPE	103.7136	99.6843	52.3177	37.6445	103.6289
RAE	0.7746	0.7800	0.4749	0.2731	0.9729
Training Data					
R^2	0.6919	0.6317	0.7439	0.9133	0.1047
R^2_{adj}	0.5925	0.5128	0.6613	0.8853	-0.1841
MSE	0.3235	0.3867	0.2688	0.0910	0.9399
RMSE	0.5687	0.6218	0.5185	0.3017	0.9695
MAE	0.4467	0.4181	0.2894	0.1851	0.6781
MAE2	0.3431	0.1929	0.1031	0.1001	0.4820
MAPE	77.5667	63.1207	35.6316	25.1662	123.2208
RAE	0.5393	0.5048	0.3494	0.2235	0.8186
All Data					
R^2	0.6557	0.5989	0.7814	0.9474	-0.0552
R^2_{adj}	0.5907	0.5233	0.7401	0.9374	-0.2543
MSE	0.3443	0.4011	0.2186	0.0526	1.0552
RMSE	0.5868	0.6333	0.4676	0.2294	1.0272
MAE	0.4879	0.4604	0.2680	0.1385	0.7153
MAE2	0.4547	0.2566	0.1186	0.1000	0.5441
MAPE	89.2441	76.9075	35.2831	22.4101	123.6039
RAE	0.6070	0.5728	0.3334	0.1723	0.8900

When Table 7 is examined, it is observed that the best model in the analyses performed for training data, test data, and all data was the "SVR radial basis". Here, the point that is required to be primarily considered is the "test data" part. The 2/3 of the dataset was used for establishing model, and through the model established, the remaining 1/3 of the dataset was used for testing in prediction. The "test data" part of Table 7 expresses the results of tests performed by 1/3 part of the dataset. When this part is examined, it is observed that the best model for the dataset discussed in the research was "SVR radial basis", the second best model was "SVR polynomial", and the third best model was "MLR". For the "SVR polynomial", being the second best model, the polynomial degree was calculated as 3. It is able to be observed in the results that there are significant differences, especially between the SVR radial basis and MLR.

The graphs of real values and predicted values for the best 3 models are shown in Figure 7-8-9 for test data, training data, and all data.

Figure 7. Support Vector Regression (kernel=rbf)

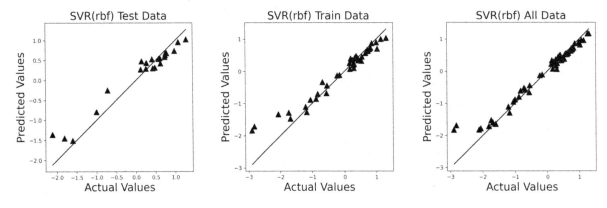

Figure 8. Support Vector Regression (kernel=polynomial, degree=3)

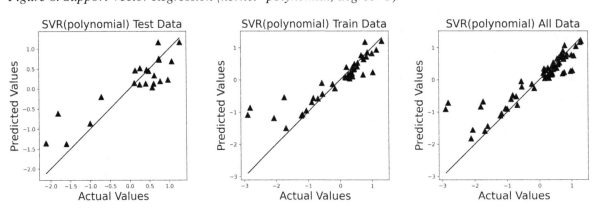

Figure 9. Multiple Linear Regression Analysis

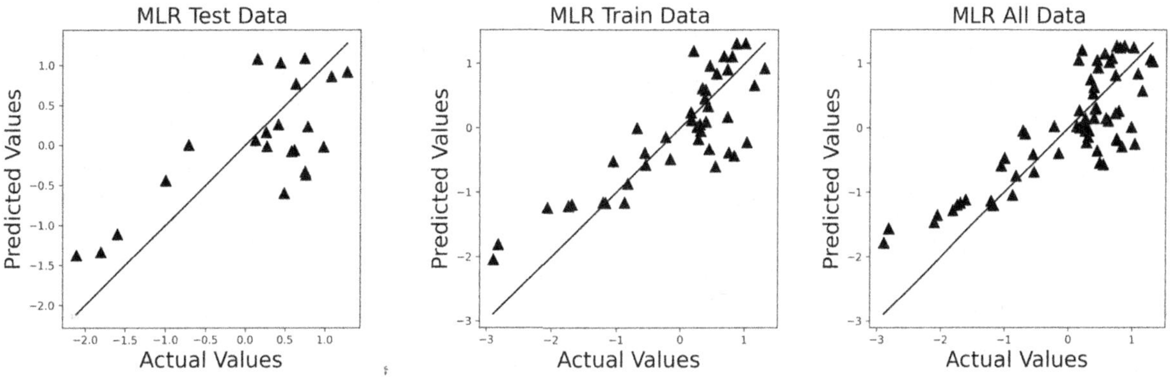

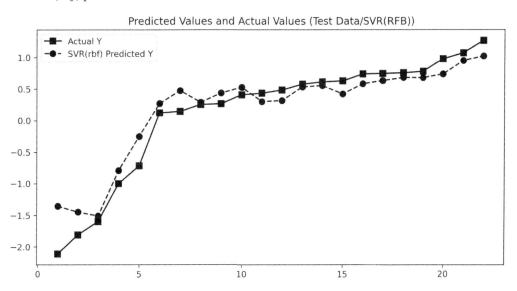

When the graphs are examined, it is observed that the distribution of the SVR (RBF) model in predicted data and real data was smoother among the models established and predicted for test data, training data, and all data. Considering the predictions of the SVR (polynomial) model, it is observed that it showed a more dispersed distribution than the SVR (RBF), but still it showed a smoother distribution than the MLR. And considering the graphs for MLR, it is able to be predicted that the values were highly dispersed and that the error rate was higher. And in Figure 10, the close course of the prediction values and the real test data, obtained by the SVR (RBF) model, which was determined as the best model, is observed. The SVR (RBF) model is able to perform better prediction compared to other models with a lower error rate.

Figure 10. SVR(rbf) prediction and test data

CONCLUSION AND RECOMMENDATIONS

In this study, the authors tried to find an answer to the question of how SVR works in different kernels. In addition to this problem, machine learning method was compared with a different statistical method. Considering the results of multiple linear regression analysis and support vector regression analysis, it was determined that the support vector regression showed much better performance with a much lower error rate. When this result is considered, it is clear that more efficient results may be obtained in the case of a combination of developing technology and machine learning methods with statistical methods. When the results of support vector regression for different kernels are examined, the RBF kernel provided the best performance in the data structure discussed in the research. For both test data, training data and all dataset, SVR (rbf) has highest R^2 and R^2_{adj} value and the lowest performance metrics which are the measures of accuracy function.

The findings obtained in this study give the same results as the studies in different fields in the literature. In their study, Muthukrishnan and Maryam (2020) compared SVR and classical regression analysis. They showed that SVR was more efficient in minimizing the error of the regression model. In a health study, Suvarna et al. (2020) used MLR and SVR to predict future number of cases of CO-VID-19. Between two models, it was seen that SVR was performed well output than linear regression. For predicting the mass of ber fruits Sattar and his friends (2021) established models using SVR, MLR and ANN methods. Findings showed that SVR and ANN models produced more precise prediction than MLR model. In another study, for the prediction of biosorption efficiency of copper, SVR and MLR were used by Parveen and her friends (2017). They showed that SVR was successfully applied to model with a good accuracy.

By the examination of other studies in the literature, it is evident that the RBF generally shows better performance compared to other kernel structures. This could be attributed to an inability to model real-world data linearly. This is valid for both classification and prediction. The model showing the second-best performance was the support vector regression with a third-degree polynomial kernel. Despite having been calculated from 3rd degree within the scope of the research, different results may be obtained in the case of the use of a polynomial kernel of a different degree in the different data structures. This method may be discussed in different research.

Besides all these determinations, a support vector regression, to be applied by removing from the model the variable not being related to the dependent variable through individually examining the effects of independent variables on the dependent variable, may give better or worse results. Similarly, this method may be addressed as a research subject for future studies.

Machine learning comes our way through more developed methods day by day. Support vector machines are just one of these methods. There are also different machine learning methods such as artificial neural networks, decision trees, random forest. These methods operate by combining machine learning and statistical methods, and they show better performance than models in which only the statistical methods are extensively used. As a result, research into machine learning methods that can be evaluated on their own merits can be conducted.

REFERENCES

Abdel-Sattar, M., Aboukarina, A. M., & Alnahdi, B. M. (2021). Application of Artificial Neural Network and Support Vector Regression in Predicting Mass of Ber Fruits (Ziziphus Mauritiana Lamk.) Based on Fruit Axial Dimensions. *PLoS One*, *16*(1), 1–15. doi:10.1371/journal.pone.0245228 PMID:33411790

Bali, V., Aggarwal, D., & Singh, S. (2021). Life Expectancy: Prediction & Analysis Using ML. *9th International Conference on Reliability, Infocom Technologies and Optimization*. 10.1109/ICRI-TO51393.2021.9596123

Ceylan, Z. (2019). Assessment of Agricultural Energy Consumption of Turkey by MLR and Bayesian Optimized SVR and GPR Models. *Journal of Forecasting*, *39*(3), 944–956.

Cortes, C., & Vapnik, V. (1995). Support Vector Networks. *Machine Learning*, *20*(3), 273–297. doi:10.1007/BF00994018

Daş,, M., Balpetek,, N., & Kavak Akpınar,, E., & Akpınar, S. (2019). Investigation of Wind Energy Potantial of Different Provinces Found in Turkey and Establishment of Predictive Model Using Support Vector Machine Regression with the Obtained Results. *Journal of the Faculty of Engineering and Architecture of Gazi University*, *34*(4), 2203–2213.

Faisal, K. K. K. F., Alomari, D. D. J. A., Alasmari, H. H. M. A., Alghamdi, H. H. S. A., & Saedi, K. K. A. S. (2021). Life Expectancy Estimation Based on Machine Learning and Structured Predictors. *AISS*. 10.1145/3503047.3503122

Farmer, L. D., & Casson, R. J. (2014). Understanding and checking the assumptions of linear regression: A primer for medical researchers. *Clinical & Experimental Ophthalmology*, *42*(6), 590–596. doi:10.1111/ceo.12358 PMID:24801277

Frenay, B., & Verleysen, M. (2011). Parameter-insensitive Kernel in Extreme Learning for Non-Linear Support Vector Regression. *Neurocomputing*, *74*(16), 2526–2531. doi:10.1016/j.neucom.2010.11.037

Guo, S., Lucas, R. M., & Ponsonby, A. (2013). A Noval Approach for Prediction of Vitamin D Status Using Support Vector Regression. *PLoS One*, *8*(11), 1–9. doi:10.1371/journal.pone.0079970

Gürsakal, N. (2013). *Çıkarımsal İstatistik, İstatistik* (Vol. 2). Dora Basım-Yayım Dağıtım Ltd. Şti.

Ingleby, F. C., Woods, L. M., Atherton, I. M., Baker, M., Ellies-Brookes, L., & Belot, A. (2021). Describing Socio-economic Variation in Life Expectancy According to An Individual's Education, Occupation and Wage in England and Wales: An Analysis of the ONS Longitudinal Study. *SSM - Population Health*, *14*, 1–9. doi:10.1016/j.ssmph.2021.100815 PMID:34027013

Jetter, M., Laudage, S., & Stadelmann, D. (2019). The Intimate Link Between Income Levels and Life Expectancy: Global Evidence from 213 Years. *Social Science Quarterly*, *100*(4), 1387–1403. doi:10.1111squ.12638

Jiang, J., Luo, L., Xu, P., & Wang, P. (2018). How Does Social Development Influence Life Expectancy? A Geographically Weighted Regression Analysis in Chine. *The Royal Society for Public Health*, *163*, 95–104.

Kabir, M. (2008). Determinants of Life Expectancy in Developing Countries. *Journal of Developing Areas*, *41*(2), 185–204. doi:10.1353/jda.2008.0013

Karacan, I., Sennaroglu, B., & Vayvay, O. (2020). Analysis of Life Expectancy Across Countries Using a Decision Tree. *EMHJ*, *26*(2), 143–151. doi:10.26719/2020.26.2.143 PMID:32141591

Karal, Ö. (2018). Compression of ECG Data by Support Vector Regression Method. *Journal of the Faculty of Engineering and Architecture of Gazi University*, *33*(2), 743–755.

Kavitha, S., Varuna, S., & Ramya, R. (2016). A Comparative Analysis on Linear Regression and Support Vector Regression. *2016 International Conference on Green Engineering and Technologies*, 1-5. 10.1109/GET.2016.7916627

Makridis, C. A., Zhao, D. Y., Bejan, C. A., & Alterovitz, G. (2021). Leveraging Machine Learning to Characterize the Role of Socio-economic Determinants on Physical Health and Well-Being Among Veterans. *Computers in Biology and Medicine*, *133*, 1–8. doi:10.1016/j.compbiomed.2021.104354 PMID:33845269

Metlek, S., & Kayaalp K. (2020). Makine Öğrenmesinde, Teoriden Örnek Matlab Uygulamalarına Kadar Destek Vektör Makineleri. Ankara: İksad Yayınevi.

Miladinov, G. (2020). Socioeconomic Development and Life Expectancy Relationship: Evidence from the EU Accession Candidate Countries. *Genus*, *76*(2), 1–20. doi:10.118641118-019-0071-0

Mirowsky, J., & Ross, C. E. (2000). Socioeconomic Status and Subjective Life Expectancy. *Social Psychology Quarterly*, *63*(2), 133–151. doi:10.2307/2695888

Muthukrishnan, R., & Maryam, J. S. (2020). Predictive Modeling Using Support Vector Regression. *International Journal of Scientific & Technology Research*, *9*(2), 4863–4865.

Nachev, A., & Teodosiev, T. (2018). Analysis of Employment Data Using Support Vector Machines. *International Journal of Applied Engineering Research: IJAER*, *13*(18), 13525–13535.

OECD. (n.d.). https://data.oecd.org

Özdamar, K. (2013). *Paket Programlarla İstatistiksel Veri Analizi Cilt 2*. Nisan Kitabevi.

Parmaksız, A. (2019). *Çoklu Doğrusal Regresyon Çözümlemesinde Farklı Korelasyon Yapılarında %80 Güç İçin Örneklem Büyüklüğünün Belirlenmesi*. Doktora Tezi. Hacettepe Üniversitesi Sağlık Bilimleri Enstitüsü.

Parveen, N., Zaidi, S., & Danish, M. (2017). Development of SVR-Based Model and Comparative Analysis with MLR and ANN Models for Predicting The Sorption Capacity of Cr(VI). *Process Safety and Environmental Protection*, *107*, 428–437. doi:10.1016/j.psep.2017.03.007

Parveen, N., Zaidi, S., & Danish, M. (2017). Support Vector Regression Prediction and Analysis of the Copper (II) Biosorption Efficiency. *Indian Chemical Engineer*, *59*(4), 295–311. doi:10.1080/0019450 6.2016.1270778

Patle, A., & Chouhan, D. S. (2013). SVM Kernel Functions for Classification. *2013 International Conference on Advances in Technology and Engineering*, 1-9.

Rencher, A. C., & Schaalje, G. B. (2007). *Linear Models in Statistics* (2nd ed.). Wiley-Interscience. doi:10.1002/9780470192610

Shaw, J. W., Horrace, W. C., & Vogel, J. (2005). The Determinants of Life Expectancy: An Analysis of the OECD Health Data. *Southern Economic Journal*, *71*(4), 768–783.

Suvarna, B., Nandipati, B. L., & Bhat, M. N. (2020). Support Vector Regression for Predicting COVID-19 Cases. *European Journal of Molecular & Clinical Medicine*, *7*(3), 4882–4893.

The World Bank. (n.d.). https://databank.worldbank.org

Timm, N. H. (2002). *Applied Multivariate Analysis*. Springer.

Tolun, S. (2008). *Destek Vektör Makineleri: Banka Başarısızlığının Tahmini Üzerine Bir Uygulama*. Doktora Tezi. İstanbul Üniversitesi Sosyal Bilimler Enstitüsü.

Vydehi, K., Manchikanti, K., Kumari, T. S., & Shah, S. K. A. (2020). Machine Learning Techniques for Life Expectancy Prediction. *International Journal of Advanced Trends in Computer Science and Engineering*, *9*(4), 4503–4507. doi:10.30534/ijatcse/2020/45942020

Weisberg, S. (2005). *Applied Linear Regression*. John Wiley & Sons. doi:10.1002/0471704091

Wu, C. H., Ho, J. M., & Lee, D. T. (2004). Travel-Time Prediction With Support Vector Regression. *IEEE Transactions on Intelligent Transportation Systems*, *5*(4), 276–281. doi:10.1109/TITS.2004.837813

Yang J., Javed A. & Vall-Llosera G. (2019). *Support Vector Machines on Noisy Intermediate Scale Quantum Computers*. ArXiv, abs/1909.11988.

Yıldırım, Y. (2018). *Destek Vektör Regresyonu ve Destek Vektör Makineleri* [Support Vector Regression and Support Vector Machines]. https://yavuz.github.io/destek-vektor-regresyonu-ve-makineleri/

Yukihiro, H., Yasunori, E., & Sadaaki, M. (2008). Support Vector Machine for Data with Tolerance based on Hard-Margin and Soft-Margin. *2008 IEEE International Conference on Fuzzy System*, 750-755.

Chapter 3
Machine Learning in Healthcare

Savitesh Kushwaha

ⓘ https://orcid.org/0000-0002-3151-1626

Postgraduate Institute of Medical Education and Research, Chandigarh, India

Rachana Srivastava

ⓘ https://orcid.org/0000-0002-5325-5555

Postgraduate Institute of Medical Education and Research, Chandigarh, India

Harsh Vats

University of Delhi, India

Poonam Khanna

Postgraduate Institute of Medical Education and Research, Chandigarh, India

ABSTRACT

Machine learning approaches are utilized in healthcare for computational decision-making in cases where critical medical data analysis is required to identify hidden linkages or anomalies that are not evident to humans. Artificial intelligence (AI) tools can assess a wide range of health data; patient data from multi-omics methods; clinical, behavioural, environmental, pharmacological data; and data from the biomedical literature to respond to research issues that necessitate a big sample size on a difficult-to-reach population. In healthcare, digitising health data has eased the development of computational models and AI systems to extract insights from the data. This chapter initially addressed the prospectus of machine learning in public health with significant focus areas. The medical devices and equipment section contain device-based modelling approaches to various diseases. The chapter also includes brief details on chatbots, wearable technologies, drug distribution systems, vending machines, and text recognition from prescriptions and medicine boxes are addressed.

DOI: 10.4018/978-1-6684-4045-2.ch003

INTRODUCTION

Machine learning (ML) is a scientific study of how computers learn from data and improve over time. It is primarily based on statistics and probability. However, it is more potent than traditional statistical approaches regarding decision-making. The information acquired from a dataset and fed to the algorithm is called features. The quality of the features provided to the algorithm determines the accuracy of the model's predictions. A machine learning developer aims to find the subset of features that best meet the purpose, boosting the model's accuracy. Machine learning, machine reasoning, and robotics are artificial intelligence methodologies and techniques. This approach is used in numerous healthcare activities using various strategies and algorithms. Revolutionary clinical decision-making is the application of machine learning to tackle clinical challenges. When machine learning is used in clinical decision-making, the system will perceive a specific individual by gathering and understanding data related to that individual's health and then reasoning on the data to recommend the best actions to maintain or improve that individual's health (Sánchez-Martínez et al., 2019).

Even if ML is poised to alter healthcare by playing a pivotal role, a few ethical considerations must be made while putting such systems in place and relying on their conclusions. The accountability and openness of such systems' decisions, the potential for group damages deriving from algorithmic bias and professional roles, and the integrity of physicians are only a few of the ethical challenges. As a result, evaluating the benefits they provide when implementing such systems, such as more efficient healthcare systems due to artificial intelligence's high and precise processing capacity at a relatively low cost, is critical. Furthermore, artificial intelligence algorithms can do computerized predictive analysis by filtering, sorting, and searching for patterns in large datasets from various sources to make quick and informed conclusions (Lysaght, Lim, Xafis, & Ngiam, 2019).

From administrative to a full-scale randomized clinical trial, ML has a wide range of possible applications in healthcare, not all of which require research ethics monitoring. In a nutshell, we're interested in clinical machine learning research involving human individuals (and/or their data). Because these classifications are difficult and, to some extent, challenged by ML approaches, it is beyond the scope of this study to provide a precise description of the distinction between "clinical" and "non-clinical," or "research" and "non-research" (McCradden et al., 2022). Machine learning targets software algorithms and gives them adaptive features to learn and reprogram based on previous experiences without human intervention. The precision of the model in machine learning is directly dependent on the amount and size of the sample data. Artificial intelligence is a process by which machines, devices, and equipment are equipped with human-like intelligence with adaptive behaviour.

MAIN FOCUS OF THE CHAPTER

The advancement of concurrent technologies like cloud/edge computing, mobile communication, and big data technology benefits ML models' potential for healthcare applications. ML, when combined with these technologies, can produce extremely accurate predicting outcomes and aid in developing human-centered intelligent solutions. These technologies can rejuvenate the healthcare business and enable remote healthcare services for rural and low-income areas. Healthcare providers generate diverse data and information regularly, making it challenging to assess and handle using "conventional methods." Machine learning and deep learning approaches effectively analyze this data for meaningful insights.

Furthermore, various data sources can supplement healthcare data, including genetics, medical data, social media, and environmental data (Qayyum, Qadir, Bilal, & Al-Fuqaha, 2021). The chapter covers machine learning implementation in various healthcare domains such as public health, healthcare technologies, diseases, surveillance, chatbots and wearable technologies. Furthermore, the chapter also includes the advantages and disadvantages of machine learning in healthcare.

Machine Learning in Public Health

Researchers and public health practitioners have begun using AI in various projects, including scanning the internet for emerging outbreaks, predicting suicide using electronic health data, detecting risk factors, disease surveillance, nutritional epidemiology, health policy and health promotion (Figure 1). Machine learning for public health can be used in investigations and biological mechanisms to establish a multivariate empirical link between disease outbreak probability and environmental conditions. Given the complex relationships and potential mediations between multi-level factors, there is an opportunity to use and develop machine learning methods for the interpretable identification and assessment of the source and magnitude of a wide range of multi-level factors in health outcomes by leveraging new data sources. The possibility of leveraging data and machine learning in efforts considering the multi-level influence around an individual is an open investigation area. For example, a large body of work in machine learning has focused on targeting the individual toward depression management, self-efficacy for weight loss, smoking cessation, and personalized nutrition based on glycemic response. Using probabilistic machine learning and deep learning approaches, it is possible to predict mortality risk, hospital readmission, and disease prognoses using pathology, imaging, or other clinical data. The prediction has also been used to answer population-level problems, most notably in disease risk mapping (Zhao et al., 2020). Clinicians, patients, and their families may use machine learning and artificial intelligence to analyze all available data, create informed, evidence-based recommendations, and participate in collaborative decision-making to determine the best strategy (Debnath et al., 2020).

Machine learning (ML) can also help detect mental health problems, diagnose, and therapy. ML approaches can open new avenues for learning human behaviour patterns, recognizing mental health symptoms and risk factors, making illness progression predictions, and customizing and improving therapies (Thieme, Belgrave, & Doherty, 2020). An essential mental health intervention can be a motivational interviewing (MI) assessment and training tool for counsellors that employs speech and language processing to automatically create ratings of therapists' MI skills from the audio of face-to-face counselling sessions. It displays the findings in an interactive visual dashboard that emphasizes the counsellors' communication strengths and faults (Hirsch, Merced, Narayanan, Imel, & Atkins).

Disease Surveillance

Topic modelling, time series forecasting and regression, classification, and clustering are four important machine learning tasks for disease surveillance or outbreak monitoring. Many disease surveillance systems still use classic (shallow) machine learning techniques, and deep learning (DL)-based algorithms outperformed classical models. Surveillance systems based on social media are superior to traditional surveillance techniques. Disease surveillance approaches based on social media often count the number of posts concerning a particular disease as an indicator of actual disease activity, using keywords like the disease name (Magumba & Nabende, 2021). The data from social network sites like Twitter and

Facebook hashtags were utilized to get the sentiment-based disease prediction through Natural Language Prediction. Although, real-time automated sentiment predictions should be made for disease-based keywords. The Google Trends data can also be extracted using programming languages for performing this type of analysis. AI-based disease surveillance can effectively identify persons who have been infected with or exposed to infectious organisms quickly. This difficulty continues one of the worst concerns that health specialists confront today. AI-based disease surveillance systems have the potential to save the economy or delay the rate of economic decline because they eliminate the need for a large population to stay at home and limit their economic contributions. Artificial intelligence approaches can estimate health indicators at individual and population levels (i.e., improving social and health policy processes). However, estimating health indicators from linked administrative data is difficult for many reasons, including a wide range of data sources and data collection methods and the availability of a large number of variables (Haneef et al., 2021).

Public health experts continue to analyze and explore sensor data and indicators from the physical world-spanning health, environmental, sociological, and economic factors, among others, to improve the timeliness and accuracy of outbreak detection and early warning systems. Keyword searches, blogs, and social networking posts have all been used extensively to use data from the internet. Twitter is a valuable source of public health surveillance data. The Twitter data feed is updated in real-time and can be collected from a vast number of users across the globe. At the same time, since tweets are frequently brief and full of incomplete and informal language, analyzing Twitter data can be difficult. Neill used a non-parametric graph scan to evaluate Twitter's heterogeneous network structure to detect hantavirus outbreaks in Chile (F. Chen & Neill, 2014). Edo-Osagie et al. mined information from Twitter for public health monitoring using an attention-based short text categorization algorithm (Edo-Osagie, Lake, Edeghere, & Iglesia, 2019). Internet-based monitoring systems are moderated, somewhat moderated, or automated. The Program for Emerging Diseases Monitoring (ProMED) (Carrion & Madoff, 2017; Yu & Madoff, 2004) is a moderated system. The Global Public Health Intelligence Network (GPHIN) (M'ikanatha et al., 2006; Mykhalovskiy & Weir, 2006), designed by the Canadian government, is a somewhat monitored system. Every day, the GPHIN processes approximately 3000 news reports. Both ProMED and GPHIN have multilingual capabilities. SENTINEL8 is a newly developed software system for real-time syndromic monitoring based on social media data, founded on current advances in machine learning and data processing. To provide situational awareness, this technology can identify disease outbreaks (Şerban, Thapen, Maginnis, Hankin, & Foot, 2019).

For estimating diabetes prevalence based on the number of reimbursements over the previous two years, a generic machine learning (ML) model was created. From a population-based epidemiological cohort (CONSTANCES) linked to the French National Health Database, a final data set of 44659 participants was chosen. In the development of this algorithm, a supervised machine learning approach was used, which included: 1. final data set selection, 2. target definition, 3. coding selected 23 variables for a given window of time, 4. splitting final data into training and test data sets, 5. variables selection, 6. training model, 7. model validation with test data set, and viii. model selection. The optimal algorithm was chosen based on the area under the receiver operating characteristic curve (AUC). The final algorithm for estimating diabetes incidence was a Linear Discriminant Analysis model based on the number of reimbursements for specified variables such as biological testing, medications, medical acts, and hospitalization without a procedure over the previous two years. This algorithm has a 62 percent sensitivity, 67 percent specificity, and 67 percent accuracy. The ML algorithms in this study were used in two other studies: to categorize and estimate the prevalence of type 1 and type 2 diabetes cases and identify the number of undiagnosed diabetes cases (Haneef et al., 2021). A deep AlexNet model was trained on sea surface temperature images and rainfall data by transfer learning to evaluate emergent spatiotemporal hotspots of dengue fever at the township level in Taiwan. On an eightfold cross-validation test dataset, our transfer learning-based algorithm overcame the overfitting problem caused by the tiny dataset and achieved 100% accuracy (Anno et al., 2019).

Health Policy

AI enables the efficient and precise handling of data with many dimensions (features) and units (feature vectors). Artificial intelligence approaches can estimate health indicators at individual and population levels (i.e., improving social and health policy processes) (Haneef et al., 2021). The use of ML in big, population-level datasets such as those from medical imaging, electronic health records (EHRs), and whole-genome research is currently the most significant contribution of AI to health policy understanding. These include ensuring adequate health and social care for an entire population through preventive techniques, disease prevention, healthy lifestyle promotion, and population screening through knowledge capture (typically in big data). Overall governance will take a patient-centred approach, with patient advocacy, workforce, and resource management, and help high-risk people get the help. Current apps can outperform existing risk scores in predicting clinical outcomes. For patients in the hundreds of thousands, these include in-hospital mortality, day unscheduled readmission, prolonged length of stay, and ultimate discharge diagnoses (Ashrafian & Darzi, 2018).

Health Promotion

The use of machine learning in modern marketing techniques demonstrates the technology's promise in health promotion. The next generation of recommender systems (decision-supporting information-filtering systems) can help people make better health decisions. The use of machine learning algorithms has been identified as providing powerful solutions to content-based analysis (based on personality information), collaborative filtering (in which past behaviour is used to predict future actions), and hybrid approaches (combining both techniques) to assess online behaviour. This information can be gathered from EHRs with consent and adherence to national legal requirements to target harmful behaviours such as the individual purchase of tobacco-based items or alcohol- or sugar-based drinks. Machine learning systems could provide quick analytics and evaluation of policy declarations. Thus, policymakers and legislators can use this information to steer the next generation's health policies. Though many machine learning systems are still in the experimental and theoretical stages, they have the potential to play the most transformational role in health governance yet (Ashrafian & Darzi, 2018). Artificial intelligence and machine learning can transform health systems, increasing efficiency and effectiveness while expanding universal health care and bettering results. To fully realize AI's and machine learning's promise and mitigate their risks, there will be a need for curated data, an enabling regulatory framework, legislative safeguards to protect individuals' rights, explicit norms on accountability, and the ability to manage strategic change (Buch, Ahmed, & Maruthappu, 2018).

COVID-19

Machine learning can significantly influence if used in more health-related jobs. The current COVID-19 epidemic has shown how multi-sectoral elements outside the clinic, such as community, social networks, and environment, are also significant in health, echoing population and public health (Mhasawade, Zhao, & Chunara, 2021). COVID-19 makes extensive use of artificial intelligence in areas such as diagnostics, public health, clinical decision making, social control, medicines, vaccine development, and monitoring, operation of other basic clinical systems in conjunction with big data patients with COVID-19, as well as their care and management (Wang et al., 2021). COVID-19 phenotypes range from little or minor symptoms and smooth recovery to fast deterioration, acute respiratory distress syndrome (ARDS), multi-organ system failure, and death. Due to the complexities of this novel disease, healthcare practitioners, patients, and their families have been obliged to immediately make vital and difficult decisions with minimal knowledge. Machine learning (ML) and artificial intelligence (AI) can better understand patient subgroups, drive clinical decision-making, and improve operational and patient-centred outcomes (Debnath et al., 2020). ML models can risk-stratify Covid patients and differentiate low-risk patients from those at higher risk of deterioration, allowing clinicians to focus on the 15% of patients who require more intensive treatment (Team, 2020). By integrating responses from symptomatic people with clinical data from electronic health records (EHRs), such as comorbidities, complaints, and demographics, a model may predict the likelihood of a confirmed COVID-19 diagnosis and its severity (including geography) (Decapprio et al., 2020).

As the number of patients grows, ML/AI techniques can construct risk scores for numerous time points based on ever-increasing continuous vitals, labs, meds, and orders. Nurses and physicians can utilize short-term predictions (4–8 hours) to prioritize care. Mid-term forecasts (12–24 hours) can assist units in identifying patients with the lowest risk of decompensation; this measure of stability can aid clinicians in making decisions about how to adjust care on the way to release and long-term models (greater than 24 hours) can assist managers in allocating valuable resources like ventilators, beds, and staffing (Debnath et al., 2020). ML/AI can help at every stage of the process by assessing the chance of admission at triage, revising risk estimations with actual data from clinical evaluation, forecasting the patient's trajectory, and the impact of early ventilator use.

Nutritional Epidemiology

In personalized nutrition, machine learning and data science hold much promise. Nutrition-related big data is being created in a variety of ways. These findings could reduce measurement error in nutritional epidemiology by providing more objective, scalable, and cost-effective data collection methods. The widespread availability of internet-connected PCs and smartphones throws up many opportunities for active data collection. Furthermore, increased big data repositories, such as those found in consumer rewards programmes and diet-tracking apps, provide the potential for secondary dietary data to be used. More longitudinal, repeated food measurements may be possible if new electronic measurement modalities are less expensive and cumbersome than existing approaches. Completely new means of dietary measurement enabled by machine learning and modern data infrastructures could improve scalability and precision. Machine learning models can automatically classify pictures of food (Sahoo et al.). Such strategies may make keeping diet records easier, more consistent, and accurate, hence boosting precision and validity. The picture/video scaling to get a precise amount of food requires extensive model training and testing on a big database of photos/videos of different foods and cuisines. Dietary data is only used in several clinical and public health prediction models. Such data could be included in predictive models to improve health outcome forecasts. Predictive models differ from most nutritional epidemiology research because they typically include all variables considered relevant for outcome prediction, are more concerned with the model's overall prediction characteristics than individual exposure variable associations and are less concerned with interpretability (Damen et al., 2016). Incorporating extensive dietary data into prediction models, especially with novel data gathering and machine learning technologies, could be a valuable and mostly untapped source of enhanced performance.

Figure 1. Public health perspectives in machine learning.

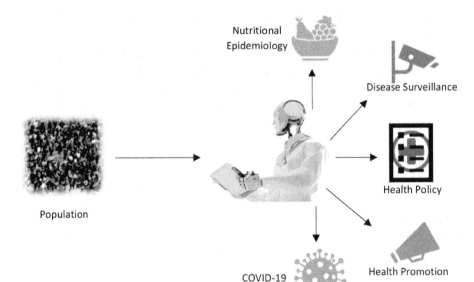

Machine Learning in Disease

Machine learning is creating and supplementing the fourth industrial revolution in which machine learning-based technology is helping transform medical devices and equipment by providing novel insights from the large amount of data generated through daily practices. These technologically equipped devices would detect and diagnose diseases with much more accuracy. They will also aid the discovery of uncommon observations for personalized healthcare development (Kaul, Enslin, & Gross, 2020). The medical devices and equipment aim to improve patient care by looking into complex and huge data and uncovering new insights using machine learning. The challenging part of this process is the regulation of medical devices and equipment. There are no harmonized regulatory standards for machine learning-based medical devices and equipment. As of now, each country independently reviews the application for it. The current regulator that approves medical devices are the FDA (Food and Drugs Administration) in the United States, the council directive 93/42/EEC in the European region, the Therapeutic products act in Switzerland and PMDA (Pharmaceuticals and Medical Devices Agency) in Japan (Chua Chin Heng et al., 2022; Muehlematter, Daniore, & Vokinger, 2021). However, regulatory harmonization became necessary in the growing need for artificial intelligence and machine learning-based devices.

There are many ways machine learning can be used in a device or system in medical devices and equipment space. Here are some applications of them:

Cardiovascular Diseases

Machine learning is increasingly used in the field of cardiovascular medicine as diagnosing, and monitoring of cardiovascular diseases is now increasingly based on non-invasive imaging with computed tomography, as these cardiac CT exams consist of hundreds of slices and to examine such a huge dataset with consistency and accuracy, we need the machine learning for interpretation. Several algorithms have been applied to daily detection and diagnosis, but most of the applied methods in cardiac CT use supervised learning. As mostly supervised learning trains a model to be optimized to provide the correct label as described in reference standard during training and will be able to predict a label to an unseen sample during testing. Coronary artery stenosis is tended to have better sensitivity and specificity with custom-built algorithms than with boosting algorithms. However, custom build algorithms do not disclose their details. So, custom-built algorithms should be transparent and replicated in several studies using the same independent variables for implementation in clinical practices. In the case of stroke prediction, SVM (Support Vector Machine) and boosting algorithms provided similar sensitivity and specificity, while SVM seems to increase accuracy in patients with stroke. The reason behind this can be the presence of discrete, linear data and a proper non-linear kernel that improves generalization or thresholding features values along a single axis, leading to highly accurate classifiers and creating a decision tree model to be more accurate. The detection of cardiac arrhythmias using ML, particularly SVM, showed promising sensitivity and specificity, as observed in several studies. It also outperforms others like CNN (Convolutional Neural Network) algorithms, logistic regression, boosting algorithm, in-house algorithms and random forest (Krittanawong et al., 2020). In the case of heart failure detection, results are inconclusive, but promising sensitivity and specificity using the SVM algorithm were shown (Rossing et al.).

Diabetic Retinopathy

The investigation of diabetic retinopathy using machine learning increased during the last decade as the screening techniques shifted towards assessing color fundus photographs (Burlina, Freund, Dupas, & Bressler, 2011; Feeny, Tadarati, Freund, Bressler, & Burlina, 2015). These fundus photographs were taken and analyzed by retina specialists or trained graders, leaving a huge margin of error due to the large diabetic population. Machine learning here provides a solution to this problem. Recently, several studies investigated machine learning in automated detection and achieving excellent high sensitivity and specificity. (Bellemo et al., 2019; Pratt, Coenen, Broadbent, Harding, & Zheng, 2016) The analysis of these studies encountered various challenges like detecting and extracting diabetic retinopathy features due to poor image quality, close localization of features, presence of red lesions and most widely, low contrast, noisy, uneven illumination and color variation images. Thus, creating a model that takes care of these background subtractions creates challenges such as system specification, operation, large-scale implementation, trade-off accuracy and efficiency. The most used algorithm for detecting diabetic retinopathy was CNN. It uses morphological processing techniques and texture analysis methods for reading fundus images. They could identify features such as hemorrhages, micro-aneurysms, hard exudates and blood vessels with very high accuracy. Several other algorithms like custom-built algorithms and CNN with SVM and a hybrid model with multiple CNN and random forest classifiers were used for detection (Islam, Yang, Poly, Jian, & Jack Li, 2020).

Breast Cancer

In recent years, machine learning in predicting axillary lymph node metastasis (ANLM) in breast cancer patients has risen exponentially. The most used algorithms in detecting ANLM were SVM, linear regression and linear discriminant analysis. The linear discriminant analysis showed the most promising sensitivity and specificity of these three (C. Chen et al., 2021). Many machine learning algorithms for breast cancer diagnosis and classification have been developed recently. To create automated diagnostic models based mostly on DL structures, the majority of the research used imaging data from computed tomography (CT), magnetic resonance imaging (MRI), X-ray radiography, and positron-emission tomography (PET) (Kourou et al., 2021). The feature extraction stage is critical because it aids in the differentiation of benign and malignant tumors. Then, picture attributes such as smoothness, coarseness, depth, and regularity are extracted by employing segmentation. Images are usually converted to binary to extract meaningful information. However, it was discovered that by doing so, several significant elements in the image vanished, resulting in the omission of crucial information. As a result, the photographs have been kept in greyscale format. The images can be translated from the time domain to the frequency domain using discrete wavelet transformation (DWT). In another study the goal of the researchers was to estimate the likelihood of relapse in breast cancer patients over a five-year period. Clinical data such as patient age, tumour size, and the number of axillary metastases were combined with seven predictive factors. Information on protein biomarkers like estrogen and progesterone receptor levels was also supplied. The researchers wanted to create an autonomous, quantitative prognostic technique that was more accurate than the traditional tumour-node-metastasis (TNM) staging scheme (De Laurentiis, De Placido, Bianco, Clark, & Ravdin, 1999). (Zheng et al., 2020) looked into and developed a CNN-based transfer learning approach for detecting breast cancer early by efficiently segmenting ROIs. Compared to other machine learning algorithms, promising results were produced with high levels of accuracy (97.2%) and a good balance of sensitivity and specificity measures.

Neurodegenerative Diseases

The diagnosis of neurodegenerative diseases is a substantial unmet need globally. The current diagnostic technologies like magnetic resonance imagining electroencephalogram produce huge quantities for detecting, monitoring, and treating neurodegenerative diseases. The analysis tends to be difficult due to the data's complexity and hugeness (Van Horn & Toga, 2014). Machine learning plays a huge role in the analysis and will continue to do so in the future. Supervised machine learning is the most applied in neurodegenerative diseases as it trains the model to use manual curation by labelling the benchmark dataset; for example, a radiologist labels a set of MRI scan images, and a neuropathologist categorizes them to set up a benchmark dataset on which machine learning builds a model to find the relationship between the input features (example, the size of brain region or blood clot in MRI scans) and label them into diseases specific. So, later, the model predicted the diseases-specific outcome in the unlabeled dataset. The most used algorithms for diagnosing Alzheimer's diseases with high sensitivity and specificity were CNN and DNN (Deep neural network). They are a better fit for image interpretation as they extract features at higher and higher levels of abstraction, combining local information and eventually integrating large-scale information across the image. The algorithm for the diagnosis of Parkinson's disease was CNN. The dementia classification and amyotrophic lateral sclerosis progression prediction were made using a hierarchical Bayesian model, SVM, random forests and variational autoencoders. These algorithms improve the consistency of diagnosis and increase the chances of treatment (Myszczynska et al., 2020).

Healthcare Technologies

Flow Cytometry

Flow cytometry is a diagnostic tool that generates information from the interaction of light with the streaming cellular suspension to classify each cell based on its size, granularity, and fluorescence by measuring elastic and inelastic scatterings (Picot, Guerin, Le Van Kim, & Boulanger, 2012). These tools generate approximately 1Tbit/s of continuous data and analyzing this type of data is a cumbersome task. Machine learning started to play a vital role in this analysis by providing new insight through image enhancement, correction, reconstruction and, more importantly, automated recognition and identification of cells. These images of cells were generally split into two classes: Images with only one cell and images with multiple cells for problem analysis. In images with multiple cells, tracking and detection become a major issue. To solve this issue, deep learning comes in very handy with two-stage models of Faster-RCNN (Ciresan, Giusti, Gambardella, & Schmidhuber, 2012) and one stage model of SSD (Caicedo et al., 2017) provide better insight into speed and accuracy. DeepLab (L. C. Chen, Papandreou, Kokkinos, Murphy, & Yuille, 2018) and Mask-RCNN (He, Gkioxari, Dollar, & Girshick, 2020) with their joint approach for segmentation and detection outshine with advantages of multitask learning. The detection and tracking task requires a real-time imaging processing algorithm based on the CNN algorithm as it directly processes the one-dimensional time-series waveforms from the imaging flow cytometer. It automatically sorts the cell with high sensitivity and specificity while taking less than a few milliseconds to classify cells and sort them accurately in real-time. In case of images with single cell, the two fundamental problems were encountered, which is classification and segmentation. To solve this issue earlier FCNNs (Fully Convolutional neural networks) was used (Li, Shen, & Yu, 2017) and recently U-net (Falk et al., 2019) and its variations started dominating cell-level counting and segmentation. Machine learning started to play a vital role in this analysis. The CNN algorithm directly processes the one-dimensional time-series waveforms from the imaging flow cytometer. It automatically sorts the cell with high sensitivity and specificity while taking less than a few milliseconds to classify cells and sort them accurately in real-time. A study published in Nature journal showed the applicability of machine learning in classifying white blood cells and epithelial cancer cells with more than 95% accuracy in a label-free fashion (Li et al.).

Biosensor for Monitoring Clinical Parameters

The biosensing field has exploded into many research areas of medical applications (Metkar & Girigoswami, 2019). The greatest appeal of biosensors is their sensitivity and specificity. Earlier biosensors used only simple regression models to analyze composition based on the biosensor's signal magnitude, but the analysis pattern has changed with the advent of machine learning (Schackart & Yoon, 2021).

Machine learning can process large datasets with complex matrices or samples very fast. In the case of biosensors, it increases the possibility of getting reasonable analytical results from heavily overlapping, noisy and low-resolution sensing data. Machine learning analyzes the raw data generated by the biosensors in several ways like categorization, anomaly detection, noise reduction and object identification with pattern recognition. Machine learning has been used to specifically enhance the imaging, Enose, Etounge and surface-enhanced Raman spectroscopy (SERS) biosensors (Cui, Yue, Zhang, Zhang, & Zhou). The algorithms used in these biosensors are principal component analysis combined with SVM and various artificial neural networks. These algorithms have shown outstanding performance in various tasks (Schackart & Yoon, 2021). Apart from the analysis, machine learning also assist in designing more desirable biosensors. The signal of surface plasmon resonance (SPR) based biosensors were amplified with usage of metamaterials that amplify the signal as the material has negative permeability and permittivity. Preparation of metamaterials with specific reflectance is critical to ensure the resonance is helpful for SPR. The Autoencoder (AE) and multilayer perceptron (MLP) are used to predict that reflectance while t-Stochastic Neighbor Embedding (t-SNE) and AE with k-means clustering for the conductance.

Chatbots

Chatbots are delivering healthcare facilities with a wide range of usage. AI-based chatbots are preliminarily used for resolving basic health-related queries. It can also help allocate useful resources to the patients, providing consultations, scheduling medical appointments, data collection, medical insurance claims, or mental health assistance (Figure 2). Chatbot algorithms require a massive dataset of queries and responses, including symptoms, diagnostics, markers, and pre-labelled treatment answers. Advanced-level chatbots like "Sensely" are also capable of voice processing and speech-based support. Mental health is the foremost concern in healthcare; it affects overall wellbeing and development. Several smartphone applications (like Woebot) use machine learning technology to provide cognitive behavioural therapy. Multilingual voice assistant-based virtual robots should be developed for easy assessment and accessibility. Natural Language Processing (NLP) technology uses human voice and speech to implement rule-based modelling with intelligent algorithms. NLP encompasses speech recognition, word sense disambiguation, named entity recognition, and sentiment analysis as data ingestion. It also has certain challenges or snags (synonyms, misspellings, abbreviations, punctuation rules, accents, etc.), making interaction difficult. Interpreting multiple medical terminologies via NLP requires careful consideration of snags and big databases with advanced computing capabilities.

Wearable Technologies

In the last decade, wearable technologies have advanced with high-tech sensors, multiple features, affordability, and information-sharing options. These devices can be fitness trackers, smartwatches, wearable ECG monitors, blood pressure monitors, biosensors, smart jewelry, smart tattoos, smart eyewear, smart headgears etc., which can measure the human body's physical and chemical features, which decipher health-related information. Wearable gadgets come in various shapes and sizes to fulfil the needs of their users. They're usually small, yet they must sense all the time. They may collect data locally or send it to a remote location for interpretation. As a result, wearables must interact safely while consuming as little power as possible. Wearable device security is a significant concern. Given the minimal processing capability of most wearable devices, a simple authentication test is required. Wearables can change medical care, resulting in more cost-effective healthcare services and longer lifespans with further development (Nahavandi, Alizadehsani, Khosravi, & Acharya, 2022). Presently, wearable technologies deal with basic AI that enables gadgets to handle specific problem-solving tasks and doesn't confer human-like intelligence. Speech recognition, visual perception and data-based decision-making are available in a few commercially available wearable gadgets. The incorporation of AI for the early prediction of diseases can be incorporated with remote reporting features. Combining nanotechnology with wearable gadgets can be a breakthrough in healthcare. The injection of nanobots in arteries and decoding its readings through a smart wristwatch could detect multiple problems inside the human body. AI-based modes to monitor single or multiple chronic diseases could be highly helpful in clinical monitoring and reduce the costs of multiple laboratory tests. The vitals of the human body is very complex, and interpreting a high level of vital fluctuation to detect accurate body conditions requires high dimensional data, which can be implemented with ML algorithms.

Figure 2. Prospects of chatbots in healthcare services.

Drug Distribution

Supply Chain

The supply chain is an integral part of the healthcare system. The supply chain's performance determines the ability of health systems to provide inexpensive and high-quality healthcare services at all delivery points. Demand can determine the actual need for vital health commodities at facility and end-user levels. Key stakeholders will need a comprehensive grasp of the short- and long-term demands after deciding which diagnostics and medications will be stocked. Managing a cold chain is a very complex process. It ensures dry ice quantity for temperature management from production till distribution to end-users. Pharmaceutical companies use advanced tracking methods and sensors to measure temperature and GPS locations. Data like traffic conditions, road conditions, airport information, vehicle specifications, weather reports, and packaging data are integrated with machine learning to tackle several challenges. It all begins with traffic and air traffic forecasting and logistical route optimization. The temperature decline of the freight can be predicted, and the packaging optimized in advance based on the parameters. Throughout delivery, the continuous temperature measurement allows for real-time monitoring and forecasting of further temperature drops. It is possible to forecast when a delivery intervention is required, especially when unexpected delays occur. The machine intelligence-based drug management ensures appropriate drug delivery and distribution conditions, reducing the extra costs to the pharma companies through automated drug quality management based on the external environment.

Prescription Text Recognition

The medicine name mentioned on its box is not interpretable/readable for all people. Through optical character recognition (OCR), it is possible to convert the captured text in images of typed, handwritten, or printed text into digitized and usable text (Figure 3). Presently, Google's open-source engine "Tesseract" is among the most efficient character recognition systems that use a neural network system. Integrating this open-source system in medicine vending machines can facilitate medicine recognition. An OCR system for reading the text on the medicine box can help provide essential medicine. The system can be built based on a text recognition system to identify the name of the medicines and search across the available medicines. Understanding the complex medical prescriptions handwritten by doctors is also a challenge. It's difficult for the patient to understand the written text without reaching a medical store. The OCR can also identify these complex handwritten prescriptions (19) so that patients can understand or buy medicine from online stores. However, there are available modelling works for OCR of doctors' writings but developing a generalized model for wider applicability is still a challenge.

Vending Machines

Artificial intelligence has advanced rapidly, and machine learning and intelligent recognition have been applied to human life (Figure 4). Vending machines are a relatively new kind of retail trade nowadays. However, numerous vending machines sell drinks and snacks in the market. Many customers' desires for medications is often sudden, and there are frequently many hospitals, queues, or urgent usage of medicines at night, this frequently causes consumers to be distressed, and many pharmacies are expensive, which often drives consumers to be concerned. Regarding issues, it is rarely available 24 hours a day, making it difficult to obtain medications. A vending machine is controlled by microcontrollers dispensing medicines, and multiple prototypes were developed to deliver medicines efficiently. Several prototypes already provided the GUI (graphic user interface), SMS-based notification services, smart medicine dispenser, integrated tracker for timely medications, etc. However, the implementation of machine learning in medicine dispensing systems is rarely addressed because it requires the development of a machine learning model which can predict medication for a wide range of patients. The diseases like the common cold, diarrhea, vomiting, digestive problems, body pains, etc., require generalized medicines which can be made available through vending machines. This concept will initially reduce the burden on healthcare facilities and may help detect disease outbreaks in any region. However, it's difficult to manually develop complicated yet parsimonious models that synthesize information from multiple data sources.

Figure 3. The OCR engine predicts the generally unrecognizable text on a doctor's prescription.

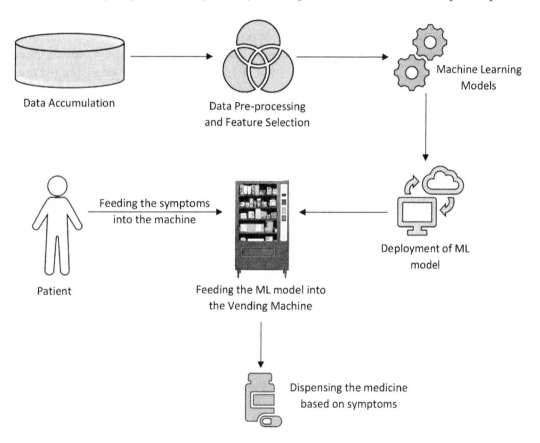

Figure 4. The brief concept of ML-based vending machine for automated symptom-based medicine prescription.

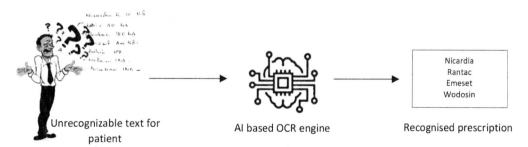

Advantages and Disadvantages of ML in Health Care

Artificial intelligence (AI) is rapidly gaining traction in health care, with applications ranging from medical practice automation to patient and resource management. As developers design AI systems to perform these activities, various risks and concerns emerge, including the risk of patient injury due to AI system mistakes, data acquisition and AI inference compromising patient privacy, and more. There are at least four roles in the medical system that AI can play.

First, AI has the potential to push the boundaries of medical knowledge and practice, allowing for previously unavailable types of care. Second, AI has the potential to democratize medical expertise, allowing a broader range of physicians to perform tasks previously only available to a small number of specialists but still well within human competence. Third, AI can automate mundane chores like paperwork, freeing clinicians time for more important tasks. Fourth, AI can allocate limited resources, directing them to the most beneficial uses (W. Price & Nicholson, 2019). While AI has a lot of potential benefits, it also has several drawbacks. The most obvious risk is that AI systems will occasionally be incorrect, resulting in patient damage or other healthcare issues. A patient could be damaged if an AI system prescribes the wrong treatment, fails to detect a tumour on a radiological exam, or allocates a hospital bed to one patient over another because it incorrectly anticipated which patient would benefit most. Large volumes of data from electronic health records, pharmacy records, insurance claims records, or consumer-generated data like activity trackers or purchase history are needed to train AI algorithms. However, health data is frequently problematic. Data is frequently dispersed across multiple platforms. Another set of dangers arises regarding privacy (W. N. Price, 2nd & Cohen, 2019). The demand for huge datasets encourages developers to acquire data from many patients. Some patients may be concerned that this data collection would infringe on their privacy, and lawsuits have been filed due to data sharing between huge health institutions and AI companies (Cohen & Mello, 2019). In healthcare AI, there are dangers of prejudice and inequality. AI systems learn from the data they've been given and can absorb biases. For example, suppose AI data is primarily collected in academic medical institutions. In that case, the resulting AI systems will know less about it and treat patients with less accuracy from populations who do not often visit academic medical centers.

FUTURE RESEARCH DIRECTIONS

The foremost requirement of machine learning and artificial intelligence is a big database and access to data, which is still inaccessible in several countries due to privacy protection laws and fear of data misuse. The data generation for implementing ML in healthcare is a multi-dimensional long-term process that requires funds and cooperation from the government and people. The next step includes data processing to minimize any influence of biasness in the database. Various methodologies are available for data pre-processing, but the accuracy may differ depending upon the data types. Detecting outliers, data augmentation, data imputation etc., may result in an error while modelling or inaccurate predictions. The complex healthcare data consists of several features that need to be addressed because implementing similar techniques on each feature may lead to overprediction/overfitting or underprediction/underfitting. The recommendation of a single machine learning algorithm might not be accurate for high-dimensional healthcare data, like numerical data, images, voices, time-series data, sentiment data etc. Therefore, specific algorithms that can be used to model and integrate one outcome into another should be done cautiously. Another important aspect of ML in healthcare is automation and self-learning, which reduce the repetitive human effort in data accumulation and processing. Establishing infrastructural support to generate high-quality data or electronic health records is essential for multi-dimensional data processing.

CONCLUSION

Machine learning is already making a significant contribution to healthcare services. Various research and industrial inventions have shown their potential to reduce the burden on healthcare facilities with cost-effectiveness. Several concepts must be focused on efficiently implementing machine learning in healthcare. Inaccurate data and misinterpretation of results will lead to a false diagnosis, false prescription, or inaccurate prediction of health-related outcomes. Therefore, it is crucial to select the domain and data before developing ML models. Before data accumulation, the multi-disciplinary team of scientists, professors, industrialists, and technologists must be considered because pre-planned data accumulation will ease data processing and ML modelling. The external validation of any output should be performed before implementing it on patients or the population. The ethical aspects are integral to healthcare services, education and research. Therefore, it should be considered at every step of machine learning implementation. Machine learning and artificial intelligence are considered the future of multiple disciplines, and their wise implementation may provide us with supplemental benefits.

ACKNOWLEDGMENT

This research received no specific grant from any funding agency in the public, commercial, or not-for-profit sectors.

REFERENCES

Anno, S., Hara, T., Kai, H., Lee, M.-A., Chang, Y., Oyoshi, K., Mizukami, Y., & Tadono, T. (2019). Spatiotemporal dengue fever hotspots associated with climatic factors in taiwan including outbreak predictions based on machine-learning. *Geospatial Health*, *14*(2). Advance online publication. doi:10.4081/gh.2019.771 PMID:31724367

Ashrafian, H., & Darzi, A. (2018). Transforming health policy through machine learning. *PLoS Medicine*, *15*(11), e1002692. doi:10.1371/journal.pmed.1002692 PMID:30422977

Bellemo, V., Lim, Z. W., Lim, G., Nguyen, Q. D., Xie, Y., Yip, M. Y. T., Hamzah, H., Ho, J., Lee, X. Q., Hsu, W., Lee, M. L., Musonda, L., Chandran, M., Chipalo-Mutati, G., Muma, M., Tan, G. S. W., Sivaprasad, S., Menon, G., Wong, T. Y., & Ting, D. S. W. (2019). Artificial intelligence using deep learning to screen for referable and vision-threatening diabetic retinopathy in Africa: A clinical validation study. *The Lancet. Digital Health*, *1*(1), e35–e44. doi:10.1016/S2589-7500(19)30004-4 PMID:33323239

Bialek, S., Boundy, E., Bowen, V., Chow, N., Cohn, A., Dowling, N., Ellington, S., Gierke, R., Hall, A., MacNeil, J., Patel, P., Peacock, G., Pilishvili, T., Razzaghi, H., Reed, N., Ritchey, M., & Sauber-Schatz, E. (2020). Severe Outcomes Among Patients with Coronavirus Disease 2019 (COVID-19) - United States. *MMWR. Morbidity and Mortality Weekly Report*, *27*(69), 343–346. doi:10.15585/mmwr.mm6912e2

Buch, V. H., Ahmed, I., & Maruthappu, M. (2018). Artificial intelligence in medicine: Current trends and future possibilities. *The British Journal of General Practice*, *68*(668), 143–144. doi:10.3399/bjgp18X695213 PMID:29472224

Burlina, P., Freund, D. E., Dupas, B., & Bressler, N. (2011). *Automatic screening of age-related macular degeneration and retinal abnormalities.* Paper presented at the 2011 Annual International Conference of the IEEE Engineering in Medicine and Biology Society.

Caicedo, J. C., Cooper, S., Heigwer, F., Warchal, S., Qiu, P., Molnar, C., Vasilevich, A. S., Barry, J. D., Bansal, H. S., Kraus, O., Wawer, M., Paavolainen, L., Herrmann, M. D., Rohban, M., Hung, J., Hennig, H., Concannon, J., Smith, I., Clemons, P. A., ... Carpenter, A. E. (2017). Data-analysis strategies for image-based cell profiling. *Nature Methods*, *14*(9), 849–863. doi:10.1038/nmeth.4397 PMID:28858338

Carrion, M., & Madoff, L. C. (2017). ProMED-mail: 22 years of digital surveillance of emerging infectious diseases. *International Health*, *9*(3), 177–183. doi:10.1093/inthealth/ihx014 PMID:28582558

Chen, C., Qin, Y., Chen, H., Zhu, D., Gao, F., & Zhou, X. (2021). A meta-analysis of the diagnostic performance of machine learning-based MRI in the prediction of axillary lymph node metastasis in breast cancer patients. *Insights Into Imaging*, *12*(1), 156. doi:10.118613244-021-01034-1 PMID:34731343

Chen, F., & Neill, D. B. (2014). Non-parametric scan statistics for event detection and forecasting in heterogeneous social media graphs. *Proceedings of the 20th ACM SIGKDD international conference on Knowledge discovery and data mining.* 10.1145/2623330.2623619

Chen, L. C., Papandreou, G., Kokkinos, I., Murphy, K., & Yuille, A. L. (2018). DeepLab: Semantic Image Segmentation with Deep Convolutional Nets, Atrous Convolution, and Fully Connected CRFs. *IEEE Transactions on Pattern Analysis and Machine Intelligence*, *40*(4), 834–848. doi:10.1109/TPAMI.2017.2699184 PMID:28463186

Chua Chin Heng, M., Aisu, N., Miyake, M., Takeshita, K., Akiyama, M., Kawasaki, R., ... Tsujikawa, A. (2022). Regulatory-approved deep learning/machine learning-based medical devices in Japan as of 2020: A systematic review. *PLOS Digital Health*, *1*(1), e0000001. Advance online publication. doi:10.1371/journal.pdig.0000001

Ciresan, D. C., Giusti, A., Gambardella, L. M., & Schmidhuber, J. (2012). *Deep Neural Networks Segment Neuronal Membranes in Electron Microscopy Images.* Paper presented at the NIPS.

Cohen, I. G., & Mello, M. M. (2019). Big Data, Big Tech, and Protecting Patient Privacy. *Journal of the American Medical Association*, *322*(12), 1141–1142. doi:10.1001/jama.2019.11365 PMID:31397838

Damen, J. A., Hooft, L., Schuit, E., Debray, T. P., Collins, G. S., Tzoulaki, I., Lassale, C. M., Siontis, G. C. M., Chiocchia, V., Roberts, C., Schlüssel, M. M., Gerry, S., Black, J. A., Heus, P., van der Schouw, Y. T., Peelen, L. M., & Moons, K. G. (2016). Prediction models for cardiovascular disease risk in the general population: Systematic review. *BMJ (Clinical Research Ed.), 353*, i2416. doi:10.1136/bmj.i2416 PMID:27184143

De Laurentiis, M., De Placido, S., Bianco, A. R., Clark, G. M., & Ravdin, P. M. (1999). A prognostic model that makes quantitative estimates of probability of relapse for breast cancer patients. *Clinical Cancer Research, 5*(12), 4133–4139. PMID:10632351

Debnath, S., Barnaby, D. P., Coppa, K., Makhnevich, A., Kim, E. J., Chatterjee, S., Tóth, V., Levy, T. J., Paradis, M., Cohen, S. L., Hirsch, J. S., Zanos, T. P., Becker, L. B., Cookingham, J., Davidson, K. W., Dominello, A. J., Falzon, L., McGinn, T., Mogavero, J. N., & Osorio, G. A. (2020). Machine learning to assist clinical decision-making during the COVID-19 pandemic. *Bioelectronic Medicine, 6*(1), 14. Advance online publication. doi:10.118642234-020-00050-8 PMID:32665967

Decapprio, D., Gartner, J., McCall, C. J., Burgess, T., Kothari, S., & Sayed, S. (2020). *Building a COVID-19 Vulnerability Index*. Cold Spring Harbor Laboratory. Retrieved from doi:10.1101/2020.03.16.20036723

Edo-Osagie, O., Lake, I. R., Edeghere, O., & Iglesia, B. l. (2019). *Attention-Based Recurrent Neural Networks (RNNs) for Short Text Classification: An Application in Public Health Monitoring*. Paper presented at the IWANN.

Falk, T., Mai, D., Bensch, R., Çiçek, Ö., Abdulkadir, A., Marrakchi, Y., Böhm, A., Deubner, J., Jäckel, Z., Seiwald, K., Dovzhenko, A., Tietz, O., Dal Bosco, C., Walsh, S., Saltukoglu, D., Tay, T. L., Prinz, M., Palme, K., Simons, M., ... Ronneberger, O. (2019). U-Net: Deep learning for cell counting, detection, and morphometry. *Nature Methods, 16*(1), 67–70. doi:10.103841592-018-0261-2 PMID:30559429

Feeny, A. K., Tadarati, M., Freund, D. E., Bressler, N. M., & Burlina, P. (2015). Automated segmentation of geographic atrophy of the retinal epithelium via random forests in AREDS color fundus images. *Computers in Biology and Medicine, 65*, 124–136. doi:10.1016/j.compbiomed.2015.06.018 PMID:26318113

Haneef, R., Kab, S., Hrzic, R., Fuentes, S., Fosse-Edorh, S., Cosson, E., & Gallay, A. (2021). Use of artificial intelligence for public health surveillance: A case study to develop a machine Learning-algorithm to estimate the incidence of diabetes mellitus in France. *Archives of Public Health, 79*(1), 168. Advance online publication. doi:10.118613690-021-00687-0 PMID:34551816

He, K., Gkioxari, G., Dollar, P., & Girshick, R. (2020). Mask R-CNN. *IEEE Transactions on Pattern Analysis and Machine Intelligence, 42*(2), 386–397. doi:10.1109/TPAMI.2018.2844175 PMID:29994331

Hirsch, T., Merced, K., Narayanan, S., Imel, Z. E., & Atkins, D. C. (2017). *Designing Contestability*. Academic Press.

Islam, M. M., Yang, H. C., Poly, T. N., Jian, W. S., & Jack Li, Y. C. (2020). Deep learning algorithms for detection of diabetic retinopathy in retinal fundus photographs: A systematic review and meta-analysis. *Computer Methods and Programs in Biomedicine, 191*, 105320. doi:10.1016/j.cmpb.2020.105320 PMID:32088490

Kaul, V., Enslin, S., & Gross, S. A. (2020). History of artificial intelligence in medicine. *Gastrointestinal Endoscopy*, *92*(4), 807–812. doi:10.1016/j.gie.2020.06.040 PMID:32565184

Kourou, K., Exarchos, K. P., Papaloukas, C., Sakaloglou, P., Exarchos, T., & Fotiadis, D. I. (2021). Applied machine learning in cancer research: A systematic review for patient diagnosis, classification and prognosis. *Computational and Structural Biotechnology Journal*, *19*, 5546–5555. doi:10.1016/j.csbj.2021.10.006 PMID:34712399

Krittanawong, C., Virk, H. U. H., Bangalore, S., Wang, Z., Johnson, K. W., Pinotti, R., Zhang, H. J., Kaplin, S., Narasimhan, B., Kitai, T., Baber, U., Halperin, J. L., & Tang, W. H. W. (2020). Machine learning prediction in cardiovascular diseases: A meta-analysis. *Scientific Reports*, *10*(1), 16057. doi:10.103841598-020-72685-1 PMID:32994452

Li, Y., Shen, L., & Yu, S. (2017). HEp-2 Specimen Image Segmentation and Classification Using Very Deep Fully Convolutional Network. *IEEE Transactions on Medical Imaging*, *36*(7), 1561–1572. doi:10.1109/TMI.2017.2672702 PMID:28237925

Lysaght, T., Lim, H. Y., Xafis, V., & Ngiam, K. Y. (2019). AI-assisted decision-making in healthcare. *Asian Bioethics Review*, *11*(3), 299–314. doi:10.100741649-019-00096-0 PMID:33717318

M'ikanatha, N. M., Rohn, D. D., Robertson, C., Tan, C. G., Holmes, J. H., Kunselman, A. R., Polachek, C., & Lautenbach, E. (2006). Use of the internet to enhance infectious disease surveillance and outbreak investigation. *Biosecurity and Bioterrorism*, *4*(3), 293–300. doi:10.1089/bsp.2006.4.293 PMID:16999590

Magumba, M. A., & Nabende, P. (2021). Evaluation of different machine learning approaches and input text representations for multilingual classification of tweets for disease surveillance in the social web. *Journal of Big Data*, *8*(1), 139. Advance online publication. doi:10.118640537-021-00528-5

McCradden, M. D., Anderson, J. A., & Stephenson, E., Drysdale, E., Erdman, L., Goldenberg, A., & Zlotnik Shaul, R. (2022). A Research Ethics Framework for the Clinical Translation of Healthcare Machine Learning. *The American Journal of Bioethics*, 1–15. doi:10.1080/15265161.2021.2013977 PMID:35048782

Metkar, S. K., & Girigoswami, K. (2019). Diagnostic biosensors in medicine – A review. *Biocatalysis and Agricultural Biotechnology*, *17*, 271–283. doi:10.1016/j.bcab.2018.11.029

Mhasawade, V., Zhao, Y., & Chunara, R. (2021). Machine learning and algorithmic fairness in public and population health. *Nature Machine Intelligence*, *3*(8), 659–666. doi:10.103842256-021-00373-4

Muehlematter, U. J., Daniore, P., & Vokinger, K. N. (2021). Approval of artificial intelligence and machine learning-based medical devices in the USA and Europe (2015–20): A comparative analysis. *The Lancet. Digital Health*, *3*(3), e195–e203. doi:10.1016/S2589-7500(20)30292-2 PMID:33478929

Mykhalovskiy, E., & Weir, L. (2006). The Global Public Health Intelligence Network and Early Warning Outbreak Detection. *Canadian Journal of Public Health*, *97*(1), 42–44. doi:10.1007/BF03405213 PMID:16512327

Myszczynska, M. A., Ojamies, P. N., Lacoste, A. M. B., Neil, D., Saffari, A., Mead, R., Hautbergue, G. M., Holbrook, J. D., & Ferraiuolo, L. (2020). Applications of machine learning to diagnosis and treatment of neurodegenerative diseases. *Nature Reviews. Neurology*, *16*(8), 440–456. doi:10.103841582-020-0377-8 PMID:32669685

Nahavandi, D., Alizadehsani, R., Khosravi, A., & Acharya, U. R. (2022). Application of artificial intelligence in wearable devices: Opportunities and challenges. *Computer Methods and Programs in Biomedicine*, *213*, 106541. doi:10.1016/j.cmpb.2021.106541 PMID:34837860

Picot, J., Guerin, C. L., Le Van Kim, C., & Boulanger, C. M. (2012). Flow cytometry: Retrospective, fundamentals and recent instrumentation. *Cytotechnology*, *64*(2), 109–130. doi:10.100710616-011-9415-0 PMID:22271369

Pratt, H., Coenen, F., Broadbent, D. M., Harding, S. P., & Zheng, Y. (2016). Convolutional Neural Networks for Diabetic Retinopathy. *Procedia Computer Science*, *90*, 200–205. doi:10.1016/j.procs.2016.07.014

Price, W., & Nicholson, I. (2019). Artificial intelligence in the medical system: Four roles for potential transformation. *Yale JL & Tech.*, *21*, 122.

Price, W. N. II, & Cohen, I. G. (2019). Privacy in the age of medical big data. *Nature Medicine*, *25*(1), 37–43. doi:10.103841591-018-0272-7 PMID:30617331

Qayyum, A., Qadir, J., Bilal, M., & Al-Fuqaha, A. (2021). Secure and Robust Machine Learning for Healthcare: A Survey. *IEEE Reviews in Biomedical Engineering*, *14*, 156–180. doi:10.1109/RBME.2020.3013489 PMID:32746371

Sahoo, D., Hao, W., Ke, S., Xiongwei, W., Le, H., Achananuparp, P., . . . Hoi, S. C. H. (2019). *FoodAI: Food Image Recognition via Deep Learningfor Smart Food Logging*. Academic Press.

Sánchez-Martínez, S., Camara, O., Piella, G., Cikes, M., Ballester, M. A. G., Miron, M., . . . Bijnens, B. (2019). *Machine learning for clinical decision-making: challenges and opportunities*. Academic Press.

Schackart, K. E. III, & Yoon, J. Y. (2021). Machine Learning Enhances the Performance of Bioreceptor-Free Biosensors. *Sensors (Basel)*, *21*(16), 5519. Advance online publication. doi:10.339021165519 PMID:34450960

Şerban, O., Thapen, N., Maginnis, B., Hankin, C., & Foot, V. (2019). Real-time processing of social media with SENTINEL: A syndromic surveillance system incorporating deep learning for health classification. *Information Processing & Management*, *56*(3), 1166–1184. doi:10.1016/j.ipm.2018.04.011

Thieme, A., Belgrave, D., & Doherty, G. (2020). Machine Learning in Mental Health. *ACM Transactions on Computer-Human Interaction*, *27*(5), 1–53. doi:10.1145/3398069

Van Horn, J. D., & Toga, A. W. (2014). Human neuroimaging as a "Big Data" science. *Brain Imaging and Behavior*, *8*(2), 323–331. doi:10.100711682-013-9255-y PMID:24113873

Wang, L., Zhang, Y., Wang, D., Tong, X., Liu, T., Zhang, S., Huang, J., Zhang, L., Chen, L., Fan, H., & Clarke, M. (2021). Artificial Intelligence for COVID-19: A Systematic Review. *Frontiers in medicine*, *8*, 704256. Advance online publication. doi:10.3389/fmed.2021.704256 PMID:34660623

Yu, V. L., & Madoff, L. C. (2004). ProMED-mail: An early warning system for emerging diseases. *Clinical Infectious Diseases*, 39(2), 227–232. doi:10.1086/422003 PMID:15307032

Zhao, Y., Wood, E. P., Mirin, N., Vedanthan, R., Cook, S. H., & Chunara, R. (2020). *Machine Learning for Integrating Social Determinants in Cardiovascular Disease Prediction Models: A Systematic Review*. Cold Spring Harbor Laboratory. doi:10.1101/2020.09.11.20192989

Zheng, J., Lin, D., Gao, Z., Wang, S., He, M., & Fan, J. (2020). Deep learning assisted efficient AdaBoost algorithm for breast cancer detection and early diagnosis. *IEEE Access: Practical Innovations, Open Solutions*, 8, 96946–96954. doi:10.1109/ACCESS.2020.2993536

Chapter 4
Lung Nodule Classification Using CT Images:
Adaptive Radial Basis Neural Network Enhanced by Red Deer Optimization Algorithm

Manaswini Pradhan
ⓘ https://orcid.org/0000-0002-4729-8233
Fakir Mohan University, India

Ranjit Kumar Sahu
AIIMS, Bhubaneswar, India

ABSTRACT

Determining lung tumor level and reducing patient mortality is a challenging task. So, the identification of benign or malignant lung nodules requires efficient and accurate methods of lung nodule diagnosis. For achieving this aim, in this paper, an adaptive radial basis neural network (RBNN) is proposed. Initially, the texture features are extracted and the extracted features are fed to the classifier to classify a nodule as benign or malignant nodule. In addition, the radial basis neural network is enhanced by using red deer optimization algorithm, which is used for optimal parameter selection. The effectiveness of the proposed approach is calculated by using different evaluation metrics. The effectiveness of the classification performance is compared with existing algorithms.

INTRODUCTION

The important leading causes of death in the world include heart disease and diabetes. Lung cancer is the leading reason of death for both men and women (McWilliams et al., 2015; Lee et al., 2009). In 2014, there were 224,210 lung and lung cancers and 159,260 deaths in the United States, accounting for 27.2% of lung cancer deaths. Petousis et al. (2019) discussed that Lung cancer is due to the uncontrolled growth

DOI: 10.4018/978-1-6684-4045-2.ch004

of lung cells. Lung nodes are defects of the spherical and circular opaque lung tissue with a diameter of 30 mm. Clinical picture processing is widely used to build expert systems for the diagnosis of many diseases, including the diagnosis of gout, the detection of parasites, and the diagnosis and rehabilitation of lung cancer(Shrestha et al. 2015; Pengo et al. 2013).

Significant studies are being conducted on using CT methods to detect lung cancer at an early stage. Wei et al. (2009) discussed that automated systems are required to detect lung cancer using computed tomography image data. A lung CT scan usually contains more than 250 images per scan. Reading this comprehensive database for all patients is difficult, time-consuming, and dangerous for radiologists. Moreover, Diciottii et al. (2008) showed about the nature of the nodes that determine the patient's fate is more complex because their shape and size vary. Sometimes they attach to vessels such as the lungs or trachea. Shi et al. (2013) explained that the exact differentiation of the lungs from the CT images is an important step in identifying the lung nodes. To this end, several techniques have been proposed for the effective measurement of the lung nodule. The exact differentiation of the lungs from the CT images is an important step in identifying the lung nodes.

Several works have been developed for the classification of lung modules as begin or malignant. Some of the works are discussed here: One of the deadliest cancers worldwide is lung cancer. Smoking is an important cause of lung cancer, but people who do not smoke also suffer from lung cancer (Hanspeter. 2001). Kelly and Mott (2015) showed in their work that the proliferation and growth of irregular cells within the tumour is lung cancer. Coughing, shortness of breath, fatigue or weight loss, and chest pain are the advanced symptoms of lung cancer. Siegel et al. (2019) discussed that although various chemotherapy regimens and target therapeutics have been developed to treat cancer, a thorough cure for locally advanced lung cancer remains a challenge. Lung cancer detection in the early stage is the most important method to increase the survival rate of patients. So, the identification of malignant lung nodules requires efficient and accurate methods of lung nodule diagnosis.

Buzug and Thorsten (2011) focussed that currently, computed tomography (CT) is one of the main diagnostic methods for image detection of lung disease. CT is one of the leading medical procedures for lung cancer. CT provides additional important information about the localization and tumour size compared to a chest radiograph Kermany et al. (2018). Using low-level chest CT images and machine learning techniques (ML), a pulmonologist has been able to diagnose lung cancer. Feng and Jiang (2022) focussed that based on CT image analysis, the traditional algorithm for detection consists of three steps, such as feature extraction, feature recognition, and diagnosis.

However, these models heavily rely on feature extraction procedures that can be difficult and time-consuming and require specialized knowledge and skills. A DL (deep learning) model gives efficient results for solving the mentioned problems. Therefore, in this chapter, an effective lung nodule diagnosis model by using lung CT images has been developed.

The rest of this chapter is arranged as follows. In the literature review section, the previous algorithms have been described which are used in lung nodule detection. In section 3, the problem methodology and the system model are discussed. In proposed methodology section describes the proposed algorithm used for lung nodule detection at an early stage. In the result and discussion section, discuss the result of each part of the proposed method. Finally, the result and discussion section is presented followed by a concise conclusion to the research and future research direction scopes.

LITERATURE REVIEW

Feng and Jiang (2022) developed chest CT image features based on lung cancer diagnosis using a deep learning model. From the results, the mask Region-based Convolutional Neural Networks-Dual Path Network RCNN-DPN model achieved improved segmentation results for CT images of lungs and also improved the diagnosis accuracy and detection efficiency. Ying Su et al. (2021) developed faster RCNN-based lung nodule detection. In this approach, the lung nodule was detected by using the Faster-RCNN model. Besides, the parameters were optimized to improve the network structure and detection accuracy. The model achieved better accuracy when compared to the other algorithms. The presented model decreases the dataset noise and improves the classification performance, but it includes the issue of dimension disasters.

Zheng et al. (2019) introduced pulmonary nodule detection using CNN in CT scans based on maximum intensity projection. To increase the results of the automatic detection of the nodule, the MIP images were used in Boo et al. (2009) approach. The authors have proved the potential of clinical screening and the integration of CNNs to enhance lung nodule detection. Kido et al. (2022) developed lung nodule segmentation using nested three-dimensional fully connected neural networks on CT images. Initially, the features are extracted from the input 3D CT image, and the region segmentation results are created by using each block encoder network. Besides, the region map is also created by using each network encoder connection. From the results, this model provides an effective lung cancer diagnosis tool. The CNN model was computationally expensive because it needs an enormous amount of CT images for CNN model training.

Huang et al. (2020) used deep transfer CNN and an ELM to diagnose a lung nodule on CT images. Benign and malignant lung nodules were classified by utilizing deep transfer CNN and ELM. From the results, this method achieved promising results with improved accuracy, specificity, and sensitivity of 94.57%, 93.69%, and 95.15% respectively. However, the machine learning classifiers and ELM model manually control an enormous amount of CT images and the interpretation consumes more time.

Zia et al. (2020) developed the detection of lung nodules in an image label class with a multi-deep model. From the results, the LIDC-IDRI database achieved sophisticated performance on the lung nodule classification problem. The empirical results showed that the model obtained better classification performance on the dataset, but the computational complexity of the developed model was comparably higher related to the traditional machine learning techniques.

Similarly, Anthimopoulos et al. (2016) developed a deep CNN-based lung pattern classification for interstitial lung diseases. For the ILD pattern classification,CNN was used in this approach. From the results, the classification effectiveness proved the ability of CNNs to analyze lung patterns. The computational complexity of the deep CNN-based ILD pattern classification model was comparably higher related to the traditional machine learning techniques.

Farahani et al. (2018) modified spatial kernelled fuzzy c-means (MSFCM) is a specific algorithm based on an obscure C-object cluster that is ideal for obtaining different representations of lung regions. Nodal identify candidates in the process of moving to all objects in the trachea. Three techniques, including multilayer perceptron (MLP), K-Nearest Neighbour (KNN), and SVM to accurately determine whether a node is a candidate node (cancer) or a node (healthy). Determining. Lung evaluates the effectiveness of a hybrid intelligent approach using data transmitted on CT images, namely: the lung image database consortium (LIDC), but it includes the issue of dimension disasters.

DaSilvaet al. (2018) discussed that the PSO algorithm was used on the convolutional neural network (CNN) to eliminate the need for a manual search, improve network performance, and change network hyper settings. This method was tested on LIDC-IDRI CT scans at 97.62%, 92.20%, 98.64%, and ROC curve area - 0.955, but the computational complexity of the developed model was comparably higher.

Liu et al. (2018) offer a CNN-based method for node type classification. The spherical shape, based on the icosahedron with the tip and the maximum distance given, forms the normal shape of the CT values in each circle. Intensive analysis based on sample values is used to obtain the approximate distance of each node. The high-frequency content measurement analysis is repeated to determine which aircraft has the most information. Built to suit node size and views, it forms the basis for creating a single CNN model and CNN model for maximum visibility. However, the machine learning classifiers model manually controls an enormous amount of CT images and the interpretation consumes more time.

Zhang et al. (2019) discussed that several complex in-depth training models have been adopted to specify the nodes to improve the performance of the gate systems. CNN models are created by automatically extracting discriminating optical features from the CT connections of the original 3D terminal. Analyzes the effectiveness of using in-depth teaching models to identify nodes by measuring the performance of multiple classifications. The results indicate the advantages of Tens net 121 and the exceptions to respiratory problems. The output time is shown by comparing the training time. The Model decreases the dataset noise and improves the classification performance, but it includes the issue of dimension disasters

Xie et al. (2019) introduced a semi-supervised adversarial classification (SSAC), which can be prepared for the classification of malignant and malignant nodes in the lungs using unknown data. This model is based on the specific application of the Pulmonary Tip Classification, a widely used semiautomatic technique that allows clinical imaging to be reduced or enhanced to perform other functions of clinical imaging based on in-depth exercise. Perform a classification. The SSIC model applies to multi-visual knowledge-based collaborative exercises aimed at describing the overall shape, form, and structure of each node and using three SSICs to perform similar characteristics in a series of nine projects. The computational complexity of the SSAC model was comparably higher related to the traditional machine learning techniques.

Xu et al. (2020) showed that multi-resolution CT drives create an image database that helps clinics identify lung nodes in an automated framework called DeepLN. A large-scale database was used to create a database that confirmed the name of the three-level description criteria. One way to diagnose lung cancer is to diagnose lung cancer in a medical database. DCNN combines high and low properties to get accurate predictions. This model needs an enormous amount of CT images for CNN model training.

Lei et al. (2020) discussed about CNN has developed a soft activation mapping (SAM) that allows you to analyze the shape and lung nodule shape and margin (LNSM) for rich features. SAM high-level feature enhancement scheme (HESAM) LNSM Scripting with advanced features. A feature of HESAM and LNSM is the more accurate localization of current methods, attractive localization than false positives, and more complex predictions. The computational complexity of the SAM model was comparably higher related to the traditional machine learning techniques.

Zheng et al. (2020) provide CNN with a scale transfer module (STM) and integrate SDM-Net with a multifunction connection feature. This network can improve small targets and replace them with different-resolution images. The evaluation data was taken from the CT database provided by ZSDB. All data show pathological symptoms and lung adenocarcinoma is divided into four risk factors: pathological adenomatous hyperplasia, localized adenocarcinoma, minimally invasive adenocarcinoma, and invasive adenocarcinoma. The results showed that the STM model obtained better classification performance on the dataset, but the computational complexity of the developed model was comparably higher related to the traditional machine learning techniques.

Cao et al. (2020) focused on two-stage CNN to determine lung nodes. The innovative U-Net segment is a major discovery of network lung nodes. The training model strategy is used to recall high coefficients without many false-positive nodes. DSCNN Architecture is based on a dual-link architecture built into three 3D-CNN classification networks for false-positive reductions.

Masood et al. (2019) studied 3DCNN and achieved excellent results against other scan sensitivity and other state-of-the-art FP systems. The current 3DCNN test performance counter is relatively high and very efficient. The ability to detect micro nodes was relatively low; therefore, micro nodes less than 3 mm were detected. Integrate data processing methods to improve the training model, achieve greater robustness and reduce the recurrence of local problems.

Tran et al. (2019) developed a classification of nodules based on DL with focal loss for accuracy improvement. In this approach, a two-dimensional DCNN was used, and also focal loss function was applied. From the results, the proposed model achieved improved accuracy of 97.2%. The increasing depth of the DCNN model causes the vanishing gradient problem.

The solution that has been described in this manuscript is an adaptive radial basis neural network (ARBNN) technique based on Red Deer Optimization (RDO) algorithm for parameter optimization to enhance the accuracy, sensitivity, specificity, an area under the curve (AUC) as compared to the existing models, which help to diagnose the lung nodules more efficiently. Given a lung nodule, the proposed system retrieves several similar CT nodules from the historical database, potentially enriched with clinical records, to facilitate the doctor in the diagnostic process.

The important steps include:
§ To propose an ARBNN-RDO-based technique to achieve better performance even for small nodules.
§ To propose a hybrid machine learning-based classifier for optimal tumour prediction.
§   To optimize multiple features to customize features to enhance the accuracy of prediction.
§ An optimization algorithm-based classifier was proposed for weight optimization.
§ The attenuated size of the nodule can differ in the long-run lung cancer danger state.

As stated earlier, the CNN model was computationally expensive and, where it requires an enormous amount of data for model training and testing. To overcome the above-stated problems, a novel automated model: an adaptive radial basis neural network model is implemented in this manuscript.

PROPOSED METHODOLOGY

Determining lung tumour levels and reducing patient mortality is a challenging task. So, the identification of a benign or malignant lung nodules requires efficient and accurate methods of lung nodule diagnosis. For achieving this aim, in this chapter, an adaptive radial basis neural network (ARBNN) is proposed. Initially, the texture features are extracted and the extracted features are fed to the classifier to classify a nodule as benign or malignant nodule. Besides, the radial basis neural network is enhanced by using the red deer optimization (RDO) algorithm which is used for optimal parameter selection. The effectiveness of the proposed approach is calculated by using different evaluation metrics. The effectiveness of the classification performance is compared with existing algorithms.

Research Gap

According to radiologists, Lung malignancy is one of the leading causes of death worldwide. However, the constant flow of medical images to hospitals is forcing radiologists to focus on quality rather than quality. This feature is obvious, but it's not the same as the gray flag symbols. Many researchers are considering automation methods using available technologies Cao et al. (2020); Masood et al.(2019); & Huang et al. (2020). Previous systems were built on traditional methods such as adaptive identification and network connectivity. Since then, hybrid machines have been operating in this area for a long time. The main concern created by such a system is the design and adoption of these features, and the complexity of these approaches is limited in their applications.

Research Contributions

To overcome the above problems, an early prediction and classification of lung nodule diagnosis on CT images based on radial basis neural network (ARBNN) is developed that is enhanced by using the red deer optimization (RDO) algorithm for parameter optimization.

Finally, the RBNN-RDO technique with different public datasets LIDC-IDRI is proposed. The comparison of the performance can be done with the existing state-of-art methods using different computational parameters viz. accuracy, precision, recall, F1-score, and false-positive rate.

Description of the Datasets

Step 1: LIDC¤IDRI Descriptions

The Digital Imaging and Communication in Medicine (DICOM) information were selected from Armato et al. (2011); Clark et al. (2013) public datasets LIDC-IDRI in the Cancer Imaging Archive (CIA). The evaluated dataset used in this study is a subset of a larger public information repository created by the National Cancer Institute. During the training process and testing phase, batches were considered and applied for optimization of the nodule and non-nodule and their location information. In this research, the nodule size 3 mm to more range and the smaller nodules with less diameter is of more clinical relevance while performing extraction of several nodule screening illustrated by Magrelli et al.(2021); Han et al., (2015).

The LIDC-IDRI database according to Anthimopoulos et al. (2016); Cao et al. (2020) in The Cancer Imaging Archive (TCIA) initiated by National Cancer Institute (NCI) contains a total of 1018 clinical thoracic CT images with more than 200,000 slices of scan size 512x512x1 for imaging research in April 2000 to develop guidelines for the creation of a CT based lung nodule reference database. Each of the scans was obtained at different potential energies within the range of 40 to 627 mA to targeted CT scans. The scans that were acquired were annotated by at least three experienced radiologists, the interpretation was based on the correlation of the XML file and the details of malignancy and locations of segmented lung nodules. For this research work, the nodules of size less than 3 mm to 30 mm were extracted according to the XML file marks. The nodules which were smaller than 3 mm in diameter are of clinical importance and has got more relevance to the nodule screening schemes, Then, 2757 nodules were cropped into different pixels of size 32x32x1 or 48x48x1 and annotated with benign and malignant lung cancer, The main aim is to publicly make accessible the LIDC/IDRI database of CT images and associated radiologist annotations, and the Dissemination of CAD for chest CT into clinical practice after successful routing the regulatory approval process.

Step 2: FAH-GMU Description

The First Affiliated Hospital of Guangxi Medical University (FAH-GMU) dataset has115 patients' pulmonary consolidation confirmed from 2016 to 2019. Samples were had with a pathology lab test and at least one CT scan. The aim was to find CT images that attained the diameter of 2mm nodule of the slice thickness and its locations were identified among 68 patients having malignant pulmonary cancer and 47 patients with benign cancer in the provided data. The outcome of the hybrid technique was compared by three radiologists to check and validate the findings.

Advantages and Limitations of the Lung Nodule Diagnosis

The important advantage of this method is that image segmentation and feature extraction is automatic with less computational loss. The CT images in .tiff format, DICOM files, are standard and communication allows the pathological diagnosis faster without any incompatibility problems.

The limitation lies in noisy image objects. Some CT scans are incomplete or left blank which does not provide sufficient information and drawing inference tends to be very difficult. Another disadvantage is that the file format used may cause intentional damage to other computer software which is malware.

Figure 1. The overall flow of the proposed classification methodology

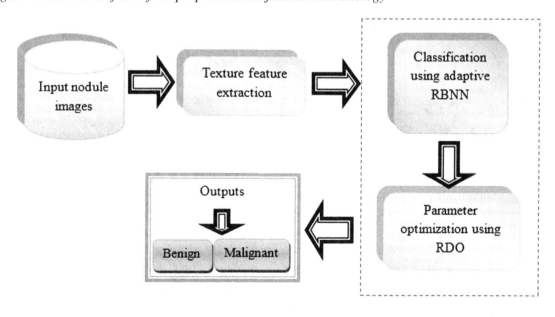

Adaptive Radial Basis Neural Network (RBNN) Based Lung Nodule Prediction

The main purpose of the proposed method is to improve the time consumption and classification results. For this aim, an adaptive radial basis neural network is developed in this approach. The overall flow of the proposed methodology is given in the below figure (1).

PRE-PROCESSING OF LUNG IMAGES IN THE CT IMAGES

In the pre-processing stage, the noise present in the images is removed using a median filter. After that, texture features are extracted from each image. In this chapter, seven texture features are extracted namely, Angular second moment, Contrast, correlation variance, Inverse Difference Moment, Sum entropy, Difference entropy, and Maximal correlation coefficient.

Figure 2. Raw CT scan images from the LIDC/IDRI database

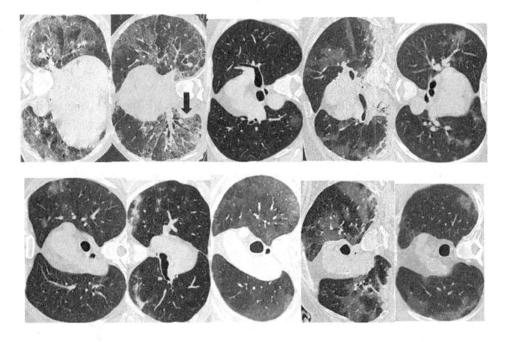

Raw CT images were collected as in figure (2) that need de-noising. Consider the CT image $I_{i,j}$, which consists of some noise. To remove the noise present in the input image, a median filter is applied. The median filter is typically used to lessen noise in an image. It is a non-linear filter that computes the median of the pixel set that falls within the filter mask. Each pixel is addressed and it is replaced using the statistical median of its $m \times n$ neighbourhood. Since the median value is computed from the neighbourhood pixel, it is more robust to outliners and does not create a new realistic pixel value, which preserves edge blurring and loss of image detail. It preserves the sharp high frequency details. It is well suited to eliminate salt and pepper noise from the image. The following are the steps for the median filter algorithm:

Steps to be followed in the median filter.

Step 1: Place a window over pixels.

Step 2: Sort the pixel's value by ascending or descending.

Step 3: Compute the median.

Step 4: The median value will be the new value of the center pixel of the window,

Step 5: Repeat the above process for all corrupting image areas.

A graphical presentation of the median filter operation is depicted in figure (3) below:

Figure 3. Graphical Representation Median filter

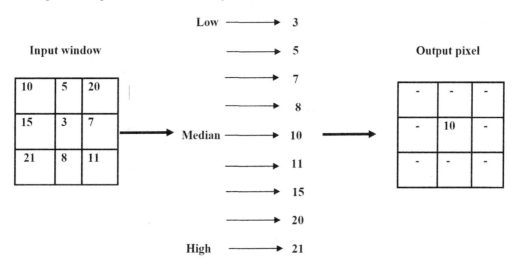

This filter works by analyzing the neighbourhood of pixels around an origin pixel like in the diagram above, for every valid pixel in an image. For this case, a 3 x 3 window, of pixels is used to calculate the output. For every pixel in the image, the window of neighbouring pixels is found. As shown in the example above, the pixel values in the window are sorted in ascending order and the median value is chosen, in this case, the median value is 50. Next, the pixel in the output image corresponding to the origin pixel in the input image is replaced with the value specified by the filter order. The value in the origin which is 70 is replaced by 50.

The effect of the median filter in removing noise is increased as the window size increase. The median filter is mathematically depicted as follows:

$$\widehat{Z}(i,j) = \underset{(s,t)\in S_{ij}}{median}\{g(s,t)\} \tag{1}$$

Where,

$\widehat{Z}(i,j)$ = median filter at a given coordinate

S_{ij} = coordinate of sub-image window of size ($m \times n$)

Feature Extraction

After the pre-processing, the texture features are extracted from each image. In this chapter, the gray-level co-occurrence matrix (GLCM) is used to extract the texture feature. George et al. (2013) formulated the GLCM that gives a joint distribution of gray-level pairs of neighbouring pixels within an image. For the computation of GLCM, first, a spatial relationship is established between two pixels, one is the reference pixel, and the other is a neighbour pixel.

Let $M(u,v)$ be the element of GLCM of a given image A of size ($a \times b$) containing the number of gray levels G^L ranging from 0 to G^L–1. Then M cab is defined as the matrix element and given by:

$$M(u,v) = \sum_{i=1}^{u}\sum_{j=1}^{v}\begin{cases}1 & \text{if } A(a,b)=u \text{ and } I^{in}(a+\Delta a, b+\Delta b)=v \\ 0 & \text{otherwise}\end{cases}$$

(2)

Where, (a,b) and $(a+\Delta a, b+\Delta b)$ are the location of the reference pixel and its neighboring pixel respectively.

According to Andre et al. (2019) each element of GLCM, $M(u,v| \Delta a, \Delta b)$ represent the relative frequency with which two pixels in a given neighbourhood separated by a distance $(\Delta a, \Delta b)$ having gray level values x and y respectively. It can be represented as $q\{u,v| D^D, \theta\}$, where the parameter DD is the distance of separation between two neighbourhood resolution cells with two pixels having intensities u and v in the image. The other parameter θ represents the direction of the neighbouring pixel concerning the pixel of reference. The parameter DD is also called set distance as it specifies the distance of all neighbouring resolution pairs contained in a set. For the texture calculation, the GLCM must be symmetrical, and each entry of the GLCM should be a probability value. In this chapter, twenty-two GLCM features are extracted from each image which is Angular Second Moment, Contrast, inverse difference moment, entropy, correlation, variance, sum average, sum variance, sum entropy, difference entropy, inertia, cluster shade, cluster prominence, Dissimilarity, homogeneity, Energy, autocorrelation, maximum probability, inverse difference normalizes, inverse difference moment normalize, information measure of correlation I and information of correlation II.

Proposed Adaptive Radial Basis Neural Network (ARBNN)

After the feature extraction process, selected features are presented to the ARBNN classifier to classify the lung nodule as benign or malignant. Broomhead & Lowe (1998) formulated the RBNN which is an effective feed-forwarded neural network. The RBNN structure has three layers namely the input layer, hidden layer, and output layer. Every hidden neuron has a radial basis function, which is consist of two parameters such as width and center position. Once the center and width are determined, the input vectors are mapped to the hidden location ($f: R^i \rightarrow R^j$). Assume that the input layer has i input units and the hidden layer has j RBF. The hidden neuron is described in the blow equation;

$$O_j(x) = \varphi\left(-\frac{x-C_J}{w_J}\right) \quad J=1,2,3\ldots j$$

(3)

Where, x is represents the input samples, C_j and w_j represents the center and width of the jth hidden neurons.

Broomhead et al. (1998)); Schwenker, F. et al. (2001) showed that RBFs are radials symmetric about a center vector since they only depend on distance from that point. The inputs to each hidden neuron are all connected in the basic form. It is usually assumed that the norm is Euclidean distance while the radial base function is Gaussian.

$$\varphi(g) = \exp\left(-\frac{g^2}{2}\right) \tag{4}$$

Where g is the variable of RBF $\varphi(.)$. The output of each RBNN is expressed in the below equation (5);

$$y_k = \sum_{J=1}^{j} d_{Jk} O_J(x) \quad k=1,2,3,\ldots,K \tag{5}$$

Where d_{Jk} is represents the relation weight among the hidden layer and output of the network. To enhance the RBNN, the parameter will be optimally selected using the red deer optimization algorithm.

Weight Optimization Using RDO Algorithm

An RDO algorithm is inspired by the mating behaviours of the red deer. The RDO algorithm follows the ability of roaring and fighting behaviours of the red deer. The process of the optimal parameter selection using RDO is described in the following steps;

Step1: Initialization

In RDO, the position of the red deer represents the position of the solution in the search space. In this work, the weight values of the RBNN are considered as the solution. The population of the solution is initialized as follows.

$$R_N = \{Y_1, Y_2, Y_3, \ldots, Y_N\} \tag{6}$$

Where Y_N denotes the Nth solution or the position of the red deer and it can be represented as the below equation (7);

$$Y_N = \{w_1, w_2, w_3, \ldots, w_i\} \tag{7}$$

Where, w_i represents the weight values of the RBNN.

Step 2: Fitness Calculation

The fitness of each solution is evaluated using classification accuracy. A good classification should have maximum accuracy. It can be expressed in the below equation (8);

$$Fitness_N = MAX(Accuracy) \tag{8}$$

If the desired fitness is not obtained, the solution is updated based on the mating behaviour of the red deer.

Step 3: Update the Solution

The solutions are updated after the fitness calculation. The following phases explain the mating process of red deer or the solution updation process.

Roar male RD: At this point, the male RD roars to increase their grace. The following equation expresses the position update of the male RD;

$$New_{male} = \begin{cases} Old_{male} + c_1 X \left((UR - LR)*c_2 \right) + LR, & \text{if } c_3 \geq 0.5 \\ Old_{male} - c_1 X \left((UR - LR)*c_2 \right) + LR, & \text{if } c_3 < 0.5 \end{cases} \tag{9}$$

The old and new location of the RD is represented as Old_{male} and New_{male}, respectively. Also, c, c_2 and c_3 denotes randomly distributed integer 0 to 1, and *UR and LR* are the upper and lower solution bounds. Using equations (10) and (11), sort the men and then create commanders and stags. Using Equation (10), calculate the number of male commanders, and the stag number is calculated according to Equation (11);

$$Num_{com} = round\{\gamma.Num_{male}\} \tag{10}$$

$$Num_{stag} = Num_{male} - Num_{com} \tag{11}$$

Where, Num_{com} and γ are representing the male count and initial value. The battle between the male commanders and stags stage is carried out using equations (12) and (13);

$$New_1 = \left(\frac{stag + com}{2} \right) + b_1 X \left((UR - LR)*b_2 \right) + LR) \tag{12}$$

$$New_1 = \left(\frac{stag + com}{2} \right) - b_1 X \left((UR - LR)*b_2 \right) + LR \tag{13}$$

After, the harems are formed by using, $Norm_n = power_n - max_i(power_i)$
The normalized power is calculated using the equation (14);

$$power_n = \left| \frac{norm_n}{\sum_i^{N_{com}} norm_i} \right| \tag{14}$$

$$Num_{narem} = round.\{power_n.Num_{hind}\} \tag{15}$$

$$Num_{harem}^{mate} = round\{\mathcal{E}.Num_{hind}\} \tag{16}$$

Generally, the mating process is formulated by

$$ffspring = \frac{(hind + com)}{2} + (UR - LR) * C,$$

where c is the random number. Hare, m is randomly selected and is denoted as K. In a harem, the number of hinds is calculated using the equation (17),

$$Num_{com} = round\{\mathcal{S}.Num_{harem_k}\} \tag{17}$$

It is used to approximate the selected harem with the elected commander. Then, select the closet by calculating the distance between the hinds and the stag. Mate the hind with the stag using equation (17).

Step 4: Termination

The solutions are updated on the mating behavior of the red deer until attaining the optimal solution. The optimal solution is obtained, and the algorithm will be terminated. The nodule size lung nodules are usually about 0.2 inches (5 millimeters) to 0.7 inches (18 millimeters) in size. Most nodules smaller than 1 cm (0.4 inches) are not visible on chest radiography and are only visible by CT. A large lung nodule, such as one that is 18 millimeters or large, is more likely to be cancerous than a smaller lung nodule. Lung nodules between 5 mm and 18 mm need to be carefully accessed. Nodules greater than 18mm in diameter should be biopsied or removed due to the 80 percent probability that they are malignant. In this case, the threshold value is taken as 0.7 inches. If the threshold values are greater than 0.7, the lung nodules are considered benign and if the threshold values are less than 0.7, the lung nodules are considered malignant. Only 3 or 4 out of 100 lung nodules end up being cancerous. The parameter settings of the ARBNN are listed as follows: maximum value of c is 1, lower bound value is 0, the minimum value of c is 0.2, population size is 22, and upper bound value is 11. Finally, the selected 1402 feature vectors are fed to the RDO to perform classification.

RESULTS AND DISCUSSION

The performance of the proposed CT image-based automatic lung nodule disease diagnosis using ARBNN_RDO optimization is analyzed in this section. The proposed approach is implemented in MATLAB version 7.12. The proposed approach is done in the windows machine having an Intel Core i5 processor with a speed of 1.6 GHz and 4 GB RAM.

Evaluation metrics

The performance of the proposed heart disease classification approach is analyzed in terms of different metrics which are listed in the below table (1).

Table 1. Performance metrics

Metrics	Formulae
Accuracy (A)	$A = \dfrac{T^P + T^N}{T^P + T^N + F^P - F^N} \times 100$
Sensitivity (S)	$S = \dfrac{T^P}{T^P + +F^N} \times 100$
Specificity (S_p)	$S_P = \dfrac{T^N}{T^N + +F^P} \times 100$
Precision (P)	$P = \dfrac{T^P}{T^P + +F^P} \times 100$
Recall (R)	$R = \dfrac{T^P}{T^P + +F^N} \times 100$
F1-Score (F)	$F = 2 \times \dfrac{Precision \times Recall}{Precision + Recall}$
False-positive irate (FPR)	$FPR = \dfrac{F^P}{F^P + +T^N} \times 100$

The results of the proposed approach are summarized in this section. In our experiment, lung CT images from the Lung Image Database Consortium (LIDC-IDRI) were used which contains 1,018 cases. 1009 cases were used to evaluate the effectiveness of the proposed method, with eight missing cases and one with damaged images. The performance of the proposed method is analyzed using various evaluation metrics such as accuracy, precision, recall, F1-score, and false-positive rate. The effectiveness of the proposed classification model is compared with the different algorithms.

Comparative Analysis of the State-of-the-Art Classifiers

In this subsection, the performance of the proposed ABNN_RDO classifier over existing classifiers is a method (Huang, et al. (2020) in terms of different metrics Accuracy, Sensitivity, Specificity, and AUC has been evaluated. The two datasets used, included the Lung Image Database Consortium and Image Database Resource Initiative (LIDC-IDRI) public database as shown in Armato et al. (2011); Clark et al. (2013), and a private database from the First Affiliated Hospital of Guangzhou Medical University in China (FAH-GMU) to verify the efficiency and effectiveness of the proposed approach.

Table 2. State-of-the-Art CNN Classifier Results on LIDC/IDRI

Classifiers	Results(%)Mean			
	Accuracy	*Sensitivity*	*Specificity*	*AUC*
ResNet50 He et al. (2016)	86.23	**98.20**	78.18	88.19
Xception Chollet et al. (2017)	**92.39**	93.69	91.52	**92.60**
NASNetMobile Tan et al. (2019)	87.68	74.77	**96.36**	85.57
MobileNetV2 Zoph et al. (2018)	82.97	69.37	92.12	80.75
EfficientNet-B5 Sandler et al. (2018)	88.77	94.59	84.85	89.72

In table (2) the classification performance of different CNN on the LIDC/IDRI database showed that the mean values measurement of ResNet50 is better for Sensitivity with 98.20%, Xception illustrated a higher accuracy of 92.39%, and AUC of 92.60%, NASNetMobile with the specificity of 96.36%. Though the ResNet50 and NASNetMobile show good performance for sensitivity and specificity respectively, they are not optimal models due to inferior metric values for accuracy and AUC. Xception is the optimal model for feature extraction using CNN because this architecture has higher sensitivity of 93.69% and a specificity of 91.52% as compared to the ResNet50 and NASNetMobile structures. The MobileNetV2 and FrricientNet-B5 show poor performance for all the cost metrics achieving low accuracy, sensitivity, specificity, and AUC as compared to the other three CNN architectures. All these models aimed at accurately determining whether a node is a candidate node (cancer) or a node (healthy) on the clinical CT scans improving the maximum visibility. However, the test results for all the classifiers are not optimal considering the various performance metric costs.

Performance Analysis

The CT scan images with 2 mm slice thickness were attained and the location of nodules was recognized by two radiologists about the nodule and non-nodule detection *from the LIDC¤IDRI* Database. Figure (4) shows the simulation results of the proposed segmentation and feature extraction process. 1st, 2nd, and 3rd columns denote the raw CT scan image, segmentation process, and feature extraction process. It depicts the enhancement of the proposed detection technique which achieves accurate detection of cancer portion in a given lung CT scan.

The effectiveness of the proposed RBNN+RDO classifier approach is analyzed in this section. The performance of the proposed model is analyzed based on different metrics such as accuracy, precision, recall, F-Score, and false-positive rate.

In this subsection, the performance of the proposed RBNN+RDO classifier is evaluated over existing classifiers Curvelet+ SVM, VGG10 method, and InceptionV3 in terms of different metrics are Accuracy, Precision, Recall, Specificity, F1-Score, and FPR. Table 2, shows that the overall effectiveness of the proposed classifier is very high over existing state-of-art classifiers. The accuracy of the proposed RBNN_RDO classifier is 98.23%, precision is 98.46%, recall is 97.7%, specificity is 98.35%, F1-score is 98.06% and FPR is 1.65 which is higher than the existing classifiers Curvelet+SVM, VGG19, and InceptionV3 respectively. The average accuracy improvement of the proposed RBNN+RDO classifier is 4.71% over existing classifiers. The average precision improvement the proposed RBNN+RDO classifier is 3.94% over existing classifiers Curvelet+SVM, VGG19 and InceptionV3. The average recall

Figure 4. Simulation results of proposed segmentation and feature extraction process. 1st, 2nd, and 3rd columns denote the raw CT scan image, segmentation process, and feature extraction process.

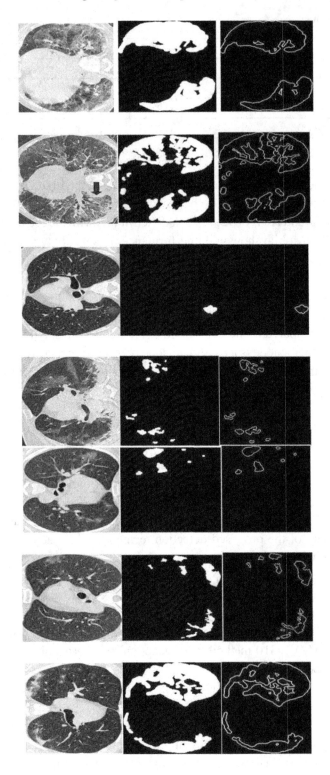

improvement of the proposed RBNN+RDO classifier is 4.98% over existing Curvelet+SVM, VGG19, and InceptionV3 classifiers. The average specificity improvement of the proposed RBNN+RDO classi-fier is 5.51% over existing Curvelet+SVM, VGG19, and InceptionV3 classifiers. The average F1-score improvement of the proposed RBNN+RDO classifier is 0.15% over existing Curvelet+SVM, VGG19, and InceptionV3 classifiers. The average FPR improvement of the proposed RBNN+RDO classifier is 3.76% over existing Curvelet+ SVM, VGG19, and InceptionV3 classifiers. *Figure 3* shows the graphical representation of the same competitive analysis.

Table 3. Comparison of lung nodule classification methods

Methods	Accuracy (%)	Precision (%)	Recall (%)	Specificity (%)	F1-score (%)	FPR (%)
Curvelet + SVM	88.27	90.12	87.69	85.94	88.89	8.6
VGG19	96.48	97.1	95.17	96.83	96.13	3.72
InceptionV3	95.81	96.35	95.3	95.76	95.85	3.87
Proposed approach	**98.23**	**98.46**	**97.7**	**98.35**	**98.06**	**1.65**
% of improvement over existing classifier	**4.71**	**3,94**	**4.98**	**5.51**	**0.15**	**3.76**

Figure 5. Performance analysis is based on various evaluation metrics.

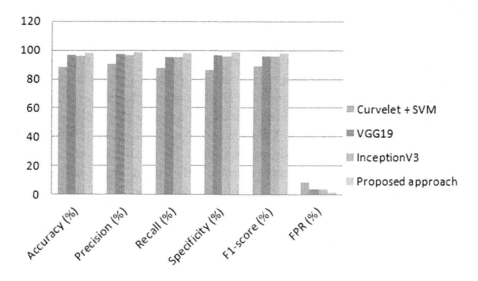

In figure 5, the effectiveness of the suggested model is analyzed based on the various evaluation metrics. In this chapter, the RBNN+RDO classifier is used. From table (3), it is clear that the suggested model achieved better classification results when compared to the other algorithms. From analyzing ac-curacy, the suggested approach achieved an accuracy of 98.23%. According to this accuracy value, it is clear that the proposed model has improved accuracy when compared to the other existing algorithms. From analyzing precision, the proposed model reached a precision of 98.46%. This shows the suggested classification method has improved precision when compared to the other algorithms. From analyzing recall and specificity, the proposed classification model achieved 97.7% recall value and 98.35% specificity. This shows the proposed model has better recall and specificity when compared to the other algorithms. Also, the proposed model achieved a minimum false positive ratio. Therefore, it showed improved performance by comparing the effectiveness of the suggested classification results.

FUTURE RESEARCH DIRECTION

In the future, an enhanced deep learning model can be presented for classification to attain a better F-measure. More research needs to be done to broaden the results to different approaches considering improvement of the model and the evaluation metrics like Negative Predictive Value (NPV), False Negative Rate (FNR), False Rejection Rate (FRR), and False Discovery Rate (FDR). A better hybrid machine learning-based technique is needed to achieve better performance even for small nodules. A hybrid machine learning-based classifier for optimal tumour prediction will be formulated as a further scope for future research direction. There is a need to optimize multiple features to customize features to enhance the accuracy of prediction. An optimization algorithm-based classifier for weight optimization can be dealt in the future. In this way, long-term lung cancer risk can be differed based on the size and attenuation of nodules.

CONCLUSION

In this chapter, the classification of lung nodules as benign or malignant based on CT images has been developed. Lung nodule identification is an important process in lung cancer disease. So, an adaptive radial basis neural network has been used for classification. To enhance the performance of the RBNN, the parameters are optimally selected by using the RDO algorithm. The performance of the proposed approach has been analyzed based on different metrics and to prove the effectiveness we compared our proposed model with different methods. The proposed approach achieved a maximum accuracy of 98.23%, maximum precision of 98.46%, maximum recall of 97.7%, maximum specificity of 98.35%, and F1 score of 98.06%. The FPR is a 1.65% of improvement over the existing classifier. This model provides accurate results and helps patients prescribe the right meditation. The results show that the proposed model achieved enhanced performance when compared to the other existing methods. Therefore, the technique can be a very helpful reference for the clinical detection of malignant and benign cancer by accessing the nodule size and shape at an early stage.

REFERENCES

Andre, E., Robicquet, A., Ramsundar, B., Kuleshov, V., DePristo, M., Chou, K., Cui, C., Carrado, G., Thrun, S., & Dean, J. (2019). A guide to deep learning in healthcare. *Nature Medicine*, *25*(1), 24–29. doi:10.103841591-018-0316-z PMID:30617335

Anthimopoulos, M., Christodoulidis, S., Ebner, L., Christe, A., & Mougiakakou, S. (2016). Lung pattern classification for interstitial lung diseases using a deep convolutional neural network. *IEEE Transactions on Medical Imaging*, *35*(5), 1207–1216. doi:10.1109/TMI.2016.2535865 PMID:26955021

Armato, S. G. III, McLennan, G., Bidaut, L., McNitt-Gray, M. F., Meyer, C. R., Reeves, A. P., Zhao, B., Aberle, D. R., Henschke, C. I., Hoffman, A., Kazerooni, E. A., MacMahon, H., van Beek, E. J. R., Yankelevitz, D., Biancardi, A. M., Bland, P. H., Brown, M. S., Engelmann, R. M., Laderach, G. E., ... Clarke, L. P. (2011). The lung image database consortium (LIDC) and image database resource initiative (IDRI): A complete reference database of lung nodules on CT scans. *Medical Physics*, *38*(2), 915–931. doi:10.1118/1.3528204 PMID:21452728

Broomhead, D. S., & Lowe, D. (1988). Multivariable functional interpolation and adaptive networks. *Complex Systems*, *2*, 321–355.

Broomhead, D. S., & Lowe, D. (1988). Radial basis functions, multi-variable functional interpolation and adaptive networks (Technical report). RSRE.

Buzug, T. M. (2011). Computed tomography.I n *Springer handbook of medical technology* (pp. 311-342). Springer.

Cao, H., Liu, H., Song, E., Ma, G., Xu, X., Jin, R., Liu, T., & Hung, C. C. (2020). A two-stage convolutional neural network for lung nodule detection. *IEEE Journal of Biomedical and Health Informatics*, *24*(7), 2006–2015. doi:10.1109/JBHI.2019.2963720 PMID:31905154

Cao, H., Liu, H., Song, E., Ma, G., Xu, X., Jin, R., Liu, T., & Hung, C. C. (2020). A two-stage convolutional neural networks for lung nodule detection. *IEEE Journal of Biomedical and Health Informatics*, *24*(7), 2006–2015. doi:10.1109/JBHI.2019.2963720 PMID:31905154

Chollet, F. (2017). Xception: Deep learning with depthwise separable convolutions. *Proceedings of the IEEE Conference on Computer Vision and Pattern Recognition*, 1251–1258. 10.1109/CVPR.2017.195

Clark, K., Vendt, B., Smith, K., Freymann, J., Kirby, J., Koppel, P., Moore, S., Phillips, S., Maffitt, D., Pringle, M., Tarbox, L., & Prior, F. (2013). The Cancer Imaging Archive (TCIA): Maintaining and operating a public information repository. *Journal of Digital Imaging*, *26*(6), 1045–1057. doi:10.100710278-013-9622-7 PMID:23884657

da Silva, G. L. F., Valente, T. L. A., Silva, A. C., de Paiva, A. C., & Gattass, M. (2018). Convolutional neural network-based PSO for lung nodule false positive reduction on CT images. *Computer Methods and Programs in Biomedicine*, *162*, 109–118. doi:10.1016/j.cmpb.2018.05.006 PMID:29903476

De, B. (2009). Computer-aided detection (CAD) of lung nodules and small tumours on chest radiographs. *European Journal of Radiology*, *72*(2), 218–225. doi:10.1016/j.ejrad.2009.05.062 PMID:19747791

Diciotti, S., Picozzi, G., Falchini, M., Mascalchi, M., Villari, N., & Valli, G. (2008). 3-D segmentation algorithm of small lung nodules in spiral CT images. *IEEE Transactions on Information Technology in Biomedicine*, *12*(1), 7–19. doi:10.1109/TITB.2007.899504 PMID:18270032

Farahani, F. V., Ahmadi, A., & Zarandi, M. H. F. (2018). Hybrid intelligent approach for diagnosis of the lung nodule from CT images using spatial kernelized fuzzy c-means and ensemble learning. *Mathematics and Computers in Simulation, 149,* 48–68. doi:10.1016/j.matcom.2018.02.001

Feng, J., & Jiang, J. (2022). Deep Learning-Based Chest CT Image Features in Diagnosis of Lung Cancer. *Computational and Mathematical Methods in Medicine, 2022,* 1–7. doi:10.1155/2022/4153211 PMID:35096129

George, A., & Rajakumar, B. R. (2013). On hybridizing fuzzy min-max neural network and firefly algorithm for automated heart disease diagnosis. *Fourth International Conference on Computing, Communications and Networking Technologies.*

Hanspeter, W. (2001). A short history of lung cancer. *Toxicological Sciences, 64*(1), 4–6. doi:10.1093/toxsci/64.1.4 PMID:11606795

He, K., Zhang, X., Ren, S., & Sun, J. (2016). Deep residual learning for image recognition. *IEEE Conference on Computer Vision and Pattern Recognition, CVPR, IEEE,* 770–778.

Huang, X., Lei, Q., Xie, T., Zhang, Y., Hu, Z., & Zhou Q. (2020). Deep Transfer Convolutional Neural Network and Extreme Learning Machine for Lung Nodule Diagnosis on CT images. *Knowledge-Based Systems, 204.*

Huang, X., Lei, Q., Xie, T., Zhang, Y., Hu, Z., & Zhou, Q. (2020). Deep transfer convolutional neural network and extreme learning machine for lung nodule diagnosis on CT images. *Knowledge-Based Systems, 204,* 106230. doi:10.1016/j.knosys.2020.106230

Kelly, L., & Mott, T. (2015). Lung cancer: Diagnosis, treatment principles, and screening. *American Family Physician, 91*(4), 250–256. PMID:25955626

Kermany, D. S., Goldbaum, M., Cai, W., Valentim, C. C., Liang, H., Baxter, S. L., McKeown, A., Yang, G., Wu, X., Yan, F., Dong, J., Prasadha, M. K., Pei, J., Ting, M. Y. L., Zhu, J., Li, C., Hewett, S., Dong, J., Ziyar, I., ... Zhang, K. (2018). Identifying medical diagnoses and treatable diseases by image-based deep learning. *Cell, 172*(5), 1122–1131. doi:10.1016/j.cell.2018.02.010 PMID:29474911

Kido, S., Kidera, S., Hirano, Y., Mabu, S., Kamiya, T., Tanaka, N., Suzuki, Y., Yanagawa, M., & Tomiyama, N. (2022). Segmentation of Lung Nodules on CT Images Using a Nested Three-Dimensional Fully Connected Convolutional Network. *Frontiers in Artificial Intelligence, 5.*

Lee, N., Laine, A. F., Mrquez, G., Levsky, J. M., & Gohagan, J. K. (2009). Potential of computer-aided diagnosis to improve CT lung cancer screening. *IEEE Reviews in Biomedical Engineering, 2,* 136–146. doi:10.1109/RBME.2009.2034022 PMID:22275043

Lei, Y., Tian, Y., Shan, H., Zhang, J., Wang, G., & Kalra, M. K. (2020). Shape and margin-aware lung nodule classification in low-dose CT images via soft activation mapping. *Medical Image Analysis, 60,* 101628. doi:10.1016/j.media.2019.101628 PMID:31865281

Liu, X., Hou, F., Qin, H., & Hao, A. (2018). Multi-view multi-scale CNNs for lung nodule type classification from CT images. *Pattern Recognition, 77,* 262–275. doi:10.1016/j.patcog.2017.12.022

Magrelli, S., Valentini, P., Rose, C. D., Morello, R., & Buonsenso, D. (2021). Classification of Lung Disease in Children by Using Lung Ultrasound Images and Deep Convolutional Neural Network. *Frontiers in Physiology*, *12*, 12. doi:10.3389/fphys.2021.693448 PMID:34512375

Masood, A., Yang, P., Sheng, B., Li, H., Li, P., Qin, J., Lanfranchi, V., Kim, J., & Feng, D. D. (2019). Cloud-based automated clinical decision support system for detection and diagnosis of lung cancer in chest CT. *IEEE Journal of Translational Engineering in Health and Medicine*, *8*, 1–13. doi:10.1109/JTEHM.2019.2955458 PMID:31929952

McWilliams, A., Beigi, P., Srinidhi, A., Lam, S., & MacAulay, C. E. (2015). Sex and smoking status effects on the early detection of early lung cancer in high-risk smokers using an electronic nose. *IEEE Transactions on Biomedical Engineering*, *62*(8), 2044–2054. doi:10.1109/TBME.2015.2409092 PMID:25775482

Pengo, T., Muñoz-Barrutía, A., & Ortiz-de-Solorzano, C. (2013). A novel automated microscopy platform for multiresolution multispectral early detection of lung cancer cells in Bronchoalveolar lavage samples. *IEEE Systems Journal*, *8*(3), 985–994. doi:10.1109/JSYST.2013.2289152

Petousis, P., Winter, A., Speier, W., Aberle, D. R., Hsu, W., & Bui, A. A. (2019). Using Sequential Decision Making to Improve Lung Cancer Screening Performance. *IEEE Access: Practical Innovations, Open Solutions*, *7*, 119403–119419. doi:10.1109/ACCESS.2019.2935763 PMID:32754420

Sandler, M., Howard, A., Zhu, M., Zhmoginov, A., & Chen, L. C. (2018). Mobilenetv2: Inverted residuals and linear bottlenecks. *Proceedings of the IEEE Conference on Computer Vision and Pattern Recognition*, 4510–4520.

Schwenker, F., Kestler, H. A., & Palm, G. (2001). Three learning phases for radial-basis-function networks. *Neural Networks*, *14*(4–5), 439–458. doi:10.1016/S0893-6080(01)00027-2 PMID:11411631

Shi, Y., Gao, Y., Yang, Y., Zhang, Y., & Wang, D. (2013). Multimodal sparse representation-based classification for lung needle biopsy images. *IEEE Transactions on Biomedical Engineering*, *60*(10), 2675–2685. doi:10.1109/TBME.2013.2262099 PMID:23674412

Shrestha, S., Petermann, J., Farrahi, T., Deshpande, A., & Giakos, G. C. (2015). Design, Calibration, and Testing of an Automated Near-Infrared Liquid-Crystal Polarimetric Imaging System for Discrimination of Lung Cancer Cells. *IEEE Transactions on Instrumentation and Measurement*, *64*(9), 2453–2467. doi:10.1109/TIM.2015.2415013

Siegel, L., Miller, K. D., & Jemal, A. (2019). Cancer statistics. *CA: a Cancer Journal for Clinicians*, *69*(1), 7–34. doi:10.3322/caac.21551 PMID:30620402

Su, Y., Li, D., & Chen, X. (2021). Lung nodule detection based on faster R-CNN framework. *Computer Methods and Programs in Biomedicine*, *200*, 105866. doi:10.1016/j.cmpb.2020.105866 PMID:33309304

Tan, M., & Le, Q. (2019). EfficientNet: Rethinking model scaling for convolutional neural networks. *Proceedings of the 36th International Conference on Machine Learning*, *97*, 6105–6114.

Tran, S., Nghiem, T. P., Nguyen, V. T., Luong, C. M., & Burie, J.-C. (2019). Improving accuracy of lung nodule classification using deep learning with focal loss. *Journal of Healthcare Engineering*, *2019*, 1–9. doi:10.1155/2019/5156416 PMID:30863524

Wei, Q., Hu, Y., Gelfand, G., & MacGregor, J. H. (2009). Segmentation of lung lobes in high-resolution isotropic CT images. *IEEE Transactions on Biomedical Engineering*, *56*(5), 1383–1393. doi:10.1109/TBME.2009.2014074 PMID:19203878

Xie, Y., Zhang, J., & Xia, Y. (2019). Semi-supervised adversarial model for benign–malignant lung nodule classification on chest CT. *Medical Image Analysis*, *57*, 237–248. doi:10.1016/j.media.2019.07.004 PMID:31352126

Xu, X., Wang, C., Guo, J., Yang, L., Bai, H., Li, W., & Yi, Z. (2020). DeepLN: A framework for automatic lung nodule detection using multi-resolution CT screening images. *Knowledge-Based Systems*, *189*, 105128. doi:10.1016/j.knosys.2019.105128

Zhang, Q., Wang, H., Yoon, S. W., Won, D., & Srihari, K. (2019). Lung nodule diagnosis on 3D computed tomography images using deep convolutional neural networks. *Procedia Manufacturing*, *39*, 363–370. doi:10.1016/j.promfg.2020.01.375

Zheng, J., Yang, D., Zhu, Y., Gu, W., Zheng, B., Bai, C., Zhao, L., Shi, H., Hu, J., Lu, S., Shi, W., & Wang, N. (2020). Pulmonary nodule risk classification in adenocarcinoma from CT images using deep CNN with scale transfer module. *IET Image Processing*, *14*(8), 1481–1489. doi:10.1049/iet-ipr.2019.0248

Zheng, S., Guo, J., Cui, X., Veldhuis, R. N. J., Oudkerk, M., & van Ooijen, P. M. A. (2019). Automatic pulmonary nodule detection in CT scans using convolutional neural networks based on maximum intensity projection. *IEEE Transactions on Medical Imaging*, *39*(3), 797–805. doi:10.1109/TMI.2019.2935553 PMID:31425026

Zia, B., Juan, Z., Zhou, X., Xiao, N., Wang, J., & Khan, A. (2020). Classification of malignant and benign lung nodule and prediction of image label class using multi-deep model. *International Journal of Advanced Computer Science and Applications*, *11*(3), 35–41. doi:10.14569/IJACSA.2020.0110305

Zoph, B., Vasudevan, V., Shlens, J., & Le, Q. V. (2018). Learning transferable architectures for scalable image recognition. *Proceedings of the IEEE Conference on Computer Vision and Pattern Recognition*, 8697–8710. 10.1109/CVPR.2018.00907

Chapter 5
Deep Learning–Based Understanding of the Complex Patterns of Cyber Attacks

Jayesh Soni

https://orcid.org/0000-0002-5740-4597

Florida International University, USA

ABSTRACT

Cybersecurity attacks are rising both in rate and complexity over time. More development and constant improvement in defensive approaches are needed to secure the operational systems against such attacks. Several malicious attacks pose severe security threats to organizations and users in today's internet age. It is vital to train enhanced malware classification systems to capture the variation in the malware type that belongs to the same family type. In this chapter, the author addresses the malware detection issue using a learning-based approach. First, the author explains various machine learning and deep learning algorithms to solve the problem. Next, the author provides practical implementation by proposing a deep learning-based framework on the open-source benchmark dataset on API calls. The dataset contains API calls during normal and malware-infected processes. The proposed framework trains a hybrid model of convolution neural network followed by long short-term memory to have a high malware detection rate.

INTRODUCTION

With the increase in digitization, the security of the devices remains a top priority. Access to recent expertise and the latest discoveries through research papers are easy nowadays with the increased proliferation of the internet high-speed network technologies. Such advanced research and findings are available to both; cybercriminals and security analyst, where each one has very different goals. Advanced research in artificial intelligence and machine learning has shown remarkable results in improving the security of such attacks. Nonetheless, cybercriminals use such findings to craft even superior, and more erudite attacks. Even a single attack from such cybercriminals would be a major success, whereas security analysts have to develop a secured system with a 100% successful detection rate. Research shows that in 2017,

DOI: 10.4018/978-1-6684-4045-2.ch005

cybercriminals impacted numerous administrations, corporates, people, and solicitations through various cyberattacks (Larson et al., 2017). Personal identification info, financial data, sensitive data were among the top stolen information. It becomes catastrophic when such information is made available publicly or sold in an illegal market. Cybercrimes are accountable for almost $400 billion in reserves whipped and budgets to lessen harms instigated by crimes (Rimo et al., 2014). With the advent of ransomware attacks, such as wannacry, attackers generate annual revenue of over $1 billion. As defense implements rapidly become outdated, it is progressively more challenging to keep up with the increased complexity of cyber-attacks. It can take days to identify an intrusion. Scalability and intricacy make such attacks challenging. Most wars between countries always have a beginning and end, whereas there is no end in cyberwar, impacting the globe. Cyberattacks are rapidly growing attacks with no sign of downfall from cybercriminals. Such criminals quickly develop new tools and techniques if the previous technique fails. From 2010 onwards, there has been a significant evolution of sophisticated malware infiltrating factories and military systems. Cyber-criminals are evolving rapidly by introducing the complex malware that outsmarts the current malware detection systems. With extraordinary evolution in ransomware, monetization of malware becomes the key. Learning-based algorithms are one of the growing areas that have a high impact in the cyber security domain, and that is the focus of this chapter. In summary, this book chapter makes the following three contributions.

1) We proposed a deep learning-based hybrid model composed of a convolution neural network followed by a long short-term memory network for malicious event detection using the Application Programming Interface (API) calls. The CNN algorithm extract the meaningful features from API calls sequences which is passed to LSTM network as input. Next, LSTM will learn the normal behavior of the system using that input. Thus, reduces the training time.
2) We performed experimental analysis on real world benchmark dataset and demonstrated that the proposed detection model achieves higher detection rate and in an optimized time compare to baseline models.

The rest of the paper is structured as follows. Section 2 provides some of the background work. Section 3 and 4 explain various machine learning and deep learning algorithms, respectively, for analyzing cyberattacks. Section 5 discusses different hyper-parameters for the neural network. Section 6 discusses the evaluation metrics. Section 7 provides an implementation of malware detection. Finally, the chapter is concluded in section 8 with future work discussion.

Background

This section discusses the recent literature that studies the malware analysis using API calls. To analyze the behavior of any application, the study of its API sequence calls is an outstanding method (Xiao et al., 2019). The considerable behavioral dissimilarity between benign and malicious processes can be captured by the sequences of API calls between processes and their underlying operating system (Ding et al., 2018). Static and dynamic signature-based techniques were used to detect malware in the past (Idika et al., 2007). The static analysis uses essential properties of the program before it is executed for malware detection. To avoid such detection algorithms, various polymorphism, encryption, and complication methods are used by malware originators (Sung et al., 2004). In the dynamic approach, the behavior of the program before and after the execution is analyzed by implementing the malware in a virtual environment to detect damaging activities. Analyzing the impact through the dynamic way is an effective way (Nataraj et al., 2011). We focused on dynamic analysis approaches. Primarily, we concentrated on examining the API sequence calls created during the execution of malware samples. Behavioral-based detection of malware exhibit practical direction toward the use of the API calls (Xiao et al., 2019). API call sequence embodies the complete course of malware behavior representing its runtime actions.

Forrest and longstaff in (Forrest et al., 1996) performed an early work on profiling benign and malicious UNIX processes. They utilize a fixed-size sequence of consecutive system calls to characterize a process. The decision of whether a process is benign or not is made by analyzing the sub-sequences of system call in lengths of 5, 6, and 11. Such usage of fixed-size lengths may lead to the misplacement of system calls, which fails to adequately capture the malicious behaviors.

Ki et al. (2015) labeled API call sequences to extract the most subjective API patterns by using sequence alignment algorithms. Distinct sub-sequence patterns were extracted using the longest common subsequence (LCS) algorithm, which was used to differentiate the program as benign or malicious. They achieved an accuracy rate of 99%. Since LCS is incompetent for longer sequences, their algorithm may become inefficient with the increased length in the sequence of API calls (Ficco, 2020).

Lu et al. (2014) transformed the sequence of API calls into the rules of regular expressions. The sequence is detected as malicious when a particular rule match with the current API sequence call. Yet, such a system can be outwitted by the modifications of the patterns.

Natural language processing (NLP) based term frequency-inverse document frequency techniques used by (Tran et al. 2017) for analysis. They provided the weights to each subsequence after dividing the sequence into n-grams. Changing the frequency of the call can easily evade such frequency-based methods (Amer, 2015).

Thus, the learning-based approach is widely used currently to detect cyberattacks. Anti-malware developers use big data and machine learning techniques (Siddiqui et al., 2018) to improve and enhance the detection system. Such learning-based techniques are efficient because different malware families share comparable behavior forms (Soni et al., 2019). Numerous feature extraction approaches are used to develop intelligent malware detection systems. Decision trees, random forest (RF), naïve bayes (Schultz et al., 2001), support vector machines (SVM) are prevalent machine learning algorithms (Soni et al., 2018). Numerous methods are explicitly intended for a particular dataset, such as the microsoft malware dataset, to achieve sophisticated performance. Some authors (Drew et al., 2016) use recent gene sequence tools for malware classification. Similarly, (Ahmadi et al., 2016) trained an xgboost classifier technique. Microsoft malware classification challenge winning team trained xgboost technique by generating the highly complex features.

Shijo and Salim (2015) mined static string feature converted it into binary form, which is used as input to the support vector machine and random forest learning-based classifiers. SVM achieved an accuracy of 98%, whereas RF achieved 97%. Detection of malware using traditional machine learning approaches has several disadvantages such as careful feature engineering and need of feature vector in specific representation form. To perform this task, an extensive expertise in the particular domain is required (Raff et al., 2018). Furthermore, once the attackers get to know the feature vectors, they can easily evades the system (Anderson et al., 2017).

Remarkably, Deep learning models have been extensively used recently for anomalous behavior detection in recent years which needs little to no feature engineering. (Omid et al., 2015) trains a deep belief network by generating unigrams of API calls to develop the dense representation. Sequence of API calls with null-terminated objects are being used as input data to train the deep neural architecture

Huang and Stokes (2016). Similarly, to predict the next API call in the sequence, different variants of RNNs are explored by Pascanu et al., 2015). (William et al., 2016) use the API calls generated during the execution of Portable Executable files and train the stacked auto-encoder network. Catak et al. (2020) and Kolosnjaji et al. (2016) developed a malware classification model by training long short-term memory (LSTM) and convolutional neural networks (CNN). An ensemble of recurrent neural networks is employed by Rhode et al. (2018) for classifying the executable as benign or malicious. Their study shows an accuracy rate of 94%. Though RNN and LSTM based algorithms show good results, the training of such a network gets complex with the increased sequence of API calls. (Vinayakumar et al. 2019). A recent method (Gibert et al., 2016) applied a convolution neural network for the same problem domain.

MACHINE LEARNING ALGORITHMS

In this modern world, numerous manual tasks are being automated today. Today's computers can accomplish surgeries, compete in chessboard games, and get more intelligent with the help of machine learning algorithms. These algorithms learn from experience rather than if and else condition. There are two types of machine learning-based algorithms, as shown in figure 1.

Figure 1. Machine Learning Algorithms

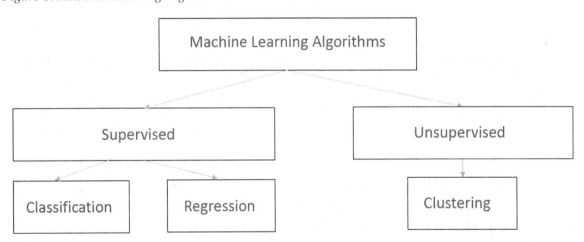

Supervised Learning

Input data is known as training data with known ground truth tags such as spam/ham or weather at a time.

Training data with a ground truth tag is used to train a model. The training is stopped when the model achieves the required accuracy. Since ground truth tags are used for training, such learning is known as supervised learning. Classification and Regression are two main types of supervised learning algorithms.

Classification: Output label is categorical, e.g., "Spam or Not Spam."
Regression: Output is actual value, e.g., Stock Price prediction.

Classification-based algorithms: Logistic Regression, Decision Trees, Random Forest, K Nearest Neighbor, Support Vector Machine, etc.

Regression-based algorithms: Decision Tree Regressor, Linear Regression, Support Vector Regressor, etc.

Unsupervised Learning

Input data does not have the ground truth tag. The model looks into the structure and patterns of the data during the training process. Such learning is used to cluster the data into different groups. An extended version is semi-supervised learning, where input data contains both ground truth and non-ground truth examples. It models the non-ground truth data by learning from ground truth data.

Clustering: It unveils the inherent structure of your data and clusters it into different groups. E.g., Clustering the test data into groups like political, weather, etc.

Unsupervised machine learning-based algorithms: KMeans++, Agglomerative Clustering, Principal Component Analysis (PCA), mixture models, etc.

DEEP LEARNING ALGORITHMS

Deep learning algorithms are a subset of machine learning algorithms that automatically generate features. They work the way the human brain works. Recently, such algorithms have shown great power in solving complex problems. Let us discuss some of the famous deep learning algorithms.

Multilayer Perceptron (MLP): They are one of the simplest neural networks (Ramchoun et al., 2016) as shown in Figure 2 and consists of the following three layers:

The input layer: A vector of features.
The hidden layers consist of N neurons.
The output layer: Output of the network.

At every node, input values are multiplied with the corresponding weights. Next, the total sum is calculated. To cope with the complexity of real-world data, the activation function is applied to the total sum. Such activation functions bring nonlinearity to map the input data to the target label.

Time Series

Recurrent neural networks (RNN): These neural network architectures (Larry et al., 2001) are specifically designed to solve the data science problem, which involves time as a critical factor. RNNs can be used in numerous time series-based solicitations such as natural language processing problems like speech recognition, text summarization, and forecasting of future values (Peddoju et al., 2020). Figure 3 represents the typical RNN architecture.

The primary difference between MLP and RNN is that the RNN takes one input time step at a time sequentially, whereas all the inputs are fed at the same time in MLP. The RNN network calculates the input data with the corresponding weights and generates a hidden state at each step. These hidden states are denoted as memory cells. This hidden state is combined with the succeeding input value to produce the output. At the end of the time series sequence, the algorithm stops. Using the hidden state information, the RNN algorithm conserves the historical info to co-relate with the recent input value.

All the weights and parameters are shared across all steps since the same RNN cell performs all the calculations for each input. The backpropagation through time (BPTT) algorithm is used for training purposes where at each step, the calculation of gradient depends on the previous steps.

Figure 2. Multi-Layer Perceptron

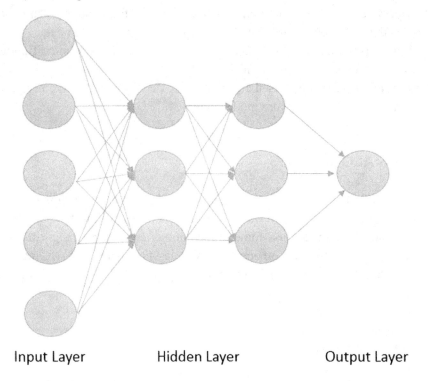

Figure 3. Recurrent Neural Network

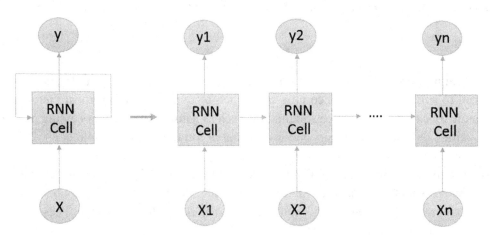

RNNs have infinite memory cells theoretically. Nevertheless, learning long-term dependencies is complex through the backpropagation algorithm and generates problems such as exploding gradient (gradient values grow very large) or vanishing (gradient values reach near zero)—the vanishing gradient results in small to no updates to the weights of the first few initial layers. The exploding gradient can be elucidated using gradient clipping, where some threshold is used to clip the gradient.

There are primarily three different variants of RNN to overcome that problem. They are:

Long Short Term Memory (LSTM): They use various gates for memory cells (Graves et al., 2005). With each input data, the memory is updated. The following four gates are aligned to the LSTM network to diminish the impreciseness of the RNN.

Input gate: It regulates the updation of new memory.
Forget gate: It accounts for the non-essential information removal.
Memory gate: It creates a new memory.
Output gate: It is used to update the hidden state with the memory cell information.

With a sample input of type b = (b_1, b_2, b_3, b_{N-1}, b_N), the gates are updated as follows:

$$(b_j, e_{j-1}, s_{j-1}) \rightarrow \left(e_j, s_j \right) \tag{1}$$

$$i_j = \tilde{A}(d_{bi} b_j + d_{ei} e_{j-1} + d_{si} z_{j-1} + k_i) \tag{2}$$

$$f_j = \tilde{A}(d_{bf} b_j + d_{ef} e_{j-1} + d_{zf} z_{j-1} + k_f) \tag{3}$$

$$z_j = f_j * z_{j-1} + i_j * tanh(d_{bz} b_j + p_{ez} e_{j-1} + k_z) \tag{4}$$

$$y_j = \tilde{A}(d_{by} b_j + d_{ey} e_{j-1} + d_{zy} z_j + k_y) \tag{5}$$

$$e_j = y_j * tanh(z_j) \tag{6}$$

The memory cell state is denoted by z, k_i, k_f, k_y, k_z are the bias units for the input gate, forget gate, output gate, and memory cell (Soni et al., 2021). Also, *e* represents previous lstm block's output and *d* represents input at a particular timestamp. Furthermore, the weight matrix is denoted by d, and the hidden layer output is denoted as e.

Imaging

Convolution Neural Network (CNN): These neural architectures (Saad et al., 2018) are widely used for image classification, segmentation, etc. However, such networks can be used to predict time series data after proper transformation. Figure 4 shows the simplified version of 1D CNN.

Figure 4. Convolution Neural Network

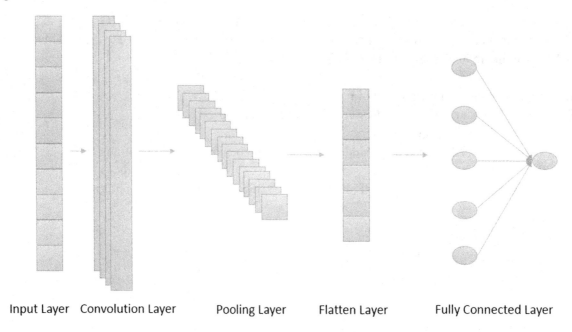

Input Layer   Convolution Layer   Pooling Layer   Flatten Layer   Fully Connected Layer

CNN has the following layers:

Convolutional layer: This layer applies the convolution operation to extract the meaningful features from the input data. It moves the kernel (feature detector) of a precise length over the one-dimensional time series array. At each step, the input is multiplied by the corresponding kernel value, and then the nonlinear activation function is applied to it.

Pooling layer: This layer preserves the temporal and spatial information and reduces the feature set.

Flatten Layer: It flattens the input from the pooling layer in one dimension.

Fully Connected Layer: The output of the flatten layer is processed by the neural network for classification, image segmentation, or object detection purposes.

Figure 5 shows the hybrid model composed of CNN followed by LSTM. The CNN network takes the complex high dimensional feature vector and extract the meaningful features, thus reduce the dimensionality of the feature vector. Next, LSTM network takes this reduced features and learn the behavior of the data.

Figure 5. Hybrid CNN with LSTM

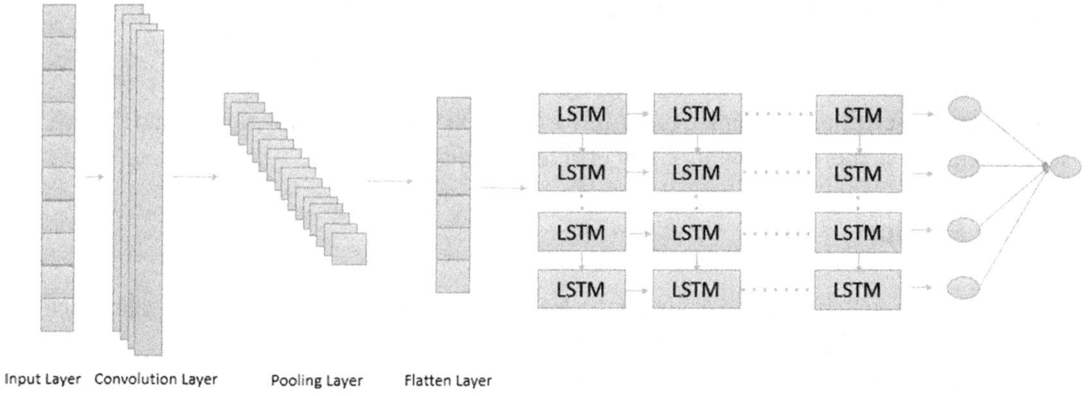

Input Layer   Convolution Layer   Pooling Layer   Flatten Layer

HYPER-PARAMETERS

To achieve optimal results, every learning-based algorithm has some hyper-parameters that must be appropriately tuned. The values for the hyper-parameters have to be set before training the model. It is one of the active research areas. Below we discuss a few of the hyper-parameters for LSTM and CNN.

1) *The number of epochs:* The total amount of time the entire dataset is passed to a neural net throughout the training period.

2) *Batch size:* In each epoch, how often to update the weight is controlled by the batch-size parameter. It is usually in the range of 32 to 256, which can vary. It means the weights updation will occur after the 32nd rows of the dataset to the 256th row of the dataset.

3) *The number of hidden layers and units:* How well a model performs on the dataset decides the number of layers and the nodes in each layer. There is an under fitting issue with a small subset of it, whereas the model tends to be over fitted when such parameters have high values. Regularization techniques can be used to find the trade-offs.

4) *Activation function:* To apply the nonlinearity, activation functions are used during the training of the neural network. ReLu is popularly used in CNN architecture. Tangent hyperbolic and sigmoid are other activation functions that can be used, and the choice depends on the task that needs to be solved.

5) *Dropout for regularization:* It prevents the overfitting of the neural network. If the dropout value is 0.2, 20% of the neurons in that layer will be deactivated during model training purposes.

It is a time inefficient process to tune the hyper-parameters manually. Thus, grid search and randomized search are two popular techniques used to speed up the tuning process.

A) *Grid Search*

The model is trained with all the parameter combinations specified during the training of the model in an exhaustive search manner in a grid search. It finds the optimal parameter values for the specified data with the applied neural architecture, but at the same time, it is computationally expensive. The computational time for the grid search rises with the increase in the size of the neural network in terms of its hidden layer.

B)   ***Random Search***
The parameter selection is sampled randomly from a specific distribution rather than the exhaustive search. Thus, it is more computationally efficient than grid search.

Evaluation Metrics

The following metrics can be used to evaluate the learning-based models where the misclassification of the malicious class data should be low.

$$\text{Recall} = \frac{TP}{TP + FN} \tag{7}$$

$$\text{Precision} = \frac{TP}{TP + FP} \tag{8}$$

$$\text{Accuracy} = \frac{TP + TN}{TP + FP + FN + TN} \tag{9}$$

$$\text{F1-Score: } 2 * \frac{Precision * Recall}{Precision + Recall} \tag{10}$$

Where TP: True positive, FN: False Negative, TN: True Negative, and FP: False Positive.

Experimental Results

This section discusses the practical implementation of using CNN-LSTM for efficient malware detection by learning its behavior using API calls. The following libraries are used for experimentation purposes.

Tensorflow: Tensorflow is an open-source library from google for deep learning and machine-learning (Joshua et al., 2017).
Keras: Keras is a wrapper on Tensorflow used by many societies worldwide. The code written in Keras is internally converted to TensorFlow for further execution. It has functional API (Application Programming Interface) and Sequential API.
Scikit-learn: Scikit-learn deals with a wide variety of learning-based algorithms (both Supervised and UnSupervised) (Padregosa et al., 2011).

Figure 6 shows the high-level framework for the implementation. It has three sections: Data Collection, Data Preprocessing, CNN-LSTM Algorithm Training, and testing with the final model.

Figure 6. Proposed Framework

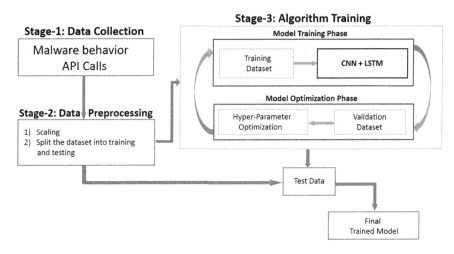

Stage1: Data Collection

The dataset is collected from Kaggle (Oliveira, 2020). It contains 42,797 malware API call sequences and 1079 benign API call sequences. The data is extracted from the cuckoo sandbox application. Each call sequence contains the first 100 consecutive API calls associated with the parent process. Table 1 shows the sample dataset.

Table 1. Sample Dataset

Hash	T_0	T_1	T_2	...	T_99	Malware
071e8c3f8922e186e57548cd4c703a5d	112	274	158	...	71	1
592e5477cb70711e90ee07587d65fe50	240	117	240	...	60	0

Each row of the dataset has a hash value in 32 bytes string format, followed by 100 API calls (T_0 to T_99) and finally a column name "Malware" where the value is 0 is for the row with benign sequences and value is 1 for the row with malicious sequences.

Stage2: Data Pre-Processing

The following two pre-processing steps are performed on the data:

1) Scaling the data value using MinMaxScalar to transform all the features with an identical scale.
2) Divide it into train and test data with 80% training and 20% for testing with stratified sampling due to the data's imbalanced nature. Table 2 shows the dataset distribution.

Table 2. Data Distribution

Type	Benign	Malware
Train	34238	863
Test	8559	216

Stage3: Algorithm Training

We use a hybrid model with a convolution neural network followed by a long, short term memory network. The first layer is the embedding layer, which learns the interdependencies between API calls. These API sequence calls are then fed to the CNN algorithm, reducing the dimension w.r.t time. Next, these reduced sequences are fed to the LSTM network to learn the sequence behavior of API calls during normal and malware-infected operations.

Figure 7 shows the overview of the model architecture. Approximately 1 million parameters are trained. The randomized Search method is used to find the optimal value of the hyper-parameters. The CNN model contains 64 filters with a kernel size of 10. Next, a max-pooling layer was applied with a pool size of 2. Finally, the LSTM layer with 480 units is applied with the dense layer at the end. ReLU (Rectifier Linear Unit) activation function is used for CNN and LSTM, whereas the sigmoid activation function is used for the last dense layer. The training data is further divided into training and validation. Figures 8 and 9 depict the accuracy and loss with the increasing epoch for the training and validation dataset. The Cohens Kappa score of the proposed model is 83.2%. This indicate that the results are impacted with the imbalance nature of the experimented dataset. Since the learning rate at epoch 10 adaptively changed to higher value, the validation accuracy drastically reduced to lower value. Overall, the model achieved a loss value of 0.0351 and an accuracy value of 0.9838.

Table 3 shows the evaluated metrics on test data with varying number of CNN filters. We trained the CNN network with number of filters being 16, 32, 64 and 128. The proposed model gave the highest accuracy with 64 filters and further increase in the filters results in overfitting of the model. Batch Size parameters has three different variants namely Batch Gradient Descent, Stochastic Gradient Descent and Mini-Batch Gradient Descent. Batch Gradient Descent takes whole dataset at once to update the weights of the model which leads to underfitting of the model. Stochastic Gradient descent update the weights after every single data row which leads to overfitting of the model. To train the model, we use mini-batch gradient descent algorithm with batch size of 32 so that the model updates the weights after every 32 rows of the data. Figure 10 shows the accuracy rate with varying batch size value. Table 4 shows the comparsion of the proposed model with the baseline models. We notice that there is constant increase in the accuracy value with increase in the batchsize value, but after the batchsize of 32, the accuracy decreases and remain stagnant around 128. Figure 11 shows corresponding confusion matrix. The model was able to classify correctly with a 95% accuracy rate on the test data.

Figure 7. Model Architecture

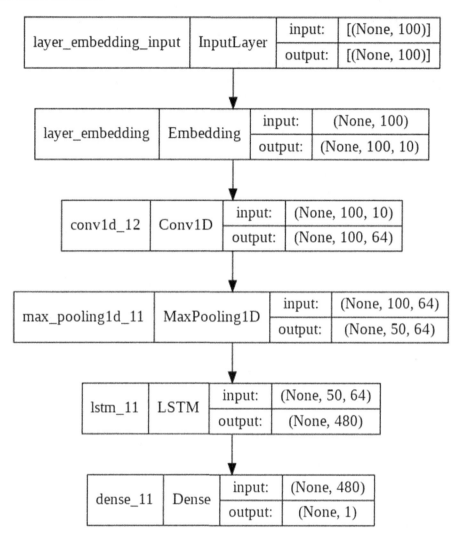

Table 3. Result Metrics on Test Data

CNN Filters	Accuracy	Precision	Recall	F1 Score
16	0.89	0.88	0.90	0.88
32	0.92	0.94	0.95	0.94
64	**0.95**	**0.99**	**0.98**	**0.98**
128	0.94	0.98	0.98	0.98

Figure 8. Accuracy with Epoch

Figure 9. Loss with Epoch

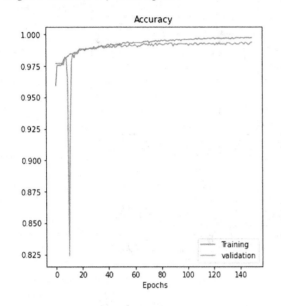
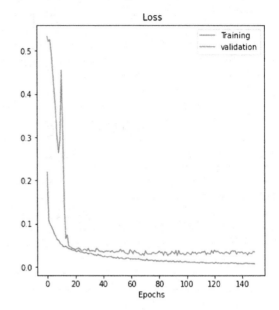

Figure 10. BatchSize

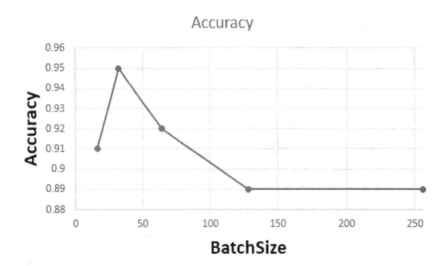

Table 4. Comparison with Baseline

Model	Accuracy	Precision	Recall	F1 Score
CNN	0.81	0.79	0.76	0.77
LSTM	0.88	0.92	0.91	0.91
CNN+LSTM	**0.95**	**0.99**	**0.98**	**0.98**

Figure 11. Confusion Matrix

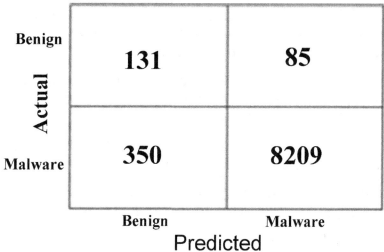

CONCLUSION AND FUTURE SCOPE

Cybersecurity is a growing concern all around the world. Cybercriminals use cutting-edge technology to break the complex system. Thus, developing an advanced technique to detect such attacks is imperative. This chapter provides details of various machine learning and deep learning algorithms that can design such advanced techniques. Next, the author proposes a framework implementation for malware detection. The open-source dataset available on Kaggle contains API sequence calls during the normal operation and malware-infected operation. The proposed framework developed a hybrid CNN followed by an LSTM network to achieve an optimal detection rate.

This work can be extended by extracting the API calls of the process by injecting multiple malicious test vectors. Furthermore, various other natural language processing-based algorithms such as Transformers and Bidirectional Encoder Representations from Transformers (BERT) can be used for comparative analysis.

REFERENCES

Ahmadi, M., Ulyanov, D., Semenov, S., Trofimov, M., & Giacinto, G. (2016, March). Novel feature extraction, selection, and fusion for effective malware family classification. *Proceedings of the sixth ACM conference on data and application security and privacy*, 183-194. 10.1145/2857705.2857713

Albawi, S., Mohammed, T. A., & Al-Zawi, S. (2017, August). Understanding of a convolutional neural network. In *2017 international conference on engineering and technology (ICET)* (pp. 1-6). IEEE.

Amer, E. (2015, August). Enhancing the efficiency of web search engines through ontology learning from unstructured information sources. In *2015 IEEE international conference on information reuse and integration* (pp. 542-549). IEEE.

Anderson, H. S., Kharkar, A., Filar, B., & Roth, P. (2017). Evading machine learning malware detection. *Black Hat.*

Angelo Oliveira. (2020). *Malware Analysis Datasets: API Call Sequences.* https://www.kaggle.com/ang3loliveira/malware-analysis-datasets-api-call-sequences.html

David, O. E., & Netanyahu, N. S. (2015, July). Deepsign: Deep learning for automatic malware signature generation and classification. In *2015 International Joint Conference on Neural Networks (IJCNN)* (pp. 1-8). IEEE. 10.1109/IJCNN.2015.7280815

Dillon, J. V., Langmore, I., Tran, D., Brevdo, E., Vasudevan, S., Moore, D., & Saurous, R. A. (2017). *Tensorflow distributions.* arXiv preprint arXiv:1711.10604.

Ding, Y., Xia, X., Chen, S., & Li, Y. (2018). A malware detection method based on a family behavior graph. *Computers & Security, 73,* 73–86. doi:10.1016/j.cose.2017.10.007

Drew, J., Moore, T., & Hahsler, M. (2016, May). Polymorphic malware detection using sequence classification methods. In *2016 IEEE Security and Privacy Workshops (SPW)* (pp. 81-87). IEEE.

Ficco, M. (2020, April). Comparing API call sequence algorithms for malware detection. In *Workshops of the International Conference on Advanced Information Networking and Applications* (pp. 847-856). Springer. 10.1007/978-3-030-44038-1_77

Forrest, S., Hofmeyr, S. A., Somayaji, A., & Longstaff, T. A. (1996, May). A sense of self for unix processes. In *Proceedings 1996 IEEE Symposium on Security and Privacy* (pp. 120-128). IEEE. 10.1109/SECPRI.1996.502675

Gibert, D. (2016). *Convolutional neural networks for malware classification.* University Rovira i Virgili.

Graves, A., Fernández, S., & Schmidhuber, J. (2005, September). Bidirectional LSTM networks for improved phoneme classification and recognition. In *International conference on artificial neural networks* (pp. 799-804). Springer. 10.1007/11550907_126

Hardy, W., Chen, L., Hou, S., Ye, Y., & Li, X. (2016). DL4MD: A deep learning framework for intelligent malware detection. In *Proceedings of the International Conference on Data Science (ICDATA)* (p. 61). The Steering Committee of The World Congress in Computer Science, Computer Engineering and Applied Computing (WorldComp).

Huang, W., & Stokes, J. W. (2016, July). MtNet: a multi-task neural network for dynamic malware classification. In *International conference on detection of intrusions and malware, and vulnerability assessment* (pp. 399-418). Springer. 10.1007/978-3-319-40667-1_20

Idika, N., & Mathur, A. P. (2007). A survey of malware detection techniques. Purdue University.

Ki, Y., Kim, E., & Kim, H. K. (2015). A novel approach to detect malware based on API call sequence analysis. *International Journal of Distributed Sensor Networks, 11*(6), 659101. doi:10.1155/2015/659101

Kolosnjaji, B., Zarras, A., Webster, G., & Eckert, C. (2016, December). Deep learning for classification of malware system call sequences. In *Australasian joint conference on artificial intelligence* (pp. 137-149). Springer. 10.1007/978-3-319-50127-7_11

Larson, S. (2017, December 20). *10 biggest hacks of 2017*. Retrieved November 3, 2018, from https://money.cnn.com/2017/12/18/technology/biggest-cyberattacksof-the-year/index.html

Louizos, C., Swersky, K., Li, Y., Welling, M., & Zemel, R. (2015). *The variational fair autoencoder*. arXiv preprint arXiv:1511.00830.

Lu, H., Zhao, B., Su, J., & Xie, P. (2014). Generating lightweight behavioral signature for malware detection in people-centric sensing. *Wireless Personal Communications*, *75*(3), 1591–1609. doi:10.100711277-013-1400-9

Medsker, L. R., & Jain, L. C. (2001). Recurrent neural networks. *Design and Applications, 5*, 64–67.

Nataraj, L., Karthikeyan, S., Jacob, G., & Manjunath, B. S. (2011, July). Malware images: visualization and automatic classification. In *Proceedings of the 8th international symposium on visualization for cyber security* (pp. 1-7). Academic Press.

Pascanu, R., Stokes, J. W., Sanossian, H., Marinescu, M., & Thomas, A. (2015, April). Malware classification with recurrent networks. In *2015 IEEE International Conference on Acoustics, Speech and Signal Processing (ICASSP)* (pp. 1916-1920). IEEE. 10.1109/ICASSP.2015.7178304

Peddoju, S. K., Upadhyay, H., Soni, J., & Prabakar, N. (2020). Natural language processing based anomalous system call sequences detection with virtual memory introspection. *International Journal of Advanced Computer Science and Applications*, *11*(5). Advance online publication. doi:10.14569/IJACSA.2020.0110559

Pedregosa, F., Varoquaux, G., Gramfort, A., Michel, V., Thirion, B., Grisel, O., & Duchesnay, E. (2011). Scikit-learn: Machine learning in Python. *Journal of Machine Learning Research, 12*, 2825–2830.

Raff, E., Barker, J., Sylvester, J., Brandon, R., Catanzaro, B., & Nicholas, C. K. (2018, June). Malware detection by eating a whole exe. *Workshops at the Thirty-Second AAAI Conference on Artificial Intelligence*.

Ramchoun, H., Ghanou, Y., Ettaouil, M., & Janati Idrissi, M. A. (2016). *Multilayer perceptron: Architecture optimization and training*. Academic Press.

Rhode, M., Burnap, P., & Jones, K. (2018). Early-stage malware prediction using recurrent neural networks. *Computers & Security, 77*, 578-594.

Rimo, T., & Walth, M. (2014). *McAfee and CSIS: Stopping Cybercrime Can Positively Impact World Economies*. McAfee.

Schultz, M. G., Eskin, E., Zadok, F., & Stolfo, S. J. (2000, May). Data mining methods for detection of new malicious executables. In *Proceedings 2001 IEEE Symposium on Security and Privacy. S&P 2001* (pp. 38-49). IEEE.

Shijo, P. V., & Salim, A. J. P. C. S. (2015). Integrated static and dynamic analysis for malware detection. *Procedia Computer Science, 46*, 804–811. doi:10.1016/j.procs.2015.02.149

Siddiqui, M., Wang, M. C., & Lee, J. (2008, March). A survey of data mining techniques for malware detection using file features. In *Proceedings of the 46th annual southeast regional conference on xx* (pp. 509-510). 10.1145/1593105.1593239

Soni, J., Peddoju, S. K., Prabakar, N., & Upadhyay, H. (2021). Comparative Analysis of LSTM, One-Class SVM, and PCA to Monitor Real-Time Malware Threats Using System Call Sequences and Virtual Machine Introspection. In *International Conference on Communication, Computing and Electronics Systems* (pp. 113-127). Springer. 10.1007/978-981-33-4909-4_9

Soni, J., & Prabakar, N. (2018). Effective machine learning approach to detect groups of fake reviewers. In *Proceedings of the 14th international conference on data science (ICDATA'18), Las Vegas, NV* (pp. 3-9). Academic Press.

Soni, J., Prabakar, N., & Upadhyay, H. (2019). *Comparative Analysis of LSTM Sequence-Sequence and Auto Encoder for real-time anomaly detection using system call sequences.* Academic Press.

Soni, J., Prabakar, N., & Upadhyay, H. (2019, December). Behavioral Analysis of System Call Sequences Using LSTM Seq-Seq, Cosine Similarity and Jaccard Similarity for Real-Time Anomaly Detection. In *2019 International Conference on Computational Science and Computational Intelligence (CSCI)* (pp. 214-219). IEEE. 10.1109/CSCI49370.2019.00043

Sung, A. H., Xu, J., Chavez, P., & Mukkamala, S. (2004, December). Static analyzer of vicious executables (save). In *20th Annual Computer Security Applications Conference* (pp. 326-334). IEEE. 10.1109/CSAC.2004.37

Tran, T. K., & Sato, H. (2017, November). NLP-based approaches for malware classification from API sequences. In *2017 21st Asia Pacific Symposium on Intelligent and Evolutionary Systems (IES)* (pp. 101-105). IEEE.

Vinayakumar, R., Alazab, M., Soman, K. P., Poornachandran, P., & Venkatraman, S. (2019). Robust intelligent malware detection using deep learning. *IEEE Access: Practical Innovations, Open Solutions*, 7, 46717–46738. doi:10.1109/ACCESS.2019.2906934

Zenati, H., Foo, C. S., Lecouat, B., Manek, G., & Chandrasekhar, V. R. (2018). *Efficient gan-based anomaly detection.* arXiv preprint arXiv:1802.06222.

ADDITIONAL READING

Drew, J., Hahsler, M., & Moore, T. (2017). Polymorphic malware detection using sequence classification methods and ensembles. *EURASIP Journal on Information Security*, *2017*(1), 1–12. doi:10.118613635-017-0055-6

Gulli, A., & Pal, S. (2017). *Deep learning with Keras.* Packt Publishing Ltd.

Kalash, M., Rochan, M., Mohammed, N., Bruce, N. D., Wang, Y., & Iqbal, F. (2018, February). Malware classification with deep convolutional neural networks. In *2018 9th IFIP international conference on new technologies, mobility, and security (NTMS)* (pp. 1-5). IEEE. 10.1109/NTMS.2018.8328749

Kolter, J. Z., & Maloof, M. A. (2006). Learning to detect malicious executables. In *Machine Learning and Data Mining for Computer Security* (pp. 47–63). Springer. doi:10.1007/1-84628-253-5_4

Oliva, A., & Torralba, A. (2001). Modeling the shape of the scene: A holistic representation of the spatial envelope. *International Journal of Computer Vision, 42*(3), 145–175. doi:10.1023/A:1011139631724

Rieck, K., Holz, T., Willems, C., Düssel, P., & Laskov, P. (2008, July). Learning and classification of malware behavior. In *International Conference on Detection of Intrusions and Malware, and Vulnerability Assessment* (pp. 108-125). Springer. 10.1007/978-3-540-70542-0_6

Ronen, R., Radu, M., Feuerstein, C., Yom-Tov, E., & Ahmadi, M. (2018). Microsoft malware classification challenge. arXiv preprint arXiv:1802.10135.

Sirigineedi, S. S., Soni, J., & Upadhyay, H. (2020, March). Learning-based models to detect runtime phishing activities using urls. In *Proceedings of 2020, the 4th International Conference on Compute and Data Analysis* (pp. 102-106). 10.1145/3388142.3388170

Soni, J., Prabakar, N., & Upadhyay, H. (2019). Feature extraction through deepwalk on weighted graph. In *Proceedings of the 15th international conference on data science (ICDATA'19)*, Las Vegas, NV.

Torralba, A., Murphy, K. P., Freeman, W. T., & Rubin, M. A. (2003, October). Context-based vision system for place and object recognition. In Computer Vision, IEEE International Conference on (Vol. 2, pp. 273-273). IEEE Computer Society. 10.1109/ICCV.2003.1238354

Xiao, F., Lin, Z., Sun, Y., & Ma, Y. (2019). Malware detection based on deep learning of behavior graphs. *Mathematical Problems in Engineering, 2019*, 2019. doi:10.1155/2019/8195395

You, I., & Yim, K. (2010, November). Malware obfuscation techniques: A brief survey. In 2010 International conference on broadband, wireless computing, communication and applications (pp. 297-300). IEEE. 10.1109/BWCCA.2010.85

KEY TERMS AND DEFINITIONS

API: Application programming interface is a list of rules and definitions for developing and integrating the application.

Encryption: It is the process of transforming the data into a secure format.

Epoch: Number of times the deep learning model goes through the dataset.

MinMaxScalar: It scales the feature value between 0 and 1.

Open Source Benchmark Dataset: Dataset available free to use for research purposes for benchmarking and validating the new proposed implementation and comparative analysis purposes.

Polymorphism: It is the concept that describes the situations when there are multiple forms of the same object.

UNIX: An operating system widely used for internet servers and workstations.

URL: Uniform resource locator refers to a file on a network computer.

Chapter 6
Machine Learning for Internet of Things–Based Smart Transportation Networks

Hammad Khawar
Baqai Medical University, Pakistan

Tariq Rahim Soomro
 https://orcid.org/0000-0002-7119-0644
Institute of Business Management (IoBM), Karachi, Pakistan

Muhammad Ayoub Kamal
Institute of Business Management (IoBM), Karachi, Pakistan

ABSTRACT

The world's population is expanding, and people want to live in cities, making city administration a difficult task. Traditional cities, with their shared characteristics, will be unable to provide human demands. Machine learning (ML) techniques are being used to increase an application's understanding and capabilities as the volume of data received rises. Smart transportation is defined as an umbrella concept that describes route optimization, parking, street lighting, and infrastructure applications in this evaluation. The purpose of this research is to present a self-contained assessment of machine learning techniques and internet of things applications in intelligent transportation to provide a clear picture of the current state of circumstances. In this chapter, the authors attempt to explain several features of smart transportation in greater depth.

INTRODUCTION

Mankind has been using different modes of travel from the very beginning such as animals, vehicles, airplanes, ships, etc. Several modes of transportation have brought serious problems for human beings as well as animals such as fatal injuries and health issues due to various kinds of pollution and anxiety

DOI: 10.4018/978-1-6684-4045-2.ch006

(Minchin, 2006). A new concept of 'Smart Transportation' has emerged and several types of research are going on to make this concept the transportation system of the future. In the IoT systems, every connected object is known as a "thing." Common components of things include physical sensors, actuators, and an integrated system with a Central processing unit. (Raza et al., 2020). Machine-to-Machine (M2M) communication is required because things must communicate with one another. Wireless technologies like Bluetooth, Wi-Fi, and ZigBee can be utilized for short-distance communication, Long-range communication may be achieved using wireless operators such as Sigfox, WiMAX, CAT M1, LoRa, NB-IoT, GPRS, GSM, 3G, 4G, LTE, and 5G (B & Petri, 2015). It is feasible to provide efficient route suggestions, quick parking bookings, cost-effective street lighting, telematics for public transportation, accident avoidance, and self-directed driving using IoT sensors implanted in a vehicle or mobile devices and devices deployed in the city. ML is a notion that has been around for a long time. Artificial Intelligence and ML are closely connected. AI is made possible through machine learning. Computer systems can learn to execute tasks like clustering, pattern recognition, categorization, predictions, and more using machine learning. Systems are taught utilizing various statistical models and algorithms to analyze a part of the data to keep track of the learning process. A machine learning technique seeks to identify a link among the characteristics and certain resultant values called labels, and the sample data is generally described by quantifiable properties called features (Mohammed et al., 2016). IoT and Machine Learning algorithms are being combined with the smart transportation field by researchers to invent all those transportation modes that can offer huge benefits to mankind and animals. To understand the developments and advancements in the smart transportation field, it is necessary to know the basics about IoT, Machine, and Deep Learning techniques and the roles these fields are playing in converting a transportation system into a smart one.

BACKGROUND

Several industry demands, as well as extensive research employing machine learning algorithms, have prepared the way for the developing topic of intelligent transportation (Karami & Kashef, 2020). Several researchers have been interested in the field of intelligent transportation, which was investigated using both machine learning and IoT approaches. Smart transportation networks are evolving with the exponential increase in the usage of IoT devices as well as the advantages obtained by applying Machine Learning methods over different applications of the smart transportation system.

IoT and Human Interaction

The Internet of Things (IoT) is a network of physical objects that are integrated with sensors, software, technology, and connection to give a platform for sharing data with other devices connected, the operator, or the producer to improve performance (Azgomi & Jamshidi, 2018). Each device connected in IoT is considered a thing, where each of these things performs some function. By creating a network of these things, IT-based services are obtained, hence called the Internet of Things. Mobile phones, microcontrollers, wearable, and wireless sensors, and nearly every other electronic item are now connected to a local network or the internet, ushering in the Internet of Things (IoT) era (Madakam et al., 2015). Several systems are now providing better and easier interaction with humans through ubiquitous computing achieved from IoT infrastructure (Kamal et al., 2019). With time, the software development of the applications that are capable of collecting all the data generated by IoT, analyzing and converting the fetched data into meaningful information using AI algorithms, has now become the demand of the current and future lifestyle. As the quantity of devices on the market grows, so does the amount of data acquired by those devices. With the growth of the Internet of Things (IoT), apps have gotten smarter, and connected devices have become more prevalent, allowing for their use in all facets of modern city life (Zantalis et al., 2019).

AI To Rescue the Cities In the Future

Nowadays, more people live in the cities than before; on average, 60% of the world's population lives inside of 5 kilometers of a city, with predictions that this percentage will climb to 70% by 2030 (Azgomi & Jamshidi, 2018). According to some reports, more than one million individuals choose cities as their preferred places to reside every week. In more industrialized nations, the figure is already much higher; for instance, in the United Kingdom, city dwellers account for almost 90% of the population (Azgomi & Jamshidi, 2018). The world's population is expanding, and people want to live in cities, making city administration a difficult task (Sánchez-Corcuera et al., 2019). Traditional cities, with numerous shared characteristics, will be unable to provide human requirements. To avoid disasters in the administration and management of cities shortly, researchers are focussed on using AI-based techniques in various systems of the cities in the future (Azgomi & Jamshidi, 2018). As a result, smart cities will be the future type of cities, gathering and processing data from a variety of sources while making appropriate judgments and sending data to all sections of the system (Neirotti et al., 2014). As a response, smart cities and their positive effects have recently received a lot of attention. Advanced analytics via AI-based algorithms are being applied in a variety of fields inside cities. This idea is a Big Data system, which is based on the flow of data that is exchanged throughout all elements of smart cities. As a result, the smart city is a sophisticated big data challenge that brings together several disciplines of study to create a unified environment (Azgomi & Jamshidi, 2018).

AI with ML and DL Methods

The word 'Artificial Intelligence (AI) was coined by John McCarthy in 1956. Hence, AI is an old but highly developing field. The idea of AI is to use computing power and make machines capable of exhibiting intelligence similar to human beings. Smartness is being increased in the applications in different applications of the smart transportation system through AI (Rivoltella, 2018). Instead of writing codes with all the possible relationships, functions, and decision logic to produce AI in computers and machines for a particular application, nowadays, AI is being produced in the systems through ML (Machine Learning) and DL (Deep Learning) algorithms due to the availability of rapidly improving programming frameworks, exponentially increasing volume of data and the large variety of powerful computing resources (Barua, 2021). With the help of ML, the system tries to derive relationships and patterns from the data that it gets from the environment, past experiences, or examples given to it explicitly by humans. In DL, machine learning is done using the concept of ANN (Artificial Neural Network) where usually, advanced ANN consisting of advanced artificial neurons is used instead of simple ANN. In a controlled environment for some applications, DL has already given performances even better than humans (Janiesch et al., 2021). A Venn diagram can be drawn through which different categories of ML algorithms can be represented, like in figure 1.

Figure 1. Venn diagram showing categories of various Machine Learning algorithms (Janiesch et al., 2021)

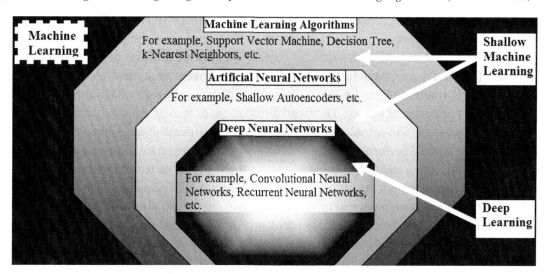

Due to the benefits of ML and DL techniques, they are being heavily deployed in IoT-based applications. ML and DL algorithms are being used to process the data generated by IoT (Azgomi & Jamshidi, 2018). Furthermore, predicting futuristic outcomes with high accuracy from the current and past information is being done also in IoT-based applications via ML and DL techniques.

Technology Areas in Smart City

The systems in a smart city can be divided into several categories. These four categories are an excellent place to start: healthcare, environment, energy, and transportation (Perboli et al., 2014). Several applications within these four areas are constantly being studied and developed such as wireless heart rate monitoring of a heart patient by smart healthcare system, air pollution level monitoring by smart environment system, intelligent automation of electrical equipment inside a smart building by a smart energy management system, smart street lights control by the smart transportation system, etc. Some applications indirectly affect multiple categories such as saving energy and the environment via smart street lights control (activating only when they are required to reduce CO_2 emission) as an application of smart transportation system, etc. Similarly, applications such as smart buildings, bring together a variety of study topics, including efficient transportation design and planning, automated control networks, smart societies, and much more (Jan et al., 2019). Figure 2 points out various applications in a smart city that are used by the smart transportation system to increase its effectiveness.

Smart Transportation System

Smart transportation is one of the most significant and difficult aspects of the smart city. Smarter transportation will be built with autonomous cars, smart roads, and infrastructure that will allow all sections of the traffic management system to interact with one another (Azgomi & Jamshidi, 2018). Route optimization, easy parking reservations, street lighting, accident prevention/detection, road abnormalities, autonomous vehicles, and infrastructure applications are all considered part of smart transportation

(Zantalis et al., 2019). Within which, road users can avoid crowded regions with effective congestion management, lowering pollution concentrations(Majumdar et al., 2021). Smart transportation is becoming an increasingly important part of modern civilizations as cities grow in size and population (Karami & Kashef, 2020). Travel habits have gotten increasingly difficult during the last few decades, particularly in megacities. To plan for municipal transportation, decision-makers need more precise and complete data (Lari, 2015). Disruption of road networks has a detrimental influence on sustainability in many cities by causing air pollution to worsen. The futuristic concept, as well as other existing Interconnected Vehicles research projects, will introduce smart and green (eco-friendly) transportation to modernity in smart cities. The control of small traffic elements will also be integrated into smart transportation systems such as traffic signs and traffic control lights to make traffic management more efficient. The results obtained by performing image processing using ML and DL techniques over the pictures and videos fetched from cameras mounted at different locations might also allow the smart transportation networks to adapt to various scenarios such as accidents, traffic congestion, severe weather conditions unsuitable for driving on a specific route, etc. Figure 3 gives an imaginative view about different elements in the environment being detected by the smart transportation system.

Figure 2. Applications linked with smart transportation systems in a smart city (Azgomi & Jamshidi, 2018)

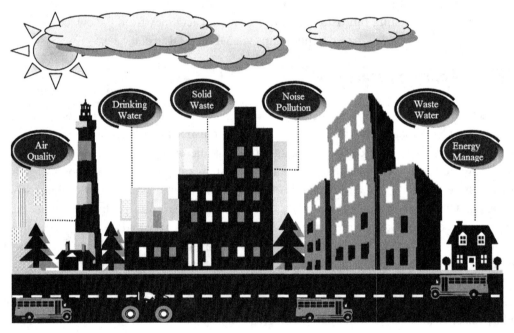

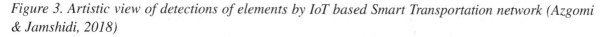

Figure 3. Artistic view of detections of elements by IoT based Smart Transportation network (Azgomi & Jamshidi, 2018)

IoT Combined with ML and DL

Without the Internet of Things, there will be no smart city. There are now data sets accessible that can be leveraged to develop smart, sustainable transportation solutions inside cities, thanks to the advent of the Internet of Things sensors (Majumdar et al., 2021). Using traditional engineering approaches, however, evaluating large data for smart control systems presents several obstacles and issues (Fleming & Purshouse, 2002). These difficulties include real-time processing of large amounts of data, quick processing, and effective decision-making and administration (Jan et al., 2019). Machine Learning (ML) techniques are being used to increase an application's understanding and capabilities as the amount of data it collects rises (Zantalis et al., 2019). Things speak with things in IoT networks so Machine-to-Machine communication (M2M) scenarios become common. Communication over short distances via wireless technologies such as Wi-Fi, ZigBee, and Bluetooth, can be done in IoT. Similarly, to achieve communication over long distances, wireless technologies like, WiMAX, LoRa, Sigfox, CAT M1, NB-IoT, GSM, GPRS, 3G, 4G, LTE, or 5G can be used in IoT with varying number of advantages and disadvantages depending upon the chosen communication technologies. As IoT deals with 'big data' and the cost of IoT node is kept to minimum, trend has shifted towards using IoT infrastructure with Machine Learning algorithms running within the infrastructure as processing tremendous amount of data through classical approaches is not feasible now. In this regard, data processing of IoT network may be done completely over some centralized server computer/node in the cloud and referred to as Cloud-computing (Kamal et al., 2020). Alternatively, the processing may be partially done over end network nodes and referred to as Edge-computing. Alternatively, heavy data processing may be done over intermediate nodes physically located close to the end network nodes and referred to as Fog computing. IoT platforms such as Kaa, ThingsBoard, DeviceHive, ThingSpeak, and Mainflux are available now and to support M2M communication in the IoT infrastructure, protocols like MQ Telemetry Transport (MQTT), Advanced Message Queuing Protocol (AMQP), Simple (or Streaming) Text Orientated Messaging Protocol (STOMP),

Constrained Application Protocol (CoAP), Extensible Messaging and Presence Protocol (XMPP), and HyperText Transfer Protocol (HTTP) are being used (Zantalis et al., 2019). In a simplified form, IoT infrastructure consists of 3 stages of processing – stage 1 (Perception layer), stage 2 (Network layer), and stage 3 (Application layer) (Dizon & Pranggono, 2021). The Perception layer consists of WSN so that the data from the environment can be sensed and measured. It may include a combination of light, humidity, motion, temperature, infrared and other types of sensors embedded in a smart object. The Network layer may be made up of mesh, star, or heterogeneous topology of these smart objects. The data of WSN inside these smart objects can be exchanged among these smart objects through gateways made from wireless technologies such as, Wireless Local Area Network (WLAN), ZigBee, (Long RAnge) LoRa, (LoRa Wide Area Network) LoRaWAN, (Narrow Band-IoT) NB-IoT or other (Low Power Wide Area Network) LPWAN technologies, etc. The transmission and reception of data may be done using GPRS, WiFi, WiMAX or some type of IoT cloud platform from where the data can be handled by centralized control system. The Application layer consists of actions to be taken against the fetched data such as; applying ML based techniques for prediction and error correction in the data, alerting concerned authorities about the current or expected abnormal scenarios (elevated pollution levels, high possibility of road accident to occur, detection of road congestion, ground water level reaching the flood level, detection of seismic activity, intensity control of smart street lights, traffic monitoring against pollution levels, fault reporting, etc).

RELATED RESEARCH WORKS

Scholars are indeed debating the major merits and downsides of numerous machine learning-based traffic monitoring and prediction models, as well as the commercial acceptance of these models to reach worldwide appeal, as well as dependability and cost savings in smart transport networks for green infrastructure (Bagloee et al., 2016). They are also studying different ways to utilize IoT infrastructure for different applications in the transportation field.

Vehicle Sharing Without IoT

Scholarly articles have also utilized the machine learning methods and proposed different vehicle sharing systems co-existing within the umbrella of the smart transportation system to promote attractive, economical, and easy mobility within urban areas such as the Bike Sharing System (BSS) through GPS or any other RF-based tracking system without using IoT. BSS, like many other transport networks, is beneficial for informing participants about station status at run time, providing information about the number of bicycles stored in each base station via web-based services, and so on. When the departure station is vacant, however, the user may be interested in knowing how the situation will develop and, in specific, whether or not a bike will arrive (and vice versa when the arrival station is full) (Scheltes & de Almeida Correia, 2017). To meet this expectation, BSS might behave as an efficient system, predicting and inferring if a motorcycle is in use and could, with a high likelihood, be delivered to the station where the client is awaiting (Bacciu et al., 2017).

Route Optimization Without IoT

Using phone calls, mobile locations, and similar records, Clustering Assessment is presently being viewed as an efficient unsupervised machine learning approach in trip distribution and generation, as well as traffic zone division, for improved Innovative Transit system efficiency (Karami & Kashef, 2020).

Route Optimization Without ML

Authors in (Al-Dweik et al., 2017) have proposed a system that uses roadside units named Scalable Enhanced Road Side Unit (SERSU) for route optimization in a smart transportation system. These units are made up of cameras, sensors to detect weather conditions, sensors to detect levels of different pollutants, and Radio Frequency modules. The system helps to reduce road jams and accidents due to severe weather conditions. These units continuously monitor traffic and weather conditions and transmit the data to Master Control Center (MCC) using 4G based mobile network, instead of using an IoT platform. These units are also capable of sending messages and alerts to the drivers such as the current speed limit set for the road on which the driver is traveling. MCC processes the received data from SERSUs and decides new speed limits and route suggestions based upon the current traffic flow speed, pollution levels, and weather conditions.

Mobile Crowd-sourcing For Transportation System

Mobile crowd-sourcing refers to the activities processed on smartphones of the crowd, usually involving GPS and Internet technologies. Google introduced this concept and provided several services to its customers such as Google Maps so that its customers can easily find the optimum route to travel to their destinations based on several criteria such as shortest distance, least traffic congestion, mode of transportation (by walk, bus, car, etc). This application uses the accelerometer, GPS, and gyroscope sensors already embedded in the mobile devices of the users, instead of fixing sensors at specific locations, to provide traffic status to its users over various routes on a real-time basis. Mobile users send their speed and location values anonymously to Google servers through the Google Maps application so that traffic-related real-time information can be predicted such as traffic congestions, etc.

Authors (Distefano et al., 2018) have also used the mobile crowd-sourcing technique to create a variant of the Ant Colony Optimization algorithm to achieve swarm-based intelligence in a transportation system. In the system, one mobile user will generate a message to lead another mobile user to a less congested area. The process of sending and following messages as a trail will continue so that the congestion is avoided by diverting the crowd to less crowded routes. In (Fan et al., 2017), researchers have focused on optimizing the remaining last mile for the traveler when he or she is reaching the destination using the crowd-sourcing technique through a mobile application named CrowdNavi. The authors point out the fact that the residents of the area have good knowledge about routes to several destinations. Using crowd-sourcing over the traveling patterns of the residents, crowd data is gathered by the proposed system. The optimum traveling route for a traveler to his/her destination, excluding the last mile of the route, is suggested by the system using Google Maps. The last mile of the route is suggested using currently fetched crowd data and landmark method.

Smart Parking Systems Without ML

For smart parking systems, several researchers have proposed IoT-based solutions without using ML techniques. In (Saarika P S, Sandhya K, 2017), authors have used ultrasonic sensors installed in each section of the parking lot to detect if that section of the parking lot is vacant or not. The data from all the sensors is sent to a cloud server using a WiFi network. The mobile application is then able to tell the user whether a vacant parking section is available or not. Simultaneously, the display on an electronic smart signboard is also updated so that the user who does not have access to his/her mobile phone can also find out whether there is a vacant parking space or not by just looking at the signboard. The authors have made the signboard out of an LED or LCD screen connected to the display output of Raspberry Pi which is in turn connected to the cloud.

Authors (Roy et al., 2016) have also used ultrasonic sensors to detect empty parking areas. The sensors are connected to Arduino Uno with a WiFi module. The data from the sensors are sent to the cloud via this WiFi module. The proposed system uses the ThingSpeak IoT platform via MQTT communication protocol for monitoring and management. The user gets information regarding vacant parking spaces on an Android-based mobile application. The user can use the application to reserve paid parking sections by paying the parking fees online through the application. Researchers (Aydin et al., 2017) have used a Genetic algorithm (GA) as an optimizing technique to get that route from a vacant parking slot to the user's position which has the shortest length. The system consists of magnetic sensors located at parking slots to detect the metallic structure of cars. On the detection of a car in a slot, the corresponding sensor sends a signal to a remote server through a gateway. Similarly, simple RFID-based parking systems can also be made in which RFID tags can be attached to all the vehicles and RFID readers can be fixed at the entrance and exit gates. Whenever the tagged vehicle exits or enters the parking area, the corresponding reader detects it and the number of vacant parking slots is incremented or decremented by 1, respectively. Similarly, line-of-sight (LoS) based Infra-red (IR) or LASER sensors can be fixed at the exit and entry gates to keep the track of the number of vacant spaces in the parking area and display it on an electronic based digit counter.

Smart Street Lighting Systems without ML

Context-aware computing plays an important role in the internet of things (Kamal et al., 2018). Street lights are important when the security and well-being of the general public are concerned. Traditional street lights consume a high level of energy. Nowadays, authorities in different cities are replacing High-Pressure Sodium (HPS) based lamps inside street lights with (Light Emitting Diode) LED-based lamps to reduce power consumption and maintenance costs while maintaining visibility levels (Dizon & Pranggono, 2021).

Authors (Dizon & Pranggono, 2021) have done case studies on the intelligent street light system of Sheffield, United Kingdom. The authors used an open-source simulator named StreetlightSim and simulated different lighting schemes available in the simulator i.e. 4 time-based light dimming schemes (Conventional, Dynadimmer, Chronosense, and Part-Night), a traffic-aware street lighting system using autonomous WSN called TALiSMaN (traffic-aware lighting scheme management network) in their work and simulated energy consumptions by these IoT based lighting schemes of the street lights. Considering the adaptive lighting system's behaviour by smart street lights, figure 4 shows a scenario when a pedestrian is detected. Figure 5 shows the adaptive lighting system's behaviour when a car is detected by the smart street lights.

Figure 4. Adaptive Lighting scheme in Smart Street Lights when S2 detects a pedestrian within its range and lights up with full brightness. The neighboring lights (S1, S3, S4, and S5) light up proportional to the distance of the pedestrian from them (Dizon & Pranggono, 2021) (Lau et al., 2015).

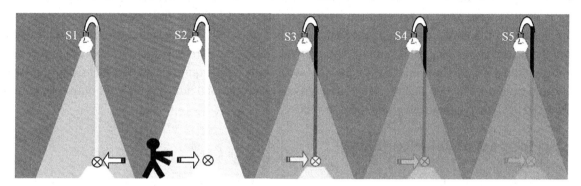

Figure 5. Adaptive Lighting scheme in Smart Street Lights when S1 detects a vehicle within its range and lights up with full brightness. The neighboring lights (S2, S3, and S4) also light up with full brightness as the car driver needs to have clear vision over long distances (Dizon & Pranggono, 2021)(Lau et al., 2015).

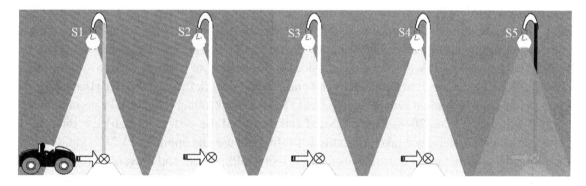

In (Maguluri et al., 2018), authors have demonstrated a smart street lighting system consisting of autonomous street lights. Each street light's lamp is turned on whenever a vehicle or pedestrian is passing by and is then turned off automatically to save energy. The detection of the object is done using IR sensors. Raspberry Pi working as a single board computer (SBC) controls the electricity supply to the lamp and is responsible for turning on or off the lamp depending upon the signals received from the sensors. The light sensor in the light is used to detect sunlight and the lamp is kept off by SBC during the daytime irrespective of the presence of any nearby object.

Authors have proposed a system (Tripathy et al., 2018) that can control its lighting by turning on, off, or dimming its lamp, depending upon the weather conditions detected by the sensors in the street light. In the proposed system, the street lights can send different types of information by connecting to a cloud-based server through WiFi. Authors have also proposed to attach cameras on these lights to increase the safety of the nearby people through surveillance. In the proposed system, emergencies can also be detected by scanning for abnormally high or low values of the sensors in the lights monitoring various properties of the environment.

A similar solution is proposed in (Jia et al., 2018) where IoT infrastructure is used. The street lights are equipped with light and IR sensors along with GPS and wireless modules. The lights use NB-IoT communication protocol to form a network among them. The light intensity is controlled by the crowd. GPS is used to send different information by each of the street lights in the system such as status of a lamp, location of the light, etc. The maintenance can be done as soon as possible whenever required by using the information. Similarly, authors (Bingol et al., 2019) have implemented LoRa communication among the street lights. The proposed system consists of street lights equipped with LED, microcontroller, and LoRa module. They upload their data to a remote controller and adjust their light output levels according to the commands received by the controller.

Social Internet of Vehicles (SIoV)

Using the concepts of Mobile Ad hoc Network (MANET) in computer communication, Vehicular Ad hoc Network (VANET) was introduced in which a wireless network gets created among parked or moving vehicles. The idea of letting the things make social relationship in the form of a network among them automatically when they share common interests (short distance among them, similar sensors data, etc,) as well as maintaining that social relationship by sharing this information among themselves, was introduced as Social IoT (SIoT). Using IoT infrastructure, the concept of the Internet of Vehicles (IoV) was introduced. SIoT applied in vehicular domains has given rise to the Social Internet of Vehicles (SIoV). SIoV has evolved intelligence in VANETs by including the concept of social relationships and uninterrupted communication among the vehicles(Butt et al., 2019). This has also greatly impacted smart transportation networks. SIoV gives various services to the drivers but generates a high volume of data. In (Jain et al., 2018), authors have proposed Vehicular Social Network Protocol (VSNP) that can be used to decrease the communication data generated due to SIoV while keeping reliable V2V communication. Authors (Chowdhury et al., 2018) have proposed and simulated the system on LabView that uses the M2M communication technique taken from the IoT infrastructure and applied to V2V communication. In the proposed system, the car transmits its location using GPS, speed, and movement direction to the neighboring cars. The car simultaneously transmits this information to a common server. By detecting a sudden change in a car's speed and transmitting an alert to the neighboring cars and/or broadcasting the presence of traffic congestion ahead to the cars on a real-time basis, chances of accidents occurring can be reduced.

Fleet Management

Researchers have proposed a system (Geetha & Cicilia, 2018) for bus fleet management. The system comprises of busses tagged with RFID, IR LOS sensors, GPS module, Texas Instrument's CC3200 microcontroller with built-in WiFi module. IR sensors are used to keep a count of the number of passengers entering and leaving the bus, GPS is used to track the location of the bus on a real-time basis and an RFID tag is used to identify the bus uniquely. The data from the sensors are sent to the microcontroller, which in turn uses a WiFi network to upload the information on a cloud server. The information suitable for the users (estimated time of arrival of the next bus, vacant space in the bus, etc,) is presented to them via electronics-based display placed at the bus station made up LCD displaying the output from its microcontroller (CC3200) as well as a mobile application.

Car-Usage Based Insurance

Vehicle telematics is a field that is inspired by telemetry in which a vehicle is tracked along with its status through the use of telecommunication devices (wireless communication technology, etc,) and computer science (computer, Internet, etc). Insurance companies are already using vehicle telematics to track how the insured car is being handled by the driver. Whenever the insurance of the car is claimed by the customer, the data collected for the car driving pattern is analyzed and the decision is made accordingly, for example, the insurance case for the customer becomes weak if the driving pattern suggests that the driver is reckless, the car has covered distance more than the limit claimable by the insurance, etc.

WAYS TO APPLY ML OVER SMART TRANSPORTATION NETWORKS

By installing various sensors into vehicles, using data of sensors already embedded in mobile devices, and combining data from various devices already installed in a smart city at various places (like, near the road-sides), IoT based transportation system can be made and the performance of vehicle telematics for the general public transportation system can be augmented. By involving ML and DL-based algorithms in IoT infrastructure, significant improvements in the application (increased accuracy in output values, reduced processing time, etc,), as well as IoT infrastructure (better network optimization, automatic load balancing, etc,), can be achieved. Transportation-related applications like vehicle tracking, long trailer tracking, freight container tracking, ships and vehicles fleet management, vehicle sharing, usage-based insurance system, etc, can be greatly improved using IoT and ML techniques. Hence, researchers are applying various ML techniques over the data created by IoT based transportation systems to increase benefits for man through increased intelligence in the system such as real-time tracking of an asset for its increased transportation security, reduced time delays in transportation services, enhanced human safety in transportation, etc. There are 4 basic ways in which an ML algorithm can be made to learn in different scenarios faced by the transportation system and then applied on the system itself to get the required outputs, as discussed below:

Supervised Learning

It is done in 2 phases. 1) training and 2) testing phase. The first training phase of the algorithm is started. In this phase, data set with known labels are given where the algorithm learns the relationships among the given data sets and labels. After the completion of the training phase, the testing phase is started in which the data to be tested is given. In this phase, the algorithm tries to predict the output values from the testing data using the relationships learned by it in the training phase.

Unsupervised Learning

It is done by giving data without labels. The algorithm tries to find patterns in the testing data and predict output values.

Semi-Supervised Learning

It is a combination of Supervised and Unsupervised learning techniques. It is done by giving data with some of the data having labels. The algorithm then tries to predict the output values.

Reinforcement Learning

It is done by inputting data with some already set parameters in the algorithm. The algorithm generates some output. The output is fed again as input. The cycle continues until the optimal output is obtained.

APPLICATIONS IN IoT BASED SMART TRANSPORTATION

Researchers are continuously working on improving smart transportation systems by applying ML and non-ML-based techniques along with different communication technologies and infrastructure such as IoT, cellular networks, etc. Table 1 enlists references to a few of the research works that have applied ML in different applications of IoT-based smart transportation networks. For Smart Lighting Systems and Smart Parking applications, there may be a shortage of ML coverage (Zantalis et al., 2019).

§   Road irregularities detection
§   Accident Detection / Prevention
§   Infrastructure
§   Route optimization and V2V communication
§   Smart Street Lighting
§   Smart Parking

Table 1. Applications in Smart Transportation System dealt with ML methods

Application	Machine Learning Based Solution
Road irregularities detection	(Gopalakrishnan, 2018), (Kulkarni et al., 2014), (Ghadge et al., 2016)
Accident Detection / Prevention	(Ghosh et al., 2017), (Kwon et al., 2018), (Liu et al., 2014), (Munoz-Organero et al., 2018), (Ozbayoglu et al., 2016), (Ryder & Wortmann, 2017), (Dogru & Subasi, 2018)
Infrastructure	(Jan et al., 2019)
Route optimization and V2V communication	(Yu et al., 2008), (Lv et al., 2014), (Sang et al., 2018)
Smart Street Lighting	(Mohandas et al., 2019), (Tukymbekov et al., 2021)
Smart Parking	(Wu et al., 2007), (Amato et al., 2017), (De Almeida et al., 2015)

Road Irregularities Detection

Bad road conditions due to surface problems lead to several traffic issues such as traffic congestion, abnormally increased air and noise pollution in specific areas due to stuck traffic flow, increased anxiety in drivers as well as passengers, etc. It may even lead to serious road accidents and vehicle damages.

Road abnormal surfaces detection usually includes the detection of bumps, large cracked patches, and holes on the roads. These problems of the roads might have arisen due to several factors such as low-quality manufacturing of the roads, severe weather conditions affecting roads, continuous use of the roads by overloaded vehicles, continual high frictional strains on specific patches on the roads, previously occurred accident causing road damage, etc. Researchers have utilized accelerometer sensor readings fetched from mobile devices and processed them using a DL-based algorithm, Feed-Forward Neural Network (FF-NN) to detect pot-holes on the roads (Kulkarni et al., 2014). Scholars have also applied to the cluster using the K-means algorithm to process irregularities of the roads to increase driving safety using the reading obtained from IoT of accelerometer sensors (Mamun et al., 2017), (Ghadge et al., 2016). Authors in (Kinabalu, 2019) have presented a performance comparison of k-NN, Random Forest (RF), and Support Vector Machine (SVM) algorithms when applied to detect road anomalies. Due to advantages and variations in the parameters involved in ML and DL based processing in IoT infrastructure, scholars have also tried to compare the performances achieved in the works of various researchers on the detection of the abnormalities of the road surface via CNN (Convolutional Neural Network) and Deep CNN (DCNN) (Gopalakrishnan, 2018).

Accident Detection / Prevention and Vehicle-To-Vehicle Communication

The statistics of road accidents are shockingly high in populated cities of the world. For example, in 2010, 32,999 people got killed, 3.9 million people got injured and 24 million vehicles were damaged by accidents involving vehicles. Hence, it is an important and time-critical aspect of a smart transportation system. Road accidents can be avoided if measures and techniques are used so that the driver stays alert while driving. The driver can be alerted at the appropriate time so that accidents can be avoided by some type of accident alert or monitoring system working on the relevant traffic data fetched and processed on a real-time basis.

Coupled Hidden Markov Model (CHMM) has been used by researchers in (Liu et al., 2014) to share information of movements among concerning vehicles with critical timings to avoid accidents. In (Oz-bayoglu et al., 2016), researchers have used data fetched from road sensors on a real-time basis and applied FF-NN, a Regression tree, and k-NN algorithms to detect road accidents. In (Dogru & Subasi, 2018), the authors have proposed a system that detects road accidents using SVM (Support Vector Machine) and ANN algorithms over Radio Frequency (FR) based V2V communication data. Authors (Kwon et al., 2018) have used Fully Connected Network (FCN) to detect blind-spot for vehicles and avoid accidents. Authors (Ghosh et al., 2017) have focused on detecting whether the driver is alert or not while driving the vehicle. The system alerts the driver immediately through a network of actuators (speakers, etc) to avoid accidents if he or she is found unconscious by applying AdaBoost, an ensemble-based supervised learning algorithm. In (Ryder & Wortmann, 2017), researchers have applied Inception Neural Network to find out the areas where the probability of accidents occurring is high. In (Munoz-Organero et al., 2018), researchers used Deep Belief Networks (DBN) to create the digital map by automatically classifying street elements such as traffic lights, roundabouts, street signs, etc, that can be used to avoid accidents. After DBN, the researchers achieved 90% accuracy in detecting street crossings 80% accuracy in the detection of traffic lights and roundabouts by using the k-NN classifier.

Infrastructure

To increase the service responsiveness of smart transportation systems, the authors built a framework for analyzing transportation data with Hadoop and Spark to handle real-time transportation data. The system is made up of four layers: data collection and acquisition, network, data processing, and application. Each layer is designed to process and manage data in a logical and orderly manner. Hadoop and Spark are used to evaluate data in the data processing layer. The data is transmitted to a smart community member using the recommended event and decision mechanism based on named data networking. The suggested system is put to the test using transportation data from a variety of reliable sources. The results reveal data processing and real-time distribution to citizens in the shortest time feasible (Jan et al., 2019).

Route Optimization and V2V Communication

One of the numerous challenges in this field of study, for example, is effectively anticipating congestion spread, which is challenging owing to the fluctuating non-linear nature of traffic flow (Majumdar et al., 2021). Other efficient and effective data gathering approaches have lately been implemented utilizing information technology, as opposed to traditional paper-based and telephone-based surveys, which are solely reliant on the accuracy of the respondents' memory of events through the questionnaire. Recent technological advancements have provided researchers with a fantastic chance to collect travel data more efficiently and effectively, saving not just time and money, but also much more data. IT-based data gathering strategies may include IoT-based data collection, which may track passengers' excursions by recording the forms of transportation utilized, as well as the origins and destinations of daily trips. For policymaking, transportation planners benefit from reliable and comprehensive travel behavior data (used modes such as car, bus, bicycle, by walk, etc) (On & Traffic, 2011). On the one hand, municipal planners and authorities have considered this problem to be a beneficial tool in carrying out their strategies to provide acceptable and enough transportation services for future travel demands. On the other hand, health officials utilize this information to develop practical and effective solutions to the global issue of obesity among individuals (Lari, 2015).

Studies have investigated a variety of artificial intelligence approaches to make transportation networks smarter, including evaluating gathered data to discriminate between transportation modes for use by passengers using a unique machine learning approach named Random Forest. With an accuracy of about 96 percent, this model can classify transportation modes such as a vehicle, buses, and walking (Lari, 2015). For the forecasting of congestion distributed throughout a roadway, long short-term memory systems have indeed been examined. Based on the vehicle speed data from traffic sensors at two sites, a model that estimates the development of congestion in a busy town over 5 minutes has been developed. These methods have an accuracy of 84–95 percent depending on the road network when the analysis is done utilizing both versions of these models, i.e. univariate and multivariate predictive models. This consistency reveals that huge short-term memory systems are capable of forecasting congestion growth on road networks, and they might be a key component of future traffic modeling systems for efficient and sustainable cities across the world (Majumdar et al., 2021). The concept of connected vehicles becomes extremely challenging when it is mapped to the real-time road scenarios for a smart transportation system using traditional engineering techniques. Hence, ML techniques are being suggested by researchers to realize such a complicated and critical scenario. To reduce traffic jams, researchers in (Sang et al.,

2018) used Markov Decision Process (MDP) method over Vehicle-to-Vehicle (V2V) communication to create groups of routes.

To predict traffic for a short duration, authors in (Budapesti Műszaki és Gazdaságtudományi Egyetem. Faculty of Transport Engineering and Vehicle Engineering. Department of Transport Technology and Economics et al., 2015) have shown multiple techniques to do it such as, Bayesian Network Seasonal Autoregressive Integrated Moving Average (BN-SARIMA), Feed Forward Neural Networks (FF-NN) and Nonlinear Auto Regressive eXogenous (NARX) models. Researchers in (Yu et al., 2008) have used a trained FF-NN model with Binary Patterns (BP) to predict changes in total travel time. Researchers in (Lv et al., 2014) have tried to predict the flow of traffic received as Big Data using the Stacked Auto Encoder method. Similarly, ARIMA, Kalman filtering, Holt winters' Exponential smoothing, Random walk, KNN Method, and variants of Deep Learning algorithms are among the ML approaches and methods that employ time series prediction to solve different difficulties in route optimizations and other smart transportation systems.

Smart Parking

An intelligent parking system will be able to tell the users about the availability and location of vacant parking lots through a mobile application and/or IoT devices based on smart electronic direction display boards so that drivers do not have to waste their time and energy in finding the vacant spot in the parking area. The system will also be able to provide its users with some kind of in-advance parking reservation system. The system will comprise several IoT devices to render these services to the users and will also be able to update the centralized system simultaneously. The system might be able to predict the availability of empty vacant slots to the users through the ML prediction process running in the background of the system. Researchers have utilized different techniques to predict vacant spaces in parking lots. Authors (Wu et al., 2007) have processed images of the parking lots using SVM and Markov Random Field (MRF) algorithms to detect free parking lots while the authors in (Amato et al., 2017) have used CNN on the image data to find the vacant lots. In (De Almeida et al., 2015), authors have applied SVM to their created dataset named PKlot so that empty parking lots can be separated from the non-empty ones.

Smart Street Lighting

Manually operating the street lights through high power on/off switch buttons or using a classical on/off scheme depending only upon the daytime is not efficient enough to save energy from these energy-hungry devices. Furthermore, using fixed light dimming scheme concerning daytime is also not efficient as it ignores various external factors such as environmental light levels and traffic flow (Dizon & Pranggono, 2021). Smart street lights are being used instead that are capable of operating in different modes by considering different external factors such as the power system's load, traffic volume, and/or environmental variables (light intensity, pollutant levels, temperature, humidity, etc). Several benefits are achieved in this way such as energy-saving, reduced air pollution, and increased public safety by proper visibility level.

The largest energy-consuming part of street lights is a lamp. Researchers are focused on using techniques to control its energy consumption so that the overall energy efficiency of the street lights is increased. Furthermore, IoT-based smart lighting with centralized monitoring can continuously monitor the status of individual lights and alert in case of any failure. The smart lights can also be managed from a remote location, depending upon the implemented management system. Alternatively, smart street lights can act autonomously by taking appropriate actions by themselves concerning the current scenario instead of waiting for commands from a remote control center to keep the efficiency of the over system at the maximum level. IoT-based smart street lights may consist of several sensors such as temperature, light intensity, humidity, CO_2 level, power dissipation, PIR sensors, etc.

Researchers in (Mohandas et al., 2019) have proposed ANN and Fuzzy controllers in smart lighting systems to increase the efficiency of decisions. The system has shown a 13.5% energy reduction. Authors in (Tukymbekov et al., 2021) have proposed LSTM (Long Short Term Memory) based smart traffic lighting system. In the proposed system, every street light has an independent power source made up of a Solar Panel and can control its light emission levels depending upon predictions done using the LSTM (Long Short Term Memory) algorithm applied over the data relating to weather forecast and the power generation levels of the connected solar panel.

Smart Traffic Lighting

Using probabilistic vehicle counting algorithm and Inverse Markov Chain, authors in (Ide et al., 2017) have proposed ML techniques-based solution to predict traffic patterns with a system having low-quality cameras to reduce the cost of the system with comparable performance. The intelligence in the smart transportation system can be increased by changing the duration of the traffic light signals (red, green, yellow) at roundabouts, lanes, and intersections by detecting the traffic pattern using ML methods applied on the fetched information through various sources such as street cameras, IoT infrastructure data through sensors of vehicles and at roads, etc. Hence, using this traffic pattern-related information, the duration of traffic lights can be automatically increased for the roads having a high probability of traffic volume as compared to other roads to provide overall smooth traffic flow.

CONCLUSION

This chapter discussed smart transportation systems and their sub-systems such as smart lighting and parking systems, etc were introduced. Basic concepts, as well as various ways in which IoT, Machine, and Deep Learning techniques are being deployed to make smart transportation systems, were presented in the chapter. The research done in the field of smart transportation was also highlighted by the chapter. The chapter also discussed different ways in which smart transportation systems can help to solve traffic problems such as traffic accidents, congestions, etc, using different communication technologies, such as ZigBee, IoT, etc. The importance of machine and deep learning methods in increasing the efficiency of these systems was also discussed. The chapter also discussed the works that have been done to enhance the performance of smart transportation systems using classical, ML, and DL-based prediction and error correction techniques. Hence, when we consider the cities of the world with the rapidly growing rates of population density, road accidents, industrialization, and IoT market, we can see the fact that smart transportation systems have become one of the major requirements of modern cities. By involving IoT and artificial intelligence via machine and deep learning techniques, smart transportation systems can achieve great success in providing safe, healthy, relatively cheap, and comfortable lifestyles for the city residents as well as creating new types of job opportunities. Hence, it can be easily said that research and development will rapidly continue over the usages of IoT infrastructure and ML techniques to analyze, solve and predict several problematic conditions involving transportation.

REFERENCES

Al-Dweik, A., Muresan, R., Mayhew, M., & Lieberman, M. (2017). IoT-based multifunctional Scalable real-time Enhanced Road Side Unit for Intelligent Transportation Systems. *Canadian Conference on Electrical and Computer Engineering*, 1–6. 10.1109/CCECE.2017.7946618

Al Mamun, M. A., Puspo, J. A., & Das, A. K. (2017). An intelligent smartphone based approach using IoT for ensuring safe driving. *ICECOS 2017 - Proceeding of 2017 International Conference on Electrical Engineering and Computer Science: Sustaining the Cultural Heritage Toward the Smart Environment for Better Future*, 217–223. 10.1109/ICECOS.2017.8167137

Amato, G., Carrara, F., Falchi, F., Gennaro, C., Meghini, C., & Vairo, C. (2017). Deep learning for decentralized parking lot occupancy detection. *Expert Systems with Applications*, 72, 327–334. doi:10.1016/j. eswa.2016.10.055

Aydin, I., Karakose, M., & Karakose, E. (2017). A navigation and reservation based smart parking platform using genetic optimization for smart cities. *ICSG 2017 - 5th International Istanbul Smart Grids and Cities Congress and Fair*, 120–124. 10.1109/SGCF.2017.7947615

Azgomi, H. F., & Jamshidi, M. (2018). A brief survey on smart community and smart transportation. *Proceedings - International Conference on Tools with Artificial Intelligence, ICTAI, 2018-Novem*, 932–939. 10.1109/ICTAI.2018.00144

Bacciu, D., Carta, A., Gnesi, S., & Semini, L. (2017). An experience in using machine learning for short-term predictions in smart transportation systems. *Journal of Logical and Algebraic Methods in Programming*, 87(November), 52–66. doi:10.1016/j.jlamp.2016.11.002

Bagloee, S. A., Tavana, M., Asadi, M., & Oliver, T. (2016). Autonomous vehicles: Challenges, opportunities, and future implications for transportation policies. *Journal of Modern Transportation*, 24(4), 284–303. doi:10.100740534-016-0117-3

Barua, H. B. (2021). Data science and Machine learning in the Clouds : A Perspective for the Future. *Journal of LATEX Templates*.

Bingol, E., Kuzlu, M., & Pipattanasompom, M. (2019). A LoRa-based Smart Streetlighting System for Smart Cities. *7th International Istanbul Smart Grids and Cities Congress and Fair, ICSG 2019 - Proceedings*, 66–70. 10.1109/SGCF.2019.8782413

Budapesti Műszaki és Gazdaságtudományi Egyetem. Faculty of Transport Engineering and Vehicle Engineering. Department of Transport Technology and Economics, Budapesti Műszaki és Gazdaságtudományi Egyetem, IEEE Hungary Section, & Institute of Electrical and Electronics Engineers. (2015). *2015 International Conference on Models and Technologies for Intelligent Transportation Systems (MT-ITS)*. Budapest University of Technology and Economics (BME), Faculty of Transport Engineering and Vehicle Engineering, Department of Transport Technology and Economics.

Butt, T. A., Iqbal, R., Salah, K., Aloqaily, M., & Jararweh, Y. (2019). Privacy Management in Social Internet of Vehicles: Review, Challenges and Blockchain Based Solutions. *IEEE Access: Practical Innovations, Open Solutions, 7,* 79694–79713. doi:10.1109/ACCESS.2019.2922236

Chowdhury, D. N., Agarwal, N., Laha, A. B., & Mukherjee, A. (2018). A Vehicle-to-Vehicle Communication System Using Iot Approach. *Proceedings of the 2nd International Conference on Electronics, Communication and Aerospace Technology, ICECA 2018, Iceca,* 915–919. 10.1109/ICECA.2018.8474909

De Almeida, P. R. L., Oliveira, L. S., Britto, A. S. Jr, Silva, E. J. Jr, & Koerich, A. L. (2015). PKLot- A robust dataset for parking lot classification. *Expert Systems with Applications, 42*(11), 4937–4949. doi:10.1016/j.eswa.2015.02.009

Distefano, S., Merlino, G., Puliafito, A., Cerotti, D., & Dautov, R. (2018). Crowdsourcing and stigmergic approaches for (swarm) intelligent transportation systems. Lecture Notes in Computer Science (Including Subseries Lecture Notes in Artificial Intelligence and Lecture Notes in Bioinformatics), 10745 LNCS, 616–626. doi:10.1007/978-3-319-74521-3_64

Dizon, E., & Pranggono, B. (2021). Smart streetlights in Smart City: A case study of Sheffield. *Journal of Ambient Intelligence and Humanized Computing, 0123456789.* Advance online publication. doi:10.100712652-021-02970-y

Dogru, N., & Subasi, A. (2018). Traffic accident detection using random forest classifier. *2018 15th Learning and Technology Conference, L and T 2018,* 40–45. 10.1109/LT.2018.8368509

Fan, X., Liu, J., Wang, Z., Jiang, Y., & Liu, X. (2017). Crowdsourced Road Navigation: Concept, Design, and Implementation. *IEEE Communications Magazine, 55*(6), 126–131. doi:10.1109/MCOM.2017.1600738

Fleming, P. J., & Purshouse, R. C. (2002). Evolutionary algorithms in control systems engineering: A survey. *Control Engineering Practice, 10*(11), 1223–1241. doi:10.1016/S0967-0661(02)00081-3

Geetha, S., & Cicilia, D. (2018). IoT enabled intelligent bus transportation system. *Proceedings of the 2nd International Conference on Communication and Electronics Systems, ICCES 2017, 2018-Janua*(Icces), 7–11. 10.1109/CESYS.2017.8321235

Ghadge, M., Pandey, D., & Kalbande, D. (2016). Machine learning approach for predicting bumps on road. *Proceedings of the 2015 International Conference on Applied and Theoretical Computing and Communication Technology, ICATccT 2015,* 481–485. 10.1109/ICATCCT.2015.7456932

Ghosh, A., Chatterjee, T., Samanta, S., Aich, J., & Roy, S. (2017). Distracted driving: A novel approach towards accident prevention. *Adv. Comput. Sci. Technol, 10*(8), 2693–2705.

Gopalakrishnan, K. (2018). Deep learning in data-driven pavement image analysis and automated distress detection: A review. *Data, 3*(3), 28. Advance online publication. doi:10.3390/data3030028

Ide, T., Katsuki, T., Morimura, T., & Morris, R. (2017). City-Wide Traffic Flow Estimation from a Limited Number of Low-Quality Cameras. *IEEE Transactions on Intelligent Transportation Systems, 18*(4), 950–959. doi:10.1109/TITS.2016.2597160

Jain, B., Brar, G., Malhotra, J., Rani, S., & Ahmed, S. H. (2018). A cross layer protocol for traffic management in Social Internet of Vehicles. *Future Generation Computer Systems*, *82*, 707–714. doi:10.1016/j.future.2017.11.019

Jan, B., Farman, H., Khan, M., Talha, M., & Din, I. U. (2019). Designing a Smart Transportation System: An Internet of Things and Big Data Approach. *IEEE Wireless Communications*, *26*(4), 73–79. doi:10.1109/MWC.2019.1800512

Janiesch, C., Zschech, P., & Heinrich, K. (2021). Machine learning and deep learning. *Electronic Markets*, *31*(3), 685–695. doi:10.100712525-021-00475-2

Jia, G., Han, G., Li, A., & Du, J. (2018). SSL: Smart street lamp based on fog computing for smarter cities. *IEEE Transactions on Industrial Informatics*, *14*(11), 4995–5004. doi:10.1109/TII.2018.2857918

Kamal, M. A., Alam, M. M., Khawar, H., & Mazliham, M. S. (2019). Play and Learn Case Study on Learning Abilities through Effective Computing in Games. *MACS 2019 - 13th International Conference on Mathematics, Actuarial Science, Computer Science and Statistics, Proceedings*, 1–6. 10.1109/MACS48846.2019.9024771

Kamal, M. A., Kamal, M. K., Alam, M., & Su'ud, M. M. (2018). Context-Aware Perspective Analysis working of RFID Anti-Collision Protocols. *Journal of Independent Studies and Research - Computing*, *2*(16), 19–32. doi:10.31645/jisrc/(2018).16.2.02

Kamal, M. A., Raza, H. W., Alam, M. M., & Mohd, M. (2020). Highlight the Features of AWS, GCP and Microsoft Azure that Have an Impact when Choosing a Cloud Service Provider. *International Journal of Recent Technology and Engineering*, *8*(5), 4124–4232. doi:10.35940/ijrte.D8573.018520

Karami, Z., & Kashef, R. (2020). Smart transportation planning: Data, models, and algorithms. *Transportation Engineering*, *2*(June), 100013. Advance online publication. doi:10.1016/j.treng.2020.100013

Kinabalu, K. (2019). *Identification of Road Surface Conditions using IoT Sensors and Machine Learning. Lecture Notes in Electrical Engineering 603 Computational Science and Technology.*

Kulkarni, A., Mhalgi, N., Gurnani, S., & Giri, N. (2014). Pothole Detection System using Machine Learning on Android. *International Journal of Emerging Technology and Advanced Engineering*, *4*(7), 360–364. http://www.ijetae.com/files/Volume4Issue7/IJETAE_0714_55.pdf

Kwon, D., Park, S., Baek, S., Malaiya, R. K., Yoon, G., & Ryu, J. T. (2018). A study on development of the blind spot detection system for the IoT-based smart connected car. *2018 IEEE International Conference on Consumer Electronics, ICCE 2018, 2018-January*, 1–4. 10.1109/ICCE.2018.8326077

Lari, A. (2015). Automated Transportation Mode Detection Using Smart Phone Applications via Machine Learning: Case Study Mega City of Tehran. *Transportation Research Board 94th Annual Meeting*, *6147*(May).

Lau, S. P., Merrett, G. V., Weddell, A. S., & White, N. M. (2015). A traffic-aware street lighting scheme for Smart Cities using autonomous networked sensors. *Computers & Electrical Engineering*, *45*, 192–207. doi:10.1016/j.compeleceng.2015.06.011

Liu, W., Kim, S. W., Marczuk, K., & Ang, M. H. (2014). Vehicle motion intention reasoning using cooperative perception on urban road. *2014 17th IEEE International Conference on Intelligent Transportation Systems, ITSC 2014*, 424–430. 10.1109/ITSC.2014.6957727

Lv, Y., Duan, Y., Kang, W., Li, Z., & Wang, F.-Y. (2014). Traffic flow prediction with big data: A deep learning approach. *IEEE Transactions on Intelligent Transportation Systems*, *16*(2), 865–873. doi:10.1109/TITS.2014.2345663

Madakam, S., Ramaswamy, R., & Tripathi, S. (2015). Internet of Things (IoT): A Literature Review. *Journal of Computer and Communications*, *03*(05), 164–173. doi:10.4236/jcc.2015.35021

Maguluri, L. P., Sorapalli, Y. S. V., Nakkala, L. K., & Tallari, V. (2018). Smart street lights using IoT. *Proceedings of the 2017 3rd International Conference on Applied and Theoretical Computing and Communication Technology, ICATccT 2017*, *3*(11), 126–131. 10.1109/ICATCCT.2017.8389119

Majumdar, S., Subhani, M. M., Roullier, B., Anjum, A., & Zhu, R. (2021). Congestion prediction for smart sustainable cities using IoT and machine learning approaches. *Sustainable Cities and Society*, *64*(September), 102500. doi:10.1016/j.scs.2020.102500

Minchin, D. (2006). *The transport and the spread of living aquatic species*. doi:10.1007/1-4020-4504-2_5

Mohammed, M., Khan, M. B., & Bashier, E. B. M. (2016). *Machine learning: algorithms and applications*. CRC Press. doi:10.1201/9781315371658

Mohandas, P., Dhanaraj, J. S. A., & Gao, X. Z. (2019). Artificial Neural Network based Smart and Energy Efficient Street Lighting System: A Case Study for Residential area in Hosur. *Sustainable Cities and Society*, *48*(January), 101499. Advance online publication. doi:10.1016/j.scs.2019.101499

Munoz-Organero, M., Ruiz-Blaquez, R., & Sánchez-Fernández, L. (2018). Automatic detection of traffic lights, street crossings and urban roundabouts combining outlier detection and deep learning classification techniques based on GPS traces while driving. *Computers, Environment and Urban Systems*, *68*(September), 1–8. doi:10.1016/j.compenvurbsys.2017.09.005

Neirotti, P., De Marco, A., Cagliano, A. C., Mangano, G., & Scorrano, F. (2014). Current trends in smart city initiatives: Some stylised facts. *Cities (London, England)*, *38*, 25–36. doi:10.1016/j.cities.2013.12.010

Ozbayoglu, M., Kucukayan, G., & Dogdu, E. (2016). A real-time autonomous highway accident detection model based on big data processing and computational intelligence. *Proceedings - 2016 IEEE International Conference on Big Data*, 1807–1813. doi:10.1109/BigData.2016.7840798

Perboli, G., De Marco, A., Perfetti, F., & Marone, M. (2014). A new taxonomy of smart city projects. *Transportation Research Procedia*, *3*(July), 470–478. doi:10.1016/j.trpro.2014.10.028

Raza, H. W., Kamal, M. A., Alam, M., & Su'ud, M. S. M. (2020). A Review Of Middleware Platforms In Internet Of Things: A Non – Functional Requirements Approach. *Journal of Independent Studies and Research Computing*. doi:10.31645/18

Rivoltella, P. C. (2018). The third age of the media. *Research on Education and Media*, *10*(1), 1–2. doi:10.1515/rem-2018-0001

Roy, A., Siddiquee, J., Datta, A., Poddar, P., Ganguly, G., & Bhattacharjee, A. (2016). Smart traffic & parking management using IoT. *7th IEEE Annual Information Technology, Electronics and Mobile Communication Conference, IEEE IEMCON 2016.* 10.1109/IEMCON.2016.7746331

Ryder, B., & Wortmann, F. (2017). Autonomously detecting and classifying traffic accident hotspots. *UbiComp/ISWC 2017 - Adjunct Proceedings of the 2017 ACM International Joint Conference on Pervasive and Ubiquitous Computing and Proceedings of the 2017 ACM International Symposium on Wearable Computers*, 365–370. 10.1145/3123024.3123199

Sánchez-Corcuera, R., Nuñez-Marcos, A., Sesma-Solance, J., Bilbao-Jayo, A., Mulero, R., Zulaika, U., Azkune, G., & Almeida, A. (2019). Smart cities survey: Technologies, application domains and challenges for the cities of the future. *International Journal of Distributed Sensor Networks*, 15(6). Advance online publication. doi:10.1177/1550147719853984

Sang, K. S., Zhou, B., Yang, P., & Yang, Z. (2018). Study of group route optimization for IoT enabled urban transportation network. *Proceedings - 2017 IEEE International Conference on Internet of Things, IEEE Green Computing and Communications, IEEE Cyber, Physical and Social Computing, IEEE Smart Data, IThings-GreenCom-CPSCom-SmartData 2017*, 888–893. 10.1109/iThings-GreenCom-CPSCom-SmartData.2017.137

Scheltes, A., & de Almeida Correia, G. H. (2017). Exploring the use of automated vehicles as last mile connection of train trips through an agent-based simulation model: An application to Delft, Netherlands. *International Journal of Transportation Science and Technology*, 6(1), 28–41. doi:10.1016/j.ijtst.2017.05.004

Tripathy, A. K., Mishra, A. K., & Das, T. K. (2018). Smart lighting: Intelligent and weather adaptive lighting in street lights using IOT. *2017 International Conference on Intelligent Computing, Instrumentation and Control Technologies, ICICICT 2017*, 1236–1239. 10.1109/ICICICT1.2017.8342746

Tukymbekov, D., Saymbetov, A., Nurgaliyev, M., Kuttybay, N., Dosymbetova, G., & Svanbayev, Y. (2021). Intelligent autonomous street lighting system based on weather forecast using LSTM. *Energy*, 231, 120902. doi:10.1016/j.energy.2021.120902

Wu, Q., Huang, C., Wang, S. Y., Chiu, W. C., & Chen, T. (2007). Robust parking space detection considering inter-space correlation. *Proceedings of the 2007 IEEE International Conference on Multimedia and Expo, ICME 2007*, 659–662. 10.1109/ICME.2007.4284736

Yu, J., Chang, G. L., Ho, H. W., & Liu, Y. (2008). Variation based online travel time prediction using clustered neural networks. *IEEE Conference on Intelligent Transportation Systems, Proceedings, ITSC*, 85–90. 10.1109/ITSC.2008.4732594

Zantalis, F., Koulouras, G., Karabetsos, S., & Kandris, D. (2019). A review of machine learning and IoT in smart transportation. *Future Internet*, 11(4), 1–23. doi:10.3390/fi11040094

KEY TERMS AND DEFINITIONS

AI: Artificial intelligence is a field of computer science and engineering in which intelligence in machines and software is artificially created.

IoT: The internet of things is a network formed by things so that they can share information among them to provide IT-based services.

LPWAN: Low power wide area network is wireless communication technology to connect low power devices over long-range with low data rate such as sensors operating on batteries, etc.

LSTM: Long short-term memory is a sub-class of RNNs (recurrent neural networks). It consists of both feed-forward and feed-back connections and handles gradient vanishing or exploding issues better than RNN.

ML: Machine learning is a branch of AI (artificial intelligence) in which the system exhibits the ability to learn from the data and experience without explicitly programming it.

RFID: Radio frequency identification is a technology in which an RFID tagged device is identified using electromagnetic signals by the RFID reader.

VANET: Vehicular ad hoc network is a wireless network formed among stationary and/or moving objects such as vehicles.

WLAN: Wireless local area network is a LAN network formed within a building between two or more devices using wireless communication technology.

Chapter 7
Semantic Tagging of Events in Video Using HNN

Parul Saxena
Madhav Institute of Technology and Science, Gwalior, India

R. S. Jadon
Madhav Institute of Technology and Science, Gwalior, India

ABSTRACT

This chapter describes the semantic tagging of events in videos using an effective combination of machine learning and neural network. Hybrid neural network architecture is proposed to consider the object features generated for each video and combine them with the LSTM model running over the label. The entire system is highly efficient for training and learning as the training dataset is optimized by applying multiple machine learning techniques. Experiments were done on the KTH dataset. Results show that the approach used gives 97% accuracy for the KTH dataset.

INTRODUCTION

Automatic human activity recognition is a major issue in public places in the field of realistic video surveillance. It is a big challenge to identify an action and mention whether it belongs to the action category. Nowadays, human activity recognition is possible by selecting appropriate features from a video (Schuldt et al., 2004, Motwani and Mooney, 2012, Marszalek et al., 2009, Ballan et al, 2011, Gao and Chen, 2010, Ji et al., 2013, and Arunnehru et al., 2018). For understanding the video, there are many surveys on human behaviour analysis (Vishwakarma and Agrawal, 2013, and Borges et al., 2013), content aware system related to sports (Shih, 2018) and video shot boundary detection (Pal et al., 2015). Recently focus is on human action recognition and prediction to detect the categories of actions from videos (Herath et al., 2017, Özyer et al., 2021, Khan et al., 2021, and Kong and Fu, 2022). Xia and Zhan (2020) focused on detailed survey on detecting time based actions using the existing datasets and methods. The work is done on offline human action detection and our focus is on online / real time detection. Few of them focus on online action detection also. Wang et al. (2021) focused on online action detection using the

DOI: 10.4018/978-1-6684-4045-2.ch007

method online time action detection that is online temporal action detection but not consider the feature selection, spatial-temporal localization and optimization of motion.

The methodology used in this paper is divided into four major sections, as shown in Figure 1. Firstly, the video is pre-processed to make it fit for the customized system, followed by the identification of semantic objects and features extraction of semantic objects (Ballan et al., 2011). After performing machine learning operations, we would have datasets that mostly contain features that will be sent to the network unit for learning the behavior of semantic objects using a hybrid neural network (HNN). At last, the system would be finalized by classification & tagging the semantic video (Ji et al., 2013).

Figure 1. Methodologies used in the system

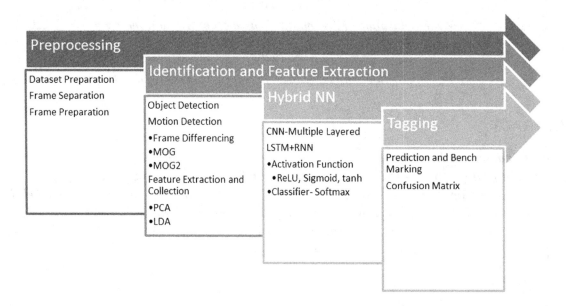

Analyzing video is different from analyzing images in a video that contain many frames in a sequence and help in gathering time based information. DNN such as convolution neural network is used to extract features due to its ability to learn representation. We are using the features of long term memory for temporal models (a variant of RNN) to detect current action by combining the previous information to the current information. RNN is still the best one for temporal action modeling. Baseline use LSTM to train video features and time based dynamics, then using the classification network RNN for anticipating the categories of actions in an iterative way. Initially, the video is pre-processed to make it fit for the customized system, followed by the identification of semantic objects and features extraction of semantic objects. After performing machine learning operations, we would have datasets that mostly contain features that will be sent to the network unit for learning the behavior of semantic objects using a hybrid neural network.

Representation of Video

In the overall video event detection problems, the focus is to interpret the characteristics of a video with the help of examining the common patterns for semantic identification. Here the issue is to extract exact data from the input videos or in other words there is need to discover a way to characterize comparable videos that have similar patterns. In order to characterize a video using this concept, a unique detector is required to be trained. For example, a human detector is wished for the "human" concept. Similarly, a "walking" detector is needed to measure the possibility of extracting a "walking" motion in a video. A common approach to developing a concept detector in video event detection is to teach a statistical model which uses a number of relevant images/videos specific to this concept. The initial entry for this statistical structure is a set of descriptors extracted from examples.

Feature Selection

Machine learning techniques have the capability to automatically select suitable concepts. The next step is Feature determination which is the most common and essential part of a machine learning concept. Feature determination reduces data dimensionality irrelevant and redundant elements using any one of the unsupervised/supervised approaches. For this type of semantic evaluation using the machine learning concept, the detector is necessary to work on the subspace which describes an event. In this work, the focus is on supervised feature selection, where the class labels, especially in our event labels, are known in advance. These all depend on their integration into the classifier with the filters, embedders and wrappers. Here filters are used to consider every characteristic separately with the help of mutual information or the correlation coefficient between features and labeled class. Basically, filters are computationally efficient and generate a feature set and feature ranking.

Tagging

Tagging is basically an act to assign a unique keyword or tag into a piece of information. Tags are metadata that label an object. This makes tags very useful to their creator as well as to the large net user community. Tags are usually selected informally and personally, depending on the application, either by the creator or by its viewer. The tags can be represented using a word along with font size/color to represent the importance of the tag (Li and Scy, 2008, Viddler, 2013, Eggink and Raimond, 2013, and Yao et al., 2013).

Video Tagging

As in Text Tagging, the contents of a website consist of words that are generally searched and indexed for categorization by search engines. Tagging requires the user to use content-related words, which are also important to the website's audience, and not to use many phrases of slang or abbreviations. Using a variety of keywords to the websites will significantly benefit the optimization of the search engine.

Similarly, videos are also labeled at the time when they are uploaded; thus, relevant captions will assist candidates without difficulty in finding them. It will be very challenging to locate videos that no longer have names or a caption with the appropriate tag via a search engine. There are many challenges that are generally faced before beginning the labeling. Tags are necessary for future purposes, especially for finding criminal events rather than the tags used for personal references. The next issue of tagging is "Semantic loss," where a folksonomy annotator is not gratified to connect all significant tags with a video, resulting in a semantic loss of text descriptions. The alternative 'batch-tag' provided by many photo-share sites also creates a problem by annotating a whole series of snapshots with a common tag. While such tags may be useful in providing a wide personal context but they are not useful to distinguish video differences, resulting in loss of semantics. Even the absence of a tag from a video description does not mean the lack of perception in that video. Similarly, for vocabulary challenges, the spontaneous preference of words to describe the same content differs between different persons and the probability that too many users use the same term is small. This repetition should be restricted to relevant keywords. Keywords must be used strategically and carefully.

Figure 2. Algorithmic Flow

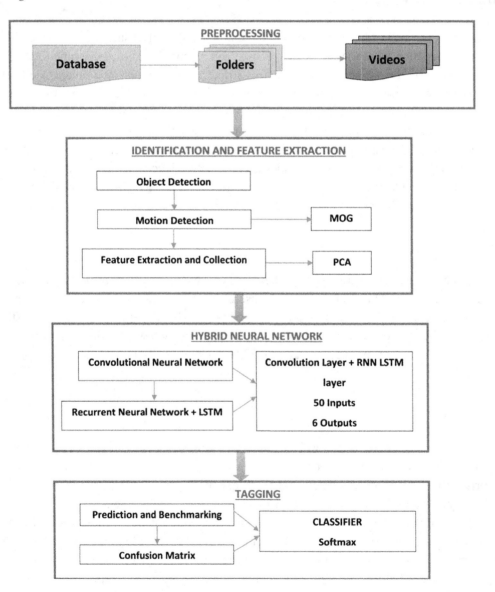

One of the ways to escape the noise and reimburse for the semantic loss is to combine visual comparison in the concept level and tag co-occurrence information with tag recommendation. The semantically or visually linked tags increase the quality of tagging. Video tagging is a complex issue that combines extracted single image features with an arbitrarily long sequence of understanding. The ability to understand the content and context (meaning) of video data is improved by tagging videos with useful metadata labels. The hybrid neural network architecture is proposed that takes into account the object features generated for each video and combine them with an LSTM model running over the label set to produce label predictions that take into account label correlation and dependence, as shown in Figure 2.

Before sending the dataset for processing by neural nets, it is the requirement to identify the semantic objects i.e., attributes that sufficiently describe the distinct identity like objects or part of objects under motion. Here we are talking about background subtraction in which the redundant background from all over the video or part of it under investigation is struck off to engrave the effective features.

For this purpose, every extracted frame is divided into two parts, background, and foreground, where the foreground consists of all the required pixels to be extracted and the background consists of all the redundant data which is not to be used. Based on this, the system will be capable of automatically detect objects using segmentation, background subtraction and tracking methods. For feature extraction and motion detection we are using MOG and PCA. It is true for the background that the colors remain same and stay longer for constant time. Hence, the pixel with low weight indicates that the pixel belongs to the foreground. While coding, we want to create an object by using the function, cv2.createBackgroundSubtractorMOG().

We are collecting all the features which are fed to the next stage by removing unnecessary noise from the pre-processing phase. For a video these features are objects in motion. This is accomplished using feature extraction techniques of machine learning from semantic objects. For this we are using PCA (Principal Component Analysis). The main concept behind PCA is to find out patterns and correlations between various features in the data set. To find a strong correlation among different variables, the last decision is made to reduce the dimensions of the data so that the significant data is still remaining. These extracted objects are used as input to the next step.

IDENTIFICATION OF SEMANTIC OBJECTS

Before sending the dataset for processing by neural nets, it is the obvious requirement to identify the semantic objects, i.e., attributes that sufficiently describe the distinct identity like objects or parts of objects under motion. This could be accomplished by multiple methods under different conditions. Here we are talking about background subtraction in which the redundant background from all over the video or part of it under investigation is struck off to engrave the effective features.

For this purpose, every extracted frame is divided into two parts, background and foreground, where the foreground consists of all the required pixels to be extracted and the background consists of all the redundant data which is not to be used. Based on this, the system will be capable of automatically detecting objects using segmentation, background subtraction and tracking methods. However, before describing the techniques, let us have a look at the frames on which we are working. We have six different classes to work with- Walking, Handwaving, Running, Jogging, Boxing and Handclapping, as shown in Figure 3 to Figure 8.

Figure 3. Frames sample of Walking

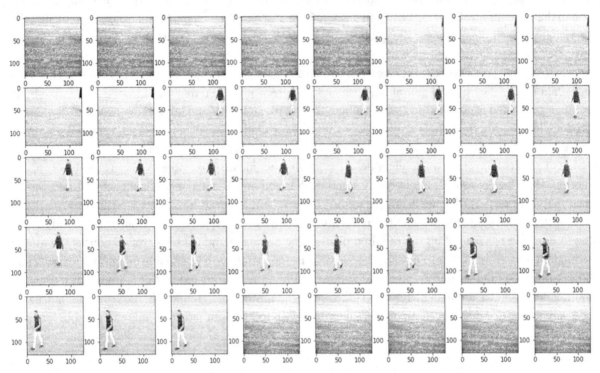

Figure 4. Frames sample of Handwaving

Figure 5. Frames sample of Running

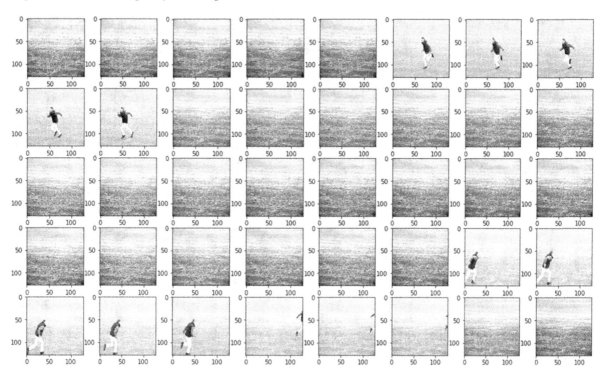

Figure 6. Frames sample of Jogging

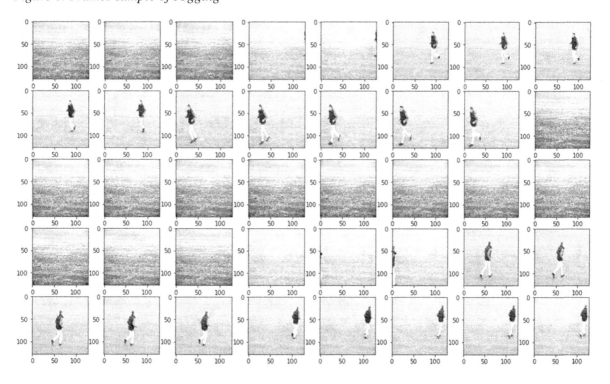

Figure 7. Frames sample of Boxing

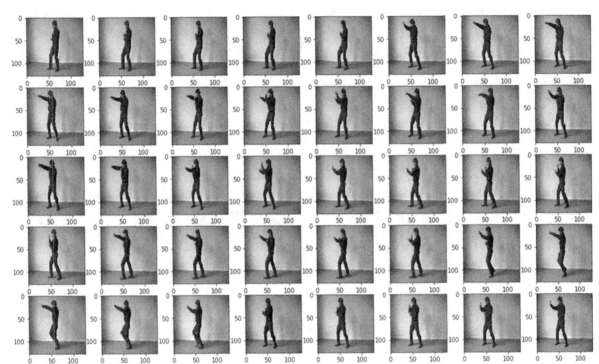

Figure 8. Frames sample of Handclapping

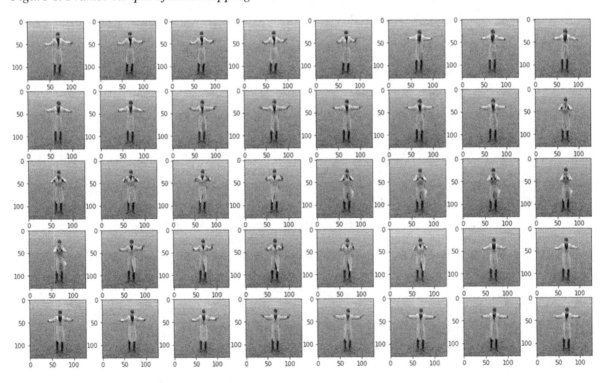

There are two popular methods of background subtraction - MOG and MOG2 background modeling algorithms. These two algorithms help us in segmenting our goal object (Hung et al., 2014, and Shao, 2006).

Background Subtraction MOG

Mixture of Gaussians is a gaussian-mixture-based segmentation also. Each background pixel is modeled with the help of a mixture of k Gaussian distributions, the range of k is from 3 to 5. Here, weights represent how long the color remains for each pixel in the frame with respect to time. It is true for a background that the colors remain the same and stay longer for a constant time. Hence, the pixel with low weight indicates that the pixel belongs to the foreground. While coding, we want to create an object by using the function cv2.createBackgroundSubtractorMOG(). This includes parameters such as history size, threshold, a quantity of Gaussian mixtures, etc and all these parameters are set with some default values. After this, we use backgroundsubtractor.apply() method to obtain foreground mask using the inner loop. Following is an instance of how to use the above-referred characteristic:

cv1.createBackgroundSubtractorMOG(history=200, nmixtures=5, backgroundRatio=0.7, noiseSigma=0)   (1)

Here, history represents the number of frames used to accumulate weights for the whole processing period, nmixture represents how many Gaussian distributions it supports in the entire video, backgroundRatio helps in differencing between back and foreground using threshold weight, the last one noiseSigma represent the 'accepted noise level.'

MOG2

MOG2 is also a background/foreground segmentation algo based on a Gaussian mixture. MOG2 has one more feature that is it select the variable amount of Gaussian distributions for every pixel (for MOG, k is the Gaussian distributions throughout the algo) and supports adaptability with varying frames due to illumination change. Similar to MOG, there are some default parameters and values for MOG2 as shown below:

cv1.createBackgroundSubtractorMOG2 (history=200, varThreshold=16, detectShadows =True)   (2)

Here, history is the same as MOG, no. of frames used to form the background. varThreshold compares the weight of the pixel on the current frame with the value on the background. Detect Shadows helps in enabling or disabling the shadow. This is also the feature of MOG2. Shadows are in gray color, as shown in Figure 9.

Figure 9. Frame sample for MOG and MOG2

FEATURE EXTRACTION OF SEMANTIC OBJECTS

For better processing of the dataset, i.e., for frames of videos by using a neural network, we will send only features to the hybrid system so that efficiency and speed could be improved. This will contain all the possible features which an object has during the change in frames (Arunnehru and Geetha, 2013). However, exact micro features like walking, jogging, hand-clapping, hand-waving, boxing, and running are not tagged in this step. This classification will only be done by the end of the training session of the hybrid neural network. In fact, that's why neural nets are used for classifying the micro features and assigning semantics to videos. All the features are collected that are fed to the next stage by removing unnecessary noise from the pre-processing phase. For a video, these features are objects in motion. This is accomplished using feature extraction techniques of machine learning from semantic objects. For this, we are using PCA (Principal Component Analysis).

Principal Components Analysis

PCA is a technique of dimension reduction. This identifies correlations and patterns in a given data set and helps in transforming data into significant lower dimensions without losing any significant information.

The main concept behind PCA is to find out patterns and correlations between various features in the data set. To find a strong correlation among different variables, the last decision is made to reduce the dimensions of the data so that the significant data is still remaining. This process is very important in solving complicated data-driven issues which involve the use of high-dimensional data sets.

Step By Step Computation of PCA

Step 1. Standardization of the Data

Standardization involves scaling our data so that all the variables and their values are in a similar range. It can be computed as:

$$S = \frac{\text{Variable price} - \text{Mean}}{\text{Standard deviation}} \tag{3}$$

Step 2. Computing the Covariance Matrix

PCA helps identify the correlation and dependencies in a data set between the features. The relationship between the variables in the data set is represented by a covariance matrix. Identifying heavily dependent variables is essential because they have biased and redundant information that reduces the model's overall performance. A covariance matrix is the d × d matrix, where d is the dimensions of the dataset. Every entry represents the covariance of the corresponding variables in the matrix.

Step 3. Compute the Eigenvectors - Eigenvalues

To determine the fundamental components of the data set, compute eigen vectors and eigen values from the covariance matrix. These components are calculated in such a way that the newly obtained variables are more significant and independent of each other. These components compress and maintain most of the efficient information that was dispersed among the initial variables.

Step 4. Computing the Principal Components

The most appropriate is the highest eigenvalue with the eigenvector and, as a result, form the first main component. Thus, the components of lesser significance can be removed to reduce the data dimensions.

The final step of principal components is to form a matrix "feature matrix," which contains all the important data variables that have the maximum data information.

Step 5. Reducing the Dimensions of the Records Set

The final step in PCA is to rearrange the original data with the final principal components representing the data set's maximum and the most significant information. To replace the original data axis with the newly formed principal components, PCA, multiply the transposition of the original dataset by the transpose feature vector obtained.

LEARNING THE BEHAVIOR OF SEMANTIC OBJECTS USING HNN

HNN represents a Hybrid Neural Network that combines the features of two popular Artificial Neural Network techniques, namely- CNN: Convolutional Neural Network and RNN: Recurrent Neural Network. Firstly, the Convolutional technique is able to extract effective features and use pooling layers; we are minimizing input frames by preserving features (Ji et al., 2013). Secondly, these processed outputs are directed to the Recurrent Neural net in the combination of LSTM (Long short term memory) for detecting the exact micro-feature from the given image, as shown in Figure 10.

Figure 10. Flow of control of the system

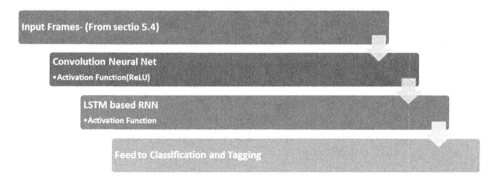

These are the neural networks and techniques which are used in constructing the HNN.

Convolutional Neural Network

It is a deep learning algo that takes an image as input, relegates significance (weights and biases) to different viewpoints/objects and distinguishes between them. Compared to other classification algorithms, ConvNet requires less pre-processing time (Karpathy et al., 2014).

Firstly the image is partitioned into multiple regions then every region is transferred to different hidden nodes, where every hidden node finds the region's pattern in the image. Kernel concludes the region and is also known as a filter. The process of convolution using a filter takes place on both the x and y-axis. Using multiple filters, various patterns are extracted from the image. When the convolution takes place throughout the whole image, the output of the one filter generates a 2-D layer of neurons called a feature map. We get one feature map from each filter. In a 3-d array, these feature layers can be mapped now this acts as an input to the further layers.

The above process is carried out by the layer present in CNN that is convolution. Now the polling layers follow up the sequence of the processed layers, reducing the output's spatial dimensions from convolutionary layers. The importance of this architecture is it helps us to convert the various contents of an image into a 1-D array. Z-Axis acts as a temporal axis for the videos. Therefore a 3-D layer that is convolutional in nature is used. Convolution maintains the connection among the pixels during the use of small squares of input data to find out object features. This is a mathematical operation involving two inputs, such as an image and filter matrix. An image matrix of dimension (height * width * dimension), a filter (f_{height} * f_{width} * d), outputs a volume dimension ((h − f_{height} + 1) * (w − f_{width} + 1) * 1)

Pooling layers and multiple convolutional layers are stacked together. When the images are too large, the number of parameters is reduced by the pooling layer. Spatial pooling is also known as down sampling or subsampling, its function is to reduce the dimension of the maps, but the essential information is retained. Max pooling, sum pooling, and the average pooling are the different forms of spatial pooling. The value is taken up by the max-pooling after the rectification of the element that is the largest in nature. It could also take the average pooling to take the biggest element. In the feature map cell, the sum pooling is used to sum up all the elements. In this, the output layer is the final layer that comes after the follow-up of the fully connected layers. Every neuron is related to the respective category that is placed in the output layer, which includes six neurons, one for each class. The major purpose of using the convolution layer is that it reduces the size of the volume that indirectly makes the computation fast, prevents overfitting and also reduces memory (Simonyan and Zisserman, 2014). Table 1 shows the parameters used in each convolutional layer, and Table 2 shows the parameters used in each pooling layer.

Working Mechanism of Long Short Term Memory

Long short term memory is an architecture based on the artificial recurrent neural network in the field of deep learning. The LSTM consists of feedback connections as compared with other neural networks. The LSTM can process both the single as well as multiple data points such as the images, videos, etc. (Liu and Shao, 2019, and Gao and Guo, 2017).

Table 1. Parameters used in the Convolutional layer

Size of Kernel	According to the input data, the window size is estimated for a single map that is converted along all axes.
Filters	This represents the number of feature maps of the layers that are convolutional in nature.
Padding	To maintain the same dimensionality, for the edges, the input is cropped to zeros.
Strides	A convolutional window should shift by the number of pixels
Activation	Specifies the function used for the layer, generally, ReLU is used because it supports non-linearity and avoids the vanishing gradient problem.

Table 2. Parameters used in pooling layer

Strides	The convolutional window should shift by the number of pixels
Size of pool	Window size.
Padding	To maintain the same dimensionality, for the edges, the input is cropped to zeros.

In general, the cell state, input gate, output gate, forgets gates are the different parts of LSTM. The cell function remembers different time intervals, the information flows into and out of the cell is processed through three gates. For the unknown duration of time to classify different processes, LSTM predicts the time series. Figure 11 shows the typical structure of LSTM.

Forget Gate

The forget gate determines which data should be kept or thrown away. The information is passed from the current input and from the previous hidden stage with the help of the sigmoid function. The output value is between 0 and 1. It is assumed that the values closer to 0 are discarded, and the values closest to 1 are preserved.

Input Gate

The input gate is used to update the cell state. At first, the current input value and the previous hidden state are passed into a sigmoid function. Now, these values decide which of the following values will be transformed into the values among 0 and 1. Here 0 means not significant and 1 means it is essential. The hidden state and the current input are put into the tanh() to squish the values among 1 and -1 to normalize the network. After this, with the tanh output, we will multiply the sigmoid output. Information that is required is decided by the sigmoid output that is to be taken from the tanh output.

Cell State

At this time, we should have sufficient information to determine the cell's state. At first, the cell state is multiplied by the forget vector in the point-wise order. In this, there is a chance of dropping the value in the cell state if this is multiplied by the value nearer to zero. Now the output (from the input gate) is taken so that a point-wise addition can be made that will update the cell state with the desired new values best suited to the neural network. This gives us the new state of the cell.

Figure 11. A Typical LSTM structure

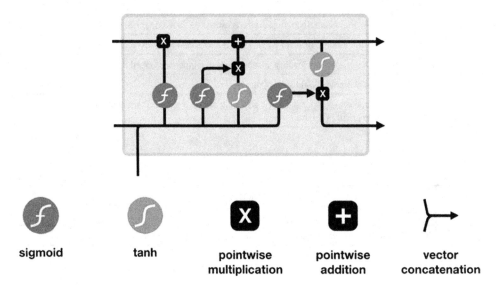

| sigmoid | tanh | pointwise multiplication | pointwise addition | vector concatenation |

Output Gate

The last one is the output gate. The next hidden state is decided at the output gate. We must remember that the information from the previous inputs is also included in the hidden state. The hidden state information is also used for predictions. At first, we pass the current input and the hidden state into the sigmoid function. And now we pass the recently updated cell state into the tanh function. To decide what the hidden state must carry, we multiply the tanh output with the sigmoid output. The hidden state is the current output. This new hidden state and the new cell state will then be moved to the next phase of the time.

The Forget gate generally decides which information should be kept from the previous steps. The input gate determines which type of information is appropriate to be added from the current stage, and to determine the next hidden state, the output gate is used.

Recurrent Neural Network

A recurrent neural network (RNN) is an artificial neural network that is mainly used in recognition of voice and for the NLP purpose. It is used in the deep learning process and in the development of various models that imitate the activity of the neurons in the human brain. In neural networks, we always assume that all the input and output are dependent on the other layers. As these neural networks perform mathematical computations, they are said to be recurrent.

Working Mechanism of RNN

Recurrent neural networks or the RNN are the most important alternative to the neural networks that are used extensively in natural language (Jiang et al., 2016, Lee and Kim, 2018, and Cho et al., 2014]. In this, input is processed by the number of layers, and the output is produced by assuming that two successive inputs are independent of each other.

This assumption, in general, is however not true in the majority of real-life scenarios. For example, one wants to predict the price of the stock at a given instant of time or wants to predict the next word in the required sequence; it is observed that the dependence on the previous observations is to be considered.

RNN is recurrent in nature; the same task is performed for each element in the given sequence, in which every output is based on the earlier computations. The information from the various calculations is calculated by the memory of the RNN. In the theoretical approach, the RNNs use the information of the long sequences, and they are limited to only a few steps in a practical approach.

In general, according to architecture, the RNN looks like shown in Figure 12. It can be observed that the multi-layer network along with each layer, represents certain observations at a given time interval t.

Figure 12. RNN nodes' unfolding

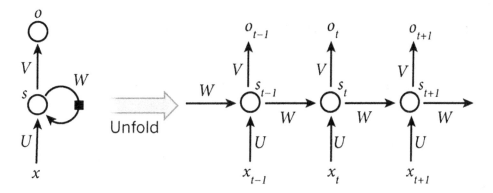

RNN is hugely successful in natural language processing (NLP), especially by using the LSTM, which looks back for a longer period of time than the RNN (Donahue et al., 2017).

Activation Function

It is the part where the machine processes its inputs by a function, namely "activation function," which could be universal in nature, i.e., independent of the problem statement. The activation function determines whether or not a neuron should be activated by measuring the weighted sum and adding bias to it. The goal of the activation function is to introduce nonlinearity into the output of a neuron so that it can learn more complex tasks and perform them. Some common activation features are ReLU, Sigmoid, Tanh, etc. Here are the activation functions which we have used in our research:

Sigmoid function is used to plot the 'S' shaped graph. Its value lies between zero and 1. Its equation is:

$$A = \frac{1}{1+e^{-x}} \qquad (4)$$

Tanh function is also referred as hyperbolic tangent function and its values lie between -1 to 1 making learning convenient for the subsequent layer. Its equation is:

$$f(x) = \tanh(x) = \frac{2}{1+e^{-2x}} - 1 \ \text{or} \ \tanh(x) = 2 \times \left(sigmoid(2x) - 1\right) \tag{5}$$

ReLU is a Rectified Linear Unit for non-linear function with a value between [0, inf]. In terms of computation, ReLU is less expensive compared to sigmoid and tanh because it uses simple mathematical operations and activates only a few neurons at a time. ReLU converges more quickly. Here linearity means that when x is high, then the slope isn't plateau or saturate. There is no issue like vanishing gradient when using different activation features like sigmoid or tanh. It's moderately activated. Because ReLU is zero for all poor inputs, it is likely for any given unit. It is frequently desirable. Its equation is:

$$f(x) = \max(0,x) \tag{6}$$

CLASSIFICATION AND TAGGING THE SEMANTIC VIDEOS

After the feeds are received from the HNN module, the system will use classifiers like SoftMax to classify the video and tag it with proper semantics to give it meaning. Let us see how the classifier works.

SoftMax

It is a type of sigmoid function used to handle classification problems. Generally used when attempting multiple classes implies that they are used to evaluate the probability of multiple classes at once. The output of the SoftMax function is given in the range of 0 and 1 for every individual class and the output is divided by them. Ideally, in the output layer of the classifier, the SoftMax is used to reach the probability of deciding the class of every input. SoftMax layer is considered the last or the final layer in a neural network.

SoftMax Terminology

The continuous output of the discrete values is obtained in the prediction process. Therefore, we get an output value Y after processing the input value X that is obtained through the network layers. It appears as shown in Figure 13.

Figure 13. Input to Output Conversion

X is taken as the input and processed through the various kinds of layers that are linear, activation, and then followed up with different layers. Now, after all the processing and the transformation processes through all the different layers of the network, we get an output value Y. This is the value Y, which is discrete in nature.

Multinomial Logistic Regression and SoftMax Classifiers

The generalization of the logistic regression is known as the SoftMax classifier. It is similar to the approach of the squared pivot loss, in which the mapping function f is considered so that the dot product of the input data x_i can be applied with the weight matrix W:

$$f(x_i, W) = W_{x_i} \tag{7}$$

These are considered to be the unnormalized log probabilities to every class label; this helps in swapping out the pivot loss function by the cross-entropy loss:

$$L_i = -log\left(e^{s_{y_i}} / \sum_j e^{s_j}\right) \tag{8}$$

Now, we will be breaking the entire function. And now the minimization of the loss function is done to the negative log value:

$$L_i = P(Y = k \mid X = x_i) \tag{9}$$

An alternative way to represent the above probability function:

$$P(Y = k \mid X = x_i) = e^{s_{y_i}} / \sum_j e^{s_j} \tag{10}$$

This is standard score function:

$$S = f(x_i, W) \tag{11}$$

This gives us the final loss value for a single data point:

$$L_i = -log\left(e^{s_{y_i}} / \sum_j e^{s_j}\right) \tag{12}$$

The algorithm is in the form of a natural algorithm as we are taking the inverse of the exponentiation. Now, we get the overall actual SoftMax function after normalization and the exponentiation process through the sum of exponents. Cross entropy loss is obtained through the negative log value.

The average of the cross-entropy loss is done by the following formula:

$$L = \frac{1}{N} \sum_{i=1}^{N} L_i \tag{13}$$

Utilizing these techniques, we would classify our results and label/tag them properly. Also, we mapped the labels to integers for simplicity of data flow and easy tagging of actions, as shown in Table 3.

Table 3. Label-Integer Mapping

Labelled Class	Mapped with Integer
Walking	0
Jogging	1
Handwaving	2
Handclapping	3
Running	4
Boxing	5

After mapping these categorical labels to integers, we will encode the classification using a one-hot encoding technique, as shown in Table 4.

Table 4. One-Hot Encoding of the labels

Labelled Class	0	1	2	3	4	5
Walking	1	0	0	0	0	0
Jogging	0	1	0	0	0	0
Handwaving	0	0	1	0	0	0
Handclapping	0	0	0	1	0	0
Running	0	0	0	0	1	0
Boxing	0	0	0	0	0	1

EXPERIMENTAL RESULTS ON KTH DATASET

Following are the environmental summary of our working system (Table 5):

Since neural net demands training, which further demands dataset to learn and work upon, we are using an open-source, freely distributed dataset, namely KTH, as shown in Figure 14, which is an action database.

Table 5. Environmental Specification of the system

S. No.	Technology/System	Source/Software
1	Dataset	KTH
2	OS	Windows 10 Pro
3	RAM	(64 GB for Training) (8 GB for testing)
4	CPU Max. Clock Speed	(16 cores for training) 4 GHz
5	Python	Version- 3.6.x
6	Libraries	OpenCV, Tensorflow, Keras, FFmpeg, Numpy, sklearn
7	Softwares used	Anaconda, Spyder, Jupyter Lab

Figure 14. KTH Dataset visual snapshot

KTH dataset is the most widely used dataset for human activity recognition in indoor and outdoor environments with a change in illumination. The following sample is taken from the dataset to describe its features. Here, this video consists of 6 types of human actions: walking, boxing, running, handclapping, jogging, and hand waving. It consists of 25 subjects with four different scenarios like s1 for indoor, s2 for outdoor among scale variation, s3 for outdoor through other clothes and s4 for indoor. Videos are recorded at 25fps frame speed with a resolution of 160*120 pixels. The dataset comprises 599 videos with 100 videos of the five categories and 99 for handclapping. On loading a single video into the memory, a NumPy array in python could be obtained with a shape of 1, 515, 120, 160, 3 which means

- One video
- 515 frames
- The spatial dimension of the video is 160*120 (width*height) in pixels
- Three channels, i.e., RGB

Figure 15. Output of a testing Video

```
Shape of the sample data: (500, 120, 160, 3)
<matplotlib.image.AxesImage at 0x7f68f83f4978>
```

```
John is clapping
```

Figure 16. Confusion Matrix

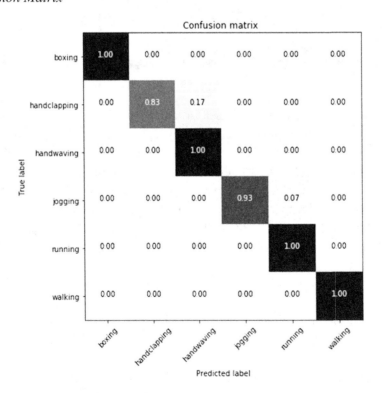

Descriptive Analysis

After training, the testing results were obtained. Output has been displayed in Figure 15, where the shape of the sample data has four parameters *(f, w, h, c)*. Here f represents the total no. of frames in the video, w and h represent the dimension of the video, i.e., width and height, respectively, c represents a number of channels. In our case, there are a total of 500 frames with 120 width and 160 height and three channels, namely- RGB. Here we are tagging our video semantically with these actions. In this Figure, we tag our video with a person who is clapping. Our model is capable of distinguishing these actions and helping in tagging our target object with these actions.

After training, we got an average accuracy of >97% on 200 testing videos. It is indeed visible in the confusion matrix shown in Figure 16, which illustrates by what fraction machine would predict the event in the video semantically.

CONCLUSION

This will show that our proposed model gives better results in predicting these actions. In fact, for 'boxing,' 'hand-waving,' 'running,' and 'walking,' 100% accurate results are obtained that means the system distinguished boxing, hand-waving, running and walking from other activities accurately and there is no confusion in predicting it. Similarly, the model differentiates running from jogging in a much better way than the benchmark model. This indicates that our model can differentiate the actions related to the movement of hands from the movement of legs.

REFERENCES

Arunnehru, J., Chamundeeswari, G., & Prasanna Bharathi, S. (2018). Human Action Recognition using 3D Motion Cuboids in Surveillance Videos. In *Proceeding of International Conference on Robotics and Smart Manufacturing* (pp. 471-477). Academic Press.

Arunnehru, J., & Geetha, M. K. (2013). Motion intensity code for action recognition in video using pca and svm. In *Proceedings of Mining Intelligence and Knowledge Exploration* (pp. 70–81). Springer. doi:10.1007/978-3-319-03844-5_8

Ballan, L., Bertini, M., & Bimbo, A. D. (2011). Event detection and recognition for semantic annotation of video. *Multimedia Tools and Applications*, *51*(1), 279–302. doi:10.100711042-010-0643-7

Borges, P. V. K., Conci, N., & Cavallaro, A. (2013). Video-based human behavior understanding: A survey. *IEEE Trans. Circ. Syst. Vid.*, *23*(11), 1993–2008. doi:10.1109/TCSVT.2013.2270402

Cho, K., Merrienboer van, B., Gülçehre, Ç., Bahdanau, D., Bougares, F., Schwenk, H., & Bengio, Y. (2014). Learning phrase representations using RNN encoder-decoder for statistical machine translation. In *Proceedings of conference on empirical methods in natural language processing* (pp. 1724–1734). 10.3115/v1/D14-1179

Donahue, J., Hendricks, L. A., Rohrbach, M., Venugopalan, S., Guadarrama, S., Saenko, K., & Darrell, T. (2017). Long-term recurrent convolutional networks for visual recognition and description. *IEEE Transactions on Pattern Analysis and Machine Intelligence*, *39*(4), 677–69. doi:10.1109/TPAMI.2016.2599174 PMID:27608449

Eggink, J., & Raimond, Y. (2013). Recent advances in affective and semantic media applications at the BBC. In *Proceedings of 14th international workshop on image analysis for multimedia interactive services* (pp 1-4). 10.1109/WIAMIS.2013.6616134

Gao, L., Guo, Z., Zhang, H., Xu, X., & Shen, H. T. (2017). Video Captioning with Attention - Based LSTM and Semantic Consistency. *IEEE Transactions on Multimedia*, *19*(9), 99. doi:10.1109/TMM.2017.2729019

Gao, Z., Chen, M., Hauptmann, A. G., & Cai, A. (2010). Comparing evaluation protocols on the KTH dataset. *Human Behaviour Understanding*, *6219*, 88–100. doi:10.1007/978-3-642-14715-9_10

Herath, S., Harandi, M., & Porikli, F. (2017). Going deeper into action recognition: A survey. *Image and Vision Computing*, *60*, 4–21. doi:10.1016/j.imavis.2017.01.010

Hung, M. H., Pan, J. S., & Hsieh, C. H. (2014). A Fast Algorithm of Temporal Median Filter for Background Subtraction. *Journal of Information Hiding and Multimedia Signal Processing*, *5*(1), 33–40.

Ji, S., Xu, W., Yang, M., & Yu, K. (2013). 3d convolutional neural networks for human action recognition. *IEEE Transactions on Pattern Analysis and Machine Intelligence*, *35*(1), 221–231. doi:10.1109/TPAMI.2012.59 PMID:22392705

Jiang, H., Lu, Y., & Xue, J. (2016). Automatic Soccer Video Event Detection Based on a Deep Neural Network Combined CNN and RNN. In *Proceedings of IEEE 28th International Conference on Tools with Artificial Intelligence*. 10.1109/ICTAI.2016.0081

Karpathy, A., Toderici, G., Shetty, S., Leung, T., Sukthankar, R., & Fei-Fei, L. (2014). Large-Scale Video Classification with Convolutional Neural Networks. In *Proceedings of the 2014 IEEE Conference* (CVPR-2014). 10.1109/CVPR.2014.223

Khan, M. A., Mittal, M., Goyal, L. M., & Roy, S. (2021). A deep survey on supervised learning based human detection and activity classiổcation methods. *Multimedia Tools and Applications*, *80*(18), 27867–27923. doi:10.100711042-021-10811-5

Kong, Y., & Fu, Y. (2022). Human action recognition and prediction: A survey. *International Journal of Computer Vision*, *130*(5), 1366–1401. Advance online publication. doi:10.100711263-022-01594-9

Lee, S., & Kim, I. (2018). *Multimodal Feature Learning for Video Captioning*. Hindawi Mathematical Problems in Engineering. doi:10.1155/2018/3125879

Li, Q., & Lu, S. C. Y. (2008). Collaborative tagging applications and approaches. *IEEE MultiMedia*, *15*(3), 14–21. doi:10.1109/MMUL.2008.54

Liu, A.-A., Shao, Z., Wong, Y., Li, J., Su, Y.-T., & Kankanhalli, M. (2019). LSTM-based multi-label video event detection. *Multimedia Tools and Applications*, *78*(1), 677–695. doi:10.100711042-017-5532-x

Marszalek, M., Laptev, I., & Schmid, C. (2009). Actions in context. In *Proceeding of CVPR 2009 - IEEE Conference on Computer Vision & Pattern Recognition* (pp.2929-2936). IEEE.

Motwani, T., & Mooney, R. (2012). Improving video activity recognition using object recognition and text mining. In *Proceeding of 20th European Conference on Artificial Intelligence* (pp. 600-605). Academic Press.

Özyer, T., Ak, D. S., & Alhajj, R. (2021). Human action recognition approaches with video datasets-A survey. *Knowledge-Based Systems*, *222*, 106995. doi:10.1016/j.knosys.2021.106995

Pal, G., Rudrapaul, D., Acharjee, S., Ray, R., Chakraborty, S., & Dey, N. (2015). Video Shot Boundary Detection: A Review. *Emerging ICT for Bridging the Future*, *2*, 119–127.

Schuldt, C., Laptev, I., & Caputo, B. (2004). Recognizing human actions: a local SVM approach. In *Proceedings of the 17th International Conference on Pattern Recognition (Vol. 3)*. IEEE Xplore. 10.1109/ICPR.2004.1334462

Shao, L. (2006). Generic Feature Extraction for Image/Video Analysis. *IEEE Conference*.

Shih, H. (2018). A survey of content-aware video analysis for sports. *IEEE Trans. Circ. Syst. Vid.*, *28*(5), 1212–1231. doi:10.1109/TCSVT.2017.2655624

Simonyan, K., & Zisserman, A. (2014). Very deep convolutional networks for large-scale image recognition. *Proceedings of ICLR*.

Viddler. (2013). *Interactive video training and practice.* https://www.viddler.com/

Vishwakarma, S., & Agrawal, A. (2013). A survey on activity recognition and behavior understanding in video surveillance. *The Visual Computer*, *29*(10), 983–1009. doi:10.100700371-012-0752-6

Wang, W., Peng, X., Qiao, Y., & Cheng, J. (2021). *An empirical study on temporal modeling for online action detection. Complex Intell. Syst.* doi:10.100740747-021-00534-3

Xia, H., & Zhan, Y. (2020). A survey on temporal action localization. *IEEE Access: Practical Innovations, Open Solutions*, *8*, 70477–70487. doi:10.1109/ACCESS.2020.2986861

Yao, T., Mei, T., Ngo, C. W., & Li, S. (2013). Annotation for free: video tagging by mining user search behavior. In *Proceedings of 21st ACM international conference on multimedia* (pp 977-986). ACM. 10.1145/2502081.2502085

NOTE

Github link of the code developed: https://github.com/Parul-1983/code.

Chapter 8
Topic Detection and Tracking Towards Determining Public Agenda Items:
The Impact of Named Entities on Event-Based News Clustering

Basak Buluz Komecoglu

https://orcid.org/0000-0001-9937-1036

Gebze Technical University, Turkey

Burcu Yilmaz

https://orcid.org/0000-0003-3643-7450

Gebze Technical University, Turkey

ABSTRACT

It is a known fact that all of the events that people in the society are exposed to while continuing their lives have important effects on their quality of life. Events that have significant effects on a large part of the society are shared with the public through news texts. With a perspective that keeps up with the digital age, the problem of automatic detection and tracking of events in the news with natural language processing methods is discussed. An event-based news clustering approach is presented for data regimentation, which is necessary to extract meaningful information from news in the form of heaps in online environments. In this approach, it is aimed to increase clustering performance and speed by making use of named entities. Additionally, an event-based text clustering dataset was created by the researchers and brought to the literature. By using the B-cubed evaluation metric on this test dataset, which consists of 930 different event groups and has a total of 19,848 news, a solution to the event-based text clustering problem was provided with an F-score of over 85%.

DOI: 10.4018/978-1-6684-4045-2.ch008

INTRODUCTION

In the digital age we live in, there is a rapid paradigm shift in information access (Nielsen & Selva, 2019). Online media, which plays one of the most significant roles in this change, has become an essential tool for the public to obtain and publish information. So much so that news and information can be provided by online news sites, mainstream media, and individual users through the internet. However, the content provided on the so-called individual text media platforms such as Twitter and blogs is of lower quality than the news texts published on online news sites. It is seen that it is insufficient to describe the events in the content (Fisher et al., 2020). The primary motivation in individually published news content is to be interesting, receive readers' reactions, and share as quickly as possible after an event has occurred. This motivation also results in the transmission of news texts that have not been confirmed, are prone to create information pollution, are far from objective information transfer, and are very open to manipulating the events in the content. Therefore, news data published online and in mainstream media has become an accurate and stable source of information for the public instead of individually shared content (Nielsen & Selva, 2019). As reported by the Reuters Institute in the Digital News Report, the acquisition of information from online media sources has increased worldwide in direct proportion to the rapid development of internet technology. The last report published in 2021 stated that the transition to a digital future accelerated with the coronavirus epidemic, and long-term trends around the rise of digital news consumption also accelerated (Newman et al., 2021).

With the advantages of providing instant access to news and offering an improved reading experience to readers, a rapid transformation process has been experienced to meet news consumption by online media platforms. These platforms, developed with web technologies, contain news that can reach a much larger audience than traditional printed media due to their dynamic nature (Nielsen & Selva,2019). With these aspects, platforms are not only tools that provide information but also appear as knowledge bases that contain data suitable for analysis for different purposes.

Almost all decision-making mechanisms at different levels, such as individuals, institutions, and governments, are affected by daily events (Chen & Wang, 2021). Therefore, it is necessary to identify and follow the news content in this digital age, which is essential for individuals, organizations, institutions, or governments. For example, for the governments, it is vital to grasp the public's views quickly and effectively on government policy, act quickly when necessary, and provide insight. In the past, the way to do this was to manually collect and analyze the news content that made up the agenda. Today, as more online media platforms are used as data sources, there has been a need to develop algorithmic approaches to cope with the exponentially increasing number of news sources and content.

Similarly, as a requirement of the competitive market, companies are faced with the need to analyze their competitors and themselves from the customer's perspective. The importance of the news reflected in the press for brand value, public opinion, and market value is beyond doubt. For this reason, it is necessary to completely assort and analyze the news reflected in the press on public and competitor analysis.

The first solution for automatic detection and tracking of hot events that constitute the agenda was presented with a Topic Detection, and Tracking (TDT) system developed because of a pilot study supported by DARPA in 1996 (Allan et al., 1998). This system has been a pioneer in defining the Topic Detection and Tracking (TDT) problem and determining a concept for solutions to be developed around this problem. There are three main concepts accepted as fundamental in TDT research (Allan,2002; Yang et al., 2009; Rasouli et al., 2020):

- Event: a reality that contains knowledge of time and space.
- Story: a news article that provides information about an event.
- Topic: an event and a series of related stories.

The three basic concepts described above led to the definition of many significant problems. These include identifying the first story about an event, obtaining the series of stories associated with that event, obtaining the plot, and identifying and grouping the stories that give information about the same event.

This book chapter discusses the problem of clustering the news of the same event published in different news sources. The solution to this problem is essential to classify the news content based on activity from the large data pile consisting of texts from different news sources. Thus, activities can be followed quickly and effectively. The approaches that have taken place so far to solve this problem in the literature have been compiled, and a method with a text clustering performance of over 85% is proposed by using named entities of the news text. The proposed method was applied to the first event-based text clustering dataset in Turkish, which was created within the scope of this research. Finally, the effects of named entities on clustering performance are examined comparatively.

BACKGROUND

Topic Detection and Tracking is a research area that aims to help search and organize newsworthy texts from different media platforms and other sources (Dai & Sun,2010). As a sub-task in achieving this goal, news with the same content should be grouped as 'stories' (Staykovski et al., 2019). Although this sub-problem, the subject of this chapter, is covered under the umbrella of Topic Detection and Tracking, it is a text clustering problem included in the natural language processing research area.

When the studies on the text clustering problem in the literature are examined, it is seen that the approaches focus on the topics by adopting a more general point of view, not the stories in the text. On the other hand, when the proposed approaches are examined, it is possible to see that they are divided into several groups. These approaches are; vector space models, k-means variations, generative algorithms, dimensionality reduction-based methods, and phrase-based methods (Andrews & Fox,2007; Blokh & Alexandrov,2017).

In the models developed for the clustering problem, homogeneous distribution of clusters, knowing the number of clusters at the beginning, sensitivity to outliers, and the volume of the corpuscles have a significant effect on the performance. For example, vector space models are pretty successful in cases where the clusters are homogeneously distributed, and the number of clusters is known initially; Generative algorithms can fail in real-life data due to their extreme sensitivity to outliers (Kömeçoğlu, Y. et al., 2020).

Another main challenge brought by the long textual nature of news content is that it contains much noise. For this reason, the approach to be developed should also focus on minimizing the noise and removing the essential elements of the event (Fonseka,2021).

In addition to all these technical requirements, it is known that finding news about the same case from many case reports forms an essential basis for public opinion analysis (Mao et al., 2021). At this point, institutions, organizations, and especially government departments are involved in a time-consuming process of manually detecting events that interest and affect people. It causes cause a tremendous waste of time to give feedback against the public's expectations. For this reason, speed is of great importance for algorithmic methods to be developed.

A NATURAL LANGUAGE PROCESSING PERSPECTIVE ON TOPIC DETECTION AND TRACKING

The main goal of the Topic Detection and Tracking problem, which was first defined by scientists in 1996 and started to be studied, was to detect and follow up on hot and new events in the news flow. However, with the increase in internet usage, it has become a problem that needs a solution for many different applications, such as analyzing public opinion from online news sources and discovering and following hot topics that cause good/bad reactions in public. Nowadays, it is a widely studied research topic for both people and institutions/organizations to reach the agenda topics instantly, access the instant hot news easily and quickly, in other words, to keep their eyes on the agenda.

The phenomenon that occurred in a certain period and in a specific location, which causes an increase in the volume of the text discussing the subject in its content, is called 'topic' (Kumaran & Allan,2004; Dou et al.,2012). The information obtained from the systems developed for the detection of these events that have an impact on the public is not only for individuals and institutions/organizations but also for countries on critical issues such as natural disasters (Sakaki et al.,2010), global epidemics (Aramaki,2011; Rosa et al.,2020), political or social events (Petkos et al.,2012; Makrehchi et al.,2013). It represents an invaluable resource in establishing and supporting rapid decision-making, raising awareness, and providing insight. Current studies addressing the event detection problem mainly focus on topic modeling and text clustering methods (Lei & Junping,2018; Kumaran & Allan,2005; Lu et al.,2012).

Based on the detection and definition of a topic containing one or more events, the solutions offered are evaluated within the framework of the 'topic tracking' problem to detect all other events related to the topic and to create a semantic chain of events. One of the biggest challenges here is that the core content of the event being tracked changes over time. When the studies dealing with this problem are examined, it is seen that while probabilistic solutions based on vectors and solutions using dynamic clustering are frequently encountered (Ren et al.,2009; Wang et al.,2006), adaptive subject tracking technologies such as GE, Dragon, and UMass have emerged in recent years (Jiang et al.,2012; Liu et al.,2020).

Event-Based News Clustering

The web environment is expanding daily, with news content spreading from large or small-scale news sources in different parts of the world. For this reason, it has become impossible to follow news texts that contain one or a series of events related to the agenda with an objective and truly informative perspective, with an individual effort. At this point, one of the most common approaches for organizing data and thus facilitating information tracking and extraction by institutions, organizations, and individuals is the use of clustering techniques.

Clustering divides any collection of entities or facts into several sub-collections based on their content similarity. The techniques used for the clustering task have proven to be proper techniques for information extraction, with their ability to discover interesting information cores and distributions in the data collection (Bouras & Tsogkas,2012). The importance of significantly reducing the data volume in carrying out the search and filtering function in Information Retrieval (IR) systems as quickly and reliably as possible is known. For this reason, clustering solutions are used to improve the results of IR systems in terms of precision/recall, primarily to deliver results that are better semantically filtered to integrated systems and the end-user and have a high potential to aid decision making.

The application of text clustering solutions specific to news contents, describing the sub-content hierarchy of a large number of news that can be accessed from hundreds of different sources, enables the detection and tracking of events. News clustering approaches focus on grouping content according to categories, usually independent of the event, as in classical text clustering problems. It is ensured that news contents are collected under basic categories similar to sports news, fire news, election news, etc. (Gwadera & Crestani,2009; Lu et al.,2011). On the other hand, another popular approach to analyzing news texts is topic modeling. This algorithmic approach is aimed to assign probabilities of belonging to specific topics to words in news documents. Thus, a list of the most relevant terms for that topic is obtained (Shomanov & Mansurova,2021; Lu et al.,2011). None of these solutions is sufficient for news experts, journalists, institutions/organizations, or citizens who focus on the events that shape the agenda. It needs much more than these solutions to filter the news of interest from the vast mass of news, to follow the evolution of the event in the content, or to be able to discover the events that are important to the public early. At this point, the need for activity-based clustering of sub-event clusters in a heap arises instead of predetermined categories. For example, instead of clustering match news, there is a need for a more specific clustering, such as 'Barcelona vs. Real Madrid match played on 24.10.2021' news clustering. For this reason, a system whose general structure is presented in Figure 1 is proposed for this problem that needs a more specific solution.

SOLUTIONS AND RECOMMENDATIONS

The problem of grouping news texts with the same event content is discussed within the scope of text clustering methods in this study's natural language processing research area. Due to the absence of a benchmark dataset in Turkish on the problem, a large-volume dataset with similar standards to datasets in different languages was brought to the literature. Then, vector space representations such as words, sentences, and documents were obtained, and density-based text clustering methods were applied. For this problem, where speed is as important as performance in the application area, the effects on clustering methods were examined using the entities representing the event in 3 different ways. All the sub-steps applied are explained in detail in the subsections. All the sub-steps applied are described in detail in the subsections, and the general structure of the proposed system is presented in Figure 1.

Turkish Event-Based Text Clustering Dataset

A benchmark dataset in Turkish was created to evaluate the performance of the event-based news clustering approach proposed in the book chapter. Although this dataset is the first in the literature, it aligns with the standards, and other researchers can use it.

A data set consisting of 19,848 news texts and 317,646 sentences in the content of which the unity of person/institution/organization, time, place, and event were ensured, and the number of clusters (the number of events) was 930. The data provider in creating this dataset is Interpress, one of Turkey's most prominent media monitoring companies. Exactly repetitive texts were removed from 40,305 news texts provided by Interpress. The filter was applied so that texts with a document length of a minimum of 500 and a maximum of 10,000 characters remain. Then, the news was automatically grouped by the citation-based real-time news grouping engine, which was recommended in the academic study (Kömeçoğlu et al.,2020) and worked with over 90% success. Among the clusters suggested by the news grouping engine, clusters with a minimum of 6 and a maximum of 105 news were filtered again from the dataset. In the last stage, verification was ensured by human validators by checking whether the news in the cluster content belonged to the same event. All of the studies carried out for clustering were tested on this dataset.

Figure 1. The proposed event-based news clustering approach

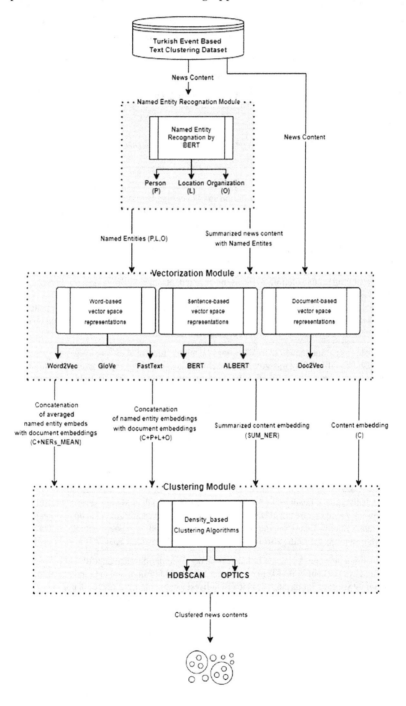

Examples of the original news text sets in the dataset are presented in Table 1. In addition, the literal translation of the cluster examples in the dataset in English is shown in Table 3 so that other researchers can easily understand them. As seen in Table 1, the subject mentioned in Cluster 1 is football players and coaches who, for various reasons, cannot attend the UEFA Europa League match of the Beşiktaş to play with the Braga. Although they have different word sequences, the cluster's three news contents also talk about the same subject. In Cluster 2, it is seen that there are news texts taken from different news sources that mention the transfer of the operating rights of the Şifalısu Recreational area to the municipality company ABİTAŞ. The news sets belonging to the Turkish Event-Based Text Clustering Dataset also contain news texts obtained from different news sources with varying sequences of words belonging to the event in the content. This dataset, which makes the study unique, promises to contribute to the literature on a Turkish. However, it also creates a limitation on the comparability of the proposed method.

Table 1. Sample news sets of the Turkish Event-Based Text Clustering Dataset

Cluster 1	
News 1	UEFA Avrupa Ligi'nde sıfır puanla grubunda son sırada yer alan Beşiktaş, bu akşam deplasmanda Braga ile oynayacağı maça önemli isimlerinden yoksun çıkacak. Siyah-beyazlı takımda sakatlıktan yeni çıkan Burak Yılmaz, Victor Ruiz, Gökhan Gönül ve N'Koudou Portekiz'e götürülmedi. Takımın parlayan iki yıldızı Atiba ve Diaby de dinlendirilme amacıyla kadroya alınmadı. Kulüpten yapılan açıklamada, "Teknik Direktörümüz Abdullah Avcı geçirdiği ağır grip nedeniyle devam eden tedavisini aksatmamak için takımımızın Braga kafilesinde yer alamamıştır. Hocamız, tedaviye vereceği cevaba göre yarın Portekiz'e gidecektir" denildi.
News 2	UEFA Avrupa Ligi'ndeki temsilcimiz Beşiktaş, bu akşam deplasmanda Braga ile karşı karşıya gelecek.Grupta 0 puanla son sırada yer alan siyah-beyazlılarda zorlu mücadelesi öncesi birçok eksik bulunuyor. Burak Yılmaz, Gökhan Gönül, Diaby, N'Koudou ve Ruiz'i kadroya almayan teknik direktör Abdullah Avcı, geçirdiği ağır gribal enfeksiyon nedeniyle kendisini de kafileye dahil etmedi. Dün, iyileşmesi durumunda Braga'ya gideceğini belirten tecrübeli teknik adam, bugün kendisini iyi hissetmediğini söyleyerek İstanbul'da kalma kararı aldı."
News 3	Avrupa Ligi'nde Braga'nın konuğu olacak Beşiktaş'ta, teknik direktör Avcı, geçirdiği ağır grip nedeniyle Portekiz'e gidemedi. Siyah Beyazlılar ilk olarak Avcı'nın düzelmesi durumunda bu ülyele gideceğini duyurdu. Ancak Siyah Beyazlılar'ın teknik patronunun durumunda bugün de düzelme olmadı. Avcı, Portekiz'e gitmedi. Beşiktaş futbol şube sorumlusu Erdal Torunoğulları da geçirdiği ameliyat nedeniyle kafilede yer alamadı. Safra kesesi rahatsızlığı nedeniyle bıçak altına yatan Torunoğulları, tedavisi nedeniyle İstanbul'da kaldı.
Cluster 2	
News 1	Son dönemde sık sık suya mikrop karışması sonucu mühürlenmesi ile gündeme gelen Şifalı Su için nihayet çalışmalar başlıyor. Akçakoca Belediyesi'nin şubat 2017'de yıllık 20 bin TL bedel ile orman işletmeden 29 yıllığına kiraladığı alanda uygulanacak sosyal proje meclis gündemine taşındı. Kasım ayı son meclis toplantısında Şifalı Su mesire yerinin yatırım ve işletmesinin belediye şirketi ABİTAŞ'a verilmesi kararlaştırıldı.
News 2	Akçakoca Belediyesinin kiraladığı D-655 Karayolu üzerindeki Şifalısu Mesire yerinin yatırım ve işletmesini belediyeye ait şirket yapacak.Akçakoca Belediye Başkanı Okan Yanmaz'ın başkanlığında kasım ayı meclis toplantısı, belediye meclis salonunda yapıldı. İmar Planı değişiklik taleplerinin ağırlıklı olarak ele alındığı toplantıda Akçakoca Belediyesinin kiraladığı şifalı su mesire yerinin yatırım ve işletmesinin belediye şirketi ABİTAŞ'a verilmesi kararlaştırıldı.
News 3	Orman Bakanlığı tarafından Akçakoca Belediyesi'ne devri yapılan Şifalısu'da artık düğmeye basılıyor. Şubat ayında, Akçakoca Belediye Başkanlığı ile Akçakoca Orman İşletme Müdürlüğü arasında imzalanan protokolle 50 dönümlük orman alanını 29 yıllığına kiralayan Akçakoca Belediyesi Şifalısu ile ilgili önemli karar aldı. Belediye meclisinin bu akşamki oturumunda gündeme gelen Şifalısu orman içi dinlenme alanının geleceğini görüşerek karara bağlayan belediye meclisi, tesisin belediye iştiraki olan ABİTAŞ'a devrine karar verdi. Şifalısu'yu ihaleye çıkarmama kararı alan belediye, tesisi kendi iştiraki olan ABİTAŞ vasıtası ile çalıştıracak.

Creation of Vector Space Representations of News Texts

Before the text clustering method can be determined according to the nature of the problem and the structure of the data, the texts should be represented in a meaningful space with real-valued vectors. Incorporating contextual information using neural network models to represent input characters, words, or sentences with real-valued vectors in a significant space is the most preferred approach in state-of-the-art studies and is the most representative approach for almost any natural language processing problem.

In the experiments, embeddings at different levels such as words, sentences, and documents for the representation of news were obtained with neural network models, and their performances were compared.

Word-Based Vector Space Representations

Perhaps one of the most critical developments that increase the ability to analyze the relationships between words, sentences, and documents is the contextual word vectors obtained through a considerable corpus. It is also possible to get vector representations of sentences and documents by obtaining word vectors.

Within the scope of the study, to preserve the semantic integrity of the words in the text and not to destroy the contextual information, the Turkish News Texts Corpus with the content of 17,470,827 sentences and 1,673,884,673 words (422,346 unique words) included in the 975,809 news texts that were created before was used. After applying preprocessing steps on this large corpus created without leaving the news domain, the Word2Vec model (Mikolov et al.,2013), frequently used in the literature, is trained. Thus, the vectors of 80,777unique words were created out of 5,262,685 words in 19,848 news. The embedding of the entire text was obtained by averaging the 100-dimensional vectors of the words in the news texts created with the Word2Vec model.

Since the Word2Vec model accepts words as the smallest unit, another model named FastText (Bojanowski et al.,2017) was also used to use N-Grams for the vector representation of words feature, allowing to achieve very high performance in tasks in agglutinative languages such as Turkish. On the other hand, the GloVe model (Pennington et al., 2014), which argues that it can create a semantically more robust word representation by combining count-based matrix factorization and local content window methods, is the last word-based vector representation used within the scope of the study. For the GloVe and FastText models, pre-trained models for Turkish were used, and embeddings of news texts were obtained by averaging the 300-dimensional word vectors.

Sentence-Based Vector Space Representations

Another primary way to create document representations is to create separate embeddings of sentences in the document and then average the resulting vector array. The resulting embedding represents the vector representing the document.

State-of-the-art pre-trained language models, BERT (Kenton & Toutanova, 2019) and ALBERT (Lan et al., 2019), were used to create the sentence representations. Bidirectional Encoder Representations from Transformers (BERT) is designed to train deep bidirectional representations from unlabeled text and is co-conditioned in both left and proper context in all its layers. Sentence-BERT (SBERT) is a modification of the pre-trained BERT language model (or other transformer models). The model derives close-size sentence embeddings in vector space for semantically similar sentences. Two models with different parameter values for the number of layers (L), the hidden layer size (H), and the attention mechanism header size (A) were presented by the Google researchers who developed the BERT model. The first of these models is named BERT Base and is designed with parameter values L=12, H=768, and A=12. The other model is the BERT Large model with parameter values L=24, H=1024, and A=16. In this study, 768-dimensional sentence vectors were created with the BERTurk and ALBERT models, a pre-trained BERT base model with 35 GB size and 44,04,976,662 tokens in the Turkish language.

Document-Based Vector Space Representations

Word2Vec does not lose the relations/proximities between words due to the conditional probability principle and working logic according to the positions of the words in the sentence. In this respect, it leads to the creation of word representations that can express semantic integrity to a large extent. After the Word2Vec method, which was revolutionary in natural language processing in 2013, can create semantic representations of the words that make up texts like never before, the 'Distributed Representations of Sentences and Documents' study was introduced by the same research group in 2014. This time, different from creating individual representations of words that make up a text, fixed-size representation vectors of documents of various sizes are directly obtained. With almost no change in Word2Vec structure, document vectors are only created by adding paragraph tokens.

The method, which is called Doc2Vec (Le & Mikolov, 2014) and enables document vectors to be obtained directly, was used within the scope of the study. As in the Word2Vec approach, document vectors are pre-trained on Turkish News Texts Corpus with the Doc2Vec method to obtain 100-dimensional representations of news texts.

Comparison of Text Clustering Methods

The clustering of news with the same content as 'stories' points to the text clustering problem within the natural language processing research field. When the studies on the text clustering problem in the literature are examined, it is seen that the approaches focus on the topics by adopting a more general point of view, not the events in the text. Benchmark datasets in the literature are similarly based on clustering of texts according to topics (for example, sports news, economic news, etc.). What is needed in this study is to cluster the news texts according to the events they contain (for example, the news of the fire in Manavgat on a specific date, the news of the new Minister of National Education, etc.). On the other hand, in the models developed for the clustering problem, homogeneous distribution of clusters, knowing the number of clusters at the beginning, sensitivity to outliers, and the volume of the corpuscles have a significant effect on the performance. For this reason, model selection for the structure of the data is also of great importance.

Another main challenge brought by the long textual nature of news content is that it contains much noise. For this reason, the approach to be developed should also focus on minimizing the noise and removing the essential elements of the event. In addition, since each 'story' is considered as a cluster in event-based news clustering problems, the number of clusters is relatively high by nature. To cope with all these difficulties, density-based HDBSCAN and OPTICS clustering methods, which do not accept the number of clusters as a parameter, were preferred.

HDBSCAN (Hierarchical Density-Based Clustering) Clustering Algorithm

DBSCAN (Density-Based Spatial Clustering of Application with Noise) clustering algorithm was designed in 1996 and is the first density-based clustering algorithm in the literature. It is based on the basic assumption that each object in a set must contain at least MinPts of objects in its neighborhood within the Eps radius. It is an algorithm designed to detect randomly shaped data sets in noisy and high-dimensional data stacks. The ε-neighborhood of a random point s in the D database is defined as in Equation 1. If the neighbors of point s contain at least a minimum number of points, then point s is defined as the seed point as in Equation 2.

$$N_{Eps} = \{n \in D \mid dist(s,n) < Eps\} \tag{1}$$

$$N_{Eps}(s) > MinPts \tag{2}$$

The DBSCAN clustering algorithm is susceptible to the Eps and MinPts parameters specified by the user, and changing the parameters leads to significant changes in the clustering results. In addition, determining whether a point is a core or not is an element that increases the I/O load considerably. The hierarchical DBSCAN clustering algorithm is one of the best alternative approaches that emerged due to the studies to eliminate these two disadvantages.

The hierarchical DBSCAN clustering algorithm performs the traditional density based DBSCAN algorithm on variable epsilon values and combines the clustering results with the most stable result over epsilon. Unlike DBCSAN, the HDBSCAN algorithm supports variable density clusters while eliminating the need to set the distance scale parameter. The HDBSCAN algorithm, which also performs very well in terms of speed, is considered an important development for density-based clustering and is actively used in studies as an excellent alternative to the frequently used DBSCAN algorithm.

The HDBSCAN algorithm only accepts a classical smoothing factor as an input parameter for density estimates, called mPts, whose behavior is well understood. Depending on the resulting density, different density levels in the cluster hierarchy will then correspond to different values of the radius ε. The kernel distance in mPts of any object (Xp Î X) in the X dataset, expressed as dcore (Xp), is the distance from Xp to mPts to its nearest neighbor (including Xp). Here, an Xp Î X is called an ε-core object for every ε value greater than or equal to the core distance with respect to x mpts (i.e., if dcore (Xp) £ ε). In addition, the Gmpts included in the HDSCAN hierarchical clustering concept, the basic steps of which are shown in Algorithm 1, is a complete graph (Campello et al.,2013). In this graph, the objects in X are represented by the vertices, and the weight of each edge is the mutual accessibility distance between the respective pair of objects dmreach (Xp, Xq) is (dmreach(Xp, Xq) = max{dcore(Xp), dcore(Xq) is d(Xp, Xq)}.

Algorithm 1. HDBSCAN main steps (Campello et al.,,2013)

Calculate the core distance in mPts for all data objects in dataset X.

Calculate a Minimum Spanning Tree (MST) of the Mutual Availability Chart (Gmpts).

To extend the MST to get the MSText graph, add a self-edge whose weight is the object's core distance from each vertex.

Extract the HDBSCAN hierarchy with a dendrogram obtained from MSText, the extended MST.

Assign a "cluster" label to all objects for the tree's root.

Iteratively remove all edges to decrease weight from the expanded MST (MSText). (in case of a bond, the edges need to be removed at the same time):

Before each removal, set the dendrogram scale value of the current hierarchical level as the weight of the edge(s) to be removed.

After each removal, assign labels to the connected component(s) containing the endpoint(s) of the removed edge(s) to get the next hierarchical level: if it still has at least one edge, assign the "noise" label to the component.

The mPts parameter mentioned in Algorithm 1 is defined with the min_cluster_size parameter in the Python package used for HDSCAN clustering in the study1. This parameter is set according to the smallest size grouping desired to be evaluated as a cluster, as its excellent value. The Turkish Event-Based Text Clustering Dataset used within the scope of the study contains a minimum of 6 and a maximum of 105 news with the same content. For this reason, min_cluster_size = 6 is set.

- **OPTICS (Ordering points to identify the clustering structure) Clustering algorithm**

OPTICS (Ordering points to identify the clustering structure) is another density-based clustering algorithm presented by Ankerst, Breunig, et al. in 1999 (Ankerst et al., 1999). The OPTICS algorithm, closely related to the DBSCAN cluster algorithm, finds the high-density core sample and expands the clusters based on these samples. Unlike DBSCAN, it tries to keep the cluster hierarchy for a variable neighborhood radius. OPTICS requires a priority queue (Min heap) size with more memory to determine the next data point closest to the data point to be processed than HDBSCAN. Thus, it addresses one of the most significant weaknesses of DBSCAN, the problem of detecting meaningful clusters in data of varying density.

The OPTICS clustering algorithm needs two initial parameters as in DBSCAN. These parameters are ε, which defines the maximum distance (radius) to be considered, and MinPts (represented as mPts in the HDBSCAN algorithm), which defines the minimum number of points required to form a cluster. The MinPts parameter used in the OPTICS algorithm is defined with the min_samples parameter in the Python package used for OPTICS clustering in the study2. This parameter is five by default, but it has been determined as six because the number of elements of the smallest sized group to be evaluated as a cluster in the studied dataset is 6. In addition, the ε parameter was determined as three because it gave the most consistent result in terms of clustering performance. The core point definition is the same as the HDBSCAN algorithm, and also, in the OPTICS algorithm, each point is assigned a core distance, which defines the distance to the MinPts-th closest point:

$$core_{dist\varepsilon,MinPts}(p) = \begin{cases} UNDEFINED & if \ |N_{\varepsilon}(p)| < MinPts \\ MinPts-th \ smallest \ distance \ in \ N_{\varepsilon}(p) & otherwise \end{cases}$$

The reachability distance of another point (s) in the data set from the point p is the distance between s and p or the kernel distance of p. Here, the larger value is determined as the reach distance.

$$reachability\_dist_{\varepsilon,MinPts}(s,p) = \begin{cases} UNDEFINED & if \; |N_\varepsilon(p)| < MinPts \\ max(core_{dist\varepsilon,MinPts}(p), dist(s,p)) & otherwise \end{cases}$$

Algorithm 2. OPTICS main steps (Ankerst et al., 1999)

Define the reach distance of each point in the database as undefined (to be calculated later)

For each "UNPROCESSED" point in the database:

Get Epsilon-neighborhood

Mark point as processed

push point to the sorted list

Look at the point's core distance: if it is not undefined (it is a seed point), look further, but if it is not a seed point, move on to the next raw point.

Initialize an empty priority queue for seed points and call the update function that sorts by reach (priority order).

For each point in the sequential priority order, get its neighbors and mark the neighboring point as processed, and exit to the sorted list. Expand the priority queue if the neighboring point is already a seed point.

Keep expanding until none of the unprocessed points no longer have a core distance (i.e., no core points).

OPTICS, whose working logic is explained in Algorithm 2, requires a priority queue (Min heap) size of memory to determine the next data point closest to the data point to be processed compared to HDBSCAN. At the same time, the nearest neighbor query cost of the OPTICS algorithm is higher than the computational cost compared to the radius query in HDBSCAN. However, the number of parameters it needs is less.

Effects of Named Entities on Text Clustering Performance

The news texts contain the subject (person/institution/organization), time, place, and action. These entities are the distinguishing elements for the separation of 'events' from one another. For this reason, using named entities in clustering news texts based on 'event' aims to ensure that the samples included in the cluster approach each other. In contrast, the samples representing different clusters are separated from other clusters as much as possible. Text clustering performance and speed are essential in hosting extensive data archives systems. At this point, another of our goals is to gain speed by reducing the volume of data to be processed.

Bidirectional Encoder Representations from Transformers (BERT) language model was used to identify named entities within the scope of the studies. It is fine-tuned with the WikiAnn dataset built using linked entities from Wikipedia pages for 282 different languages, with named entity tags for Person, Organization, and Location on the BERTurk model, which is pre-trained for Turkish. The performance of the trained BERT-based NER model[3] is over 94%, according to the two different test datasets applied.

The named entities in the text were used in 3 different ways, as listed below, and their performances were compared.

1. **Summarizing Text with Named Entities (SUM_NER):** The BERT language model trained for the NER task determines the text's person, location, or organization entities. Sentences with at least one named entity tag were identified and summarized by keeping only these sentences in the text content and cleaning the other sentences (which do not contain any named entities). Thus, by keeping the descriptive information of the news in the text, it was ensured that the sentences with general expressions were reduced and the size of the text to be studied was reduced. While the total number of sentences for 19,848 news items is 317,646, the total number of sentences containing at least one named entity is 158,784. Thus, there was a 50% reduction in the number of sentences.

Figure 2. Effects of summarization with NER

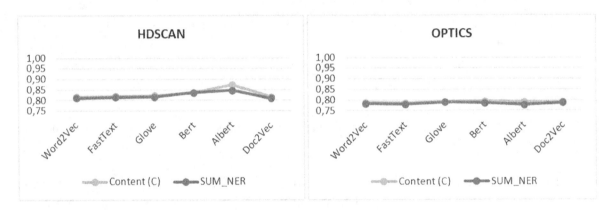

2. **Concatenation of Named Entity Embeddings with Document Embeddings (Content+P+L+O):** Sentence embeddings were obtained using different word, sentence, and document-based space representation methods, as mentioned in detail in the section "Creating vector space representations of news texts." However, there are studies carried out to include information such as person/ organization/organization, time, and place, which play a significant role in distinguishing events, on representation in a sense, to include them in burials obtained from named entities as news text representation. In this context, the entities defined as Person, Location, and Organization in the sentences in the news article were determined by the BERT model and separated according to their categories. Each entity's representation was obtained (with the word/sentence/document-based representation method used to obtain the document vector). The individual representation vectors of Person, Location, and Organization were obtained by calculating the averages of the embeddings of the entities included in each category. The obtained representations were added end-to-end with the document vector, and a news representation was obtained, which could be formulated as "Document + Person + Location + Organization."

3.   **Concatenation of Named Entity Embeds Averaged by Document Embeddings (Content+NERs_ MEAN):** Unlike the previous method, a single named entity embedding is obtained by averaging the individual Person, Location, and Organization vectors. This resulting embedding is concatenated with the document representation.

Density-based HDBSCAN and OPTICS clustering methods were applied over the space vector representations of the news content extracted at different levels (word, sentence, document) and with different models. Named entities with distinctive features of the events in the news content were used in 3 different ways.

Figure 3. Effects of the NER embeddings on Event-based Text Clustering (for word-based vector representations).

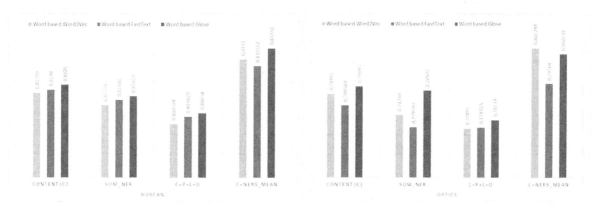

In Table 2, precision, recall, and f-score values according to the B-cubed evaluation metric. Findings obtained according to the results;

- According to the results obtained, the OPTICS clustering method showed lower performance than the HDBSCAN clustering method in all experiments.

- While a 50% gain was achieved in the number of sentences processed in the text summarization method with named entities, a decrease in performance was observed only in the ALBERT model. As seen in Figure 2, there is no significant performance loss for any other model.

- The method of Concatenation named entity embeddings with document embedding caused the vector size to increase by three times. It is also observed that the model's sensitivity against named entities increased. Decreased precision values and increased recall values show that this sensitivity has led to the inclusion of news that contains the same person/institution or the exact location information in the same cluster, even though the event is different.

- Document embedding to reduce the sensitivity of named entities and the method of adding averaged named entity embeddings end-to-end (Content+NERs_MEAN) increased performance for all other models and both clustering algorithms, except for the ALBERT model, as seen in Figure 3.

Table 2. Effects of named entities on text clustering performance

	Vect.	HDBSCAN			OPTICS		
		Precision	Recall	F-Score	Precision	Recall	F-Score
Content							
Word-based	**Word2Vec**	0.87724	0.766252	0.81799	0.81899	0.76078	0.78881
	FastText	0.8653	0.7789	0.8198	0.794898	0.77633	0.785507
	Glove	0.87429	0.77668	0.8226	0.82491	0.7596	0.79093
Sentence based	**Bert**	0.89440	0.78746	0.83753	0.82093	0.76946	0.79436
	Albert	0.91212	0.83792	0.87345	0.78683	0.79256	0.78968
Document based	**Doc2Vec**	0.86908	0.76813	0.815495	0.81518	0.765404	0.7895
Summarizing text with named entities (SUM_NER)							
Word-based	**Word2Vec**	0.86487	0.76373	0.81116	0.80754	0.75969	0.78288
	FastText	0.855617	0.776264	0.81401	0.788189	0.770814	0.779404
	Glove	0.86412	0.7732	0.81614	0.81508	0.765883	0.78971
Sentence based	**Bert**	0.8843	0.79295	0.83614	0.79492	0.77566	0.78518
	Albert	0.88701	0.81096	0.84728	0.76682	0.78857	0.77755
Document based	**Doc2Vec**	0.86097	0.763103	0.80909	0.80412	0.7701	0.78674
Concatenation of named entity embeddings with document embeddings (Content+P+L+O)							
Word-based	**Word2Vec**	0.76196	0.84333	0.800588	0.72543	0.84098	0.77894
	FastText	0.7789486	0.83206	0.804629	0.728065	0.838327	0.779315
	Glove	0.77629	0.83934	0.80658	0.728117	0.843074	0.78139
Sentence based	**Bert**	0.8067	0.841362	0.82366	0.71517	0.83622	0.77097
	Albert	0.82619	0.8463	0.83613	0.71251	0.82881	0.76627
Document based	**Doc2Vec**	0.7723	0.83771	0.80367	0.72298	0.8388	0.7766
Concatenation of named entity embeds averaged by document embeddings (Content+NERs_MEAN)							
Word-based	**Word2Vec**	0.82693	0.84773	0.8372	0.76433	0.84311	0.801799
	FastText	0.826292	0.8407367	0.833452	0.746501	0.842684	0.79168
	Glove	0.83825	0.84866	0.84342	0.762207	0.84196	0.800101
Sentence based	**Bert**	0.86895	0.8372	0.85278	0.75816	0.80805	0.78231
	Albert	0.84562	0.83315	0.83934	0.718425	0.805039	0.75927
Document based	**Doc2Vec**	0.83346	0.84773	0.840536	0.75289	0.84468	0.79615

In addition to the findings listed above, in the tests conducted within the scope of the study, it has been seen that the named entities in the texts are essential for TDT problems. Especially in the 2nd test, which is the text summarization approach with named entities, there is no significant difference between the clustering performance obtained by embedding only the sentences containing named entities and the performance obtained by embedding the entire content reveals this. Determining essential elements such as a person, organization, and location in the 'event' phenomenon in named entity detection is critical for all problems that fundamentally examine this phenomenon. The study was carried out in Turkish, which is a language with few resources and is difficult to process due to its agglutinative language structure. This has created the limitation of this work on the dataset. Still, on the other hand, it is pleasing that a new dataset has been brought to a complex language for the development of language technologies. The language structure is quite different from the widely used languages such as English, and the absence of a directly comparable experimental dataset resulted in the tests being compared only within the same dataset but with different embedding types and clustering methods.

FUTURE RESEARCH DIRECTIONS

TDT paves the way for governments to act quickly to analyze the events in society without losing time, follow the other events that develop around an event and increase the welfare level accordingly. Technical solutions in the literature have been compiled, analyzed, and compared for this research area, which offers solutions for application areas with high social impact potential. Moreover, examples of applications related to the subject for different levels of society such as individuals, institutions, and the state are also included. The effects of these practices on increasing the welfare level of the community and the progress of civilization were discussed. Finally, an event-based news clustering approach using state-of-the-art technology is presented. In addition, the effects of named entities with this solution on the speed and performance of news clustering approaches are examined. Thus, while making a technical contribution to the literature, a dataset in Turkish, which is considered a low-resource language, has also been brought to the literature.

Future studies are planned to display a holistic approach by conducting studies on incident detection and the follow-up of detected incidents. It is predicted that event follow-up mechanisms will significantly impact the early detection of the consequences of events in news texts and have high social impacts. On the other hand, it should be determined as an important application area for institutions/organizations in a competitive environment to follow the market and quickly detect and follow information about competitors through news texts. We argue that integrating incident detection and follow-up mechanisms into applications specialized in the field of work of institutions/organizations will make a significant contribution.

CONCLUSION

In this book chapter, we argue that the Topic Detection and Tracking problem and the sub-tasks within the scope of this problem will play a significant role in extracting valuable information from extensive online data that will have a substantial impact on the identification of social issues and public opinion analysis in producing fast and effective solutions. In addition, we present an integrative framework that synthesizes the solution methods for the event-based news clustering sub-problem, which is essential in obtaining information from online news sources, which are accepted as social information sources in the digital age. We produce an algorithmic solution with a text grouping perspective within the natural language processing research area to automatically bring together those that point to the same event among the stories obtained from hundreds of different news sources and compiled in a heap. This solution generates text representations with state-of-the-art pre-trained language models and then uses density-based clustering algorithms. We consider not only clustering performance but also speed as an essential criterion. For this reason, we use the named entities in the text, which determine the scope of the activity, in 3 different ways. We comparatively examine the effects of each on clustering performance and speed.

ACKNOWLEDGMENT

Interpress Media Monitoring Agency has been a data provider in preparing the data set brought to the literature and has shared thousands of news texts with researchers.

REFERENCES

Allan, J. (2002). Topic detection and tracking: event-based information organization. In *Topic detection and tracking: event-based information organization* (pp. 1–16). Springer Science and Business Media. doi:10.1007/978-1-4615-0933-2_1

Allan, J., Carbonell, J., Doddington, G., Yamron, J., & Yang, Y. (1998). Topic detection and tracking pilot study: final report. In *Proceedings of the DARPA broadcast news transcription and understanding workshop* (pp. 194–218). Academic Press.

Ankerst, M., Breunig, M. M., Kriegel, H. P., & Sander, J. (1999). OPTICS: Ordering points to identify the clustering structure. *SIGMOD Record*, *28*(2), 49–60. doi:10.1145/304181.304187

Aramaki, E., Maskawa, S., & Morita, M. (2011, July). Twitter catches the flu: detecting influenza epidemics using Twitter. In *Proceedings of the 2011 Conference on empirical methods in natural language processing* (pp. 1568-1576). Academic Press.

Blokh, I., & Alexandrov, V. (2017). News clustering based on similarity analysis. *Procedia Computer Science*, *122*, 715–719. doi:10.1016/j.procs.2017.11.428

Bojanowski, P., Grave, E., Joulin, A., & Mikolov, T. (2017). Enriching word vectors with subword information. *Transactions of the Association for Computational Linguistics*, *5*, 135–146. doi:10.1162/tacl_a_00051

Bouras, C., & Tsogkas, V. (2012). A clustering technique for news articles using WordNet. *Knowledge-Based Systems*, *36*, 115–128. doi:10.1016/j.knosys.2012.06.015

Campello, R. J., Moulavi, D., & Sander, J. (2013, April). Density-based clustering based on hierarchical density estimates. In *Pacific-Asia conference on knowledge discovery and data mining* (pp. 160–172). Springer. doi:10.1007/978-3-642-37456-2_14

Chen, C. C., & Wang, H. C. (2021). Adapting the influences of publishers to perform news event detection. *Journal of Information Science*. doi:10.1177/01655515211047422

Dai, X., & Sun, Y. (2010, October). Event identification within news topics. In *2010 International Conference on Intelligent Computing and Integrated Systems* (pp. 498-502). IEEE.

Dou, W., Wang, X., Ribarsky, W., & Zhou, M. (2012, October). Event detection in social media data. In *IEEE VisWeek Workshop on Interactive Visual Text Analytics-Task Driven Analytics of Social Media Content* (pp. 971-980). IEEE.

Fisher, C., Flew, T., Park, S., Lee, J. Y., & Dulleck, U. (2020). Improving trust in news: Audience solutions. *Journalism Practice*, 1–19.

Fonseka, W. P. I. (2021). *Automated News Clustering Using an Unsupervised Learning Model* (Doctoral dissertation).

Gwadera, R., & Crestani, F. (2009, November). Mining and ranking streams of news stories using cross-stream sequential patterns. In *Proceedings of the 18th ACM conference on information and knowledge management* (pp. 1709-1712). 10.1145/1645953.1646210

Jiang, L., Zhang, H., & Yang, X. (2012). Research on semantic text mining based on domain ontology. In *Proc. Int. Conf. Comput. Comput. Technol. Agricult.* Berlin, Germany: Springer.

Kenton, J. D. M. W. C., & Toutanova, L. K. (2019, May). Bert: Pre-training of deep bidirectional transformers for language understanding. In *Proceedings of NAACL-HLT* (pp. 4171-4186). Academic Press.

Kömeçoğlu, Y., Kömeçoğlu, B. B., & Yılmaz, B. (2020, August). Real-Time News Grouping: Detecting the Same-Content News on Turkish News Stream. In *International Online Conference on Intelligent Decision Science* (pp. 14-25). Springer.

Kumaran, G., & Allan, J. (2004, July). Text classification and named entities for new event detection. In *Proceedings of the 27th annual international ACM SIGIR conference on research and development in information retrieval* (pp. 297-304). 10.1145/1008992.1009044

Kumaran, G., & Allan, J. (2005, October). Using names and topics for new event detection. In *Proceedings of Human Language Technology Conference and Conference on Empirical Methods in Natural Language Processing* (pp. 121-128). 10.3115/1220575.1220591

Lan, Z., Chen, M., Goodman, S., Gimpel, K., Sharma, P., & Soricut, R. (2019). *Albert: A lite bert for self-supervised learning of language representations.* arXiv preprint arXiv:1909.11942.

Le, Q., & Mikolov, T. (2014, June). Distributed representations of sentences and documents. In *International conference on machine learning* (pp. 1188-1196). PMLR.

Lei, S. H. I., & Junping, D. U. (2018). Social network bursty topic discovery based on RNN and topic model. *Journal of Communication*, *39*(4), 189.

Liu, W., Jiang, L., Wu, Y., Tang, T., & Li, W. (2020). Topic detection and tracking based on event ontology. *IEEE Access: Practical Innovations, Open Solutions*, 8, 98044–98056. doi:10.1109/ACCESS.2020.2995776

Lu, R., Xiang, L., Liu, M. R., & Yang, Q. (2012). Discovering news topics from microblogs based on hidden topics analysis and text clustering. *Pattern Recognition and Artificial Intelligence*, *25*(3), 382–387.

Lu, Y., Mei, Q., & Zhai, C. (2011). Investigating task performance of probabilistic topic models: An empirical study of PLSA and LDA. *Information Retrieval*, *14*(2), 178–203. doi:10.100710791-010-9141-9

Makrehchi, M., Shah, S., & Liao, W. (2013, November). Stock prediction using event-based sentiment analysis. In *2013 IEEE/WIC/ACM International Joint Conferences on Web Intelligence (WI) and Intelligent Agent Technologies (IAT)* (Vol. 1, pp. 337-342). IEEE. 10.1109/WI-IAT.2013.48

Mao, C., Liang, H., Yu, Z., Huang, Y., & Guo, J. (2021). A Clustering Method of Case-Involved News by Combining Topic Network and Multi-Head Attention Mechanism. *Sensors (Basel)*, *21*(22), 7501. doi:10.339021227501 PMID:34833580

Mikolov, T., Chen, K., Corrado, G., & Dean, J. (2013). *Efficient estimation of word representations in vector space*. arXiv preprint arXiv:1301.3781.

Newman, N., Fletcher, R., Schulz, A., Andi, S., Robertson, C. T., & Nielsen, R. K. (2021). *Reuters Institute Digital News Report 2021*. Reuters Institute for the Study of Journalism.

Nicholas, O. (2007). *Andrews and Edward A. Fox: Recent Developments in Document Clustering. Technical Report*. Virginia Tech.

Nielsen, R., & Selva, M. (2019). *More important, but less robust? Five things everybody needs to know about the future of journalism*. Academic Press.

Pennington, J., Socher, R., & Manning, C. D. (2014, October). Glove: Global vectors for word representation. In *Proceedings of the 2014 conference on empirical methods in natural language processing (EMNLP)* (pp. 1532-1543). 10.3115/v1/D14-1162

Petkos, G., Papadopoulos, S., & Kompatsiaris, Y. (2012, June). Social event detection using multimodal clustering and integrating supervisory signals. In *Proceedings of the 2nd ACM International Conference on Multimedia Retrieval* (pp. 1-8). 10.1145/2324796.2324825

Rasouli, E., Zarifzadeh, S., & Rafsanjani, A. J. (2020). WebKey: A graph-based method for event detection in web news. *Journal of Intelligent Information Systems*, *54*(3), 585–604. doi:10.100710844-019-00576-7

Ren, X. D., Zhang, Y. K., & Xue, X. F. (2009, May). Adaptive topic tracking technique based on K-modes clustering. *Comput. Eng.*, *35*(9), 222–224.

Rosa, R. L., De Silva, M. J., Silva, D. H., Ayub, M. S., Carrillo, D., Nardelli, P. H., & Rodríguez, D. Z. (2020). Event detection system based on user behavior changes in online social networks: Case of the COVID-19 pandemic. *IEEE Access: Practical Innovations, Open Solutions*, *8*, 158806–158825. doi:10.1109/ACCESS.2020.3020391 PMID:34812354

Sakaki, T., Okazaki, M., & Matsuo, Y. (2010, April). Earthquake shakes Twitter users: real-time event detection by social sensors. In *Proceedings of the 19th international conference on world wide web* (pp. 851-860). 10.1145/1772690.1772777

Shomanov, A. S., & Mansurova, M. E. (2021). Parallel news clustering and topic modeling approaches. *Journal of Physics: Conference Series*, *1727*(1), 012018. doi:10.1088/1742-6596/1727/1/012018

Staykovski, T., Barrón-Cedeno, A., Da San Martino, G., & Nakov, P. (2019). Dense vs. Sparse Representations for News Stream Clustering. In Text2Story@ ECIR (pp. 47-52). Academic Press.

Wang, Y., Liu, J., Huang, Y., & Feng, X. (2016, July). Using hashtag graph-based topic model to connect semantically-related words without cooccurrence in microblogs. *IEEE Transactions on Knowledge and Data Engineering, 28*(7), 1919–1933. doi:10.1109/TKDE.2016.2531661

Yang, C. C., Shi, X., & Wei, C. P. (2009). Discovering event evolution graphs from news corpora. *IEEE Transactions on Systems, Man, and Cybernetics. Part A, Systems and Humans, 39*(4), 850–863. doi:10.1109/TSMCA.2009.2015885

ADDITIONAL READING

Cai, Z., Wang, J., & He, K. (2020). Adaptive density-based spatial clustering for massive data analysis. *IEEE Access: Practical Innovations, Open Solutions, 8*, 23346–23358. doi:10.1109/ACCESS.2020.2969440

Hoang, T. A., Vo, K. D., & Nejdl, W. (2018, October). W2E: a worldwide-event benchmark dataset for topic detection and tracking. In *Proceedings of the 27th ACM International Conference on Information and Knowledge Management* (pp. 1847-1850). 10.1145/3269206.3269309

Saeed, Z., Abbasi, R. A., Maqbool, O., Sadaf, A., Razzak, I., Daud, A., Aljohani, N. R., & Xu, G. (2019). What's happening around the world? a survey and framework on event detection techniques on Twitter. *Journal of Grid Computing, 17*(2), 279–312. doi:10.100710723-019-09482-2

Xiang, W., & Wang, B. (2019). A survey of event extraction from text. *IEEE Access: Practical Innovations, Open Solutions, 7*, 173111–173137. doi:10.1109/ACCESS.2019.2956831

KEY TERMS AND DEFINITIONS

B-Cubed: An evaluation metric, which can evaluate the precision and recall for every data point in clustering on a given dataset according to ground truth.

Cluster: A group of similar objects (data points) belonging to the same cluster. They have similar characteristics in the cluster but are different from the objects in other clusters.

Density-Based Clustering: An unsupervised learning technique that identifies distinctive clusters which includes data objects spread in the data space over a contiguous region of a high density of objects.

Embedding: A term used to represent words/sentences/documents for NLP applications. It is typically in the form of a real-valued vector and used for encoding the meaning of the word/sentence/document.

Information Retrieval: The process, methods, and procedures of accessing and retrieving sufficient information from information system resources on a query given by the user.

Named-Entity Recognition: A process or task in NLP where the text is parsed through to find entities that can be put under categories like a person, organizations, locations, etc.

Noise: Unwanted variation, irrelevant information.

Pre-Trained Language Model: Language models used to learn universal language representations. It has been trained with large-scale corpora to perform specific language tasks.

ENDNOTES

[1]   https://github.com/scikit-learn-contrib/hdbscan

[2]   https://scikit-learn.org/stable/modules/generated/sklearn.cluster.OPTICS.html

[3]   https://github.com/snnclsr/ner

APPENDIX

Table 3. Sample news sets of the Turkish Event-Based Text Clustering Dataset (in English)

Cluster 1	
News 1	Beşiktaş, which is in the last place in its group with zero points in the UEFA Europa League, will be deprived of important names in the away match against Braga this evening. Burak Yılmaz, Victor Ruiz, Gökhan Gönül, and N'Koudou, who had just come out of injury in the black and white team, were not taken to Portugal. The two shining stars of the team, Atiba and Diaby were not included in the squad for rest. In the statement made by the club, it was said, "Our technical director, Abdullah Avcı, was not able to take part in our team's Braga group in order not to disrupt his ongoing treatment due to the severe flu. According to his response to the treatment, our teacher will go to Portugal tomorrow."
News 2	Beşiktaş, our representative in the UEFA Europa League, will face Braga on the road this evening. Coach Abdullah Avcı, who did not include Burak Yılmaz, Gökhan Gönül, Diaby, N'Koudou, and Ruiz in the squad, did not include himself in the squad due to the severe flu infection he had. The experienced coach, who stated yesterday that he would go to Braga if he got better, said he did not feel well today and decided to stay in Istanbul.
News 3	In Beşiktaş, which will be the guest of Braga in the Europa League, coach Avcı could not go to Portugal due to the severe flu he had. Black and Whites first announced that he would go to this country if the hunter got better. However, the situation of the technical boss of the Black and Whites did not improve today. The hunter did not go to Portugal. Beşiktaş football branch manager Erdal Torunoğulları was also unable to take part in the convoy due to the surgery he had. Torunoğulları, who was under the knife due to gallbladder disease, stayed in Istanbul due to his treatment.
Cluster 2	
News 1	Work is finally starting for Şifalısu, which has recently come to the fore with its sealing due to microbes mixing with water. The social project to be implemented in the area that Akçakoca Municipality rented from the forest management for 29 years with an annual cost of 20 thousand TL in February 2017 was brought to the council's agenda. At the last council meeting in November, it was decided to hand over the investment and management of the Şifalı Su promenade to the municipality company ABİTAŞ.
News 2	A municipality-owned company will invest in and operate the Şifalısu Recreation area on the D-655 Highway, leased by the Akçakoca Municipality. At the meeting, in which the requests for changes in the Zoning Plan were mainly discussed, it was decided to give the investment and management of the healing water resort rented by the Akçakoca Municipality to the municipality company ABİTAŞ.
News 3	Now the button is pressed in Şifalısu, which was transferred to the Akçakoca Municipality by the Ministry of Forestry. In February, Akçakoca Municipality, which leased 50 decares of forest area for 29 years with the protocol signed between Akçakoca Municipality and Akçakoca Forestry Management Directorate, took an important decision regarding Şifalısu. The municipal council, which discussed the future of the Şifalısu forest recreation area, which came to the agenda in this evening's meeting of the municipal council, decided to transfer the facility to ABİTAŞ, which is the municipality's subsidiary. The municipality, which has decided not to tender Şifalısu, will operate the facility through its own subsidiary ABİTAŞ.

Chapter 9
Deep Learning for Information Extraction From Digital Documents:
An Innovative Approach to Automatic Parsing and Rich Text Extraction From PDF Files

Yavuz Kömeçoğlu
iD https://orcid.org/0000-0002-3048-8364
Kodiks Bilişim, Turkey

Serdar Akyol
Kodiks Bilisim, Turkey

Fethi Su
Kodiks Bilisim, Turkey

Başak Buluz Kömeçoğlu
iD https://orcid.org/0000-0001-9937-1036
Gebze Technical University, Turkey

ABSTRACT

Print-oriented PDF documents are excellent at preserving the position of text and other objects but have difficulties in processing. Processable PDF documents will provide solutions to the unique needs of different sectors by paving the way for many innovations such as searching within documents, linking with different documents, or restructuring in a format that will increase the reading experience. In this chapter, a deep learning-based system design is presented that aims to export clean text content, separate all visual elements, and extract rich information from the content without losing the integrated structure of content types. While the F-RCNN model using the Detectron2 library was used to extract the layout, the cosine similarities between the wod2vec representations of the texts were used to identify the related clips, and the transformer language models were used to classify the clip type. The performance values on the 200-sample data set created by the researchers were determined as 1.87 WER and 2.11 CER in the headings and 0.22 WER and 0.21 CER in the paragraphs.

DOI: 10.4018/978-1-6684-4045-2.ch009

INTRODUCTION

Technology refers to the body of information that is used to produce useful products and to design new products, or all the physical processes that transform inputs into outputs and the social arrangements accompanying this transformation. The role of technology in the field of international competition has become so decisive that today the classification of economic development has gradually turned into technology producing and non-producing countries. The most important subject of today's technological development is data and its processing. The huge increase in data volume and data diversity, the fact that even simple daily activities produce data, require very large volumes of warehouses to store this data. At the same time, the processing of these data and the ability to quickly analyze them for the purpose make the dimensions important in terms of data storage and processing capacity. The analysis of data and the size of the data are also factors affecting competition in areas such as trade, energy, and economy. For this reason, to obtain economic value from big data, it is important to process the correct data with advanced analytical methods, to keep up with the new developing technologies with the machine learning method, and to affect the decision-making processes.

In many countries, the ecosystem, which includes public institutions/organizations, the private sector, and academia, sets targets for artificial intelligence applications and quality data. Big data collection platforms, increasing the capacity of analysis and decision making and implementation accordingly, and creating problem pools for sectors are the main ones (Ferrara et al.,2014; Chang et al.,2006). Access to quality data by extracting valuable information from data is a core mission of many businesses intelligence services that require large-scale document processing. Understanding the documents included in the business processes in terms of page layout allows the establishment of the contextual structure at the stage of semantically interpreting the document terms in it. In this book chapter, the focus is on PDF, which is the most preferred document format open to sharing electronically for security reasons, since the possibility of making changes and editing the document is limited. PDF is the most widely used format for book, magazine, newspaper, and article-like document formats and is developed by Adobe Systems. On the other hand, it is largely kept in unstructured PDF format in the scientific literature (Jimeno Yepes et al., 2021). This format, which is very suitable for preserving basic visual elements, also has great difficulties in terms of automatic processing of these visual contents by machines. Extracting non-natural language content such as figures and tables, which often provide a summary and worthwhile information, as well as text in formatted formats with a focus on visuality, from a PDF file is another challenge. To provide comprehensive information extraction, it is necessary to determine the document layout and to parse the visually enriched texts and non-natural language content in a machine-structured format with background and other special formal features. Based on this need, the authors make use of the information contained in PDF documents with a complex layout, image processing, and deep learning methods in this book chapter and propose a solution that enables the document outline to be determined, parsed into elements, defined as a clip, and the title, subtitle, image, and actual text content of the clip itself to be output in reading order.

Background

Documents in PDF format, which contain information from many different industries such as academic articles, medical documents, insurance documents, newspapers, and magazines, are accepted as the main source of information both online and offline. Although it is a very useful format for different users to access the basic visual and textual elements of the document in terms of being independent of the operating system and the environment, it is not a format that can be understood by machines (Jimeno Yepes et al.,2021). The sub-steps traditionally followed in converting a PDF document into a machinable and machine-understandable format can be listed as follows: Separating the pages into structural and logical units, tagging the detected regions according to their types (e.g. title, text, images, lines, tables), and finally, gathering all the elements belonging to the same articles together to produce output in a structured format according to the reading order (Zeni & Weldemariam,2017).

Evaluation datasets such as BE-Arabic-9K (Elanwar et al.,2021), DocBank (Li et al.,2020), and PubLayNet (Zhong et al.,2019) are designed for the task of determining the page layout in PDF documents, where image processing and natural language processing can produce solutions together, have been published. These datasets are important in developing new methods and measuring and comparing their performance. On the other hand, there are many rule-based systems for detecting and segmenting document objects (Hashmi et al.,2020; Constantin et al.,2013; Ahmad et al.,2016), but these systems fail to detect objects in documents with complex layouts. The use of deep learning methods, especially convolutional neural networks, has created a great improvement in object detection performance compared to rule-based systems (Liebl & Burghardt,2021). While deep neural networks take advantage of the visual differences between object classes, they cannot provide sufficient performance alone for objects framed by text. Object detection provides classes and locations of objects based on bounding boxes, while segmentation is defined as the task of sharply delineating objects at the pixel level. In complex layouts where objects overlap, this task is quite challenging, and it is seen in the literature that specially designed segmentation masks for each object category are used to increase the performance of deep neural networks in the separation of these objects (Biswas et al.,2021).

In the literature review for this book chapter, it was not seen that the layout information in the PDF source code was used in the studies to increase the performance of image processing techniques. It is seen that OCR technologies are frequently used in the literature in separating the characters as clean text from the text blocks that make up the majority of the content in many different document types (Yuan et al.,2020; Singh et al.,2021). The sensitivity of OCR technologies to font types and background designs makes it difficult to obtain a clean text. For this reason, studies have focused on trying to eliminate erroneous texts with natural language processing methods (März et al.,2021). Obtaining the representations of the texts in sub-tasks such as determining the related ones from the separated text blocks, determining the continuation of the document existing on the same or different pages, and then determining the vectoral similarities with various distance metrics are the most frequently used methods (Farouk,2020; Kenter & De,2015)

Another sub-task in determining the page layout in PDF documents is categorizing the text according to its subject. There are many studies in the literature, especially on the classification of news texts according to their subjects, and the classification ability of deep neural networks is quite high for this problem. The ability to create context-specific representations with trainable models such as Word2Vec, and subsequently, language models that present the entire language structure in a single framework after 2018 have led to great performance increases in many sub-problems, including classification in the field of natural language processing. With this increase, human performance has now been surpassed on many evaluation datasets (Mikolov et al.,2013; Devlin et al.,2018).

AUTOMATIC PARSING SYSTEM OF DIGITALLY PRODUCDED PDF DOCUMENTS

The focus of this book chapter is the extraction of rich text on PDF documents with automatic element parsing and machine learning and computer vision methods to automate repetitive, value-added work in our world where digital transformation is becoming more and more indispensable. With the proposed method, the targeted content will be automatically parsed from the PDF document containing more than one content. Thus, documents such as newspapers, magazines, books, and research in PDF format will be automatically divided into clips and presented in output formats for the specific needs of different sectors. For all these purposes, the challenges to be overcome are listed below. To overcome the listed difficulties and exhibit an integrated approach, a unique system design was carried out in which different modules were brought together.

- It is very difficult to process PDF documents with complex layouts such as newspapers, as existing PDF extraction methods remain at the level of text or table extraction.
- Few studies have been done on extracting the raw text from the source of the PDF.
- Studies in literature are at the level of rendering PDF pages as images, determining the outline of the page over the image, and reading texts with optical character reading (OCR) solutions.
- Pre-trained neural network models show very poor performance for newspaper-specific outlines.
- The order of news clips on the page and the problem of determining the reading order within the clip itself is one of the problems that must be overcome.
- The problem of determining which news clip the pictures belong to is one of the problems that has not been studied.

SOLUTIONS AND RECOMMENDATIONS

Within the scope of this book chapter, it is aimed to design a system that includes all the functions of extracting all elements such as textual content, and images, identifying their types, and extracting rich text in PDF format documents designed as complex layouts.

The system will have the basic functions of determining the outline of the document, parsing the text regions, and obtaining the data in these regions in an OCR-error-free manner, automatically classifying the elements that are parsed by the layout according to categories such as advertisements, columns, news, advertisements. It will include approaches to be developed using computer vision and deep learning techniques.

It is aimed to obtain structured data that can meet the unique needs of many different sectors, not only in terms of separating different types of elements in the document content but also in terms of obtaining the rich content obtained in workable formats.

The system is designed in 2 main modules listed below:

1. Extracting the layout of a full-page PDF document and splitting it into clips
2. Separating the clips into titles, subtitles, content, and pictures

System Modules

Extracting Layout of PDF Document:

The Detectron2 library developed by the Facebook AI Research team was used (Wu et al.,2019) to obtain the document layout by separating the borders of the clips in the full-page PDF document. Detectron2 includes state-of-the-art object detection and segmentation algorithms.

There are many state-of-the-art deep learning models trained with PRImA Layout Analysis Dataset (Antonacopoulos et al.,2009), PubLayNet Dataset (Zhong et al.,2019), HJDataset (Shen et al.,2020) TableBank (Li et al.,2019) and The Newspaper Navigator Dataset (Lee et al.,2020) for segmentation task in Detectron2 library.

The Faster-RCNN (F-RCNN) deep learning model trained with The Newspaper Navigator Dataset was used in the study to determine the borders of the nested clip and picture areas in newspaper-like documents with a complex layout, and thus parse the outline of the page. An example of the segmentation model applied on a full-page newspaper image and separated from the borders of all elements is shown in Figure 1 and Figure 2.

Figure 1. Layout example as a result of the segmentation model of a full-page newspaper

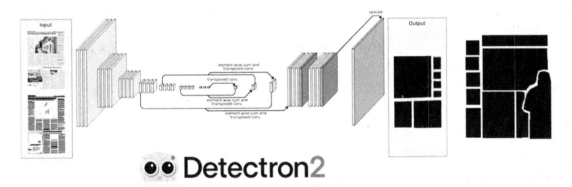

F-RCNN is one of the pinnacles of R-CNN object detector architectures and this deep learning model is built on the logic of Region Proposal as shown in Figure 3. In this methodology, suitable areas are distinguished by an antecedent segmentation and the object detection algorithm is trained on the segmented areas. The underlying idea is that each segment in the picture represents an autonomous object.

Parsing PDF Elements

Existing systems treat each page of PDF documents as an image file and try to obtain the text over the image with OCR technologies. Since OCR is very sensitive to fonts and background images, it causes noisy data. Searchability is very low due to recognition errors in texts obtained using OCR.

Figure 2. Layout example as a result of the segmentation model of a full-page newspaper

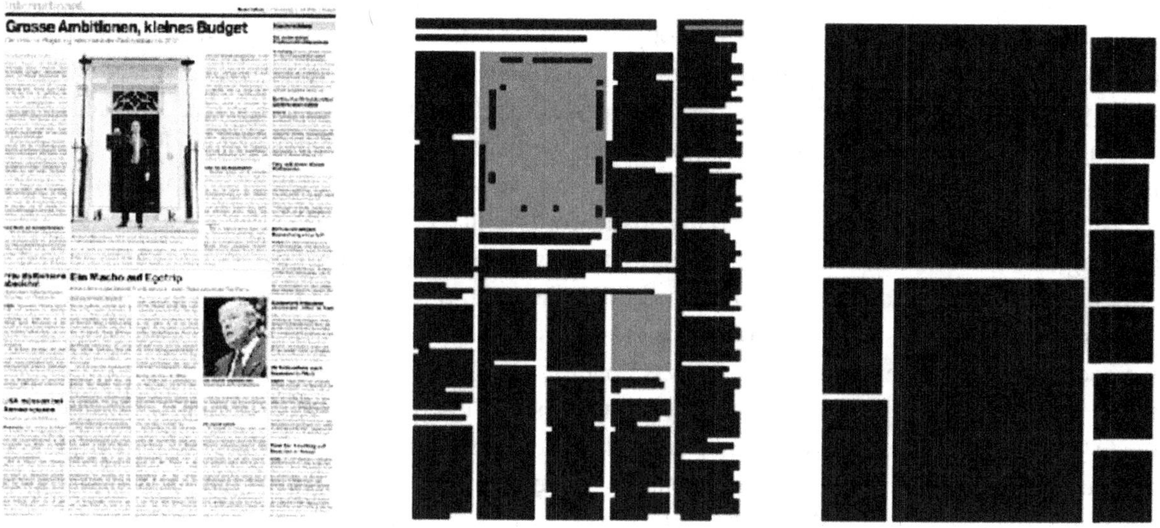

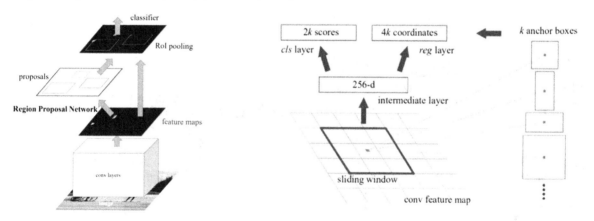

Figure 3. Left: R-CNN is a converged network in which the RPN module acts as the "attention". Right:: Region Proposal Network (RPN) (Ren et.al,2015)

In the system presented as a solution, object information specific to the PDF format document's own format was used to determine the picture and text borders within each clip in the outlined documents. At the point of obtaining the texts in the document is a complete and error-free manner, the raw text in the PDF was processed instead of the OCR technology. On the other hand, vector drawings other than text, horizontal and vertical lines, and pictures are extracted from the source code of the PDF together with the coordinate information and converted into an analyzable format.

Detecting Clip Areas and Reading Order

It is the function of automatic detection of objects, lines, blocks, and the order between items to separate the parts such as news and advertisements in the content of the document to be processed, without destroying their integrity. In the implementation of this function, the coordinates of the clip areas were determined by using image processing techniques as well as the coordinate information of the elements in the source code of the PDF file. First, the font size of all the words was ordered from smallest to largest by using the font information of each word, and the words with the two smallest font sizes were accepted as paragraphs, and the words with the largest font size were accepted as the title. To be able to segment only the paragraphs, taking into account the cases where the title or paragraph texts and the pictures overlap, black rectangles in sizes surrounding the words were drawn on a blank white background, using the coordinates of the texts. This process was done separately by grouping them according to the font size. Paragraph regions were segmented into font sizes on these reproduced images as grayscale with the OTSU Thresholding Method (Yuan et al.,2016) and 35px kernel size was determined as a result of experimental studies. An example of segmentation of subheading and paragraph regions of a newspaper news clip is shown in Figure 4. The segmented text regions are arranged in reading order from left to right and top to bottom. A healthy text was obtained by combining the texts in the text regions according to the reading order.

Figure 4. Segmentation of subheading and paragraph regions of a newspaper news clip

Detection of Clip Information

It is the function of automatically detecting the clip's (if any) features such as title, summary/full text, and image. In the implementation of this function, as well as the coordinate information of the elements in the PDF, the segmented areas according to the font sizes and the font sizes are considered. An example of classification of the title, subtitle, paragraph, and image regions of a newspaper news clip is shown in Figure 5.

In addition, as shown in Figure 6, noisy texts in which more than one same character is added to create shadows in print-oriented PDFs are transformed into clean text with normalization methods in natural language processing and RegEx methods.

Figure 5. Classification example of a newspaper news clip in the form of title/spot/text/picture

Figure 6. Classification example of a newspaper news clip in the form of title/spot/text/picture

Detection of Related Clips

It is the function of automatic detection of clips on different pages of the PDF format document, which are the continuation of each other as shown in Figure 7. A news article that is summarized on the homepage is not always found on the inner page addressed, or it cannot be easily determined which clip it refers to among the clips on the inner pages. For this, natural language processing methods based on text similarity were used. An example of a follow-up story on the inside page of news on the headline is shown in Figure 6.

Before performing any learning process, the most commonly used text preprocessing steps such as tokenization, removal of stop-words from the text, and stemming were carried out with the Python implementation of the Zemberek (Akın & Akın,2007) library for the Turkish language and for other languages, the natural language processing library developed by the researchers based on the NLTK (Bird et al., 2009) library.

Vector representations of pre-processed texts were created with the word2vec (Mikolov et al.,2013) model trained by the researchers. Within the scope of the study, the Turkish News Texts Corpus, which was created by the researchers in their previous studies (Kömeçoğlu et al.,2020), was used to preserve the semantic integrity of the words in the text, and thus the news texts, and not to destroy the contextual information. After applying a series of pre-processing steps to the Turkish News Texts Corpus, which has 17,470,827 sentences and 1,673,884,673 words (422,346 unique words) in 975,809 news texts, the Word2Vec model, which is frequently used in the literature, is trained. The embedding of the entire text was obtained by averaging the 100-dimensional vectors of the words in the texts created with the Word2Vec model.

In subtasks such as identifying the related text blocks from the parsed text blocks, and determining the continuation of the document on the same or different pages (such as a newspaper article with a continuation on a different page), correlations were made according to the cosine similarity scores of the vectors (Kömeçoğlu et al.,2020). The cosine similarity score represents the similarity/uniqueness between two vectors in an inner product space. The cosine of the angle between two vectors roughly determines whether the vectors point in the same direction and is often one of the most commonly used methods to measure document similarity in text analysis. Let x and y be the two vectors whose similarity score is to be measured. In this case, the cosine similarity of the two vectors is calculated by Formula 1. and $\|x\|$ represents the Euclidean form of vector x (Han et al.,2011).

$$sim(x,y) = \frac{x.y}{\|x\|\|y\|} \tag{1}$$

Detection of Clip Content-Type

The content of the clip is related to the economy, sports, health, etc. It is the function of automatic classification according to possible categories. This function addresses the traditional text classification problem. Although there are many supervised learning methods regarding the text classification problem in the literature, clip types have been determined using state-of-the-art transformers-based language models within the scope of this study. Transformer-based deep learning approaches can classify categories with very high performance by considering the entire context of the text.

Figure 7. There is a continuation of a news headline on page 12.

In this sub-function, SVM and Bert-based classification models trained with the Interpress Turkish News Category Dataset (270K - Lite Version) (Kömeçoğlu & Akyol,2021), which were brought to the literature by the researchers, were used (Kömeçoğlu & Akyol,2021).

Within the scope of the study, before using the SVM model, the texts were converted to lowercase, cleaning e-mail addresses, numbers, and punctuation marks, and deleting stop words, respectively. As input to the SVM model, 1-3 char n-grams and 2–6-word n-grams are used by concatenating. Linear kernel and auto gamma hyper parameters are preferred. The performance of the training set was determined as 94%.

On the other hand, the classification of the clip content type was carried out by utilizing the state-of-the-art transformer-based BERT language model. The pre-processing steps applied this time are the deletion of URL, e-mail, and punctuation marks, as well as the cleaning of words with less than 2 characters in length. The data, which has passed through the preprocessing steps and is ready for training, has been tokenized with the Transformers BERT tokenizer. During tokenization, padding, special tokens, and an attention mask were applied. Adam was used as the optimizer and the model was trained for 4 epochs by determining the learning rate as 5e-5 (Devlin et al.,2018) as discussed in the original article. 97% success was achieved on the training set.

RESULTS

The datasets in PDF format used in related studies in the literature were created from scanned books or documents focused on OCR problems. Layout-oriented datasets were also created to include the coordinate information of the related species as a picture. In this study, the main success criterion is the error-free export of texts. In this context, a test dataset consisting of 200 samples was created, with full-page non-image, digitally produced PDF documents and texts in the documents separated as title and content. The parsed results of the document in PDF format in the test set are presented in APPENDIX-1, APPENDIX-2, and APPENDIX-3. System performance has been evaluated on this test set. Since the performance of the system is determined by the error-free export rate of the texts, the OCR error calculation metrics in the literature were examined and the performance in this study was evaluated according to the Character Error Rate (CER) and Word Error Rate (WER) scores based on title and paragraph. (Morris et al.,2004).

Character error rate (CER) is a metric that gives the error rate on a character basis between the reference text and the OCR output to measure the performance in Speech Recognition, Machine Translation systems or OCR studies. The lower the CER value, the better the performance of the OCR model. The CER evaluation metric, whose formula is given in Formula 2, is calculated based on the following:

S= number of words changed in sentence/number of letter changes in a word
D = Number of deleted words in the sentence / Number of deleted letters in the word
I = Number of words added to the sentence / Number of letters added to the word
L = Total number of words in the sentence / Total number of letters in the word

$$CER = (S + D + I) / L \tag{2}$$

Word Error Rate (WER) is the same success metric as CER and gives the error rate on a word basis. If we formulate one by one, the Formula-3 will be as follows:

$$WER = (S + D + I) / L \tag{3}$$

The average results of the entire test set by title and content are shown in Table-1 below.

Table 1. Average word and character error rates of the 200-sample test set based on title and content

	WER (%)	CER (%)
Title	187.25	211.43
All Paragraphs	22.56	21.32

Examples of the extraction ability of the system can be seen in Figure 8, Figure 9, and the reference (ground truth) and output (prediction) results of the texts and WER and CER percentage scores based on title and paragraph can be seen in Table 2. and Table-3.

Figure 8. The parsed version of a news clip from Hürriyet newspaper dated 13.09.2021

Deep Learning for Information Extraction From Digital Documents

Table 2. GT and prediction results and WER and CER values of the news clip in Figure 8

Sample (Figure-8)	Ground Truth	Prediction	WER (%)	CER (%)
Title	ÇUVAL ÇUVAL ÇALDILAR 2.4 MILYONLUK 289 CEP TELEFONU	ÇUVAL ÇUVAL ÇALDILAR 2.4 MILYONLUK 289 CEP TELEFONU	0	0
Paragraph	İSTANBUL Ataşehir'de bulunan bir teknoloji mağazasına 6 Eylül 2021 günü giren hırsızlar, mağazadaki cep telefonlarını çuvallara doldurarak kayıplara karıştı. 289 adet çeşitli marka ve modelde 2 milyon 400 bin lira değerinde cep telefonunun çalındığını belirten işletme sahipleri, şikâyetçi oldu. Asayiş Şube Hırsızlık Büro Amirliği ekipleri, işyerinde parmak izi incelemesi yaptı. Daha sonra işyeri ve çevredeki sokakların kamera görüntüleri toplandı. Kamera görüntülerinde, hırsızların çuvallara doldurdukları cep telefonlarını mağazaya geldikleri bir otomobile koyarak kaçtıkları belirlendi. TOPLAM 81 SUÇ KAYDI ÇIKTI Kamera görüntülerinden hırsızların kimlikleri tespit edildi. Düzenlenen operasyonda 7 suç kaydı olan Mehmet M. (22), 27 suç kaydı olan ve 5 suçtan aranan Umut G. (37), 2 suç kaydı olan Cem S. (26) ve 45 suç kaydı olan Murat Ö. (39) gözaltına alındı. Operasyonda 2 tabanca, 2 telsiz ve çalınan bazı telefonlar ele geçti. Adliyeye sevk edilen 4 kişi tutuklandı. Çetin AYDIN / İSTANBUL	İSTANBUL Ataşehir'de bulunan bir teknoloji mağazasına 6 Eylül 2021 günü giren hırsızlar, **mağa zadaki** cep telefonlarını çuvallara doldurarak kayıplara karıştı. 289 adet çeşitli marka ve modelde 2 milyon 400 bin lira değerinde cep telefonunun çalındığını belirten işletme sahipleri, şikâyetçi oldu. Asayiş Şube Hırsızlık Büro **Amir liği** ekipleri, işyerinde parmak izi incelemesi yaptı. Daha sonra işyeri ve çevredeki sokakların **kame ra** görüntüleri toplandı. Kamera görüntülerinde, hırsızların çuvalla ra doldurdukları cep telefonlarını mağazaya geldikleri bir otomobile koyarak kaçtıkları belirlendi. TOPLAM 81 SUÇ KAYDI ÇIKTI Kamera görüntülerinden hırsız ların kimlikleri tespit edildi. **Düzen lenen** operasyonda 7 suç kaydı olan Mehmet M. (22), 27 suç kaydı olan ve 5 suçtan aranan Umut G. (37), 2 suç kaydı olan Cem S. (26) ve 45 suç kaydı olan Murat Ö. (39) gözaltına alındı. Operasyonda 2 tabanca, 2 telsiz ve çalınan bazı telefonlar ele geçti. Adliyeye sevk edilen 4 kişi tutuklandı. **m** Çetin AYDIN / ISTANBUL	9.09	0.69

Table 3. GT and prediction results and WER and CER values of the news clip in Figure 9

Sample (Figure-9)	Ground Truth	Prediction	WER (%)	CER (%)
Title	İHRACATTA TARİHİ REKOR	İHRACAT TA İHRACAT TA TARİHİ REKOR	16.66	68.18
Paragraph	2018 yılı için ihracat hedefini 7 milyar dolar belirleyen Gaziantep ihracat hedefine emin adımlarla ilerliyor. TİM tarafından açıklanan Kasım ayı ihracat rakamlarına göre Gaziantep'ten, Kasım ayında 665 milyon 673 bin dolarlık ihracat gerçekleştirildi. 3'te	2018 yılı için ihracat hedefini 7 milyar dolar belirleyen Gaziantep ihracat hedefine emin adımlarla ilerliyor. TİM tarafından açıklanan Kasım ayı ihracat rakamlarına göre Gaziantep'ten, Kasım ayında 665 milyon 673 bin dolarlık ihracat gerçekleştirildi. 3'te	0	0

Figure 9. The parsed version of a news clip from Gaziantep Güneş newspaper dated 03.12.2018

FUTURE RESEARCH DIRECTIONS

Although the issue of determining the page layout in PDF documents is a less studied problem in the literature, it has a widespread use potential that can cut almost every sector horizontally, including media monitoring, education, law, academia, and many more public institutions. As a result of this, it is a valuable study topic in the global and commercial sense.

Media monitoring agencies are the organizations that record and analyze the messages, news, and advertisements published about the people, institutions, and organizations they serve by following all the printed and digital press organs. The business process of separating news on documents with a very complex layout, especially in magazines and newspapers, requires a lot of workforces. In addition, news clips that cannot be obtained in a processable format are not suitable for information extraction, although they are manually extracted. For this reason, it is an important area of use for the system developed in terms of both increasing efficiency and obtaining data that can be processed in a format that can enable information extraction.

Libraries are service businesses that perform the tasks of collecting information from all kinds of information sources and archiving and distributing information to users who need information. Storing documents such as books, which are out of print, in a complete, noise-free, and processable form, in digital archives will meet an important need in preventing the loss of works and facilitating access to information for those who will work on them.

They are platforms where newspapers and magazines can be purchased and read online by subscription method. The experience of reading the publications uploaded as PDF by end-users as e-publishing with PDF viewers is quite tiring. Thanks to a tool that will be based on the system design presented within the scope of the study, the news will be accessed separately instead of full-page viewing. Thus, a better reading experience will be provided to the reader. In addition, since the texts are in an editable format, it will be possible to make different filters according to the needs of the reader.

In future studies, it is aimed to successfully separate different document types such as invoices and catalogs, unlike academic articles, plain texts, or newspapers. The dataset created within the scope of the study will be diversified and the number of samples will be increased and shared so that researchers can benefit.

CONCLUSION

With the system design presented in the book chapter, an approach to obtaining clean and rich text for digitally produced PDFs without using OCR software is presented. It was observed that the texts were exported with an average of 1.8725 WER and 2.1143 CER values on a headline basis, and 0.2256 WER and 0.2132 CER values on a paragraph basis, on a 200-sample dataset consisting of news clips in newspapers the researchers.

Using the image processing and deep learning methods from the information embedded in the documents in PDF format, it is possible to determine the outline of the document, separate the elements, define the clip for the detected elements, to obtain the title, subtitle, picture and actual text content of the clip itself in the reading order.

In the results obtained at the end of the study, it is seen that healthier texts can be obtained from raw data for PDFs produced in digital media. The potential to be used for different purposes increases with the fact that the text obtained with this study can be reproduced to provide a better reading experience thanks to the font type, font size, and word-based coordinate information. Converting the texts in the PDF to a searchable one and exporting richer data in addition to the text are provided. Thus, it will pave the way for many different studies such as linking different documents.

ACKNOWLEDGMENT

The research was supported by Interpress Media Monitoring Company as a data provider.

REFERENCES

Ahmad, R., Afzal, M. T., & Qadir, M. A. (2016, May). Information extraction from PDF sources based on rule-based system using integrated formats. In *Semantic web evaluation challenge* (pp. 293–308). Springer. doi:10.1007/978-3-319-46565-4_23

Akın, A. A., & Akın, M. D. (2007). Zemberek, an open source NLP framework for Turkic languages. *Structure (London, England)*, *10*, 1–5.

Antonacopoulos, A., Bridson, D., Papadopoulos, C., & Pletschacher, S. (2009, July). A realistic dataset for performance evaluation of document layout analysis. In *2009 10th International Conference on Document Analysis and Recognition* (pp. 296-300). IEEE. 10.1109/ICDAR.2009.271

Bird, S., Klein, E., & Loper, E. (2009). *Natural language processing with Python: analyzing text with the natural language toolkit*. O'Reilly Media, Inc.

Biswas, S., Riba, P., Lladós, J., & Pal, U. (2021). Beyond document object detection: Instance-level segmentation of complex layouts. *International Journal on Document Analysis and Recognition*, *24*(3), 269–281. doi:10.100710032-021-00380-6

Chang, C. H., Kayed, M., Girgis, M. R., & Shaalan, K. F. (2006). A survey of web information extraction systems. *IEEE Transactions on Knowledge and Data Engineering*, *18*(10), 1411–1428. doi:10.1109/TKDE.2006.152

Constantin, A., Pettifer, S., & Voronkov, A. (2013, September). PDFX: fully-automated PDF-to-XML conversion of scientific literature. In *Proceedings of the 2013 ACM symposium on document engineering* (pp. 177-180). ACM.

Devlin, J., Chang, M. W., Lee, K., & Toutanova, K. (2018). *Bert: Pre-training of deep bidirectional transformers for language understanding*. arXiv preprint arXiv: 1810.04805.

Elanwar, R., Qin, W., Betke, M., & Wijaya, D. (2021). Extracting text from scanned Arabic books: A large-scale benchmark dataset and a fine-tuned Faster-R-CNN model. *International Journal on Document Analysis and Recognition*, *24*(4), 349–362. doi:10.100710032-021-00382-4

Farouk, M. (2020). Measuring text similarity based on structure and word embedding. *Cognitive Systems Research*, *63*, 1–10. doi:10.1016/j.cogsys.2020.04.002

Ferrara, E., De Meo, P., Fiumara, G., & Baumgartner, R. (2014). Web data extraction, applications and techniques: A survey. *Knowledge-Based Systems*, *70*, 301–323. doi:10.1016/j.knosys.2014.07.007

Han, J., Pei, J., & Kamber, M. (2011). *Data mining: concepts and techniques*. Elsevier.

Hashmi, A. M., Afzal, M. T., & ur Rehman, S. (2020, November). Rule Based Approach to Extract Metadata from Scientific PDF Documents. In *2020 5th International Conference on Innovative Technologies in Intelligent Systems and Industrial Applications (CITISIA)* (pp. 1-4). IEEE.

Jimeno Yepes, A., Zhong, P., & Burdick, D. (2021, September). ICDAR 2021 Competition on Scientific Literature Parsing. In *International Conference on Document Analysis and Recognition* (pp. 605-617). Springer. 10.1007/978-3-030-86337-1_40

Kenter, T., & De Rijke, M. (2015, October). Short text similarity with word embeddings. In *Proceedings of the 24th ACM international on conference on information and knowledge management* (pp. 1411-1420). ACM.

Kömeçoğlu, Y., & Akyol, S. (2021). *Turkish News Category Classification.* https://github.com/kodiks/turkish-news-classification

Kömeçoğlu, Y., & Akyol, S. (2021). *Turkish News Category Dataset (270K - Lite Version).* https://huggingface.co/datasets/interpress_news_category_tr_lite

Kömeçoğlu, Y., Kömeçoğlu, B. B., & Yılmaz, B. (2020, August). Real-Time News Grouping: Detecting the Same-Content News on Turkish News Stream. In *International Online Conference on Intelligent Decision Science* (pp. 14-25). Springer.

Lee, B. C. G., Mears, J., Jakeway, E., Ferriter, M., Adams, C., Yarasavage, N., . . . Weld, D. S. (2020). *The newspaper navigator dataset: extracting and analyzing visual content from 16 million historic newspaper pages in chronicling America.* doi:10.1145/3340531.3412767

Li, M., Cui, L., Huang, S., Wei, F., Zhou, M., & Li, Z. (2019). *Tablebank: A benchmark dataset for table detection and recognition.* arXiv preprint arXiv: 1903.01949.

Li, M., Xu, Y., Cui, L., Huang, S., Wei, F., Li, Z., & Zhou, M. (2020). *DocBank: A benchmark dataset for document layout analysis.* doi:10.18653/v1/2020.coling-main.82

Liebl, B., & Burghardt, M. (2021, January). An Evaluation of DNN Architectures for Page Segmentation of Historical Newspapers. In *2020 25th International Conference on Pattern Recognition (ICPR)* (pp. 5153-5160). IEEE. 10.1109/ICPR48806.2021.9412571

März, L., Schweter, S., Poerner, N., Roth, B., & Schütze, H. (2021, September). Data Centric Domain Adaptation for Historical Text with OCR Errors. In *International Conference on Document Analysis and Recognition* (pp. 748-761). Springer. 10.1007/978-3-030-86331-9_48

Mikolov, T., Chen, K., Corrado, G., & Dean, J. (2013). *Efficient estimation of word representations in vector space.* arXiv preprint arXiv: 1301.3781.

Morris, A. C., Maier, V., & Green, P. (2004). From WER and RIL to MER and WIL: improved evaluation measures for connected speech recognition. *Eighth International Conference on Spoken Language Processing.* 10.21437/Interspeech.2004-668

Ren, S., He, K., Girshick, R., & Sun, J. (2015). Faster r-cnn: Towards real-time object detection with region proposal networks. *Advances in Neural Information Processing Systems*, 28.

Shen, Z., Zhang, K., & Dell, M. (2020). A large dataset of historical japanese documents with complex layouts. In *Proceedings of the IEEE/CVF Conference on Computer Vision and Pattern Recognition Workshops* (pp. 548-549). 10.1109/CVPRW50498.2020.00282

Singh, A., Pang, G., Toh, M., Huang, J., Galuba, W., & Hassner, T. (2021). TextOCR: Towards large-scale end-to-end reasoning for arbitrary-shaped scene text. In *Proceedings of the IEEE/CVF Conference on Computer Vision and Pattern Recognition* (pp. 8802-8812). 10.1109/CVPR46437.2021.00869

Wu, Y., Kirillov, A., Massa, F., Lo, W., & Girshick, R. (2019). *Detectron2*. https://github.com/facebookresearch/detectron2

Yuan, J., Li, H., Wang, M., Liu, R., Li, C., & Wang, B. (2020, August). An OpenCV-based Framework for Table Information Extraction. In *2020 IEEE International Conference on Knowledge Graph (ICKG)* (pp. 621-628). IEEE.

Yuan, X., Martínez, J. F., Eckert, M., & López-Santidrián, L. (2016). An improved Otsu threshold segmentation method for underwater simultaneous localization and mapping-based navigation. *Sensors (Basel)*, *16*(7), 1148. doi:10.339016071148 PMID:27455279

Zeni, M., & Weldemariam, K. (2017). Extracting information from newspaper archives in Africa. *IBM Journal of Research and Development*, *61*(6), 12–1. doi:10.1147/JRD.2017.2742706

Zhong, X., Tang, J., & Yepes, A. J. (2019, September). Publaynet: largest dataset ever for document layout analysis. In *2019 International Conference on Document Analysis and Recognition (ICDAR)* (pp. 1015-1022). IEEE. 10.1109/ICDAR.2019.00166

ADDITIONAL READING

Binmakhashen, G. M., & Mahmoud, S. A. (2019). Document layout analysis: A comprehensive survey. *ACM Computing Surveys*, *52*(6), 1–36. doi:10.1145/3355610

Nasar, Z., Jaffry, S. W., & Malik, M. K. (2018). Information extraction from scientific articles: A survey. *Scientometrics*, *117*(3), 1931–1990. doi:10.100711192-018-2921-5

KEY TERMS AND DEFINITIONS

Layout: It is the name given to the placement and order of the elements in the document.

Ngram (N-Gram): It is the general name given to consecutive arrays consisting of n elements. In the context of NLP and computational linguistics, the elements that make up n-grams can be selected as words, syllables, phonemes or letters in a spoken text or written text. The variable expressed with n represents the value for which the repetition is controlled, while the gram corresponds to the weight of this repeated value in the array.

Optical Character Recognition (OCR): A technology of converting mechanical and handwriting to digital text character by character on scanned images.

Portable Document Format (PDF): A document format developed by Adobe that can preserve the layout of all the elements in it independently of hardware and operating system and can be viewed on any system.

RegEx: The abbreviation of the term "regular expression". It is a string of characters developed in theoretical computer science and formal language theory that allows to create patterns for matching, locating, and managing text.

APPENDIX

Figure 10. Parsed version of a news clip from Gaziantep Güneş newspaper dated 03.12.2018

Figure 11. Parsed version of a news clip from Hürriyet newspaper dated 13.09.2021

Figure 12. Parsed version of a news clip from 2 Eylül newspaper dated 30.11.2018

Yine genç ve yakışıklı

Nabi Avcı, daha önce Büyükşehir adayı için "Genç ve yakışıklı bir adayımız olacak" sözünü hatırlatarak, "Neticede öyle oldu. Tecrübeli, sorun üreten değil, çözüm odaklı çalışan bir aday. Eskişehirliler Burhan Sakallı'yı çok iyi tanıyor" dedi

AK Parti Eskişehir Milletvekili Prof.Dr. Nabi Avcı, ES TV'de katıldığı canlı yayında, ilk olarak Kanal 26'nın canlı yayınında söylediği sözlere gönderme yaparak, "Genç, yakışıklı bir adayımız olacak' demiştim son görüşmemizde. Neticede oldu. Tecrübeli. Sorun üreten değil, çözüm odaklı çalışan bir aday. Eskişehirliler Burhan Sakallı'yı çok iyi tanıyor. AK Parti'nin çok uygun bir adayla seçime girdiğine inanıyorum. Beraber çalışacağı ilçe belediye başkanları da açıklanınca çok güzel çalışacaklarına inanıyorum" dedi.

Nabi Avcı, "Eskişehir'in önümüzdeki dönemde taze ve heyecanlı bir yönetime kavuşacağına inanıyorum. Burhan bey ve ilçe belediye başkanlarımız, genç ve yeni kadrolarla, toplumun her kesimine dokunan, kadınlara büyük temsil imkanı sağlayan, şehrin tüm dinamiklerini de içine alan, onlarla bir-

Büyükşehir kadroları yorgun

NABİ Avcı ayrıca Büyükşehir Belediyesi ile ilgili, "4 seçim kazanarak, aynı zamanda bu kadrolar 4 dönemdir iş başında demektir. Bu da, 20 yıldır Eskişehir'i, Eskişehir Büyükşehir Belediyesi'ni bu kadro yönetiyor. Peki bu 20 yılda Türkiye'de neler değişti? Bu kadar cumhurbaşkanı, başbakan, genel müdür, şehirler değişirken, Eskişehir 20 yıldır aynı kalması... İlk dönem yeni başlama diyelim, ikinci dönem de devam edilebilir, ama 20 yıl kardeşim, yorulur insan... O yorgunluk Eskişehir Büyükşehir Belediyesi kadrolarında görülüyor. Bu kaçınılmaz bir şey. Bu yorgunluk o kadar nüksetmiş ki, geçmişte popülist görülen bir takım uygulamalar üzerinden, seçmene yeni bir

neyecan görüntüsü verilmeye çalışılıyor. Asfalt dökmeler, durak olan yere yine durak koymak... Ama tüm ilçelerimiz bu fırsattan istifade etsinler. Büyükşehir Başkanı can havliyle bir şeyler yapmaya çalışıyor. Ne istiyorlarsa yaptırsınlar. İlçelere açılıyoruz diyorlar ya... İlçelerimiz ne veriliyorsa alsınlar, her ihtiyacı da talep etsinler. Çünkü bu seçim döneminde ne alırlarsa kârdır. Eskişehir'de belediye böyle bir seçim ekonomisine girdi, vatandaş istifade etsin. Mesela 20 senedir bağlanmayan su şimdi bağlanıyor. Olsun, yapsınlar. Ama 31 Mart'tan sonra bunların gerçeği, hesaplı kitaplı uygulamaları başlayacak inşallah" diye konuştu.

Bırakın bunları. Türkiye'nin böyle bir derdi yok. Kimse birbirinin sakalına, eteğine, örtüsüne, askısına karışmıyor. Eskişehir'de hiç karışılmaz. Eskişehirli sevmez böyle şeyleri. Şimdi Burhan Sakallı 10 yıldır belediye başkanlığı yaptı. Tarihi bölgeyi restore etti, kadınlara istihdam olanakları yarattı... Bunları konuş. Belki CHP'de bu söylemlerle gaza getireceğiniz yüzde 3'lük bir kesim vardır. AK Parti'de de olabilir böyle bir yüzde 3. Ama Eskişehirliler onları asimile etmiştir, idare eder. Onların üzerinden bu kavga başlamaz, ayıp" dedi.

ikte çözüm üreten bir yönetim felsefesiyle işe koyulacak" dedi.

ESKİŞEHİRLİLERİN ZEKASINA, TERBİYESİNE HAKARET

kişehir için doğru kriter... Biz belediye başkanı seçe-

ceğiz. Bir komutan, toplumsal hareket lideri filan seçmeyeceğiz. Eskişehir'de vatandaş gündelik hayatındaki sıkıntıları çözecek bir belediye başkanı seçmek istiyor" derken, Büyükerşen'in bazı açıklamalarına atıfta bulunarak, "Eskişehir'in sorunları belli, sen de diyorsun ki

Laik misin, değil misin... Bu cambaza bak hikayesidir. Hakikaten gücüme gidiyor, yakıştıramıyorum. Böyle bir propagandayı, söylemi Eskişehirlilerin zekasına ve birlikte yaşama terbiyesine hakaret gibi görüyorum. Eskişehirliler birbirilerine sen o musun, bu musun demez.

ESKİŞEHİR TÜRKÜLERİ NEZAKETLE ELEŞTİRİR

Nabi Avcı ayrıca, "Eskişehir türküleri adam ağlatmaz. Sitem olur, ama neşelidir. Birbirini iğneler, ama bunu nezaket içinde yapar. Tadında, üslubunda eleştirir" diye konuştu.

Chapter 10
Prediction of Formation Conditions of Gas Hydrates Using Machine Learning and Genetic Programming

Anupama Kumari

🆔 https://orcid.org/0000-0003-2318-6090

Indian Institute of Technology, Roorkee, India

Mukund Madhaw

Independent Researcher, India

Vishnu S. Pendyala

🆔 https://orcid.org/0000-0001-6494-7832

San Jose State University, USA

ABSTRACT

The formation of gas hydrates in the pipelines of oil, gas, chemical, and other industries has been a significant problem for many years because the formation of gas hydrates may block the pipelines. Hence, the knowledge of the phase equilibrium conditions of gas hydrate became necessary for the economic and safe working of oil, gas, chemical industries. Various thermodynamic approaches with various mathematical techniques are available for the prediction of formation conditions of gas hydrates. In this chapter, the authors have discussed the least square support vector machine and artificial neural network models for the prediction of stability conditions of gas hydrates and the use of genetic programming (GP) and genetic algorithm (GA) to develop a generalized correlation for predicting equilibrium conditions of gas hydrates.

DOI: 10.4018/978-1-6684-4045-2.ch010

INTRODUCTION

The oil and gas industry pipelines face various flow assurance difficulties in the subsea networks of pipelines. It includes the treatment of multiple deposits of solids in the subsea flowlines from the fluid streams of hydrocarbon. These flow assurance problems may be caused by gas hydrate formation, slugging, degradation, wax, scales, etc. Out of these problems, the appearance of gas hydrates is of grave concern. A suitable environment with high pressure and low temperature in the marine climate of the oil and gas industry is the primary cause of the gas hydrate formation. Hence, deep-water flow preservation became a severe problem for these industries (Kumari, Khan, Misra, Majumder, & Arora, 2020).

Gas hydrates are solid crystalline materials formed after trapping the guest molecules inside the cage-like structure formed by water molecules. Methane (CH_4), Ethane (C_2H_6), Propane (C_3H_8), Nitrogen (N_2), Carbon Dioxide (CO_2), and Hydrogen Sulphide (H_2S) are the most available guest molecules which can form the gas hydrates (Kumari et al., 2020). These hydrates are abundant in nature. The stability of hydrates crystals is because of the Vander Waals force, which occurs because of no bonding between the water and gas molecules (Kumari, Hasan, Majumder, Arora, & Dixit, 2021). The significant deposits for the formation of in situ gas hydrates are the deep ocean regions and the permafrost zones. About 97% of gas hydrate deposits are in the form of submarine sediments (Ke & Chen, 2019). The gas hydrates are also known as clathrate. The word clathrate comes from the Greek word "Khlatron." The meaning of this Greek word is the shield.

Sir Humphrey Davy discovered the gas hydrates in 1810 (E. D. Sloan, 1998), which remain stable at temperatures higher than 273.15 K. The gas hydrate has become a significant research interest for academics and the business sector by considering many factors. Gas hydrates could become a vast energy source because the amount of energy stored in the gas hydrates is twice the total quantity of all the other forms of energy available on the earth (Chong, Yang, Babu, Linga, & Li, 2016). The gas hydrate can also become a threat to the atmosphere and environment after the accidental dissociation of methane gas from the hydrate deposits (Giustiniani, Tinivella, Jakobsson, & Rebesco, 2013). Some other applications of gas hydrates are the capture and storing of hydrate-based carbon (Cai, Pethica, Debenedetti, & Sundaresan, 2016), seawater desalination (M. S. Khan, Lal, Sabil, & Ahmed, 2019), hydrogen storage (Lee et al., 2011), distribution and storage of natural gas (Gbaruko, Igwe, Gbaruko, & Nwokeoma, 2007), and the advanced form of air conditioning systems (Fournaison, Delahaye, Chatti, & Petitet, 2004).

The formation of natural gas hydrates in the pipelines is a critical and challenging issue because of the reformation of hydrates in the production pipelines because of the higher pressure and lower temperature. The research on gas hydrates requires multiscale analysis because of the thermodynamic and phase equilibrium features of gas hydrates (Englezos, 1993).

FORMATION CONDITION OF GAS HYDRATES

Gas hydrates crystallize at high pressure and low temperature after capturing the methane or other hydrocarbon gases by the lattice structure of water molecules. The gas hydrate formation requires enough concentration of gas. The gas solubility in water and the ionic strength of water are dominant factors in forming gas hydrates (Kvenvolden, 1993). The specific temperature-pressure regime controls the stability of gas hydrates. The significant areas available for the formation of Gas hydrates are mainly continental margins where methane-bearing fluids and sufficient organic carbon are available (Davie, Zatsepina, & Buffett, 2004). The released methane gas in the shallower zones of the earth is encaged inside the cages of the crystal lattice of water molecules at high pressure and lower temperature.

The favorable environments in the permafrost deposits are due to the low temperature and high pressure because of the lower surface and the presence of sediments. These factors prepared desired conditions for the gas hydrate formation in the earth's subsurface. At some depths in the tropical regions, the temperature at the sea bottom decreases substantially from the detected temperature at the sea's surface. The width of the water column creates desired pressure condition for the gas hydrate formation in the subsurface of the earth. There is the requirement of enough accessible methane gas having non-solubility of methane gas in the water in both environments for the gas hydrate formation. The oceans' shallower zones release methane gas because of the biochemical and microbial decay of disposing of organic materials in the bottom sediments. It may also leak because of the discharge of the natural gases from the gas-bearing deposits and shallow oil (Thakur & Rajput, 2010).

Gas hydrates are stable at in situ conditions of desired pressure-temperature values in the subsurface earth. The upper limit of the thickness of the stability zone of the gas hydrates is the seafloor and regions enclosed at the convergence of the geothermal gradient curve, and the lower limit is the equilibrium with pure and seawater. The other parameters on which the stability of gas hydrates depends are the temperature at the sea bottom, the water salinity, composition, and local geology. The accurate estimation of the width of the stability zone of the gas hydrate is difficult because the above parameters show different in situ conditions and cannot be predicted accurately (Thakur & Rajput, 2010). There are two phases (Solid-phase and vapor phase) present in the hydrate, which is in equilibrium thermodynamically. The solid and vapor phase equilibrium arises under specific pressure and temperature conditions for the desired gas. The water is present in vapor form only in natural gas and other liquid hydrocarbons. There are some different phases, such as liquid water, liquid hydrocarbon, and water ice, because of the water content of the natural gas. These additional phases are also in equilibrium with the solid-phase and vapor phases. Figure 1 shows the phase diagram for gas hydrate.

BACKGROUND

Considerable literature is available on measuring the formation condition of gas hydrates. The basic model for predicting equilibrium conditions of gas hydrates is the Vander Waal Platteeuw and Chen-Guo models (Sinehbaghizadeh, Javanmardi, Roosta, & Mohammadi, 2019). However, these models are not sufficiently accurate for the forecast. In addition to these available traditional methods, machine learning models may also be used for predicting equilibrium conditions of gas hydrates. As we describe in the following sections, the machine learning models have the potential to improve prediction accuracy. For instance, Artificial Neural Networks (ANN) and Least-Squares Support Vector Machine (LSSVM) models were recently used to predict hydrate formation conditions with significant success (Xu, Jiao, Zhang, Huffman, & Wang, 2021).

Figure 1. Phase Diagram (Collett, Lewis, & Uchida, 2000)

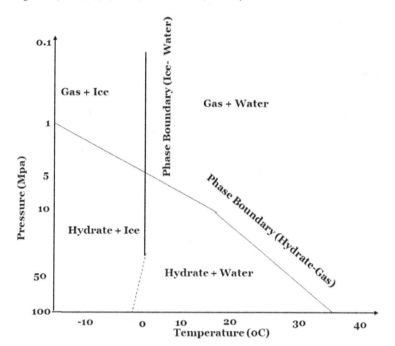

PREDICTING GAS HYDRATES FORMATION CONDITIONS

Natural gas hydrate formation is like a thermodynamical operation that connects temperature, pressure, and gas composition. Thermodynamic rules can predict the pressure or temperature for hydrate formation. The temperature and pressure are the main parameters for analyzing hydrate stability conditions. Hydrate will form at low pressure if the quantity of heavy components in natural gas is enhanced. Many datasets are available in the literature for gas hydrates' formation conditions, which can help predict the formation conditions of gas hydrates through Genetic Programming (E. Dendy Sloan & Koh, 1998).

Genetic programming can develop different nonlinear correlation models using pressure-temperature data, forming the gas hydrates. Each data set includes two groups randomly: training and test sets. The training data set is used to produce the prediction model, and the test set checks the prediction efficiency of the developed model. This tool performs the multi-gene symbolic regression analysis by generating the central equation and then crossing over the best equation and producing the best equation to estimate the formation conditions of gas hydrates. The formation temperature, pressure data, and molecular weight are the inputs for the genetic programming, and then the subset correlation can be obtained with the excellent value of evaluation parameters (Abooali & Khamehchi, 2017).

Other than conventional thermodynamic models, various statistical and mathematical algorithms are available to predict the hydrate stability conditions. Genetic programming (Abooali & Khamehchi, 2017), Artificial Neural Networks (ANN), and generalized regression neural networks are well-known tools (Zahedi, Karami, & Yaghoobi, 2009) for estimating hydrate formation conditions. But genetic programming is one of the most effective methods for predicting and optimizing processes with sound capability. Genetic programming can easily predict the formation conditions of gas hydrates without any nested terms. The nested terms can give complicated background calculations and intensive calculations (S. H. Khan, Kumari, Chandrajit, & Amit, 2020).

DATASET AND PRE-PROCESSING

Abundant research literature is available on predicting gas hydrates' formation conditions by genetic programming. Abooali and Khamehchi developed three new data-based models for predicting the formation temperature of natural gas hydrate as a function of equilibrium pressure and molecular weight of gas using genetic programming with an acceptable error percentage (Abooali & Khamehchi, 2017). Khan et al. 2020 developed a new correlation by genetic programming to predict the formation pressure of hydrates with a reasonable error percentage (S. H. Khan et al., 2020). Cao et al. 2020 combined the genetic algorithm and support vector machine to develop a new model for estimating gas hydrate formation conditions with a slight average relative deviation (Cao, Zhu, Li, & Han, 2020).

The genetic algorithm's first step for predicting the stability conditions of gas hydrates is guessing the random correlation or function of pressure, temperature, and specific gravity of gas and the initial values of constants. The fitness of the process depends upon the calculated value of the selected function for each constant. A more suitable value of constants with the low values of the fitness function is determined and then allowed to perform the next step. The columns selected for the dataset are pressure, temperature, and specific gravity or molecular weight of gases. In machine learning, dimensionality is the number of features of the data set. Feature selection helps remove irrelevant dimensions from the selected data sets. Dimensionality reduction slashes the number of random variables or attributes down while preserving the significant characteristics of the data. In a genetic algorithm, dimensionality reduction is achieved by the mutation and crossover of the datasets. The normalization technique calculates the optimum values of the constants for the manipulation of data. Data manipulation is performed by increasing or decreasing the range of data before it goes to the next step.

The best method for predicting phase equilibria conditions of gas hydrates is by experimentation. The experimental observation of gas hydrates' pressure and temperature conditions for various gas compositions is not usually feasible. Hence, the calculation of equilibrium conditions of gas hydrates by using correlation techniques is needed.

Two experimental techniques are available to study the phase equilibria of gas hydrates. The first is a dynamic method, where a given gas is injected inside a chamber continuously at favorable gas hydrate formation conditions, usually at low temperatures. The formation of gas hydrates stops the continuous flow of gas from the enclosure at the desired pressures to equilibrate the system to form gas hydrates. After the formation of gas hydrates, the pressure or temperature of the system can be decreased or increased, respectively (Kumari, Madhaw, Majumder, & Arora, 2021). The second is a static method, which shows the growth of gas hydrate crystals in an autoclave or stationary high-pressure vessel. In this method, the study uses the controlled temperature and pressure of the cell. This method applies to studying the phase equilibria of gas hydrates because of the ease of measuring intensive properties (Kumari, Madhaw, Majumder, & Arora, 2021).

This chapter discusses the applicability of LSSVM, ANN, and genetic programming as essential mathematical tools for predicting hydrate formation conditions. These tools are particularly helpful from a big data point of view when the dataset has wide ranges of pressure, temperature, and molecular weight of gases. GA, ANN, and LSSVM have been used to model the relationship between the growth rate of methane hydrate, pressure, and temperature.

ARTIFICIAL NEURAL NETWORKS FOR GAS HYDRATES PREDICTION

Artificial neural networks (ANNs) use various computational units called neurons parallelly connected in an enormous structure. They do not require an explicit conceptualization of the physical or mathematical relationships. These neural networks are established to be universal functional approximators, that is, they can compute any function f(x) approximately, where x represents the inputs. The neural networks are used as a computational algorithm to learn, organize, generalize, and cluster data (Blackwell & Chen, 2009). The frequently used neural networks are the feed-forward neural networks (FNN) which contain one input and output layer and a number of hidden layers in between (Schmitz, Zemp, & Mendes, 2006). The FNNs are flexible, simple, and easy to use, and these networks can execute differentiable and continuous mathematical functions, which can minimize the error analysis (Zahedi et al., 2009). The ideal number of neurons in the hidden layer is a hyperparameter of the FNNs that needs to be determined. Few neurons generate a network with low accuracy, and a higher number can lead to overfitting and then a poor standard of extrapolation and interpolation. Methods such as Bayesian regularization with a Levenberg-Marquardt algorithm apply with the FNNs to overcome the disadvantage (Marquardt, 1963).

The neural network's input layer accepts normalized input data and forwards it to the hidden layers of the network. The network processes these data from the input layer with the help of weighted interconnections between the neurons in the layers. In a fully connected network, every i^{th} neuron in a kth layer can be attached to every neuron in the adjoining layers. The ith neuron in the kth hidden layer executes the summation of all weighted inputs and propagates the result, typically through a nonlinear activation function f. This process is expressed as equation (1). The propagations continue in this fashion on the adjoining neurons of the next hidden layer and eventually, the output neurons. Like in any machine learning task, the data sets are subdivided into training, validation, and test data sets. The training data set is used to determine the network's parameters. The validation data set is used to fine-tune the model's performance. After the model gets trained, the test data is used to evaluate the performance of the trained model. All the biases and synaptic weights are initialized randomly. During the process of training the network, an optimization algorithm adjusts the synaptic weights until the error in the predicted output is minimized (Chapoy, Mohammadi, & Richon, 2007).

$$O_j = f(\sum w_{ji} x_i + b_j) \tag{1}$$

where w_{ji} is the weight, x_i is the input value, b_j is the threshold value, and f is the activation function.

The output from one neuron becomes the input to the neuron in the next layer. This simple arrangement of the interconnected neurons arranged in layers is powerful enough to approximate any mathematical function of the inputs. The layers of neurons and their interconnections using linear and non-linear transformations can convert the input data to any desired output. For instance, input pixel values of images can be converted to probabilities of the image being that of a lion or a tiger. For this, the weights of the interconnections obviously need to change to suit the desired output. The weights of the neural network are adjusted by an optimization algorithm, for example, stochastic gradient descent using backpropagation, in order to minimize the error between the generated and actual values of the target. A common function to compute the error often used in machine learning regression problems when the output values are continuous is the mean square error, which is the average value of the squared difference between the network's output and the true output in the training dataset.

$$Error = \frac{1}{N}\sum_{i=1}^{N}(P_i - C_i)^2 \tag{2}$$

In the above equation, N is the number of training data, P_i and C_i are the targeted and calculated output, respectively (Ghavipour, Ghavipour, Chitsazan, Najibi, & Ghidary, 2013). Figure 2 shows a schematic of a three-layered neural network.

Figure 2. A three-layered neural network (Kumari, Madhaw, Majumder, & Arora, 2021)

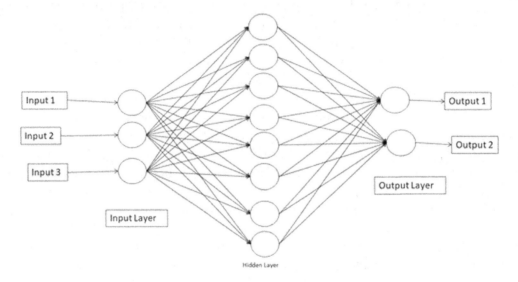

Elgibaly and Elkamel 1998 calculated the formation pressure of the gas hydrate with an average error of 19%. They also evaluated the amount of thermodynamic inhibitors required in a different system (Elgibaly & Elkamel, 1998). Chapoy et al. 2007 used ANN to predict formation conditions of natural gas hydrate in the absence and presence of inhibitors (Chapoy et al., 2007). Moradi et al. 2013 fitted an ANN model to the experimental data of the gas hydrates of binary hydrocarbon mixtures (Moradi, Nazari, Alavi, & Mohaddesi, 2013). Mohammadi and Richon 2010 and Mohammadi, Belandria, and Richon developed ANN models to predict hydrogen and methane hydrate formation conditions in the presence of the promoters (tert-butylamine and tetrahydrofuran). The results of the ANN model are not well fitted with the results of the thermodynamic models (Mohammadi, Belandria, et al., 2010; Mohammadi & Richon, 2009).

Babakhani et al. 2015 observed a relative error of 1.02% after evaluating an ANN model (Babakhani, Bahmani, Shariati, Badr, & Balouchi, 2015). Mohammadi et al. 2010 calculated the formation conditions of tetrahydrofuran and methane, nitrogen or carbon dioxide hydrate, hydrogen, and tetra-n-butyl ammonium bromide hydrate. The developed ANN model evaluates the acid gas systems and obtained satisfactory results (Babakhani et al., 2015; Ghavipour et al., 2013; Mohammadi, Martínez-López, & Richon, 2010; ZareNezhad & Aminian, 2012). Rebai et al. 2019 developed an ANN model to calculate the thermodynamic properties depending on the formation of gas hydrates for more mixtures. The developed model also evaluated some thermodynamic properties of gas hydrates, such as viscosity (Rai, Majumdar, DasGupta, & De, 2005; Rebai, Hadjadj, Benmounah, Berrouk, & Boualleg, 2019), density, compressibility factor (Bouchard & Granjean, 1995), vapor pressure (Laugier & Richon, 2003), heat transfer coefficient (Potukuchi & Wexler, 1997) and vapor-liquid equilibrium (Ganguly, 2003; Petersen, Fredenslund, & Rasmussen, 1994; Sablani, Baik, & Marcotte, 2002; Sharma, Singhal, Ghosh, & Dwivedi, 1999).

Heydari et al. 2006 and Zahedi et al. 2009 trained an ANN model to calculate the hydrate formation temperature (Heydari, Shayesteh, & Kamalzadeh, 2006) (Zahedi et al., 2009). Mehrizadeh used ANNs to predict the formation conditions of gas hydrate in the presence of thermodynamic inhibitors (Mehrizadeh, 2020). Soroush et al. 2015 used the ANN model to predict the formation temperature of the natural gas hydrate. They observed a total mean square error of 0.349 only (Soroush et al., 2015). Mesbah et al. 2017 developed a supervised learning algorithm, namely, MLP ANN, to predict the dissociation pressure of the semi-clathrate hydrate for carbon dioxide and its binary mixtures. They observed the AARD% of 3.13 and overall R^2 as 0.9961(Mesbah, Soroush, & Roham, 2017).

Several datasets for the stability conditions of gas hydrates were used to develop an ANN. The main parameters for applying ANN to determine stability conditions of gas hydrates are temperature, pressure, and the specific gravity of the gas. The training and testing set apply to the experimental data points of gas hydrates. The input layer of the ANN takes features like the pressure and specific gravity of gases. The number of hidden layers is a hyperparameter and depends on the data set. If the input parameters for developing an artificial neural network are pressure and specific gravity of gases, and then the temperature will be the output parameter. The hyperparameters of an artificial neural network are the variables that determine the topology of the neural network and the variables that determine the neural network's training step. The number of hidden units is a hyperparameter too, and these hyperparameters are set before the training step and before optimizing weights and bias terms. The hidden layers are the layers between the input and output layers, and the optimum number of hidden layers depends upon the minimum error value.

The following steps are involved in setting up an ANN model for prediction.

1. Input data comprising temperature and specific gravity of gases is selected based on the experiments. This is the ground truth from which the training, validation, and test datasets are obtained.
2. The target variable is pressure.
3. The input data become the input for the neural network, and the target variable becomes the target for the output of the ANN.
4. The topology of the neural network model depends on the number of layers and the number of neurons in each layer. These "hyperparameters" are chosen accordingly.
5. Levenberg-Marquardt Backpropagation is commonly used for training the network.
6. The predicted outputs from ANN are compared with the expected predictions from the training data and loss calculated.
7. The training process progresses in iterations until the loss computed based on the training data is minimized and the network parameters are determined.
8. The selected parameters apply to the neural network for the dataset's training, testing, and validation.

9.   The above procedure repeats for multiple configurations to determine the best hyperparameters.

THE LEAST-SQUARES SUPPORT VECTOR MACHINE

Vapnik's support vector machine (SVM) builds upon the statistical learning theory (V. N. Vapnik, 1999). SVM is a supervised machine learning method, and LSSVM is the reformulation of SVM. LSSVM uses the least-squares objective function, thereby circumventing quadratic programming (Yarveicy & Ghiasi, 2017a). SVM is a skilful learning method adopted for regression analysis and classification in machine learning. Still, the main drawback of the SVM method is its complexity in the computational procedure (V. Vapnik, 1999). This mathematical tool can solve several complex problems, from the nonlinear function approximation to pattern classification. This algorithm obtains an optimum hyperplane with the minimum distance from the actual data by projecting the input features to a higher dimension in case the data is not linearly separable (Soroush, Mesbah, Shokrollahi, Bahadori, & Ghazanfari, 2014). In this method, the chances for overfitting are less, and there is no need for multiple adjustable parameters (Cortes & Vapnik, 1995). LSSVM is generally preferred over SVM for scalability reasons.

The solution of quadrating encoding equations increases the complications in the optimization procedure. The LSSVM reduces the complexity of SVM and then enhances the speed. Then LSSVM model performs the linear calculations by linear encoding. The network results after resolving given fixed linear equalities in the LSSVM algorithm (Suykens and Vandewalle, 1999). The LSSVM can operate on large data sets with acceptable accuracy by changing the inequality constraints with the equality constraints (Pelckmans et al., 2002). The regression error adapts as an additional constraint in the LSSVM algorithm. This error calculates by the difference between the predicted and experimental data (Pelckmans et al., 2002).

Suppose a data set with the given equation (3) in which x and y are the input data points. (For the gas hydrates, x and y should be temperature and specific gravity of gases.)

$$D = \{(x_1, y_1) \ldots (x_k, y_k) \ldots (x_N, y_N), x_k \in R^n, y_k \in R\} \tag{3}$$

Equation (3) is generalized by the following equation of nonlinear function (4)

$$f(x) = wg(x) + b \tag{4}$$

Equation $w \in R^{nh}$ is the weight vector in the initial weight space, b is the bias term, $g(\circ): R^n \rightarrow R^{nh}$ is the nonlinear mapping, and n_h is the space dimension. This optimization problem is given by

$$\min J(w, e) = \frac{1}{2} w^T w + \frac{1}{2} \mu \sum_{k=1}^{n} e_k^2 \tag{5}$$

μ is the relative weight of the summation of the errors calculated during regression after comparing the weight of the regression.

The above equation (5) gives the constraints of equation (6)

$$y_k = (w^T g(x)) + b + e_k, \quad k=1,2,...,n \tag{6}$$

In equation (6), e_k is the error, w^T is the weight matrix transpose, and $\mu \geq 0$ is the regularization constant. After solving (equation (6)) in the (equation (5))

$$L_{LSSVM} = \frac{1}{2} w^T w + \frac{1}{2} \mu \sum_{k=1}^{n} e_k^2 - \sum_{k=1}^{n} \beta_k \left\{ \left(w^T g(x) \right) + b + e_k - y_k \right\} \tag{7}$$

The Lagrangian multipliers $\beta_k \in R$. The conditions needed for the optimization are given in equation (8) to equation (11).

$$\frac{\partial L_{LSSVM}}{\partial b} = 0 \rightarrow \sum_{K=1}^{n} \beta_k = 0 \tag{8}$$

$$\frac{\partial L_{LSSVM}}{\partial w} = 0 \rightarrow w = \sum_{K=1}^{n} \beta_k g(x_k) \tag{9}$$

$$\frac{\partial L_{LSSVM}}{\partial \beta_k} = 0 \rightarrow \left(w^T g(x) \right) + b + e_k - y_k = 0 \dots\dots, \left(k = 1, \dots\dots.n \right) \tag{10}$$

$$\frac{\partial L_{LSSVM}}{\partial e_k} = 0 \rightarrow \beta_k = \mu e_k, \quad \left(k = 1, \dots\dots n \right) \tag{11}$$

Equation (12) will obtain after assuming a linear regression relationship for the independent and dependent variables.

$$y = \sum_{K=1}^{n} \beta_k x_k^T x + b \tag{12}$$

We use a kernel function for the dot product in equation (12) to enhance the applicability.

$$y = \sum_{K=1}^{n} \beta_k K(x_k, x) + b \tag{13}$$

The Kernel function of $K(x_i,x)$ is the dot product of vectors $g(x_i)$ and $g(x)$ in the higher dimensional space (equation (14))

$$K(x,x_k) = g(x)g(x_k)^T \tag{14}$$

The RBF kernel given in equation (15) and the polynomial kernel given in equation (16) are popularly used in the LSSVM model.

$$K(x,x_k) = \exp(x_k - x^2 / \sigma^2)$$ (15)

$$K(x,x_k) = (1 + x^T x_k / c)^d$$ (16)

The σ^2 is the squared width. It is a hyperparameter. In the polynomial kernel, d is the degree, which is also a hyperparameter.

Figure 3 shows the steps involved in developing the LSSVM model to predict the stability conditions of gas hydrates. The algorithm starts with the empty feature set, and then after each iteration, this adds the feature. The regularization (μ) and the kernel (σ^2) parameters should specify before the training step.

Figure 3. Schematic diagram of the LSSVM model (Kumari, Madhaw, Majumder, Arora, & Dixit, 2021)

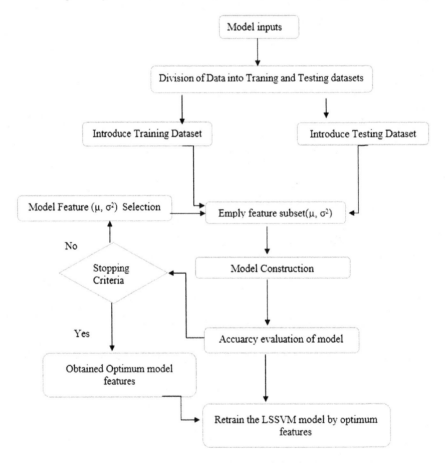

Mesbah et al. 2017 used the LSSVM model based on the gas hydrate structure and provided an effective algorithm with a squared correlation coefficient of 0.9918 (Mesbah, Soroush, & Rezakazemi, 2017). Baghban et al. 2016 applied the LSSVM model to the Katz Chart data points and predicted the formation temperature of gas hydrates with a squared correlation coefficient of 0.9973 and minimum square error of 0.778634 (Baghban et al., 2016). Yarveicy and Ghiasi 2017 utilized a model that uses extremely randomized trees to predict the formation conditions of gas hydrate of different gases formed in pure water, salts, and alcohols. This model provides a squared correlation coefficient of greater than 96 and a percentage absolute relative deviation (%ARD) between 0.04 and 0.32 (Yarveicy & Ghiasi, 2017b). Mohammadi et al. applied the LSSVM model to estimate phase equilibria for the CO_2, CH_4 or C_2H_6 hydrate in porous media (Mohammadi et al., 2012).

GENETIC ALGORITHM

The Genetic Algorithm (GA) was developed in 1975 by John Holland, supported by the concept of the artificial system (Holland, 1992). This algorithm is appropriate for searching and optimization problems. GA performs various operations, and every procedure carries multiple techniques, which give different results due to the diverse nature of methods (Abbasi & Hashim, 2016). An off-shoot of GA called Genetic programming (GP) is a robust methodology whose programming procedure depends upon biological generation systems. It is an efficient technique applied in different optimization and mathematical problems. Genetic Programming (GP) is a popular technique to determine correlations in modeling projects. Genetic Programming (GP) solves a problem by generating a population randomly using mathematical equations like genes. These genes are chromosome-like structures of syntactic trees from the input data. GP develops several genes usually instead of one to enhance the accuracy of the prediction. A developed multi-gene network contains one or more genes and this provides more specific functions frequently than the additional developed models with one monolithic GP tree. Figure 4 shows an example of a simple tree structure.

Figure 4. An Example of the Tree structure for Genetic Programming (S. H. Khan et al., 2020)

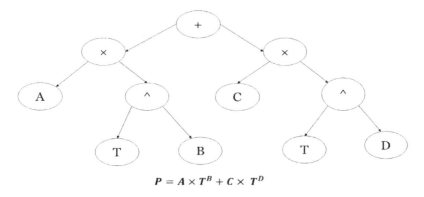

$$P = A \times T^B + C \times T^D$$

The genetic algorithm endeavors to obtain the optimal solution to a given problem. The algorithm is quite widely used in economics, bioinformatics, and data sciences. Genetic Algorithms employ ideas from the theory of human genetics. These algorithms provide a heuristic approach to solving complex problems, and these can also be used to optimize the results. The Genetic Algorithm depends upon Initialization, Selection, Crossover, Mutation, and Termination (Figure 5).

Figure 5. Steps involved in Genetic Algorithm

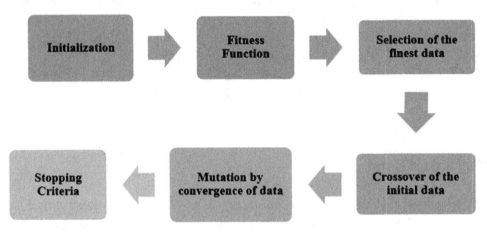

Initial Population

The algorithm starts with initializing data sets (population), and each data is a solution to the given problem. A group of parameters or variables characterizes each piece of information.

Fitness Function

A fitness function uses to check the fitness of data. This fitness function identifies the ability of a data to compete with the other data. The probability of data identification for reproduction depends on its fitness value.

Selection

The fittest data sets are selected and then sent for the following data generation in the selection step. Data with a high fitness value have more chances to be chosen for reproduction. Two pairs of data are selected based on their fitness value for the next step.

Crossover

The most significant step in the genetic algorithm is crossover. A crossover point is selected randomly for each data set to be mated.

Mutation

Some data sets send for the mutation with a low random probability. The mutation maintains diversity within the data sets and avoids premature convergence of data.

Termination

The genetic algorithm stops when the data converge and then provides solutions for the given problem.

Hence, a genetic algorithm is an optimization technique applied to find input data sets to obtain the best output. Figure 6 shows a schematic representation of all steps involved in the genetic algorithm.

Figure 6. Representation of steps for Genetic Algorithm

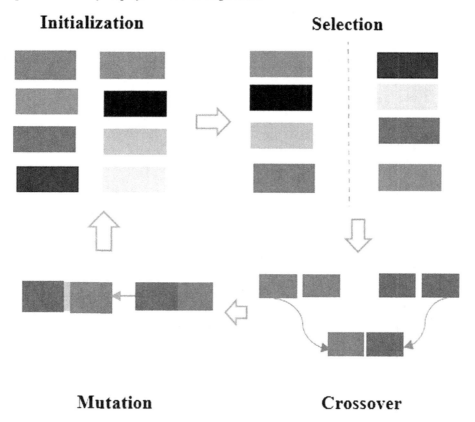

GP technique is a symbolic regression method. The algorithm itself explores the model and fits the constants afterward. In ordinary regressions, the structure of the model must be stated by the user and subsequently fitted to the model constants. The inclusive status of the primary model is attained by the weighted summation of every available function after the generation of the first population randomly. The genes with a biased term constitute these functions: the bias and weight terms obtained by the standard least square method. The first accepted population may not provide a good prediction; the structure often requires updating, and the unusable functions change with others. Hence, the algorithm goes through the best executing trees and then improves the network to obtain a new population. New structures create the genes in the new population and repeat the summation of the weights of all newly developed genes. Then the new bias and weight term are predicted. The regeneration process performs repeatedly, and then the mathematical functions are also iterated to obtain new populations. This iteration will stop after solving the problem successfully (Jain, 2017). Figure 7 shows the overall flowchart of GP.

Figure 7. Overall Flowchart for Genetic Programming

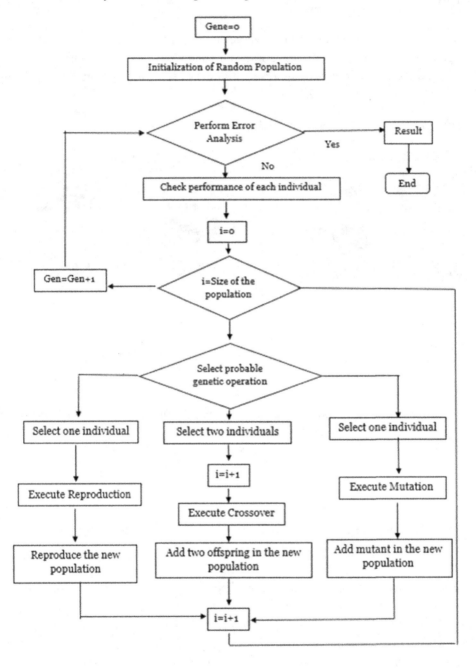

Searson developed a free, open-source tool to perform genetic programming in MATLAB software. This tool creates the nonlinear correlation to determine the temperature for the hydrate formation. A toolbox "GPTIPS" develops for multi-gene symbolic regression problems. All the required steps of GP perform to obtain the best correlation. For each subset, input data, including experimental sets of hydrate formation Pressure, temperature, and Molecular weight, were provided to the GP program. Correlation for this subset acquires the desired accuracy.

Abooali and Khamehchi 2019 applied three new data-based models using genetic programming to predict the formation temperature of natural gas hydrates as a function of the molecular weight of gas and equilibrium pressure of gas hydrates. They observed the correlation coefficient value as 09673 for the 891 experimental data items. Abbasi and Hashim 2015 developed a model using genetic programming to predict the formation conditions of gas hydrates in subsea pipelines in the presence and absence of inhibitors (Abbasi & Hashim, 2015). Khan et al. 2020 developed a correlation for predicting the formation pressure of gas hydrates with the RMSE value of 0.68 (S. H. Khan et al., 2020).

EVALUATION CRITERIA

The perfection of the newly obtained model obtain by some familiar statistical measures like average absolute relative deviation percent (AARD%), squared correlation coefficient (R^2) (Cao et al., 2020), root means square deviation (RMSD) (Abooali & Khamehchi, 2017) and absolute average deviation (AAD%) (Seif & Kamran-pirzaman, 2020). The Low values of AARD% and RMSD and high value of R^2 prefers for evaluating the model.

$$\text{AARD}(\%) = \frac{100}{N} \sum_{i=1}^{N} \left| \frac{Experimental - Predicted}{Experimental} \right| \tag{17}$$

$$\text{RMSD} = \sqrt{\frac{\sum_{i=1}^{N} |Experimental - Predicted|^2}{N}} \tag{18}$$

$$R^2 = 1 - \frac{\sum_{i=1}^{N} |Experimental - Predicted|^2}{\sum_{i=1}^{N} |Experimental - Predicted|} \tag{19}$$

$$\text{AAD} = \frac{1}{N} \sum_{i=1}^{N} \left| \frac{Experimental - Predicted}{Experimental} \right| \tag{20}$$

N indicates the number of all data points (Kumari et al., 2020).

APPLICATION OF GENETIC PROGRAMMING FOR GAS HYDRATES

Another technique for predicting the stability condition of gas hydrates uses a correlation model developed through genetic programming. GP randomly generates a population of different programs shown by trees. Each tree set generates a new population using mutation, crossing over with the best-performing trees to obtain a new data set (Koza, 1994). To determine the equilibrium condition of gas hydrates by GP, pressure or temperature and specific gravity or molecular weight of gas are the input variables, and temperature or pressure are output variables. Several steps perform to obtain a correlation, such as the primary population of the program, fitness evaluation of each program, development of the following population by mutation, crossover, and reproduction. These steps repeat many times until the termination criteria are met. The following are the important steps to achieving the GP.

1. Generate the initial population randomly from a predefined set of functions as f= (-, /, sin, cos etc) and termination function, t= (T, constant).
2. Set the size of the initial population.
3. Evaluate the programs by ramped half and half methods with some depth value. It creates disturbed and small trees.
4. Perform the error analysis of each program using the error evaluation criteria.
5. Perform the reproduction of the next generation in a probabilistic manner.
6. Perform the crossover events using the standard GP crossover method by randomly choosing a node as the crossover point.
7. Perform the mutation by applying the standard GP mutation by randomly selecting a particular program's mutation point and constant probability distribution.
8. Remove and replace another tree from the mutation point.
9. Repeat 3 to 8 steps until the termination criteria are satisfied.

Several correlations develop for the stability conditions of gas hydrates using genetic programming (Table 1). These correlations obtain by performing the genetic algorithm on the data sets.

Various researchers applied the Genetic Algorithm with the Artificial Neural Network and LSSVM model to find a new correlation for predicting stability conditions of gas hydrates. The combination of Genetic Algorithms can enhance the capability of ANN and LSSVM models. Various points consider during the development of GA-ANN and GA-SVM models, such as diversity in data points, selection of variables, and optimizing parameters. Modeling gas hydrate formation conditions can be improved by considering the operational requirements and various optimization algorithms. This adaption can give the method better accuracy than the available methods.

DISCUSSION

The above-discussed algorithms have some advantages and disadvantages for determining the stability conditions of gas hydrates. The LSSVM is considered the most powerful and reliable algorithm. The following points are some benefits of LSSVM over ANN.

1. The LSSVM model has better chances of convergence to the optimum value.
2. LSSVM is a standard algorithm that obtains a relatively quick estimation of the solution.
3. There is no requirement to know the network topology in advance like for ANN.
4. LSSVM is less prone to overfitting.
5. There is no requirement to select the number of hidden nodes.
6. LSSVM has acceptable generalization performance.
7. LSSVM has a smaller number of adjustable hyperparameters.
8. The LSSVM model follows convex optimization procedures. (Mohammadi et al., 2012)

Table 1. Available correlations developed with the genetic algorithm for the prediction of the stability condition of gas hydrates

S.No.	Correlation		References
1	1. $16.04 \leq M_w \leq 28.966$ (Except methane and propane) $$T = 10.38\ln\left((P+6.711388)\,M_w\right) + 3.507\ln\left|M_w - 2\ln\left(M_w\right) - 12.01\right|$$ $$-34.11\ln\left|\ln\left(M_w - 13.45\right)\right| + 0.7009\ln\left|M_w - \ln\left(M_w\right) - 13.932642\right| \quad (21)$$ $$+10.58\ln\left|M_w - \ln\left(M_w^2 + 3.664M_w\right) - 12.01\right| - 35.34$$ 2. $28.966 \leq M_w \leq 58.1203$ (Except methane and propane) $$T = 691.6\ln\left(P + \ln\left(P^2 + 2P\right)\right) + 0.0003531(P^2 - \ln \mid M_w$$ $$-P - \ln\left(P + M_w\right)\mid) - 0.08179 P\ln\left(P\right) + 258\ln \mid M_w^2 - 3M_w \quad (22)$$ $$+ P\left|-645.6\ln\left(P\left(M_w + 2\right) + \ln\left|M_w - P\right|\right) + 7.063M_w\ln\left|\ln\right|\ln\left(2P\right)\right| \mid + 170.5$$ 3. For methane and propane $$T = 3405\ln \mid \ln(M_w + \ln\left|P - 8.948\right|)$$ $$\left|-800.6\ln\left(\left(M_w + \ln\left(P + 4.637\right)\right) \times \ln\left(M_w - 9.399\right)\right) + 126.6\ln\right| \quad (23)$$ $$11.65143 + \ln\left(M_w\right) - M_w \mid -878.5$$ The temperature is in ^{0}F, and the pressure is in psia. The molecular weight (Mw) ranges obtain by performing the genetic algorithm. These data depend on the minimum value of error obtained from each set. In these equations, the ⏐ represents the absolute operator.		(Abooali & Khamehchi, 2017)
2	For γ ranges from 0.656 to 0.787, and a pressure range from 0.58 to 8.68 MPa $$\frac{1000}{T} = 4.343295 + 1.0734 \times 10^{-3} \times P - 9.1984 \times 10^{-2} \times \ln\left(P\right) - 1.071989 \times \gamma_g \quad (24)$$ The temperature in K and Pressure in MPa.		(Sun, Chen, Lin, & Guo, 2003)
3	$$T_K = 242 \times \gamma_g^{\,0.2} \times P_{kPa}^{0.021} \quad (25)$$ The temperature in K and Pressure in kPa.		(Chavoshi, Safamirzaei, & Pajoum Shariati, 2018)
4	$$T_{0_F} = -20.928 + 13.623\left(lnP_{psia}\right) + 29.67\left(ln\gamma_g\right) - 0.006\left(P_{psia}\right)\left(\gamma_g\right)^2 + 4.14$$ $$\times 10^{-6}(P_{psia}^{\,2}\left(\gamma_g\right)^3 + 0.979\left(lnP_{psia}\right)\left(ln\gamma_g\right) + 0.19\left(P_{psia}\right)\left(\gamma_g\right) + 1.25$$ $$\times 10^{-20}(P_{psia}^{\,6}\left(\gamma_g\right)^8 + 0.001(lnP_{psia})^5 + 281.743\left(\gamma_g\right)^7 + 1.25 \quad (26)$$ $$\times 10^{-27}(P_{psia}^{\,8}\left(\gamma_g\right)^8 + 7.24 \times 10^{-28}(P_{psia}^{\,8}\left(\gamma_g\right)^7 + 0.002(lnP_{psia})^6\left(ln\gamma_g\right)^8$$ $$+1.84 \times 10^{-5}(lnP_{psia})^7\left(ln\gamma_g\right)^4 + 0.792\left(lnP_{psia}\right)\left(ln\gamma_g\right)^3$$ The temperature in ^{0}F, and the pressure in psia.		(Khamehchi, Shamohammadi, & Yousefi, 2013)

continues on following page

Table 1. Continued

S.No.	Correlation		References
5	$P = 83904.22 \times T^{1.788} + 23529.51 \times T^{2.136} - 59133.632$ $\times T^{2.0435} + 2.0435 \times e^{\frac{-1218.998}{T}} - 74357563.76 \times e^{\frac{-1331.419}{T^{(1-2)^*}}}$ The temperature in K and Pressure in MPa.	(27)	(S. H. Khan et al., 2020)

Where
M_w – Molecular weight of the gas
T- Temperature
P- Pressure
γg *Specific Gravity of Gas*

The genetic algorithm can be developed alone or in combination with LSSVM and ANN for better performance of the models. The genetic algorithm can be used as an optimization process to minimize the error obtained in applying the LSSVM and ANN model.

EXPERIMENTAL DATA

The experimental data points for predicting the phase equilibrium of gas hydrate used for the modeling are from the Katz chart (D. L. Katz, 1945; D. L. V. Katz, 1959) and Sloan (E. Dendy Sloan & Koh, 1998). The temperature and pressure range for the modeling was 273.7 K to 303.1 K and 0.6 MPa to 62.85 MPa, respectively, and the range of gravities of gas was between 0.57 to 0.86.

The radial basis function (RBF) was applied as the kernel function to develop the LSSVM model. The results of the LSSVM model are further optimized by the added genetic algorithm in the LSSVM model.

The following table 2 shows the error obtained in developing LSSVM, ANN, and GA algorithms to predict stability conditions of methane gas hydrates. Several data points are used from the literature to see the applicability of these algorithms. The error obtained after applying the LSSVM model is minimal compared to the ANN and Genetic Algorithm.

Table 2. AAD (%) obtained by different methods

	(Abooali & Khamehchi, 2017)	(Sun et al., 2003)	(Chavoshi et al., 2018)	(Khamehchi et al., 2013)	(S. H. Khan et al., 2020)	ANN	LSSVM
AAD (%)	0.9439	0.9813	0.8791	0.9609	0.32	0.9782	0.2134

CONCLUSION

This chapter discussed different models for predicting formation conditions of natural gas hydrates dependent upon the pressure and molecular weight of the gas. A compelling new model created by genetic programming seems to be one of the most effective mathematical-statistical methods for this problem domain. The wide ranges of pressure, temperature, and molecular weight can increase the prediction ability of the developed models. Applying genetic programming to estimate phase equilibrium conditions can help design an economical technology for the dissociation of gas hydrates. Exploring gas from gas hydrates can fulfill the world's energy requirement for many centuries. This technique applies to the gas hydrate system containing salts, inhibitors, and promoters. There is scope for expansion of the application of genetic programming for the gas hydrate system with inhibitors, promoters, and many more. The solutions discussed in this chapter can help alleviate the problem of hydrate formation in pipelines of oil and gas industries.

REFERENCES

Abbasi, A., & Hashim, F. M. (2015). Prediction of hydrate formation conditions in the subsea pipeline with genetic algorithm. *Proceedings of the 2015 International Conference on Technology, Informatics, Management, Engineering and Environment, TIME-E 2015*, 133–136. 10.1109/TIME-E.2015.7389761

Abbasi, A., & Hashim, F. M. (2016). Prediction of hydrate formation conditions in subsea pipeline with genetic algorithm. *Proceedings of the 2015 International Conference on Technology, Informatics, Management, Engineering and Environment, TIME-E 2015*, 133–136.

Abooali, D., & Khamehchi, E. (2017). New predictive method for estimation of natural gas hydrate formation temperature using genetic programming. *Neural Computing & Applications*, 1–10.

Babakhani, S. M., Bahmani, M., Shariati, J., Badr, K., & Balouchi, Y. (2015). Comparing the capability of artificial neural network (ANN) and CSMHYD program for predicting of hydrate formation pressure in binary mixtures. *Journal of Petroleum Science Engineering*, *136*, 78–87. doi:10.1016/j.petrol.2015.11.002

Baghban, A., Namvarrechi, S., Phung, L. T. K., Lee, M., Bahadori, A., & Kashiwao, T. (2016). Phase equilibrium modelling of natural gas hydrate formation conditions using LSSVM approach. *Petroleum Science and Technology*, *34*(16), 1431–1438. doi:10.1080/10916466.2016.1202966

Blackwell, W. J., & Chen, F. W. (2009). *Neural networks in atmospheric remote sensing*. Artech House.

Bouchard, C., & Granjean, B. P. A. (1995). A neural network correlation for the variation of viscosity of sucrose aqueous solutions with temperature and concentration. *Lebensmittel-Wissenschaft + Technologie*, *28*(1), 157–159. doi:10.1016/S0023-6438(95)80029-8

Cai, L., Pethica, B. A., Debenedetti, P. G., & Sundaresan, S. (2016). Formation of cyclopentane methane binary clathrate hydrate in brine solutions. *Chemical Engineering Science*, *141*, 125–132. doi:10.1016/j.ces.2015.11.001

Cao, J., Zhu, S., Li, C., & Han, B. (2020). Integrating support vector regression with genetic algorithm for hydrate formation condition prediction. *Processes (Basel, Switzerland)*, *8*(5), 1–11. doi:10.3390/pr8050519

Chapoy, A., Mohammadi, A. H., & Richon, D. (2007). Predicting the hydrate stability zones of natural gases using artificial neural networks. *Oil & Gas Science and Technology-Revue de l'IFP*, *62*(5), 701–706. doi:10.2516/ogst:2007048

Chavoshi, S., Safamirzaei, M., & Pajoum Shariati, F. (2018). Evaluation of empirical correlations for predicting gas hydrate formation temperature. *Gas Processing Journal*, *6*(2), 15–36.

Chong, Z. R., Yang, S. H. B., Babu, P., Linga, P., & Li, X.-S. (2016). Review of natural gas hydrates as an energy resource: Prospects and challenges. *Applied Energy*, *162*, 1633–1652. doi:10.1016/j.apenergy.2014.12.061

Collett, T. S., Lewis, R., & Uchida, T. (2000). Growing interest in gas hydrates. *Oilfield Review*, *12*(2), 42–57.

Cortes, C., & Vapnik, V. (1995). Support-vector networks. *Machine Learning*, *20*(3), 273–297. doi:10.1007/BF00994018

Davie, M. K., Zatsepina, O. Y., & Buffett, B. A. (2004). Methane solubility in marine hydrate environments. *Marine Geology*, *203*(1–2), 177–184. doi:10.1016/S0025-3227(03)00331-1

Elgibaly, A. A., & Elkamel, A. M. (1998). A new correlation for predicting hydrate formation conditions for various gas mixtures and inhibitors. *Fluid Phase Equilibria*, *152*(1), 23–42. doi:10.1016/S0378-3812(98)00368-9

Englezos, P. (1993). Clathrate hydrates. *Industrial & Engineering Chemistry Research*, *32*(7), 1251–1274. doi:10.1021/ie00019a001

Fournaison, L., Delahaye, A., Chatti, I., & Petitet, J.-P. (2004). CO2 hydrates in refrigeration processes. *Industrial & Engineering Chemistry Research*, *43*(20), 6521–6526. doi:10.1021/ie030861r

Ganguly, S. (2003). Prediction of VLE data using radial basis function network. *Computers & Chemical Engineering*, *27*(10), 1445–1454. doi:10.1016/S0098-1354(03)00068-1

Gbaruko, B. C., Igwe, J. C., Gbaruko, P. N., & Nwokeoma, R. C. (2007). Gas hydrates and clathrates: Flow assurance, environmental and economic perspectives and the Nigerian liquified natural gas project. *Journal of Petroleum Science Engineering*, *56*(1–3), 192–198. doi:10.1016/j.petrol.2005.12.011

Ghavipour, M., Ghavipour, M., Chitsazan, M., Najibi, S. H., & Ghidary, S. S. (2013). Experimental study of natural gas hydrates and a novel use of neural network to predict hydrate formation conditions. *Chemical Engineering Research & Design*, *91*(2), 264–273. doi:10.1016/j.cherd.2012.08.010

Giustiniani, M., Tinivella, U., Jakobsson, M., & Rebesco, M. (2013). Arctic ocean gas hydrate stability in a changing climate. *Journal of Geological Research*, (783969), 1–10.

Heydari, A., Shayesteh, K., & Kamalzadeh, L. (2006). Prediction of hydrate formation temperature for natural gas using artificial neural network. *Oil and Gas Business,* 1–10.

Holland, J. H. (1992). *Adaptation in natural and artificial systems: an introductory analysis with applications to biology, control, and artificial intelligence.* MIT Press. doi:10.7551/mitpress/1090.001.0001

Jain, S. (2017). Introduction to genetic algorithm & their application in data science. *Analytics Vidhya,* 1–31.

Katz, D. L. (1945). Prediction of conditions for hydrate formation in natural gases. *Transactions of the AIME, 160*(1), 140–149. 10.2118/945140-G

Katz, D. L. V. (1959). *Handbook of natural gas engineering*. McGraw-Hill.

Ke, W., & Chen, D. (2019). A short review on natural gas hydrate, kinetic hydrate inhibitors and inhibitor synergists. *Chinese Journal of Chemical Engineering, 27*(9), 2049–2061. doi:10.1016/j.cjche.2018.10.010

Khamehchi, E., Shamohammadi, E., & Yousefi, S. H. (2013). Predicting the hydrate formation temperature by a new correlation and neural network. *Gas Processing, 1*(1), 41–50. Retrieved from https://www.sid.ir/en/Journal/ViewPaper.aspx?ID=418945

Khan, M. S., Lal, B., Sabil, K. M., & Ahmed, I. (2019). Desalination of seawater through gas hydrate process: An overview. *Journal of Advanced Research in Fluid Mechanics and Thermal Sciences, 55*(1), 65–73.

Khan, S. H., Kumari, A., Chandrajit, G. D., & Amit, B. M. (2020). Thermodynamic modeling and correlations of CH_4, C_2H_6, CO_2, H_2S, and N_2 hydrates with cage occupancies. *Journal of Petroleum Exploration and Production Technology*, (0123456789). doi:10.1007/s13202-020-00998-y

Koza, J. R. (1994). Genetic programming as a means for programming computers by natural selection. *Statistics and Computing, 4*(2), 87–112. doi:10.1007/BF00175355

Kumari, A., Hasan, S., Majumder, K. C. B., Arora, A., & Dixit, G. (2021). Physio - chemical and mineralogical analysis of gas hydrate bearing sediments of Andaman Basin. *Marine Geophysical Research*, 1–12. doi:10.1007/s11001-020-09423-9

Kumari, A., Khan, S. H., Misra, A. K., Majumder, C. B., & Arora, A. (2020). Hydrates of Binary Guest Mixtures: Fugacity Model Development and Experimental Validation. *Journal of Non-Equilibrium Thermodynamics, 45*(1), 39–58. doi:10.1515/jnet-2019-0062

Kumari, A., Madhaw, M., Majumder, C. B., & Arora, A. (2021). Artificial Neural Network: A New Tool for the Prediction of Hydrate Formation Conditions. In Applications of Nature-Inspired Computing in Renewable Energy Systems (pp. 95–115). Academic Press.

Kumari, A., Madhaw, M., Majumder, C. B., Arora, A., & Dixit, G. (2021). *Application of statistical learning theory for thermodynamic modeling of natural gas hydrates*. Petroleum. doi:10.1016/j.petlm.2021.10.005

Kvenvolden, K. A. (1993). *A primer on gas hydrates* (Vol. 1570). US Geological Survey.

Laugier, S., & Richon, D. (2003). Use of artificial neural networks for calculating derived thermodynamic quantities from volumetric property data. *Fluid Phase Equilibria, 210*(2), 247–255. doi:10.1016/S0378-3812(03)00172-9

Lee, H., Lee, J., Kim, D. Y., Park, J., Seo, Y.-T., Zeng, H., & Moudrakovski, I. L. (2011). *Tuning clathrate hydrates for hydrogen storage. Materials For Sustainable Energy: A Collection of Peer-Reviewed Research and Review Articles from Nature Publishing Group*. World Scientific.

Marquardt, D. W. (1963). An algorithm for least-squares estimation of nonlinear parameters. *Journal of the Society for Industrial and Applied Mathematics, 11*(2), 431–441. doi:10.1137/0111030

Mehrizadeh, M. (2020). Prediction of gas hydrate formation using empirical equations and data-driven models. *Materials Today: Proceedings*. Retrieved from doi:10.1016/j.matpr.2020.06.058

Mesbah, M., Soroush, E., & Rezakazemi, M. (2017). Development of a least squares support vector machine model for prediction of natural gas hydrate formation temperature. *Chinese Journal of Chemical Engineering, 25*(9), 1238–1248. doi:10.1016/j.cjche.2016.09.007

Mesbah, M., Soroush, E., & Roham, M. (2017). *Phase equilibrium modeling of semi-clathrate hydrates of the CO 2 + H 2 / CH 4 / N 2 + TBAB aqueous solution system*. Academic Press.

Mohammadi, A. H., Belandria, V., & Richon, D. (2010). Use of an artificial neural network algorithm to predict hydrate dissociation conditions for hydrogen+ water and hydrogen+ tetra-n-butyl ammonium bromide+ water systems. *Chemical Engineering Science, 65*(14), 4302–4305. doi:10.1016/j.ces.2010.04.026

Mohammadi, A. H., Eslamimanesh, A., Richon, D., Gharagheizi, F., Yazdizadeh, M., Javanmardi, J., Hashemi, H., Zarifi, M., & Babaee, S. (2012). Gas hydrate phase equilibrium in porous media: Mathematical modeling and correlation. *Industrial & Engineering Chemistry Research, 51*(2), 1062–1072. doi:10.1021/ie201904r

Mohammadi, A. H., Martínez-López, J. F., & Richon, D. (2010). Determining phase diagrams of tetrahydrofuran+ methane, carbon dioxide or nitrogen clathrate hydrates using an artificial neural network algorithm. *Chemical Engineering Science, 65*(22), 6059–6063. doi:10.1016/j.ces.2010.07.013

Mohammadi, A. H., & Richon, D. (2009). Methane hydrate phase equilibrium in the presence of salt (NaCl, KCl, or CaCl2) + ethylene glycol or salt (NaCl, KCl, or CaCl2) + methanol aqueous solution: Experimental determination of dissociation condition. *The Journal of Chemical Thermodynamics, 41*(12), 1374–1377. doi:10.1016/j.jct.2009.06.012

Mohammadi, A. H., & Richon, D. (2010). Hydrate phase equilibria for hydrogen+ water and hydrogen+ tetrahydrofuran+ water systems: Predictions of dissociation conditions using an artificial neural network algorithm. *Chemical Engineering Science, 65*(10), 3352–3355. doi:10.1016/j.ces.2010.02.015

Moradi, M. R., Nazari, K., Alavi, S., & Mohaddesi, M. (2013). Prediction of equilibrium conditions for hydrate formation in binary gaseous systems using artificial neural networks. *Energy Technology (Weinheim), 1*(2-3), 171–176. doi:10.1002/ente.201200056

Pelckmans, K., Suykens, J. A. K., Van Gestel, T., De Brabanter, J., Lukas, L., Hamers, B., & De Moor, B. (2002). LS-SVMlab: a matlab/c toolbox for least squares support vector machines. Tutorial. KULeuven-ESAT.

Petersen, R., Fredenslund, A., & Rasmussen, P. (1994). Artificial neural networks as a predictive tool for vapor-liquid equilibrium. *Computers & Chemical Engineering, 18*, S63–S67. doi:10.1016/0098-1354(94)80011-1

Potukuchi, S., & Wexler, A. S. (1997). Predicting vapor pressures using neural networks. *Atmospheric Environment, 31*(5), 741–753. doi:10.1016/S1352-2310(96)00203-8

Rai, P., Majumdar, G. C., DasGupta, S., & De, S. (2005). Prediction of the viscosity of clarified fruit juice using artificial neural network: A combined effect of concentration and temperature. [Elsevier.]. *Journal of Food Engineering, 68*(4), 527–533. doi:10.1016/j.jfoodeng.2004.07.003

Rebai, N., Hadjadj, A., Benmounah, A., Berrouk, A. S., & Boualleg, S. M. (2019). Prediction of natural gas hydrates formation using a combination of thermodynamic and neural network modeling. *Journal of Petroleum Science and Engineering, 182*(March), 106270. doi:10.1016/j.petrol.2019.106270

Sablani, S. S., Baik, O.-D., & Marcotte, M. (2002). Neural networks for predicting thermal conductivity of bakery products. *Journal of Food Engineering, 52*(3), 299–304. doi:10.1016/S0260-8774(01)00119-4

Schmitz, J. E., Zemp, R. J., & Mendes, M. J. (2006). Artificial neural networks for the solution of the phase stability problem. *Fluid Phase Equilibria, 245*(1), 83–87. doi:10.1016/j.fluid.2006.02.013

Seif, M., & Kamran-pirzaman, A. (2020). Prediction of Gas and Refrigerant Hydrate Equilibrium Conditions With and Without Thermodynamic Inhibitors Using Simple Empirical Correlations. *Journal of Petroleum Science and Technology, 10*, 61–72.

Sharma, R., Singhal, D., Ghosh, R., & Dwivedi, A. (1999). Potential applications of artificial neural networks to thermodynamics: Vapor–liquid equilibrium predictions. *Computers & Chemical Engineering, 23*(3), 385–390. doi:10.1016/S0098-1354(98)00281-6

Sinehbaghizadeh, S., Javanmardi, J., Roosta, A., & Mohammadi, A. H. (2019). Estimation of the dissociation conditions and storage capacities of various sH clathrate hydrate systems using effective deterministic frameworks. *Fuel, 247*, 272–286. doi:10.1016/j.fuel.2019.01.189

Sloan, E. D. (1998). Physical / Chemical Properties of Gas Hydrates. *Gas Hydrates. Relevance to world margin stability and climatic change, 624*(5), 191–196.

Soroush, E., Mesbah, M., Shokrollahi, A., Bahadori, A., & Ghazanfari, M. H. (2014). Prediction of methane uptake on different adsorbents in adsorbed natural gas technology using a rigorous model. *Energy & Fuels, 28*(10), 6299–6314. doi:10.1021/ef501550p

Soroush, E., Mesbah, M., Shokrollahi, A., Rozyn, J., Lee, M., Kashiwao, T., & Bahadori, A. (2015). Evolving a robust modeling tool for prediction of natural gas hydrate formation conditions. *Journal of Unconventional Oil and Gas Resources, 12*, 45–55.

Sun, C.-Y., Chen, G.-J., Lin, W., & Guo, T.-M. (2003). Hydrate formation conditions of sour natural gases. *Journal of Chemical & Engineering Data, 48*(3), 600–602. doi:10.1021/je020155h

Thakur, N. K., & Rajput, S. (2010). *Exploration of gas hydrates: Geophysical techniques.* Springer Science & Business Media.

Vapnik, V. (1999). *The nature of statistical learning theory.* Springer science & business media.

Vapnik, V. N. (1999). An overview of statistical learning theory. *IEEE Transactions on Neural Networks, 10*(5), 988–999. doi:10.1109/72.788640 PMID:18252602

Xu, H., Jiao, Z., Zhang, Z., Huffman, M., & Wang, Q. (2021). Prediction of methane hydrate formation conditions in salt water using machine learning algorithms. *Computers & Chemical Engineering, 151*, 107358. doi:10.1016/j.compchemeng.2021.107358

Yarveicy, H., & Ghiasi, M. M. (2017a). Modeling of gas hydrate phase equilibria: Extremely randomized trees and LSSVM approaches. *Journal of Molecular Liquids, 243*, 533–541. doi:10.1016/j.molliq.2017.08.053

Yarveicy, H., & Ghiasi, M. M. (2017b). Modeling of gas hydrate phase equilibria: Extremely randomized trees and LSSVM approaches. *Journal of Molecular Liquids, 243*, 533–541. doi:10.1016/j.molliq.2017.08.053

Zahedi, G., Karami, Z., & Yaghoobi, H. (2009). Prediction of hydrate formation temperature by both statistical models and artificial neural network approaches. *Energy Conversion and Management, 50*(8), 2052–2059. doi:10.1016/j.enconman.2009.04.005

ZareNezhad, B., & Aminian, A. (2012). Accurate prediction of sour gas hydrate equilibrium dissociation conditions by using an adaptive neuro fuzzy inference system. *Energy Conversion and Management, 57*, 143–147. doi:10.1016/j.enconman.2011.12.021

KEY TERMS AND DEFINITIONS

γ_g: Gas-specific gravity.
AARD%: Average absolute relative deviation.
ANN: Artificial neural network.
ARD%: Absolute relative deviation.
GA: Genetic algorithm.
GP: Genetic programming.
HFT: Hydrate formation temperature.
LSSVM: Least-squares support vector machine.
R^2: Squared correlation coefficient.
RBF: Radial basis function.
RMSD: Root mean square deviation.

Chapter 11
The Role of Big Data Analysis and Machine Learning in Marketing Communications:
A Case Study of Amazon

Ali Ayci

Ankara Yıldırım Beyazıt Universtiy, Turkey

Shivam Tyagi

Amazon, USA

ABSTRACT

Technological and commercial developments in the 21ˢᵗ century have increased the demands and expectations of consumers. Big data analysis and machine learning can play a critical role in establishing healthy communication. The insights obtained from big data analysis and ML models can help in making marketing communication more personalized and useful to customers. In this chapter, the authors present an exploratory analysis of the role of big data and ML in the marketing communication of enterprises. For this, Amazon, which provides big data analysis infrastructures to other businesses which are big data users, is being researched as a case study. This study is one of the first studies in the literature to examine the significance of big data and ML in marketing communication and investigate the obstacles encountered when using them. The insights presented in this chapter will help professionals in the marketing communication domain to better understand how they can utilize big data and ML models to make a significant impact on their customers and sales.

INTRODUCTION

Experts estimate that consumers receive an average of between 4,000 and 10,000 marketing messages per day (Simpson, 2017). While on one hand consumers are exposed to thousands of marketing messages every day, each consumer expects a personal approach from the companies. At the same time,

DOI: 10.4018/978-1-6684-4045-2.ch011

considering that the target audience of the enterprises is large, how is it possible for the enterprises to communicate with their target audiences in a healthy and effective manner in line with their goals, with personal judgments, past estimates, and unfounded assumptions? In the big data era we live in, computer scientists, physicists, economists, mathematicians, political scientists, informatics, sociologists and other scientists strive to access the enormous amount of information produced about people, objects and their interactions.

The interaction of billions of people using computers, GPS devices, cell phones and medical devices creates an ever-increasing flood of data, and many of these interactions occur through the use of mobile devices in the developing world, used by people whose needs and habits have not been adequately understood until now (WorldEconomicForum, 2012). Scientists across disciplines, businesses, public and private institutions are exploring the potential benefits of analyzing genetic sequences, social media interactions, health records, phone records, government records, and other digital traces left by humans (Boyd and Crawford, 2012, p. 662; Saggi and Jain, 2018, p. 758). Although there is no official definition (De Mauro, Greco and Grimaldi, 2016, p. 122), Big data is a resource that generates new ideas by quickly obtaining and analyzing different sources such as humans and machines (EU, 2021) and ultimately big data is the information asset used to be turned into value (De Mauro at all. 2016, p. 122). Big data is data management that cannot be solved with traditional databases due to the increasing volume, velocity and variety (Amazon, 2021a). Big data can be divided into structured and unstructured big data. Structured data comes in a defined format and offers clear answers. In user-generated content, structured data typically has ratings and data from responses such as totally agree, strongly disagree continues to be useful to marketers.

However, there are also negative aspects of structured big data. For example, the target audience may be uncomfortable with being forced to answer, or people may not be able to accurately and fully express the answer they would like to give (Bendle and Wang, 2016, p. 118). Unlike structured data, unstructured data is not ready and comes in a form that must be processed to be usable. Such unstructured data is often rich and exciting but can be extremely difficult to use. Managers trying to guess what consumers are thinking by browsing these reviews will often create overly biased estimates. When the volume of reviews is very high, reading all reviews can present significant practical difficulties (Bendle and Wang, 2016, p. 118). With the use of big data analysis in businesses, the benefits of creating value for the company, reducing costs, producing innovative solutions, launching new products or services, creating customer value, helping marketing decisions, personalization in the marketing mix can be achieved (Benoit, Lessmann and Verbeke, 2020, p. 235). Understanding the wishes and needs of the target audience is one of the areas where businesses can benefit from big data analysis. On the one hand, businesses use communication tools (Social media, websites, consumer forums, etc.) as large data collection areas, on the other hand, they give their messages regarding their marketing strategies with these marketing communication tools. In other words, big data is both a field where data is collected and a field where data is created. With this feature, big data analysis is becoming an increasingly important channel in terms of marketing communication tools for enterprises.

The findings show that research in big data applications for marketing is at the embryonic stage and therefore more direct efforts towards business need to be developed for big data to evolve in the field of marketing (Erevelles, Fukawa and Swayne, 2016, p. 897). Research is needed to clearly identify the pros and cons of enterprises' big data investments (Amado, at all, 2018, p. 6). When evaluating big data investments, first of all, the benefits of big data for businesses should be revealed. In this study, first of all, a general perspective is presented in order to reveal how and for what purpose big data can be used in marketing communications. Until recently, big data investments had to be met with business resources, and academic studies were based on high investment values and limited opportunities for businesses. However, today, some leading companies providing big data analysis services are bringing their services and capabilities with other businesses at affordable costs. In this context, Amazon and Amazon Personalize (AP) are researched as a case study in order to investigate the service scopes and usability of outsourcing organizations for the use of big data in marketing communications. technically and practically. The reason why Amazon is included in the research is that it is one of the businesses that use big data and big data analysis most effectively, and more importantly, it provides big data analysis infrastructure services to other businesses, especially SMEs. It makes big data applications more accessible for companies. Because Amazon is a business that markets its services online, the business' website is used as the data source for the exploratory research within the scope of this article. Finding detailed technical information about the services offered on the Amazon web page also provides convenience in accessing information. This study is one of the few studies in the international literature that deals with marketing communication and big data analysis. New and up-to-date studies are needed because consumer expectations, which is one of the most important areas of use of big data, are constantly changing and technology and actors in big data analysis are constantly developing.

BIGDATA, MACHINE LEARNING AND MARKETING COMMUNICATION FROM MARKETING ASPECTS

Marketing Communications and Big Data Needs

Traditionally, marketing has always been a field in which data plays an important role. Since the 1980s, with the development and cheapening of computing technologies, more business processes have been digitized and the data produced and captured by the devices have been made available to marketing researchers and practitioners. Customer choice modelling, market basket analysis, estimation of price (cross) elasticities, etc. have emerged and evolved with the increasing availability of various types of data (Benoit, et al., 2020, p. 236). While deciding on the target customer profile in marketing, defining information sources, and ensuring customer participation in product design, businesses benefit from big data (Zhan, et al, 2018, p. 584). Big data analytics is a powerful analytical tool to understand market and customer needs for products or services and enable them to make better decisions (Saggi and Jain, 2018, p. 782) and serves as a tool to identify customer value creation strategies, define an overall marketing strategy, develop product concept features, identify value creation opportunities, and develop customer value metrics (Smith and Colgate, 2007, p. 15). The main research topic of marketing is to understand the target audience correctly. Based on the results of field research; while 88 per cent of IT managers believe their organization truly understands its customers, only 61 per cent of consumers believe that companies understand their needs (Talend, 2021). Big data analysis offers important opportunities for businesses to understand and respond to consumers' needs and expectations in a timely and accurate manner. (Buganza, Trabucchi and Pellizzoni, 2020, p. 58). Big data is the biggest opportunity that changes the rules of the marketing and sales ecosystem and allows us to understand the target audience in more detail since the internet became mainstream nearly 25 years ago (McKinsey, 2015, p. 4). As machine learning evolves and analyzes different types of data faster; Big data is playing a more central role in marketing than ever before, making the pace of development of marketing messages a more important revenue item for the business (Luenendonk, 2019). Prior to the recent interest of businesses in analyzing marketing data at a large scale, rapid advances in network and database technology have led to the development of a variety of software applications. This technology not only allowed business processes to be further integrated by interconnected computers but also stimulated interest in analyzing data where the volume and diversity are large, such as the growth of the internet, interacting with potential and existing customers, gathering information about competitors (Benoit, at al, 2020, p. 236). While marketers are trying to use big data analysis commercially, it is seen that the interest of academicians on the subject has increased in the literature. According to the results of Amado et al.'s (2018: 6) study of 1560 articles published between 2010 and 2015 on the use of big data in marketing, big data in marketing has received increasing attention over the years and the number of publications doubles every year compared to the previous year. As a result of the use of big data in marketing activities by researchers and practitioners, businesses have made significant gains. The results of the research conducted by Suoniemi et al. (2020) on 301 marketing managers reveal that the use of big data improves firm performance by improving the firm's market-oriented capabilities.

The main way to make businesses competitive and differentiate them in an internationally competitive environment is healthy communication with the target audience. Marketing communications can provide a sustainable competitive advantage to any organization that taps into its potential (Mihaela, 2015, p. 1447). Marketing communication is the coordinated use of promotional messages and related media to communicate with a market, where marketing communication messages are communicated through one or more channels such as digital media, printed materials, radio, television, direct mail, and personal selling (AMA, 2021). Integrated marketing communication, which expresses the harmony of communication tools in the business, is an activity that allows creating profitable customer relations and creates value for the product/brand or company. It aims to ensure the consistency of the message conveyed through various communication tools such as advertising, sales promotion, direct marketing, public relations, online communication (Mihaela, 2015, p. 1949).

Customer Oriented Marketing

In customer-oriented marketing, it is aimed to collect consumer information, to make effective inferences as a result of detailed analysis of this information, to predict the future from the analysis of past customer interactions, and finally to respond to customer needs in real-time (Gulati and Oldroyd, 2005, p. 97). For this purpose, customer-oriented marketing and customer-oriented communication become more effective with big data analysis, which is one of the most effective data collection and analysis methods. The increased focus on customer experience arises due to the complexity of the communication process as customers interact with companies through multiple channels and numerous touchpoints in the media, due to the redundancy of tools and messages in marketing communication. (Lemon and Verhoef, 2016, p. 69). The integration of technology and big data into business strategy increases the complexity of marketing communications and fosters the need for advanced marketing performance analytics (Buhalis and Volchek, 2021, p. 1). Effective management of the complexity in the communication process is possible with big data analysis tools. Big data enables strategic communicators to analyze the needs, views, attitudes and behaviors of their stakeholders in greater detail. From planning to evaluation, big data analytics make enterprise communication more analytical and potentially more strategic.

Communication professionals use advanced analytics tools to capture and process the needs, opinions, attitudes and user behavior of target groups from all over the world. Marketers by connecting this data to market data can monitor the changing perceptions of their companies, brands and products in different countries and this in more or less real-time. Insights from big data analytics allow companies to conduct more personalized communications in marketing, public relations and internal communications than in the past (Wiencierz and Röttger, 2018, p. 43). A study was conducted by Wiencierz and Röttger (2018, p, 42) with 35 big data and social media analytics experts on the use of big data in the field of communication, and the results of the research show that big data offers benefits to marketing communication practitioners in four main areas. a) providing communicators with a wider knowledge base for situation analysis b) formulating database-based strategies c) automated communication applications d) providing evaluation based on larger data stocks. Marketers benefit from big data analytics in individual product and brand communication, online touchpoint analytics, predictive analytics of product and label message spread, topic or content marketing identification, real-time processing of customer data for online marketing, market share determination through share analytics, and effective communication. In order for big data analysis to be successful in marketing communication, it should be clear which of the goals of the business serves the big data, it should be repeated several times until the results of the efforts such as data generation, extraction and analysis are compatible with the determined goal, and interdepartmental cooperation should be supported (Wiencierz and Röttger, 2018, p. 42).

Behavior-oriented Marketing

The analysis of consumer behavior is of great importance in the effectiveness of advertising decisions, which is one of the leading marketing communication tools. While advertisements in traditional media can present common content regardless of differences, advertisements can be personalized with big data technology, allowing the delivery of advertisements suitable for the region, culture and person (Yavuz and Erdoğan-Gençyürek, 2019, p. 214). Behavioral advertising is one way to better target the most valuable consumers. For example, if past purchasing behavior in one product category is positively correlated with product preference in another category, consumers who purchased the previous category may be more heavily advertised (Shen and Villas-Boas, 2018). Netflix, one of the most valuable media companies in the world, owes its success to its impressive customer retention rates, and the secret of Netflix's customer retention is that it is more successful in determining what they want by communicating effectively with its viewers compared to its competitors. Netflix collects data from its 151 million subscribers and applies data analytics models to explore customer behavior and purchasing patterns, then uses this information to recommend movies and TV shows based on their subscribers' preferences and more than 75% of audience activity is based on personalized recommendations with offers delivered through different marketing communication tools (Dixon, 2019). At the macro level, the two main components of interactive integrated marketing communication are big data marketing information and its technical system and interactive marketing communication plans (Tang, 2020). Social media is the medium where big data is most active with marketing communication. After the analysis of the big data obtained from social media, communication with the target audience is established with different marketing communication tools in line with the strategies compatible with the business objectives and this is a continuous cycle. In other words, while marketing communication tools are used to provide big data, it is also a basic tool used for effective communication after the analysis of big data (Figure 1).

Figure 1. Big Data Usage Cycle in Marketing Communications. Source: (Authors, 2022)

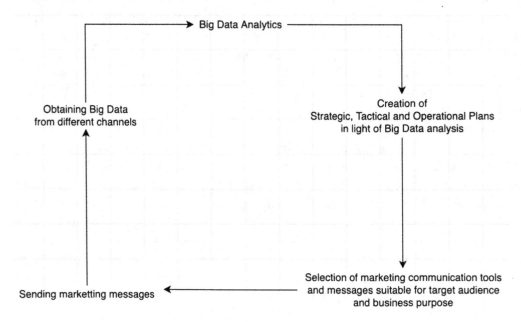

It is seen that different people, institutions and organizations have made big data analysis in social media the building block of their communication strategies and have achieved significant success. Coca-Cola is able to respond to its customers in real-time by analyzing and evaluating the information of Twitter users around the world, using services from Sysomos, a social media analytics business. Former US President Obama predicted the intentions and tendencies of undecided voters by using the Boatbuilder system, which can manage various databases in the 2008 elections, closely analyzed the voter movement and responded to them with a direct communication strategy in real-time and won the US presidential election (Bitnine, 2016). The critical point in the effective design and implementation of these steps and the development of strategies is to collect and analyze as much qualified information as possible from the target audience. With big data analysis, businesses can fully understand consumers' concerns, reach opinions about competitors and the industry, and find the opportunity to build their marketing communications on these findings.

Active vs Passive Recipient's Impact on Marketing

In the era of social commerce, the first part of the 21st century, the basic idea is that customers do not become passive recipients of information from marketers, but interact with each other and with the business to influence consumer purchasing and business decisions. These interactions can take the form of product reviews, product usage descriptions, "homemade ads", blogs, and other consumer-initiated contributions (Fader and Winer, 2012, p. 369). Businesses need to develop timely and effective strategic responses to contributions such as consumer review information, as silence to incoming messages is often not a solution (Chen and Xie, 2008, p. 488). It now has access not only to purchasing and marketing mix data but also to rich information about how consumers interact with each other and the products/services they consume. This provides a much more complete picture of the effects on buyers and has the potential to significantly improve modelling efforts and ultimately marketing decisions (Fader and Winer, 2012, p. 369). Because analysis of social media data provides valuable information for marketing research purposes, businesses should use this data as a form of exploratory research (Malthouse, et al, 2013, p. 270). By observing what consumers write about products in a category, firms can better understand the online discussion and marketing opportunities, market structure, competitive landscape, and characteristics of their own and competitors' products (Netzer, et al, 2012, p. 521). Businesses soon realized the potential of using internet-based social networks to influence customers and incorporated social media marketing communications into their strategies to strengthen their businesses (Moro, Rita and Vala, 2016, p. 3341). A system that can predict the impact of individual posts would be a valuable advantage in promoting products and services (Chen and Xie, 2008, p. 477). 12 factors can be used to measure the performance of social media posts (Table 1).

Table 1. Social Media Posts Performance Aspects. Source: (Moro et al. 2016, p. 3343)

Characteristic	Indicator
Full access to the post	Number of people who saw the post on the page
	The number of times a post is viewed regardless of whether it is clicked or not. People can see more than one.
Total views	They are the impressions of the same article. For example, someone might see a page update in their news feed once, and then see it a second time if a friend shares it.
Users interacting	The number of people (unique users) who clicked anywhere on a post.
Consumers	The number of people who clicked anywhere on a post
Post consumption	Number of clicks anywhere on a post
Impressions of people who like a page	Total impressions from people who only liked a page
Reach of people who like a page	The number of people who saw a page post because they liked that page (unique users).
People who like a page and are interested in a post	The number of people who liked a page and clicked anywhere on a post (Unique users).
Comments	Number of comments on the post
Likes	Number of likes on the post
Shares	Number of posts shared
Total interactions	Total of likes, "comments and shares"

This dataset is also linked to all phases of branding (cognitive, affective and cognitive phases) and shows that predictions about social media interaction can also be used to predict brand building. Managers will be able to use this information to make informed decisions about the posts they publish, increasing their impact and thus contributing to successful brand communication and brand building (Moro, et al., 2016, p. 3350).

METHODOLOGY

Within the scope of this study, the technical dimensions of big data analysis and machine learning in marketing communication, the problems experienced and the future perspective will be investigated. As a research method, exploratory analysis will be conducted to obtain data by in-depth interview method from experts who work in Amazon. Afterwards, as a case study, Amazon AP, which is the product Amazon offers to other businesses, will be analyzed in accordance with the information provided by the experts, the information obtained from the product and its web page. In face-to-face interviews, the participants were asked to answer in-depth 15 questions spanning over different paradigms including marketing problems and big data, ML solutions, services used and offered by Amazon itself, problems they encounter and the future of machine learning and big data in marketing communication.

Technical Aspects Of Marketing Communication With Bigdata And Machine Learning

While the rapid growth in user content on the Internet has a huge impact on marketing practice at the same time, brand managers are no longer able to fully control the messages they use (Fader and Winer, 2012, p. 369; Malthouse, at al., 2013, p. 270). The huge amount of data makes it difficult to track and measure information, and this rich but unstructured set of consumer data is qualitative in nature. A combination of a text mining device and a network analysis framework can be used to overcome these challenges (Netzer, et al, 2012, p. 521). Unstructured big data from online product reviews are generated in real-time, easily accessible, and contain the messages consumers want managers to hear. Analyzing such data has the potential to revolutionize market research and competitive analysis, but how can the messages be deduced? How can large amounts of data be concentrated on insights to help drive business strategy? How can large amounts of data be concentrated on insights to help drive business strategy?

Data Collection

Different types of data can shed light on different aspects of CX. Depending on the requirement, clients can decide what type of data to be collected on their websites. As in this study, we are focussing on marketing communication, customer interaction and behavioral data is of importance and thus we will focus on strategies to collect that data. For big data applications, customer data is collected in three ways, asking customers directly, by tracking data indirectly and by acquiring data from other companies. There are tools which can be enabled in a website to track what item the customer is looking at, which buttons and links he/she clicked and how much time the customer spent over a specific section or webpage. All these data points when fed into a big data analysis tool or ML algorithm can generate insights that can help in understanding and tracking user interests and behavior.

But there are some hurdles that companies face during the data collection phase. With the latest development in privacy controls and new regulations being placed by governments, data collection is becoming a more and more challenging task. In research, it has been observed that after Apple provided an option to customers to block any type of data tracking, almost 25% of customers have opted out of it. This is a huge impact as it means 25% less data for training models. Government regulations like CCPA and GDPR give power to customers for the right to be forgotten. This brings an obligation on companies to delete a customer's data when opted. Due to these new controls and regulations, data collection needs to be very transparent. Indirect tracking of data and selling of data is not encouraged to practice. True that data collection is a matter of concern but also it has a big role to play in improving CX by helping in identifying patterns in customer behavior and hence allowing companies to create targeted offers and advertisements. Companies like Facebook, Snapchat and Twitter which earn most of their revenue by advertisements are on the receiving end of the push towards privacy controls. They are working on changing their underlying architecture to minimize the impact. In this direction data collection methods like interviews, surveys, GPS based location tracking and data collection through IoT devices are being used more and more.

Data Preprocessing

Most of the time raw data available is not suitable to be used in machine learning models as is. Data preprocessing is a very essential part of the whole process. The quality of inferences directly depends on the quality of the data. If the data is incomplete or incoherent, the results will be unreliable. To ensure that proper inferences are derived, a lot of effort is dedicated to data preprocessing. There are certain techniques like sampling and imputation to clean and prepare data before being used as input to ML models. Once the data is validated to be in good form, the ML model is trained and tested using this data for analysis.

Figure 2. Data Preprocessing. Source: (Authors, 2022)

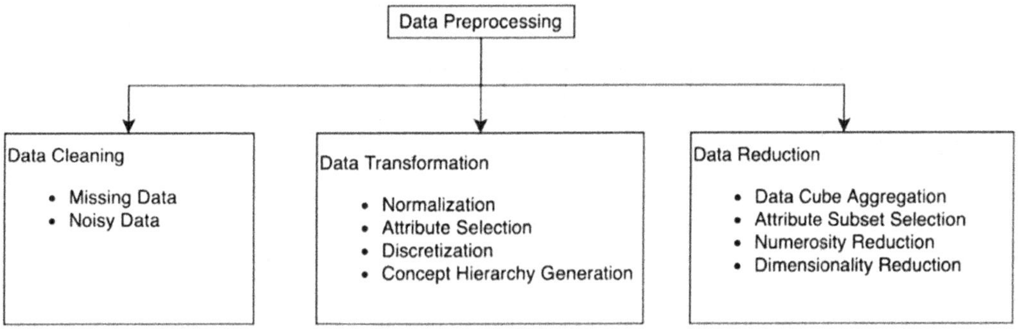

Source: (Authors, 2022)

For training machine learning models, the data is divided into train, test and validation data. There are many ways to do this. Like data can be divided into 70:15:15 shares where 70% data will be used for training, 15% data for testing and 15% for validation. In another approach, there can be overlapping sets that will have some data in common. In some approaches the data set is divided into N number of sets and training is performed using a certain number of sets each time.

There are three main challenges of any data pre-processing stage which can be defined by three Vs, Volume, Variety and Velocity. As their literal meanings, volume means amount of data, variety means different types of data and velocity signifies the speed with which data is processed. All three of these directly impact the data preprocessing step and the quality of results hence obtained. In today's world where IoT and sensors are all around us, millions of data points are obtained every second. To save, identify, filter and process these data points requires a lot of computing resources. Today hardware designers are working on creating more and more efficient processors to speed up the calculations and hence provide results as quickly as possible. With these advancements in computing power, processing large amounts of data has become possible. But even then as the data increases with every day, new approaches are being researched. Distributed processing is one such field where companies like Google and Amazon have excelled a lot.

Figure 3. Training, Validation and Testing Dataset
Source: (Authors, 2022)

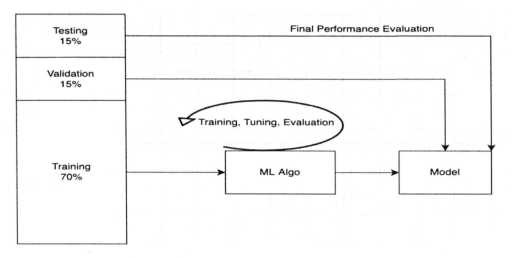

Distributed Data Processing

There are a lot of softwares for big data analysis. Spark is an open-source distributed computing framework used to analyze big data quickly. Its ability to divide the task among workers to process chunks of data in parallel allows it to analyze large amounts of data quickly, hence making it apt for big data applications. For marketing, communication spark can be used to analyze the data of millions of customers in real-time and thus provide inferences that can be integrated with marketing messages instantly. Engineers and scientists can use Spark APIs to analyze user data from different sources to generate insights (Alzahrani, 2021). Hadoop is another distributed data processing framework that uses maps and reduces algorithms to distribute tasks and combine results to get final inferences. The main difference between Hadoop and Spark is the place where data is stored. Spark saves data in RAM while Hadoop uses a hard disk to save data. This makes Spark faster than Hadoop. Thus Spark is good for applications that need real-time inferences while Hadoop is used for applications that require batch processing. Amazon EMR or Elastic Map Reduce service is another big data platform based on Hadoop that provides the capability to run distributed data processing jobs using open source frameworks like Spark. Amazon EMR distributes tasks among virtual servers Amazon EC2 instances and saves data on Amazon S3. Due to being on the cloud, this service has the capability to scale up and down dynamically depending on the requirement. Although these programs are not very expensive to acquire, professionals are needed to use them.

Data Analysis Models for Marketing Communication

Artificial intelligence tools driven by machine learning algorithms are rapidly transforming the business world and this transformation is increasing the interest of researchers. Machine learning methods have flexible model structures that can handle large-scale and unstructured data and provide strong predictive performance (Ma and Sun, 2020, p. 481). Although it is argued that big data will remove the human factor (Akçan, 2016, p. 311) or not (Altunışık, 2015, p. 72), it is a fact that it will enrich the human factor qualitatively. Marketing communication consists of three main types of content, text, images and videos. There are different approaches to analyze each of these types effectively using AI. In this section, we will discuss some of the models for each data type and how they can impact marketing communication.

Text Data

Text analysis of user-generated content provides access to information provided by active, content-producing consumers, providing useful information from the social structure of a brand's follower base, regardless of whether it creates or consumes content. This is particularly useful for predicting perceptual traits that consumers may be less likely to mention in brand conversations rather than key product features (Culotta and Cutler, 2016, p. 347). In order to make these analyzes, Twitter is a very important tool in big data analysis, as it is popular, relevant, social connections are public, and organized as it is organized by users into topic-based lists (Culotta and Cutler, 2016, p. 348). Unlike traditional transaction data, social media is a difficult medium to research due to data volume, diversity and speed (Arrigo, Liberati and Mariani, 2021). Big data analysis and suggestions can be made by people as well as artificial intelligence tools can be used. There are many AI approaches to analyze text data today. Topic-based analysis is one such methodology where an AI model tries to find a topic for each section of the text and then derives an overall topic. This is also known as topic modeling. Latent Dirichlet Allocation (LDA) is a good example of this approach.

LDA is a statistical model that works on the problem of topic discovery. It works by changing each word to its root lexical forms and then checking which topic they relate to. For example Fly, Flying, Flies, Flew will all be converted to Fly and then the system can correlate that word to most probable topics like a bird or plane. So whenever there is an ambiguous situation like this, LDA will try to predict probabilities of all probable topics and present them to us. Plate annotations can be used to represent such probabilistic graphical models (Blei et al. 2003).

In the representation of LDA, their is only one observable variable in the whole process, all others are latent variables which are inferred. There are three levels in LDA, corpus, document (outer box) and words(inner box). LDA can analyze large amounts of text and identify content by focusing on attributes that do not appear with a certain weight. For example, in examining a graphic text, it can be analyzed by focusing 70% on the story and 30% on the graphics. Collecting content from a large number of consumers allows us to understand what is on the minds of consumers collectively, from which it can be revealed what consumers care about and which features are viewed positively or negatively. Thus, for example, if advertisements will be given in newspapers, healthy communication will be established by providing the target audience to concentrate on the areas that the business wants to concentrate on while saving on advertising expenses by including the features that the target audience sees positive. LDA is able to map the relative strategic positions of competitors in the minds of consumers where they matter most (Bendle and Wang, 2016, p. 115). Any method that tries to understand the message must extract the common themes between the interpretations and thus bring together the unseen qualities expressed at various levels of abstraction. As one of the effective methods of this grouping, LDA has similarities with the principal component methods performed in customer surveys in terms of extracting common core characteristics. The advantage of the method is that it works with a large amount of unstructured data where not every customer review has most attributes. While LDA is somewhat technical, it is relatively easy to implement for statistically trained analysts and the data required for analysis can be accessed from social media. Without in-house expertise, data can be easily and relatively inexpensively purchased from third parties. LDA reveals the hidden nature of the invisible attributes behind comments. This provides more insight into what consumers think, telling management which areas of the customer experience need attention (Bendle and Wang, 2016, p. 123). Thus, very critical information is obtained in terms of strategic communication decisions.

Image Data

Advanced machine learning algorithms integrated with big data power recommendation systems on e-commerce sites and content platforms like Amazon and Netflix. Learning engines analyze and tag billions of images on social media sites like Facebook. Automatic bidding algorithms analyze a user's profile on a millisecond timescale to determine the most appropriate bid for ad serving; chatbots engage in human-like conversations with customers to maintain relationships and loyalty (Ma and Sun, 2020, p. 482). Despite significant advances and growing interest, the use of machine learning methods for big data in marketing is still at an early stage and current work is somewhat scattered. For example, there is no consensus on how machine learning methods should be incorporated into marketing research (Ma and Sun, 2020, p. 482). One challenge with using big data in marketing communications is that while automation can be more efficient for businesses, people still want to talk to people (Ariker and Manuel, 2015, p. 99).

Video Data

The ability of machine learning methods to handle unstructured big data is quite high and unstructured media data (text, audio, video recordings), consumer monitoring data, network data, hybrid data created by the combination of different data are transformed into unique information for marketing managers by machine learning tools (Ma and Sun, 2020, p. 497). Video-based analysis derives real-time inferences by analyzing the customer videos for behavior patterns that can then be materialized for enhancing marketing communication. With the increase in computation power now it is possible to analyze video data with more speed and in more volume. Thus it is apt time to use video-based analysis to derive useful insights. One tool that can be used to benefit from video data in marketing communication is the Video-Based Automatic Suggestion (VAR) System. The system uses a camera that captures the customer's behavior in front of the mirror to make inferences about their preferences based on facial expressions and clothing viewed by consumers at points in time. Second, the system identifies customers with preferences similar to the focus customer from a database of shoppers whose preferences, purchasing and/or evaluation decisions are known. Finally, recommendations are made to the focal customer based on the preferences of these like-minded customers and their purchasing and/or evaluation decisions. Each of the three steps can be implemented in various variations, and a retail chain can choose the very specific configuration that best serves its purpose (Lu, Xiao, and Ding, 2016, p. 484).

General design of the VAR system can be understood by example where a video feed from the changing room can analyze the behavior of the customers and their likings. Then the insights can be used to recommend better choices in marketing communication. If the VAR system is to be implemented in Walmart which has 10526 branches and 2.3 million employees in 24 countries (Walmart, 2021), the size of the data and the scope of its analysis will be understood. Unknown to the consumer, a significant part of the purchasing journey is guided by automated systems.

Search results are generated by an advanced Google ranking system, determined in part by advertisers' bids automatically generated using bidding machines (Ma and Sun, 2020, p. 481). Content on websites is customized according to user profile and questions are answered by chatbots. Reviews read by consumers stand out because they are deemed useful by a rating algorithm, and ads they see repeatedly are delivered through retargeting algorithms with real-time bidding. Coupons offering personalized prices to a consumer are generated just in time by the pricing engine. Finally, their posts on social media are collected by social listening engines and analyzed for emotion and feedback. These automated systems that make instant and context-dependent decisions are artificial intelligence tools implemented using state-of-the-art machine learning algorithms.

CASE STUDY: AMAZON AS A MARKETING COMMUNICATION SYSTEM PROVIDER

Founded in 1994 as a bookselling site, Amazon sold books to people in the US and 45 different countries in its first month (Hartmans, 2021). With 1.3 million employees today, Amazon generated $21.3 billion in annual sales of more than $386 billion in 2020 (Fortune, 2021). Amazon ranks second in the Fortune top 500 list with a market capitalization approaching $2 Trillion (Fortune, 2021). As a leader in customer experience innovation and defining many aspects of customer experience, Amazon is reorganizing its marketing activities around AI and machine learning efforts, not only taking things to the next level but showing how other businesses can do the same. Amazon provides big data analysis services to other large, medium and small businesses as well as serving the American Space and Aviation Administration (NASA) with its solutions based on big data analysis (Morgan, 2018). One of the most effective uses of big data and analytics, Amazon collects more than 2,000 historical and real-time data points on every order, using machine learning algorithms to find transactions with high fraud probability and stopping millions of dollars of fraudulent transactions every year (InsideBigData, 2019). Sharing this information alone is part of Amazon's effective marketing communication for the long-term relationship, not the instantaneous one.

Amazon Personalize (AP) As A Marketing Communication Tool

Amazon provides infrastructure for the use and analysis of big data to other businesses through its AP service. AP makes it easy for businesses to create applications that can offer a wide variety of personalization experiences, such as specific product recommendations, personalized product rankings, and customized direct marketing. AP is a fully managed machine learning service by training, tuning and deploying custom machine learning (ML) models beyond strict static rules-based recommendation systems to provide customized recommendations to customers in industries such as retail, media, entertainment (Amazon, 2021b).

Deep Dive Into AP's Client Space

Amazon Personalize is a service that Amazon provides to its clients who want to obtain recommendations based on their user data. Though AP is being used by companies in many fields most of the AP clients come from two main industries, media entertainment and retail. Amazon pioneered personalization in e-commerce more than 20 years ago so it is a natural fit, bringing the Amazon Personalized service to retail clients, with all the historical learning and experience. Due to Amazon's vast experience in retail, AP has been developed in such a way that it resonates very well with the requirements and expectations of its retail clients(Jory, 2022).

In media entertainment, the scope of AP's use cases is very broad. AP's clients can be media companies that are streaming video on demand or streaming sports or streaming short videos. In addition to these, there are use cases where clients are streaming music or textual data like news and articles. An example of an AP client is Discovery, which is using AP to personalize all aspects of their user experience including recommendations on the content rails. Down under, AP doesn't really care if it's a product client is trying to sell, a video client is trying to stream or a song client is trying to get people to listen to. It just looks at how users are interacting with those items within the client's environment including its application, emails, web app, mobile app and so on (Jory, 2022). The results obtained from AP depend a lot on the quality of data that is fed into the models. The data is owned by the client. AP provides algorithms in which clients can ingest their own data to obtain insights. AP is not like other services which provide already pre-trained models in the form of APIs which clients can call. AP takes the data from the client, uses the recipes to create a trained model. For this clients can save data in AWS S3 buckets or other storage services. The information obtained from Amazon's cloud storage service and the Personalize interface is analyzed and presented to the company, with the models optimized with the right parameters, and presented to the company simultaneously with the models. With AP service clubbed with other AWS services, Amazon has provided an easy-to-use and highly scalable platform that helps clients to generate recommendations for users. By providing the necessary infrastructure, Amazon manages the entire pipeline, including processing data, recognizing features, using the best algorithms, training, optimizing and hosting models (Amazon, 2021b). So in the end, every client has their own dedicated trained model. The focus of AP is on providing the clients with a quality ML model which can be used by them to generate useful insights(Expert, 2022).

The easy integration of the system with different marketing communication tools is a very important feature and it ensures that the people who use the system are not directed to only one communication tool. The most important question in mind is the confidentiality of information, and businesses may rightly be concerned about the confidentiality of shared information. (Altunışık, 2015, p. 61). Amazon's offering for businesses states that the data will be privately and securely encrypted and will only be used to generate recommendations to customers and will not be shared with customers or Amazon. com. (Amazon, 2021b). The benefits of applying big data analytics for the retail industry are listed as follows: Personalizing user home pages with product recommendations based on their shopping history, suggesting similar items on product details pages to help users find what they are looking for easily, helping users quickly find relevant new products, deals and promotions, improving marketing communication through personalization of push notifications and marketing emails with individualized product recommendations, improving sales with relevant product rankings and high-quality up-sell/cross-sell suggestions in the cart (Amazon, 2021b).

Data

One important aspect of the data is temporal details. AP can analyze the temporal details in real-time to help the clients understand the evolving nature of customer interaction. This temporality aspect is really powerful because it allows AP to understand how customer interests are changing over time in contrast to the collaborative filtering approach that's just using a matrix of items. "When did the customer interact" becomes really important when the client is looking to capture "what the customer is interested in now" as opposed to two weeks ago. Sophisticated combination of data and various ML models which are called recipes are used by AP under the hood to provide clients with the best results. These recipes are structured targeting different personalization use cases and hence provide a wide choice of selection to clients(Expert, 2022). Temporal aspect is a groundbreaking discovery as it allows the model to understand the evolving intent of a customer and can predict what he may buy next or alongwith an item already in his cart. This knowledge helps AP models to provide solid recommendations to clients.

There's another aspect to the data that clients can provide to AP and it's very powerful. It is what is called contextual data. This data is very specific to an interaction. Usually clients need to provide a user ID and item ID and a timestamp when a user interacts with an item at a particular time. But the client can also provide additional data about that interaction like when did the interaction occur? Like seasonality, is it winter, fall or spring. So if a client is selling clothing, user interest varies based on the weather conditions for that season. Another example is day of the week, where consumers consume video content differently on weekends. Maybe they watch long movies with their family. But on weekday mornings, maybe they're looking for short 30-minute news clips or sitcoms, whether commuting to work. This type of data. Device type is another really common contextual data. So are customers consuming content on their mobile phones, or on their desktops, or maybe on their set-top boxes. All of this contextual information can help AP learn the nuances of how the same user interacts differently based on different contexts. This allows AP to make even more relevant recommendations based on the current context when you're providing those recommendations. The dynamic filters included in the system create better user experiences by allowing clients to tailor the business rules for each user when recommendations are created, providing the opportunity for clients to control the recommendations in real-time while responding to the individual needs and preferences of the users (Chwastek, Pooniwala and Ashman, 2020).

Examining the customers, it is seen that AP users are international companies (Subway, Yamaha, Dominos etc.). However, the presence of promotions, free apps, training, free trials, minimum fees and no commitments shows that the AP target audience includes other businesses. The potential for SMEs to access these services is very exciting. These developments show that easy and relatively inexpensive applications started to exist shortly after Altunışık (2015) found that "it is extremely difficult to obtain and benefiting from its benefits is extremely difficult, but also very troublesome". AP offers personalized impressions, similar products, personalized redirection, personalized promotions/notifications for businesses using its own infrastructure (Amazon, 2021b).

LotteMart, one of the users of the AP system, is a supermarket chain in South Korea with 189 stores and more than 600,000 users, including an online store (Lottemart, 2021). AP enabled LotteMart to improve the customer experience with tailored recommendations. By focusing only on datasets for predefined interactions, users and items helped Lottemart in time savings tune to almost 50% of what they used to spend earlier in getting insights from the data. The use of coupons, a tool of marketing communication, has more than doubled since the introduction of personalized recommendations. In addition, there was a 1.7-fold increase in the frequency of new product sales. (Park and Hwang, 2020). By using the AP system at Subway, the fast-food restaurant with branches in 100 countries, can offer personalized recommendations to its customers without the need for machine learning expertise of company personnel(Amazon, 2021b). It is a fact that subjects such as big data, artificial intelligence, data mining, and machine learning are complex and require expertise. It is seen that there are simple package customization services that include all these concepts in the AP system and will be sufficient for the use of the enterprise in practice. AP is now being used in a variety of fields spanning blogs in which the users share their information, training videos, visuals, frequently asked questions and answers sections, certified training programs, customer service support consisting of professional experts, and many others(Amazon, 2021b).

With the effective use of AP, it is seen that the communication with the target audience of the enterprise can be improved in a more effective, fast and healthy way, which can be relatively cost-effective. With the AP product in the literature, as a result of big data analysis, the subject of determining marketing activities: limited access to big data, trust problem, costs, complexity, lack of necessary skills (Boyd and Crawford, 2012, p. 662; Fosso et al. 2015, p. 244; Johnson, 2012; Altunışık, 2015, p. 61; Ariker, Breuer, and McGuire, 2015, p. 91) are partly eliminated.

In the growing space of media and retail which sees most of the AP clients, competition is very fierce. With time it is getting extremely easy for customers to switch from one provider to another. Customer experience was never as important as it is in today's market. It is very essential for providers that they give the customer the best quality and experience. For this using APs recommendations, clients can segment customers that have an affinity for the promoted items. This gives a much better chance of engagement of customers, increasing the probability of getting an open click and then conversion to an order. It's like every customer have their own dedicated, trained model to them (Expert 2, 2022). This is also what differentiates AP from other competitors who provide recommendations as an out of the box SAAS which can be used by calling an API. Since these AP alternates have to focus on end to end products, they somewhere lose the focus on quality of big data analysis and that is where AP excels. These services will provide clients with already built-in libraries that clients have no control to modify as per their use case. So having this one model fits all use-case approach is not correct as every client might have different demographics that will be impacting the sales. AP's approach to personalize the model to individual client and not group them as part of segmented solution brings out the quality recommendations(Expert 1: 2022).

Amazon Personalize (AP) Technical Operating Process

Process Start with first conversation. Every customer that is planning to use Amazon personalized service, Amazon does a touch point meeting to set and decide the things. Amazon starts engaging with a client that's actually looking to use personalized advertising to improve their marketing. So using that user segmentation capability of Amazon mentioned earlier AP enables clients to more intelligently target users that would have an affinity for products that they are trying to promote.

The goal of different AP teams as a whole, including operations, developers, and solution architects is to make the service so easy that clients don't need them at all. Because of this tenet AP have a lot of customers that self adopt the service which means they organically read about the service usings documentation, blog posts and sample codes. AP is so simple to use that most of the time clients never have to contact AP teams at all. Being simple is APs core mission.

Moving to the data being consumed in AP services, clients bring their own data. AP is an industry agnostic tool. Any client can bring their own data and start playing with the recipes provided by AP. AP requires interaction and behavioral data to generate quality recommendations. These data points can be as simple as time a user stayed on an item page. AP takes these datasets and trains the model behind the scene. Different use cases that can benefit from this design are item recommendations based on similarity, popularity and other parameters. Clients have the option to either use already available recipes for some of these common use cases or create their own. AP provides the ability to clients to create multiple versions for testing and then productionalize the best model by using it as an API endpoint from their website to get the inferences(Expert 2, 2022).

The challenges that clients face while working with AP are similar to what they will face with any ML service. The quality of ML service is usually measured by the quality of its recommendations. Quality of recommendations depends a lot on the quality of data used to train and test the models. are usually related to integration issues on either client side or Amazon side. To achieve data quality, clients usually require to do some feature engineering, data cleaning and other data preparation activities. AP is very smart and takes care of feature engineering for clients. Clients can bring their raw data and AP will feature engineer the parameters, perform data splitting for training and evaluation providing performance metrics. Clients however need to develop capability on their side to cache the results, to handle the AP recommendation flow, scaling of application, integrating the application with AP API, and how to productionalize the whole flow. All these tasks need to be taken care of by the client itself.

Selection of Metadata

Selecting the right meta data for the use-case while using AP service can be a game changer in targeted marketing communication. This allows AP clients to optimize results and generate more customer relevant recommendations. This section discusses how to select the right meta data depending on different aspects of a use-case. Right metadata plays a crucial role in training and testing of models. High quality of data ensures high quality results and optimized models. Right metadata allows models to identify patterns of user behavior and preferences. Due to availability of the same data from multiple sources, one needs to compare and determine which data set to use and which to ignore. When a customer visits a website, different aspects of his behavior are captured. This includes data points like how long he was on a web page, how long he hovered over a certain image, which items he added to his wish list etc. All these data points are collected but not all will be useful for every use-case. A proper selection can help in identifying the customer preferences and hence will help in personalized recommendations.

AP has different combinations of models and datasets which are together called recipes. Different recipes lead to different recommendations. Irrespective of the recipe an AP client chooses, there are three main type of data sets that AP deals with. These are, user data, item data and user-item interactions. User data can have metadata like, age, gender, location, ethnicity etc. Similarly, items will have metadata like, size, color, originated from, price etc. The third and most revealing type of dataset is user-item interaction. This dataset will have metadata like, time spent on the item page, item added to wish list etc. The minimum number of interactions Amazon Personalize expects in order to start making recommendations is 1,000 interactions from a minimum of 25 users(Hood and Cleopas, 2020).

Table 2. Different AP Data Types. Source: (Hood & Cleopas, 2020)

Dataset Type	Required Fileds	Reserved Keywords
User	USER_ID (string)	
Item	ITEM_ID (string)	CREATION_TIMESTAMP (long)
Interactions	USER_ID (string) ITEM_ID (string) TIMESTAMP (long)	EVENT_TYPE (string) IMPRESSION (string) EVENT_VALUE (float, null)

Usually there are two types of users that visit a website, guest users and member users. It is always more optimal to use data from members as they are authenticated as well as easy to track then guest or anonymous user. In AP, each data set has set specific requirements and a schema needs to be defined. This ensures a proper expected structure of data and parameters which AP can then use.

One of the latest feature that has been launched is user segmentation (AWS re:Invent, 2021) . Clients can train the models to segment users liking a particular item. So rather than asking what a particular customer will buy, the problem statement becomes, who are all the prospective customers of a specific item. This changes the whole game because now rather than sending email of the prospective items to the customer, clients can send out marketing emails to all the prospective clients of an item. So from a client's perspective these will look like generalized communication to a user segment, but from a customer's perspective this will look like a personalized email of the items he/she likes.

Recommendation Models

In the previous section we discuss how careful and well researched data selection can lead to quality recommendations and optimized models. There are two recommendation models that are used in AP, collaborative filtering and content-based filtering. Collaborative filtering focuses on the user similarities. If two users show similar patterns and interests, then the recommendations to one user depends on the products that other similar users have bought. On the other hand, in content based filtering, focus is one finding similarities between items. The recommendations are the items having similar metadata as the one that the customer likes. Due to the intrinsic differences in the approach, both these models used different data. Collaborative filtering uses user data while content based filtering uses item data. A hybrid model will use both of these data sets.

While a quality data set results in optimized model, quantity of data also makes a big difference too. Too much data will result in creating noise in model while too less data will create an underperforming model. If meta data that has no relation to user is included in training data set, it makes it harder for the learning algorithm to find a relevant pattern in the data. So this displays how a wrong approach in metadata selection can make it hard for algorithms to find patterns and learn anything from data. Recommendations generated by such a model which is developed using skewed, non-relevant data will not be as personalized as expected.

Findings and Suggestions

Marketing communication plays a very critical part in sales of any business. Sales in the soul of any company. A good marketing campaign can make or break the yearly sales revenue. Thus it is of utmost importance that any insight that can be used to make marketing messages as effective as possible must be utilized. Big data analysis holds this capability to provide useful insights into customer behavior and thus helping create personalized marketing communication. From our analysis of different aspects of using big data analysis to drive marketing campaigns we present some important findings in this section.

One of the most important findings is the impact of metadata on the quality of insights. Specific use cases require specific types of data and thus it is very important to carefully choose the metadata. This is challenging as it is not always easy to find the required parameters. In such cases work arounds like interpolation, mutation and other such techniques can be used to get inferential data which is close to the actual data. Another important finding is the selection of models to process the data and get insights. A single model cannot cater to all use cases. So deciding which will be the best model is a challenge. With this the challenge to train the model in such a way that we can minimize any noise comes into picture. This is closely related with the quantity and quality of data. To decide how much data will be sufficient to properly train a model needs a lot of iterations and validations. Last but not the least the requirement of high speed processing of big data to get quick real-time results is another frontier on which a lot of advancement is required. All these problems bring up the question of cost-benefit analysis of using big data insights in making targeted marketing campaigns more efficient and personalized. No doubt it will bring a lot of value in terms of increased sales and high rate of customer acquisition for the companies.

CONCLUSION

Big data analysis is a very important tool for marketing communication at the point of timely and accurate understanding and the response of consumers whose needs and expectations are constantly increasing. With the development of communication technologies and increasing competition, the messages sent to the consumers and the feedback of the consumers are getting more complex day by day and businesses have to give more importance to healthy communication. Online commerce is increasing very rapidly, and many aspects of communication and product recommendations in online stores are becoming more important. The comments made by the users are read by millions of people within a few minutes, and millions of replies are received to these comments, and if there is no strategic and instant intervention, processes leading to the bankruptcy of the enterprises can be experienced. Big data has a very critical function for effective marketing communication in this environment. Identifying consumer requests, needs, observing comments, complaints and satisfaction, and as a result, determining communication strategies will increase the effectiveness of marketing communication for the business while reducing costs on the other hand. The business will be able to make effective interventions for the right target audience with the right tools.

In addition to this, attention should be paid to the fact that people prefer to talk to people, especially when making decisions about digital communication strategies after big data analysis. Until recently, serious IT personnel, technical equipment, additional personnel, etc. were required by businesses to enable them to collect, analyze and interpret big data in millions of channels within their own structure. Today, outsourced services make big data analytics services relatively accessible to businesses. In the AP example, free usage rights, discounts, training, protocols to ensure security/privacy are indicators that infrastructure services will be offered to a much wider audience at affordable costs.

In this study, big data analysis and machine learning in marketing communication are discussed with different dimensions. In future studies, it is evaluated that big data analysis, which will be carried out by using primary data, will be beneficial to the literature and practitioners in research on the use cases in the marketing communications of the enterprises, the obstacles encountered while using it, and the solution proposals.

REFERENCES

Akçan, B. (2016). Big Data: Producers and Consumers. *New Media Studies*, (2).

Altunışık, R. (2015). Big Data: My Source of Opportunities or New Bundle of Problems? *Yildiz Social Science Review*, *1*(1), 45–76.

Alzahrani, S. M. (2021). Big Data Analytics Tools: Twitter API and Spark. *2021 International Conference of Women in Data Science at Taif University (WiDSTaif)*, 1-6. 10.1109/WiDSTaif52235.2021.9430205

AMA. (2021). *American Marketing Association*. https://www.ama.org/topics/marcom/

Amado, A., Cortez, P., Rita, P., & Moro, S. (2018). Research Trends on Big Data in Marketing: A Text Mining and Topic Modeling Based Literature Analysis. *European Research on Management and Business Economics*, *24*(1), 1–7. doi:10.1016/j.iedeen.2017.06.002

Amazon. (2021a). *What is Big Data*. https://aws.amazon.com/tr/big-data/what-is-big-data/

Amazon. (2021b). *Personalize*. https://aws.amazon.com/tr/personalize/

Ariker, M., Breuer, P., & McGuire, T. (2015). *How to Get the Most from Big Data? McKinsey. In Marketing & Sales Big Data, Analytics, and the Future of Marketing & Sales*. McKinsey.

Ariker, M., & Manuel, N. (2015). Want Big Data Sales Programs to Work? Get emotional. In Marketing & Sales Big Data, Analytics, and the Future of Marketing & Sales. McKinsey.

Arrigo, E., Liberati, C., & Mariani, P. (2021). Social Media Data and Users' Preferences: A Statistical Analysis to Support Marketing Communication. *Big Data Research*, 24.

Bendle, N., & Wang, X. (2016). Uncovering the Message from the Mess of Big Data. *Business Horizons*, *59*(1), 115–124. doi:10.1016/j.bushor.2015.10.001

Benoit, D. F., Lessmann, S., & Verbeke, W. (2020). On Realizing the Utopian Potential of Big Data Analytics for Maximizing Return On Marketing İnvestments. *Journal of Marketing Management*, *36*(3-4), 233–247. doi:10.1080/0267257X.2020.1739446

Bitnine. (2016). *Introduction About Big Data Marketing*. https://bitnine.net/blog-useful-information/introduction-about-big-data-marketing

Blei, D. M., & Ng, Y. A., & Jordan M. (2003). Latent Dirichlet Allocation. *Journal of Machine Learning Research*, *3*(4–5), 993–1022. doi:10.1162/jmlr.2003.3.4-5.993

Boyd, D., & Crawford, K. (2012). Critical Questıons for Big Data. *Information Communication and Society*, *15*(5), 662–679. doi:10.1080/1369118X.2012.678878

Buganza, T., Trabucchi, D., & Pellizzoni, E. (2020). Limitless Personalization: The Role of Big Data İn Unveiling Service Opportunities. *Technology Analysis and Strategic Management*, *32*(1), 58–70. do i:10.1080/09537325.2019.1634252

Buhalis, D., & Volchek, K. (2021). Bridging Marketing Theory and Big Data Analytics: The Taxonomy of Marketing Attribution. *International Journal of Information Management*, *56*, 1–14. doi:10.1016/j. ijinfomgt.2020.102253

Chen, Y., & Xie, J. (2008). Online Consumer Review: Word-of-Mouth as a New Element of Marketing Communication Mix. *Management Science*, *54*(3), 477–491. doi:10.1287/mnsc.1070.0810

Chwastek, M., Pooniwala, P., & Ashman, S. (2020). *Amazon Personalize Now Supports Dynamic Filters for Applying Business Rules to Your Recommendations on the Fly.* https://aws.amazon.com/tr/blogs/ machine-learning/amazon-personalize-now-supports-dynamic-filters-for-applying-business-rules-to-your-recommendations-on-the-fly/

Culotta, A., & Cutler, J. (2016). Mining Brand Perceptions from Twitter. *Marketing Science*, *35*(3), 343–362. doi:10.1287/mksc.2015.0968

De Mauro, A., Greco, M., & Grimaldi, M. (2016). A Formal Definition of Big Data Based on İts Essential Features. *Library Review*, *65*(3), 122–135. doi:10.1108/LR-06-2015-0061

Dixon, M. (2019). *How Netflix Used Big Data and Analytics to Generate Billions.* https://seleritysas. com/blog/2019/04/05/how-netflix-used-big-data-and-analytics-to-generate-billions/

Erevelles, S., Fukawa, N., & Swayne, L. (2016). Big Data Consumer Analytics and The Transformation of Marketing. *Journal of Business Research*, *69*(2), 897–904. doi:10.1016/j.jbusres.2015.07.001

EU. (2021). *Big Data: Definition, Benefits, Challenges (infographics).* https://www.europarl.europa.eu/ news/en/headlines/society/20210211STO97614/big-data-definition-benefits-challenges-infographics

Fader, P., & Winer, R. (2012). Introduction to The Special Issue on The Emergence and Impact of User-Generated Content. *Marketing Science*, *31*(3), 369–371. doi:10.1287/mksc.1120.0715

Fortune. (2021). *Fortune 500.* https://fortune.com/company/amazon-com/fortune500/

Fosso, W. S., Akter, S., Edwards, A., Chopin, G., & Gnanzou, D. (2015). How 'Big Data' Can Make Big Impact: Findings from A Systematic Review and A Longitudinal Case Study. *International Journal of Production Economics*, *165*, 234–246. doi:10.1016/j.ijpe.2014.12.031

Gulati, R., & Oldroyd, J. B. (2005). The Quest for Customer Focus. *Harvard Business Review*, 92–101. PMID:15807042

Hartmans, A. (2021). *Jeff Bezos Originally Wanted To Name Amazon 'Cadabra,' And 14 Other Little-Known Facts About The Early Days Of The E-Commerce Giant.* Businessinsider: https://www.businessinsider.com/jeff-bezos-amazon-history-facts-2017-4

Hood, A., & Kleopas, I. (2020). *Selecting the right metadata to build high-performing recommendation models with Amazon Personalize.* https://aws.amazon.com/blogs/machine-learning/selecting-the-right-metadata-to-build-high-performing-recommendation-models-with-amazon-personalize/

InsideBigData. (2019). *How Amazon Used Big Data to Rule E-Commerce.* https://insidebigdata. com/2019/11/30/how-amazon-used-big-data-to-rule-e-commerce/

Johnson, E. J. (2012). Big Data + Big Analytics = Big Opportunity: Big Data is Dominating the Strategy Discussion for Many Financial Executives. As These Market Dynamics Continue to Evolve, Expectations Will Continue to Shift About What Should Be Disclosed, When and to Whom. *Financial Executive, 28*(6).

Lemon, N., & Verhoef, C. (2016). Understanding Customer Experience Throughout the Customer Journey. *Journal of Marketing,* (80), 69-96. doi:10.1509/jm.15.0420

Lottemart. (2021). https://www.lotteon.com/p/display/main/lottemart?mall_no=4&chno=100195&ch_ dtl_no=1000617

Lu, S., Xiao, L., & Ding, M. (2016). A Video-Based Automated Recommender (VAR) System for Garments. *Marketing Science, 35*(3), 484–510. doi:10.1287/mksc.2016.0984

Luenendonk, M. (2019). *Uses of Big Data in Marketing.* https://www.cleverism.com/best-uses-big-data-marketing/

Ma, L., & Sun, B. (2020). Machine Learning and AI in Marketing – Connecting Computing Power to Human Insights. *International Journal of Research in Marketing, 37*(3), 481–504. doi:10.1016/j.ijres-mar.2020.04.005

Malthouse, E. C., Haenlein, M., Skiera, B., & Zhang, E. W. (2013). Managing Customer Relationships in The Social Media Era: Introducing The Social CRM house. *Journal of Interactive Marketing, 27*(4), 270–280. doi:10.1016/j.intmar.2013.09.008

McKinsey. (2015). *Marketing & Sales Big Data, Analytics and the Future of Marketing & Sales.* https:// www.mckinsey.com

Mihaela, E. O. (2015). *The Influence of the Integrated Marketing Communication on The Consumer Buying Behavior. Procedia Economics and Finance.*

Morgan, B. (2018). *How Amazon Has Reorganized Around Artificial Intelligence And Machine Learning.* https://www.forbes.com/sites/blakemorgan/2018/07/16/how-amazon-has-re-organized-around-artificial-intelligence-and-machine-learning/?sh=4f75f1573618

Moro, S., Rita, P., & Vala, P. (2016). Predicting Social Media Performance Metrics and Evaluation of The İmpact On Brand Building: A Data Mining Approach. *Journal of Business Research, 69*(9), 3341–3351. doi:10.1016/j.jbusres.2016.02.010

Netzer, O., Feldman, R., Goldenberg, J., & Fresko, M. (2012). Mine Your Own Business: Market structure Surveillance Through Text Mining. *Marketing Science, 31*(3), 521–543. doi:10.1287/mksc.1120.0713

Park, S., & Hwang, K. (2020). *Increasing Customer Engagement and Loyalty With Personalized Coupon Recommendations Using Amazon Personalize.* https://aws.amazon.com/tr/blogs/machine-learning/ increasing-customer-engagement-and-loyalty-with-personalized-coupon-recommendat ions-using-amazon-personalize/

Saggi, G. M., & Jain, S. (2018). A Survey Towards An Integration of Big Data Analytics to Big Insights. *Information Processing & Management*, *54*(5), 758–790. doi:10.1016/j.ipm.2018.01.010

Shen, Q., & Villas-Boas, J. (2018). Behavior-based Advertising. *Management Science*, *64*(5), 2047–2064. doi:10.1287/mnsc.2016.2719

Simpson, J. (2017). *Finding Brand Success In The Digital World.* https://www.forbes.com/sites/forbesagencycouncil/2017/08/25/finding-brand-success-in-the-digital-world/? sh=774a012626e2

Smith, J. B., & Colgate, M. (2007). Customer Value Creation: A Practical Framework. *Journal of Marketing Theory and Practice*, *15*(1), 7–23. doi:10.2753/MTP1069-6679150101

Suoniemi, S., Meyer-Waarden, L., Munzel, A., & Straub, A. R. (2020). Big Data and Firm Performance: The Roles of Market-directed Capabilities and Business Strategy. *Information & Management*, *57*(7), 103365. doi:10.1016/j.im.2020.103365

Talend. (2021). *Big Data in Marketing 101: Why it's Important, Where it's Going, and How to Get Started.* https://www.talend.com/resources/big-data-marketing/

Tang, Q. (2020). Construction of Interactive Integrated Communication Marketing System in Big Data Era. *Journal of Physics: Conference Series*, *1550*(3), 1550. doi:10.1088/1742-6596/1550/3/032142

Walmart. (2021). https://corporate.walmart.com/our-story/our-locations

Wiencierz, C., & Röttger, U. (2018). *Big Data-Based Strategic Communication.* https://www.akademischegesellschaft.com/fileadmin/webcontent/Presse/1803_Comm_Director_CW_UR_2018_BD_based_Strat_Comm.pdf

WorldEconomicForum. (2012). *Big Data, Big Impact: New Possibilities for International Development.* http://www3.weforum.org/docs/WEF_TC_MFS_BigDataBigImpact_ Briefing_ 2012.pdf

Yavuz, V., & Erdoğan-Gençyürek, M. (2019). *Advertising Applications on Internet News Sites.* Current Marketing Studies. in Image Publishing House.

Zhan, Y., Tan, K. H., Ji, G., & Tseng, L. C. (2018). A Big Data Framework for Facilitating Product Innovation Processes. *Business Process Management Journal*, (270), 577–595.

Compilation of References

Abbasi, A., & Hashim, F. M. (2015). Prediction of hydrate formation conditions in the subsea pipeline with genetic algorithm. *Proceedings of the 2015 International Conference on Technology, Informatics, Management, Engineering and Environment, TIME-E 2015*, 133–136. 10.1109/TIME-E.2015.7389761

Abbasi, A., & Hashim, F. M. (2016). Prediction of hydrate formation conditions in subsea pipeline with genetic algorithm. *Proceedings of the 2015 International Conference on Technology, Informatics, Management, Engineering and Environment, TIME-E 2015*, 133–136.

Abdel-Sattar, M., Aboukarina, A. M., & Alnahdi, B. M. (2021). Application of Artificial Neural Network and Support Vector Regression in Predicting Mass of Ber Fruits (Ziziphus Mauritiana Lamk.) Based on Fruit Axial Dimensions. *PLoS One*, *16*(1), 1–15. doi:10.1371/journal.pone.0245228 PMID:33411790

Abooali, D., & Khamehchi, E. (2017). New predictive method for estimation of natural gas hydrate formation temperature using genetic programming. *Neural Computing & Applications*, 1–10.

Adedeji, O., & Wang, Z. (2019). intelligent Waste Classification System Using Deep Learning Convolutional Neural Network. *Procedia Manufacturing*, *35*, 607–612. doi:10.1016/j.promfg.2019.05.086

Ahmadi, M., Ulyanov, D., Semenov, S., Trofimov, M., & Giacinto, G. (2016, March). Novel feature extraction, selection, and fusion for effective malware family classification. *Proceedings of the sixth ACM conference on data and application security and privacy*, 183-194. 10.1145/2857705.2857713

Ahmad, R., Afzal, M. T., & Qadir, M. A. (2016, May). Information extraction from PDF sources based on rule-based system using integrated formats. In *Semantic web evaluation challenge* (pp. 293–308). Springer. doi:10.1007/978-3-319-46565-4_23

Akçan, B. (2016). Big Data: Producers and Consumers. *New Media Studies*, (2).

Akın, A. A., & Akın, M. D. (2007). Zemberek, an open source NLP framework for Turkic languages. *Structure (London, England)*, *10*, 1–5.

Al Mamun, M. A., Puspo, J. A., & Das, A. K. (2017). An intelligent smartphone based approach using IoT for ensuring safe driving. *ICECOS 2017 - Proceeding of 2017 International Conference on Electrical Engineering and Computer Science: Sustaining the Cultural Heritage Toward the Smart Environment for Better Future*, 217–223. 10.1109/ICECOS.2017.8167137

Albawi, S., Mohammed, T. A., & Al-Zawi, S. (2017, August). Understanding of a convolutional neural network. In *2017 international conference on engineering and technology (ICET)* (pp. 1-6). IEEE.

Al-Dweik, A., Muresan, R., Mayhew, M., & Lieberman, M. (2017). IoT-based multifunctional Scalable real-time Enhanced Road Side Unit for Intelligent Transportation Systems. *Canadian Conference on Electrical and Computer Engineering*, 1–6. 10.1109/CCECE.2017.7946618

Allan, J., Carbonell, J., Doddington, G., Yamron, J., & Yang, Y. (1998). Topic detection and tracking pilot study: final report. In *Proceedings of the DARPA broadcast news transcription and understanding workshop* (pp. 194–218). Academic Press.

Allan, J. (2002). Topic detection and tracking: event-based information organization. In *Topic detection and tracking: event-based information organization* (pp. 1–16). Springer Science and Business Media. doi:10.1007/978-1-4615-0933-2_1

Altunışık, R. (2015). Big Data: My Source of Opportunities or New Bundle of Problems? *Yildiz Social Science Review*, *1*(1), 45–76.

Alzahrani, S. M. (2021). Big Data Analytics Tools: Twitter API and Spark. *2021 International Conference of Women in Data Science at Taif University (WiDSTaif)*, 1-6. 10.1109/WiDSTaif52235.2021.9430205

AMA. (2021). *American Marketing Association*. https://www.ama.org/topics/marcom/

Amado, A., Cortez, P., Rita, P., & Moro, S. (2018). Research Trends on Big Data in Marketing: A Text Mining and Topic Modeling Based Literature Analysis. *European Research on Management and Business Economics*, *24*(1), 1–7. doi:10.1016/j.iedeen.2017.06.002

Amato, G., Carrara, F., Falchi, F., Gennaro, C., Meghini, C., & Vairo, C. (2017). Deep learning for decentralized parking lot occupancy detection. *Expert Systems with Applications*, *72*, 327–334. doi:10.1016/j.eswa.2016.10.055

Amazon. (2021a). *What is Big Data*. https://aws.amazon.com/tr/big-data/what-is-big-data/

Amazon. (2021b). *Personalize*. https://aws.amazon.com/tr/personalize/

Amer, E. (2015, August). Enhancing the efficiency of web search engines through ontology learning from unstructured information sources. In *2015 IEEE international conference on information reuse and integration* (pp. 542-549). IEEE.

Anair, D., Martin, J., Pinto, M. C., & Goldman, J. (2020, February 25). *Ride-Hailing Climate Risks*. Union of Concerned Scientists. https://www.ucsusa.org/resources/ride-hailing-climate-risks

Anderson, H. S., Kharkar, A., Filar, B., & Roth, P. (2017). Evading machine learning malware detection. *Black Hat*.

Andre, E., Robicquet, A., Ramsundar, B., Kuleshov, V., DePristo, M., Chou, K., Cui, C., Carrado, G., Thrun, S., & Dean, J. (2019). A guide to deep learning in healthcare. *Nature Medicine*, *25*(1), 24–29. doi:10.103841591-018-0316-z PMID:30617335

Angelo Oliveira. (2020). *Malware Analysis Datasets: API Call Sequences*. https://www.kaggle.com/ang3loliveira/malware-analysis-datasets-api-call-sequences.html

Ankerst, M., Breunig, M. M., Kriegel, H. P., & Sander, J. (1999). OPTICS: Ordering points to identify the clustering structure. *SIGMOD Record*, *28*(2), 49–60. doi:10.1145/304181.304187

Anno, S., Hara, T., Kai, H., Lee, M.-A., Chang, Y., Oyoshi, K., Mizukami, Y., & Tadono, T. (2019). Spatiotemporal dengue fever hotspots associated with climatic factors in taiwan including outbreak predictions based on machine-learning. *Geospatial Health*, *14*(2). Advance online publication. doi:10.4081/gh.2019.771 PMID:31724367

Anthimopoulos, M., Christodoulidis, S., Ebner, L., Christe, A., & Mougiakakou, S. (2016). Lung pattern classification for interstitial lung diseases using a deep convolutional neural network. *IEEE Transactions on Medical Imaging*, *35*(5), 1207–1216. doi:10.1109/TMI.2016.2535865 PMID:26955021

Antonacopoulos, A., Bridson, D., Papadopoulos, C., & Pletschacher, S. (2009, July). A realistic dataset for performance evaluation of document layout analysis. In *2009 10th International Conference on Document Analysis and Recognition* (pp. 296-300). IEEE. 10.1109/ICDAR.2009.271

Aramaki, E., Maskawa, S., & Morita, M. (2011, July). Twitter catches the flu: detecting influenza epidemics using Twitter. In *Proceedings of the 2011 Conference on empirical methods in natural language processing* (pp. 1568-1576). Academic Press.

Ariker, M., & Manuel, N. (2015). Want Big Data Sales Programs to Work? Get emotional. In Marketing & Sales Big Data, Analytics, and the Future of Marketing & Sales. McKinsey.

Ariker, M., Breuer, P., & McGuire, T. (2015). *How to Get the Most from Big Data? McKinsey. In Marketing & Sales Big Data, Analytics, and the Future of Marketing & Sales*. McKinsey.

Armato, S. G. III, McLennan, G., Bidaut, L., McNitt-Gray, M. F., Meyer, C. R., Reeves, A. P., Zhao, B., Aberle, D. R., Henschke, C. I., Hoffman, A., Kazerooni, E. A., MacMahon, H., van Beek, E. J. R., Yankelevitz, D., Biancardi, A. M., Bland, P. H., Brown, M. S., Engelmann, R. M., Laderach, G. E., ... Clarke, L. P. (2011). The lung image database consortium (LIDC) and image database resource initiative (IDRI): A complete reference database of lung nodules on CT scans. *Medical Physics*, *38*(2), 915–931. doi:10.1118/1.3528204 PMID:21452728

Arrigo, E., Liberati, C., & Mariani, P. (2021). Social Media Data and Users' Preferences: A Statistical Analysis to Support Marketing Communication. *Big Data Research,* 24.

Arunnehru, J., Chamundeeswari, G., & Prasanna Bharathi, S. (2018). Human Action Recognition using 3D Motion Cuboids in Surveillance Videos. In *Proceeding of International Conference on Robotics and Smart Manufacturing* (pp. 471-477). Academic Press.

Arunnehru, J., & Geetha, M. K. (2013). Motion intensity code for action recognition in video using pca and svm. In *Proceedings of Mining Intelligence and Knowledge Exploration* (pp. 70–81). Springer. doi:10.1007/978-3-319-03844-5_8

Ashrafian, H., & Darzi, A. (2018). Transforming health policy through machine learning. *PLoS Medicine*, *15*(11), e1002692. doi:10.1371/journal.pmed.1002692 PMID:30422977

Aydin, I., Karakose, M., & Karakose, E. (2017). A navigation and reservation based smart parking platform using genetic optimization for smart cities. *ICSG 2017 - 5th International Istanbul Smart Grids and Cities Congress and Fair*, 120–124. 10.1109/SGCF.2017.7947615

Azgomi, H. F., & Jamshidi, M. (2018). A brief survey on smart community and smart transportation. *Proceedings - International Conference on Tools with Artificial Intelligence, ICTAI, 2018-Novem*, 932–939. 10.1109/ICTAI.2018.00144

Babakhani, S. M., Bahmani, M., Shariati, J., Badr, K., & Balouchi, Y. (2015). Comparing the capability of artificial neural network (ANN) and CSMHYD program for predicting of hydrate formation pressure in binary mixtures. *Journal of Petroleum Science Engineering*, *136*, 78–87. doi:10.1016/j.petrol.2015.11.002

Bacciu, D., Carta, A., Gnesi, S., & Semini, L. (2017). An experience in using machine learning for short-term predictions in smart transportation systems. *Journal of Logical and Algebraic Methods in Programming*, *87*(November), 52–66. doi:10.1016/j.jlamp.2016.11.002

Baghban, A., Namvarrechi, S., Phung, L. T. K., Lee, M., Bahadori, A., & Kashiwao, T. (2016). Phase equilibrium modelling of natural gas hydrate formation conditions using LSSVM approach. *Petroleum Science and Technology*, *34*(16), 1431–1438. doi:10.1080/10916466.2016.1202966

Bagloee, S. A., Tavana, M., Asadi, M., & Oliver, T. (2016). Autonomous vehicles: Challenges, opportunities, and future implications for transportation policies. *Journal of Modern Transportation*, *24*(4), 284–303. doi:10.100740534-016-0117-3

Bali, V., Aggarwal, D., & Singh, S. (2021). Life Expectancy: Prediction & Analysis Using ML. *9th International Conference on Reliability, Infocom Technologies and Optimization*. 10.1109/ICRITO51393.2021.9596123

Ballan, L., Bertini, M., & Bimbo, A. D. (2011). Event detection and recognition for semantic annotation of video. *Multimedia Tools and Applications*, *51*(1), 279–302. doi:10.100711042-010-0643-7

Barua, H. B. (2021). Data science and Machine learning in the Clouds : A Perspective for the Future. *Journal of LATEX Templates*.

Bellemo, V., Lim, Z. W., Lim, G., Nguyen, Q. D., Xie, Y., Yip, M. Y. T., Hamzah, H., Ho, J., Lee, X. Q., Hsu, W., Lee, M. L., Musonda, L., Chandran, M., Chipalo-Mutati, G., Muma, M., Tan, G. S. W., Sivaprasad, S., Menon, G., Wong, T. Y., & Ting, D. S. W. (2019). Artificial intelligence using deep learning to screen for referable and vision-threatening diabetic retinopathy in Africa: A clinical validation study. *The Lancet. Digital Health*, *1*(1), e35–e44. doi:10.1016/S2589-7500(19)30004-4 PMID:33323239

Bendle, N., & Wang, X. (2016). Uncovering the Message from the Mess of Big Data. *Business Horizons*, *59*(1), 115–124. doi:10.1016/j.bushor.2015.10.001

Benoit, D. F., Lessmann, S., & Verbeke, W. (2020). On Realizing the Utopian Potential of Big Data Analytics for Maximizing Return On Marketing İnvestments. *Journal of Marketing Management*, *36*(3-4), 233–247. doi:10.1080/0267257X.2020.1739446

Bialek, S., Boundy, E., Bowen, V., Chow, N., Cohn, A., Dowling, N., Ellington, S., Gierke, R., Hall, A., MacNeil, J., Patel, P., Peacock, G., Pilishvili, T., Razzaghi, H., Reed, N., Ritchey, M., & Sauber-Schatz, E. (2020). Severe Outcomes Among Patients with Coronavirus Disease 2019 (COVID-19) - United States. *MMWR. Morbidity and Mortality Weekly Report*, *27*(69), 343–346. doi:10.15585/mmwr.mm6912e2

Bingol, E., Kuzlu, M., & Pipattanasompom, M. (2019). A LoRa-based Smart Streetlighting System for Smart Cities. *7th International Istanbul Smart Grids and Cities Congress and Fair, ICSG 2019 - Proceedings*, 66–70. 10.1109/SGCF.2019.8782413

Bird, S., Klein, E., & Loper, E. (2009). *Natural language processing with Python: analyzing text with the natural language toolkit*. O'Reilly Media, Inc.

Biswas, S., Riba, P., Lladós, J., & Pal, U. (2021). Beyond document object detection: Instance-level segmentation of complex layouts. *International Journal on Document Analysis and Recognition*, *24*(3), 269–281. doi:10.100710032-021-00380-6

Bitnine. (2016). *Introduction About Big Data Marketing*. https://bitnine.net/blog-useful-information/introduction-about-big-data-marketing

Blackwell, W. J., & Chen, F. W. (2009). *Neural networks in atmospheric remote sensing*. Artech House.

Blei, D. M., & Ng, Y. A., & Jordan M. (2003). Latent Dirichlet Allocation. *Journal of Machine Learning Research*, *3*(4–5), 993–1022. doi:10.1162/jmlr.2003.3.4-5.993

Blokh, I., & Alexandrov, V. (2017). News clustering based on similarity analysis. *Procedia Computer Science*, *122*, 715–719. doi:10.1016/j.procs.2017.11.428

Bojanowski, P., Grave, E., Joulin, A., & Mikolov, T. (2017). Enriching word vectors with subword information. *Transactions of the Association for Computational Linguistics*, *5*, 135–146. doi:10.1162/tacl_a_00051

Borges, P. V. K., Conci, N., & Cavallaro, A. (2013). Video-based human behavior understanding: A survey. *IEEE Trans. Circ. Syst. Vid.*, *23*(11), 1993–2008. doi:10.1109/TCSVT.2013.2270402

Bouchard, C., & Granjean, B. P. A. (1995). A neural network correlation for the variation of viscosity of sucrose aqueous solutions with temperature and concentration. *Lebensmittel-Wissenschaft + Technologie*, *28*(1), 157–159. doi:10.1016/S0023-6438(95)80029-8

Bouras, C., & Tsogkas, V. (2012). A clustering technique for news articles using WordNet. *Knowledge-Based Systems*, *36*, 115–128. doi:10.1016/j.knosys.2012.06.015

Boyd, D., & Crawford, K. (2012). Critical Questions for Big Data. *Information Communication and Society*, *15*(5), 662–679. doi:10.1080/1369118X.2012.678878

Bratsas, C., Grau, J. M. S., Koupidis, K., Giannakopoulos, K., Kaloudis, A., & Aifadopoulou, G. (2019, December). A Comparison of Machine Learning Methods for the Prediction of Traffic Speed in Urban Places. *Sustainability*, *12*(1), 142. doi:10.3390u12010142

Broomhead, D. S., & Lowe, D. (1988). Radial basis functions, multi-variable functional interpolation and adaptive networks (Technical report). RSRE.

Broomhead, D. S., & Lowe, D. (1988). Multivariable functional interpolation and adaptive networks. *Complex Systems*, *2*, 321–355.

Buch, V. H., Ahmed, I., & Maruthappu, M. (2018). Artificial intelligence in medicine: Current trends and future possibilities. *The British Journal of General Practice*, *68*(668), 143–144. doi:10.3399/bjgp18X695213 PMID:29472224

Budapesti Műszaki és Gazdaságtudományi Egyetem. Faculty of Transport Engineering and Vehicle Engineering. Department of Transport Technology and Economics, Budapesti Műszaki és Gazdaságtudományi Egyetem, IEEE Hungary Section, & Institute of Electrical and Electronics Engineers. (2015). *2015 International Conference on Models and Technologies for Intelligent Transportation Systems (MT-ITS)*. Budapest University of Technology and Economics (BME), Faculty of Transport Engineering and Vehicle Engineering, Department of Transport Technology and Economics.

Buganza, T., Trabucchi, D., & Pellizzoni, E. (2020). Limitless Personalization: The Role of Big Data İn Unveiling Service Opportunities. *Technology Analysis and Strategic Management*, *32*(1), 58–70. doi:10.1080/09537325.2019.1634252

Buhalis, D., & Volchek, K. (2021). Bridging Marketing Theory and Big Data Analytics: The Taxonomy of Marketing Attribution. *International Journal of Information Management*, *56*, 1–14. doi:10.1016/j.ijinfomgt.2020.102253

Burlina, P., Freund, D. E., Dupas, B., & Bressler, N. (2011). *Automatic screening of age-related macular degeneration and retinal abnormalities*. Paper presented at the 2011 Annual International Conference of the IEEE Engineering in Medicine and Biology Society.

Butt, T. A., Iqbal, R., Salah, K., Aloqaily, M., & Jararweh, Y. (2019). Privacy Management in Social Internet of Vehicles: Review, Challenges and Blockchain Based Solutions. *IEEE Access: Practical Innovations, Open Solutions*, *7*, 79694–79713. doi:10.1109/ACCESS.2019.2922236

Buzug, T. M. (2011). Computed tomography.I n *Springer handbook of medical technology* (pp. 311-342). Springer.

Caicedo, J. C., Cooper, S., Heigwer, F., Warchal, S., Qiu, P., Molnar, C., Vasilevich, A. S., Barry, J. D., Bansal, H. S., Kraus, O., Wawer, M., Paavolainen, L., Herrmann, M. D., Rohban, M., Hung, J., Hennig, H., Concannon, J., Smith, I., Clemons, P. A., ... Carpenter, A. E. (2017). Data-analysis strategies for image-based cell profiling. *Nature Methods*, *14*(9), 849–863. doi:10.1038/nmeth.4397 PMID:28858338

Cai, L., Pethica, B. A., Debenedetti, P. G., & Sundaresan, S. (2016). Formation of cyclopentane methane binary clathrate hydrate in brine solutions. *Chemical Engineering Science*, *141*, 125–132. doi:10.1016/j.ces.2015.11.001

Campello, R. J., Moulavi, D., & Sander, J. (2013, April). Density-based clustering based on hierarchical density estimates. In *Pacific-Asia conference on knowledge discovery and data mining* (pp. 160–172). Springer. doi:10.1007/978-3-642-37456-2_14

Cao, H., Liu, H., Song, E., Ma, G., Xu, X., Jin, R., Liu, T., & Hung, C. C. (2020). A two-stage convolutional neural network for lung nodule detection. *IEEE Journal of Biomedical and Health Informatics*, *24*(7), 2006–2015. doi:10.1109/JBHI.2019.2963720 PMID:31905154

Cao, J., Zhu, S., Li, C., & Han, B. (2020). Integrating support vector regression with genetic algorithm for hydrate formation condition prediction. *Processes (Basel, Switzerland)*, *8*(5), 1–11. doi:10.3390/pr8050519

Carrion, M., & Madoff, L. C. (2017). ProMED-mail: 22 years of digital surveillance of emerging infectious diseases. *International Health*, *9*(3), 177–183. doi:10.1093/inthealth/ihx014 PMID:28582558

Cauwer, C. D., Coosemans, T., Verbeke, W., Faid, S., & Mierlo, J. V. (2017). A Data-Driven Method for Energy Consumption Prediction and Energy-Efficient Routing of Electric Vehicles in Real-World Conditions. *Energies*, *10*(5), 608. doi:10.3390/en10050608

Ceylan, Z. (2019). Assessment of Agricultural Energy Consumption of Turkey by MLR and Bayesian Optimized SVR and GPR Models. *Journal of Forecasting*, *39*(3), 944–956.

Chang, C. H., Kayed, M., Girgis, M. R., & Shaalan, K. F. (2006). A survey of web information extraction systems. *IEEE Transactions on Knowledge and Data Engineering*, *18*(10), 1411–1428. doi:10.1109/TKDE.2006.152

Chapoy, A., Mohammadi, A. H., & Richon, D. (2007). Predicting the hydrate stability zones of natural gases using artificial neural networks. *Oil & Gas Science and Technology-Revue de l'IFP*, *62*(5), 701–706. doi:10.2516/ogst:2007048

Chavoshi, S., Safamirzaei, M., & Pajoum Shariati, F. (2018). Evaluation of empirical correlations for predicting gas hydrate formation temperature. *Gas Processing Journal*, *6*(2), 15–36.

Chen, C. C., & Wang, H. C. (2021). Adapting the influences of publishers to perform news event detection. *Journal of Information Science*. doi:10.1177/01655515211047422

Chen, C., Qin, Y., Chen, H., Zhu, D., Gao, F., & Zhou, X. (2021). A meta-analysis of the diagnostic performance of machine learning-based MRI in the prediction of axillary lymph node metastasis in breast cancer patients. *Insights Into Imaging*, *12*(1), 156. doi:10.118613244-021-01034-1 PMID:34731343

Chen, F., & Neill, D. B. (2014). Non-parametric scan statistics for event detection and forecasting in heterogeneous social media graphs. *Proceedings of the 20th ACM SIGKDD international conference on Knowledge discovery and data mining*. 10.1145/2623330.2623619

Chen, J., Zeng, G.-Q., Zhou, W., Du, W., & Lu, K.-D. (2018, June). Wind speed forecasting using nonlinear-learning ensemble of deep learning time series prediction and extremal optimization. *Energy Conversion and Management*, *165*, 681–695. doi:10.1016/j.enconman.2018.03.098

Chen, L. C., Papandreou, G., Kokkinos, I., Murphy, K., & Yuille, A. L. (2018). DeepLab: Semantic Image Segmentation with Deep Convolutional Nets, Atrous Convolution, and Fully Connected CRFs. *IEEE Transactions on Pattern Analysis and Machine Intelligence*, *40*(4), 834–848. doi:10.1109/TPAMI.2017.2699184 PMID:28463186

Chen, X., Zheng, H., Chen, X., & Wang, Z. (2021). Exploring impacts of on-demand ridesplitting on mobility via real-world ridesourcing data and questionnaires. *Transportation*, *48*(4), 1541–1561. doi:10.100711116-018-9916-1

Chen, Y., & Xie, J. (2008). Online Consumer Review: Word-of-Mouth as a New Element of Marketing Communication Mix. *Management Science*, *54*(3), 477–491. doi:10.1287/mnsc.1070.0810

Cho, K., Merrienboer van, B., Gülçehre, Ç., Bahdanau, D., Bougares, F., Schwenk, H., & Bengio, Y. (2014). Learning phrase representations using RNN encoder-decoder for statistical machine translation. In *Proceedings of conference on empirical methods in natural language processing* (pp. 1724–1734). 10.3115/v1/D14-1179

Chollet, F. (2017). Xception: Deep learning with depthwise separable convolutions. *Proceedings of the IEEE Conference on Computer Vision and Pattern Recognition*, 1251–1258. 10.1109/CVPR.2017.195

Chong, Z. R., Yang, S. H. B., Babu, P., Linga, P., & Li, X.-S. (2016). Review of natural gas hydrates as an energy resource: Prospects and challenges. *Applied Energy*, *162*, 1633–1652. doi:10.1016/j.apenergy.2014.12.061

Chou, J. S., & Tran, D.-S. (2018, December 5). Forecasting energy consumption time series using Machine Learning techniques based on usage patterns of residential householders. *Energy*, *165*(B), 709-726. doi:10.1016/j.energy.2018.09.144

Chowdhury, D. N., Agarwal, N., Laha, A. B., & Mukherjee, A. (2018). A Vehicle-to-Vehicle Communication System Using Iot Approach. *Proceedings of the 2nd International Conference on Electronics, Communication and Aerospace Technology, ICECA 2018, Iceca*, 915–919. 10.1109/ICECA.2018.8474909

Chua Chin Heng, M., Aisu, N., Miyake, M., Takeshita, K., Akiyama, M., Kawasaki, R., ... Tsujikawa, A. (2022). Regulatory-approved deep learning/machine learning-based medical devices in Japan as of 2020: A systematic review. *PLOS Digital Health*, *1*(1), e0000001. Advance online publication. doi:10.1371/journal.pdig.0000001

Chwastek, M., Pooniwala, P., & Ashman, S. (2020). *Amazon Personalize Now Supports Dynamic Filters for Applying Business Rules to Your Recommendations on the Fly*. https://aws.amazon.com/tr/blogs/machine-learning/amazon-personalize-now-supports-dynamic-filters-for-applying-business-rules-to-your-recommendations-on-the-fly/

Ciresan, D. C., Giusti, A., Gambardella, L. M., & Schmidhuber, J. (2012). *Deep Neural Networks Segment Neuronal Membranes in Electron Microscopy Images*. Paper presented at the NIPS.

Clark, K., Vendt, B., Smith, K., Freymann, J., Kirby, J., Koppel, P., Moore, S., Phillips, S., Maffitt, D., Pringle, M., Tarbox, L., & Prior, F. (2013). The Cancer Imaging Archive (TCIA): Maintaining and operating a public information repository. *Journal of Digital Imaging*, *26*(6), 1045–1057. doi:10.100710278-013-9622-7 PMID:23884657

Cohen, I. G., & Mello, M. M. (2019). Big Data, Big Tech, and Protecting Patient Privacy. *Journal of the American Medical Association*, *322*(12), 1141–1142. doi:10.1001/jama.2019.11365 PMID:31397838

Collett, T. S., Lewis, R., & Uchida, T. (2000). Growing interest in gas hydrates. *Oilfield Review*, *12*(2), 42–57.

Constantin, A., Pettifer, S., & Voronkov, A. (2013, September). PDFX: fully-automated PDF-to-XML conversion of scientific literature. In *Proceedings of the 2013 ACM symposium on document engineering* (pp. 177-180). ACM.

Cortes, C., & Vapnik, V. (1995). Support Vector Networks. *Machine Learning*, *20*(3), 273–297. doi:10.1007/BF00994018

Culotta, A., & Cutler, J. (2016). Mining Brand Perceptions from Twitter. *Marketing Science*, *35*(3), 343–362. doi:10.1287/mksc.2015.0968

da Silva, G. L. F., Valente, T. L. A., Silva, A. C., de Paiva, A. C., & Gattass, M. (2018). Convolutional neural network-based PSO for lung nodule false positive reduction on CT images. *Computer Methods and Programs in Biomedicine*, *162*, 109–118. doi:10.1016/j.cmpb.2018.05.006 PMID:29903476

Dai, X., & Sun, Y. (2010, October). Event identification within news topics. In *2010 International Conference on Intelligent Computing and Integrated Systems* (pp. 498-502). IEEE.

Damen, J. A., Hooft, L., Schuit, E., Debray, T. P., Collins, G. S., Tzoulaki, I., Lassale, C. M., Siontis, G. C. M., Chiocchia, V., Roberts, C., Schlüssel, M. M., Gerry, S., Black, J. A., Heus, P., van der Schouw, Y. T., Peelen, L. M., & Moons, K. G. (2016). Prediction models for cardiovascular disease risk in the general population: Systematic review. *BMJ (Clinical Research Ed.), 353*, i2416. doi:10.1136/bmj.i2416 PMID:27184143

Daş,, M., Balpetek,, N., & Kavak Akpınar,, E., & Akpınar, S. (2019). Investigation of Wind Energy Potantial of Different Provinces Found in Turkey and Establishment of Predictive Model Using Support Vector Machine Regression with the Obtained Results. *Journal of the Faculty of Engineering and Architecture of Gazi University, 34*(4), 2203–2213.

David, O. E., & Netanyahu, N. S. (2015, July). Deepsign: Deep learning for automatic malware signature generation and classification. In *2015 International Joint Conference on Neural Networks (IJCNN)* (pp. 1-8). IEEE. 10.1109/IJCNN.2015.7280815

Davie, M. K., Zatsepina, O. Y., & Buffett, B. A. (2004). Methane solubility in marine hydrate environments. *Marine Geology, 203*(1–2), 177–184. doi:10.1016/S0025-3227(03)00331-1

De Almeida, P. R. L., Oliveira, L. S., Britto, A. S. Jr, Silva, E. J. Jr, & Koerich, A. L. (2015). PKLot-A robust dataset for parking lot classification. *Expert Systems with Applications, 42*(11), 4937–4949. doi:10.1016/j.eswa.2015.02.009

De Laurentiis, M., De Placido, S., Bianco, A. R., Clark, G. M., & Ravdin, P. M. (1999). A prognostic model that makes quantitative estimates of probability of relapse for breast cancer patients. *Clinical Cancer Research, 5*(12), 4133–4139. PMID:10632351

De Mauro, A., Greco, M., & Grimaldi, M. (2016). A Formal Definition of Big Data Based on İts Essential Features. *Library Review, 65*(3), 122–135. doi:10.1108/LR-06-2015-0061

De, B. (2009). Computer-aided detection (CAD) of lung nodules and small tumours on chest radiographs. *European Journal of Radiology, 72*(2), 218–225. doi:10.1016/j.ejrad.2009.05.062 PMID:19747791

Debnath, S., Barnaby, D. P., Coppa, K., Makhnevich, A., Kim, E. J., Chatterjee, S., Tóth, V., Levy, T. J., Paradis, M., Cohen, S. L., Hirsch, J. S., Zanos, T. P., Becker, L. B., Cookingham, J., Davidson, K. W., Dominello, A. J., Falzon, L., McGinn, T., Mogavero, J. N., & Osorio, G. A. (2020). Machine learning to assist clinical decision-making during the COVID-19 pandemic. *Bioelectronic Medicine, 6*(1), 14. Advance online publication. doi:10.118642234-020-00050-8 PMID:32665967

Decapprio, D., Gartner, J., McCall, C. J., Burgess, T., Kothari, S., & Sayed, S. (2020). *Building a COVID-19 Vulnerability Index*. Cold Spring Harbor Laboratory. Retrieved from doi:10.1101/2020.03.16.20036723

Demirbas, A., Alamoudı, R. H., Ahmad, W., & Sheıkh, M. H. (2016). Optimization of municipal solid waste (MSW) disposal in Saudi Arabia. *Energy Sources. Part A, Recovery, Utilization, and Environmental Effects, 38*(13), 1929–1937. doi:10.1080/15567036.2015.1034385

Devlin, J., Chang, M. W., Lee, K., & Toutanova, K. (2018). *Bert: Pre-training of deep bidirectional transformers for language understanding*. arXiv preprint arXiv: 1810.04805.

Diciotti, S., Picozzi, G., Falchini, M., Mascalchi, M., Villari, N., & Valli, G. (2008). 3-D segmentation algorithm of small lung nodules in spiral CT images. *IEEE Transactions on Information Technology in Biomedicine, 12*(1), 7–19. doi:10.1109/TITB.2007.899504 PMID:18270032

Dillon, J. V., Langmore, I., Tran, D., Brevdo, E., Vasudevan, S., Moore, D., & Saurous, R. A. (2017). *Tensorflow distributions*. arXiv preprint arXiv:1711.10604.

Ding, Y., Xia, X., Chen, S., & Li, Y. (2018). A malware detection method based on a family behavior graph. *Computers & Security*, *73*, 73–86. doi:10.1016/j.cose.2017.10.007

Distefano, S., Merlino, G., Puliafito, A., Cerotti, D., & Dautov, R. (2018). Crowdsourcing and stigmergic approaches for (swarm) intelligent transportation systems. Lecture Notes in Computer Science (Including Subseries Lecture Notes in Artificial Intelligence and Lecture Notes in Bioinformatics), 10745 LNCS, 616–626. doi:10.1007/978-3-319-74521-3_64

Dixon, M. (2019). *How Netflix Used Big Data and Analytics to Generate Billions*. https://seleritysas.com/blog/2019/04/05/how-netflix-used-big-data-and-analytics-to-generate-billions/

Dizon, E., & Pranggono, B. (2021). Smart streetlights in Smart City: A case study of Sheffield. *Journal of Ambient Intelligence and Humanized Computing*, *0123456789*. Advance online publication. doi:10.100712652-021-02970-y

Dogru, N., & Subasi, A. (2018). Traffic accident detection using random forest classifier. *2018 15th Learning and Technology Conference, L and T 2018*, 40–45. 10.1109/LT.2018.8368509

Donahue, J., Hendricks, L. A., Rohrbach, M., Venugopalan, S., Guadarrama, S., Saenko, K., & Darrell, T. (2017). Long-term recurrent convolutional networks for visual recognition and description. *IEEE Transactions on Pattern Analysis and Machine Intelligence*, *39*(4), 677–69. doi:10.1109/TPAMI.2016.2599174 PMID:27608449

Dou, W., Wang, X., Ribarsky, W., & Zhou, M. (2012, October). Event detection in social media data. In *IEEE VisWeek Workshop on Interactive Visual Text Analytics-Task Driven Analytics of Social Media Content* (pp. 971-980). IEEE.

Drew, J., Moore, T., & Hahsler, M. (2016, May). Polymorphic malware detection using sequence classification methods. In *2016 IEEE Security and Privacy Workshops (SPW)* (pp. 81-87). IEEE.

Edo-Osagie, O., Lake, I. R., Edeghere, O., & Iglesia, B. l. (2019). *Attention-Based Recurrent Neural Networks (RNNs) for Short Text Classification: An Application in Public Health Monitoring*. Paper presented at the IWANN.

Eggink, J., & Raimond, Y. (2013). Recent advances in affective and semantic media applications at the BBC. In *Proceedings of 14th international workshop on image analysis for multimedia interactive services* (pp 1-4). 10.1109/WIAMIS.2013.6616134

Elanwar, R., Qin, W., Betke, M., & Wijaya, D. (2021). Extracting text from scanned Arabic books: A large-scale benchmark dataset and a fine-tuned Faster-R-CNN model. *International Journal on Document Analysis and Recognition*, *24*(4), 349–362. doi:10.100710032-021-00382-4

Elgibaly, A. A., & Elkamel, A. M. (1998). A new correlation for predicting hydrate formation conditions for various gas mixtures and inhibitors. *Fluid Phase Equilibria*, *152*(1), 23–42. doi:10.1016/S0378-3812(98)00368-9

Englezos, P. (1993). Clathrate hydrates. *Industrial & Engineering Chemistry Research*, *32*(7), 1251–1274. doi:10.1021/ie00019a001

Environment - Solutions for Environmental Sustainability - 2013 IBM Corporate Responsibility Report. (n.d.). *IBM*. Retrieved February 19, 2022, from https://www.ibm.com/ibm/responsibility/2013/environment/solutions-for-environmental-sustainability.html

Erevelles, S., Fukawa, N., & Swayne, L. (2016). Big Data Consumer Analytics and The Transformation of Marketing. *Journal of Business Research*, *69*(2), 897–904. doi:10.1016/j.jbusres.2015.07.001

EU. (2021). *Big Data: Definition, Benefits, Challenges (infographics)*. https://www.europarl.europa.eu/news/en/headlines/society/20210211STO97614/big-data-definition-benefits-challenges-infographics

Fader, P., & Winer, R. (2012). Introduction to The Special Issue on The Emergence and Impact of User-Generated Content. *Marketing Science*, *31*(3), 369–371. doi:10.1287/mksc.1120.0715

Faisal, K. K. K. F., Alomari, D. D. J. A., Alasmari, H. H. M. A., Alghamdi, H. H. S. A., & Saedi, K. K. A. S. (2021). Life Expectancy Estimation Based on Machine Learning and Structured Predictors. *AISS*. 10.1145/3503047.3503122

Falk, T., Mai, D., Bensch, R., Çiçek, Ö., Abdulkadir, A., Marrakchi, Y., Böhm, A., Deubner, J., Jäckel, Z., Seiwald, K., Dovzhenko, A., Tietz, O., Dal Bosco, C., Walsh, S., Saltukoglu, D., Tay, T. L., Prinz, M., Palme, K., Simons, M., ... Ronneberger, O. (2019). U-Net: Deep learning for cell counting, detection, and morphometry. *Nature Methods*, *16*(1), 67–70. doi:10.103841592-018-0261-2 PMID:30559429

Fan, X., Liu, J., Wang, Z., Jiang, Y., & Liu, X. (2017). Crowdsourced Road Navigation: Concept, Design, and Implementation. *IEEE Communications Magazine*, *55*(6), 126–131. doi:10.1109/MCOM.2017.1600738

Farahani, F. V., Ahmadi, A., & Zarandi, M. H. F. (2018). Hybrid intelligent approach for diagnosis of the lung nodule from CT images using spatial kernelized fuzzy c-means and ensemble learning. *Mathematics and Computers in Simulation*, *149*, 48–68. doi:10.1016/j.matcom.2018.02.001

Farmer, L. D., & Casson, R. J. (2014). Understanding and checking the assumptions of linear regression: A primer for medical researchers. *Clinical & Experimental Ophthalmology*, *42*(6), 590–596. doi:10.1111/ceo.12358 PMID:24801277

Farouk, M. (2020). Measuring text similarity based on structure and word embedding. *Cognitive Systems Research*, *63*, 1–10. doi:10.1016/j.cogsys.2020.04.002

Feeny, A. K., Tadarati, M., Freund, D. E., Bressler, N. M., & Burlina, P. (2015). Automated segmentation of geographic atrophy of the retinal epithelium via random forests in AREDS color fundus images. *Computers in Biology and Medicine*, *65*, 124–136. doi:10.1016/j.compbiomed.2015.06.018 PMID:26318113

Feng, J., & Jiang, J. (2022). Deep Learning-Based Chest CT Image Features in Diagnosis of Lung Cancer. *Computational and Mathematical Methods in Medicine*, *2022*, 1–7. doi:10.1155/2022/4153211 PMID:35096129

Ferrara, E., De Meo, P., Fiumara, G., & Baumgartner, R. (2014). Web data extraction, applications and techniques: A survey. *Knowledge-Based Systems*, *70*, 301–323. doi:10.1016/j.knosys.2014.07.007

Ficco, M. (2020, April). Comparing API call sequence algorithms for malware detection. In *Workshops of the International Conference on Advanced Information Networking and Applications* (pp. 847-856). Springer. 10.1007/978-3-030-44038-1_77

Fisher, C., Flew, T., Park, S., Lee, J. Y., & Dulleck, U. (2020). Improving trust in news: Audience solutions. *Journalism Practice*, 1–19.

Fleming, P. J., & Purshouse, R. C. (2002). Evolutionary algorithms in control systems engineering: A survey. *Control Engineering Practice*, *10*(11), 1223–1241. doi:10.1016/S0967-0661(02)00081-3

Fonseka, W. P. I. (2021). *Automated News Clustering Using an Unsupervised Learning Model* (Doctoral dissertation).

Forrest, S., Hofmeyr, S. A., Somayaji, A., & Longstaff, T. A. (1996, May). A sense of self for unix processes. In *Proceedings 1996 IEEE Symposium on Security and Privacy* (pp. 120-128). IEEE. 10.1109/SECPRI.1996.502675

Fortune. (2021). *Fortune 500*. https://fortune.com/company/amazon-com/fortune500/

Fosso, W. S., Akter, S., Edwards, A., Chopin, G., & Gnanzou, D. (2015). How 'Big Data' Can Make Big Impact: Findings from A Systematic Review and A Longitudinal Case Study. *International Journal of Production Economics*, *165*, 234–246. doi:10.1016/j.ijpe.2014.12.031

Fournaison, L., Delahaye, A., Chatti, I., & Petitet, J.-P. (2004). CO2 hydrates in refrigeration processes. *Industrial & Engineering Chemistry Research*, *43*(20), 6521–6526. doi:10.1021/ie030861r

Frenay, B., & Verleysen, M. (2011). Parameter-insensitive Kernel in Extreme Learning for Non-Linear Support Vector Regression. *Neurocomputing*, *74*(16), 2526–2531. doi:10.1016/j.neucom.2010.11.037

Friedman, J. H. (2001). Greedy Function Approximation: A Gradient Boosting Machine. *Annals of Statistics*, *29*(5), 1189–1232. doi:10.1214/aos/1013203451

Frost, S., Tor, B., Agrawal, R., & Forbes, G., A. (2019, October). CompostNet: An Image Classifier for Meal Waste. *IEEE Global Humanitarian Technology Conference (GHTC)*, 1-4. 10.1109/GHTC46095.2019.9033130

Fukushima, A., Yano, T., Imahara, S., Aisu, H., Shimokawa, Y., & Shibata, Y. (2018, August). Prediction of energy consumption for new electric vehicle models by Machine Learning. *IET Intelligent Transport Systems*, *12*(9), 1751–956X. doi:10.1049/iet-its.2018.5169

Ganguly, S. (2003). Prediction of VLE data using radial basis function network. *Computers & Chemical Engineering*, *27*(10), 1445–1454. doi:10.1016/S0098-1354(03)00068-1

Gao, L., Guo, Z., Zhang, H., Xu, X., & Shen, H. T. (2017). Video Captioning with Attention - Based LSTM and Semantic Consistency. *IEEE Transactions on Multimedia*, *19*(9), 99. doi:10.1109/TMM.2017.2729019

Gao, Z., Chen, M., Hauptmann, A. G., & Cai, A. (2010). Comparing evaluation protocols on the KTH dataset. *Human Behaviour Understanding*, *6219*, 88–100. doi:10.1007/978-3-642-14715-9_10

Gbaruko, B. C., Igwe, J. C., Gbaruko, P. N., & Nwokeoma, R. C. (2007). Gas hydrates and clathrates: Flow assurance, environmental and economic perspectives and the Nigerian liquified natural gas project. *Journal of Petroleum Science Engineering*, *56*(1–3), 192–198. doi:10.1016/j.petrol.2005.12.011

Geetha, S., & Cicilia, D. (2018). IoT enabled intelligent bus transportation system. *Proceedings of the 2nd International Conference on Communication and Electronics Systems, ICCES 2017, 2018-Janua*(Icces), 7–11. 10.1109/CESYS.2017.8321235

George, A., & Rajakumar, B. R. (2013). On hybridizing fuzzy min-max neural network and firefly algorithm for automated heart disease diagnosis. *Fourth International Conference on Computing, Communications and Networking Technologies*.

Ghadge, M., Pandey, D., & Kalbande, D. (2016). Machine learning approach for predicting bumps on road. *Proceedings of the 2015 International Conference on Applied and Theoretical Computing and Communication Technology, ICATccT 2015*, 481–485. 10.1109/ICATCCT.2015.7456932

Ghavipour, M., Ghavipour, M., Chitsazan, M., Najibi, S. H., & Ghidary, S. S. (2013). Experimental study of natural gas hydrates and a novel use of neural network to predict hydrate formation conditions. *Chemical Engineering Research & Design*, *91*(2), 264–273. doi:10.1016/j.cherd.2012.08.010

Ghosh, A., Chatterjee, T., Samanta, S., Aich, J., & Roy, S. (2017). Distracted driving: A novel approach towards accident prevention. *Adv. Comput. Sci. Technol*, *10*(8), 2693–2705.

Gibert, D. (2016). *Convolutional neural networks for malware classification*. University Rovira i Virgili.

Giustiniani, M., Tinivella, U., Jakobsson, M., & Rebesco, M. (2013). Arctic ocean gas hydrate stability in a changing climate. *Journal of Geological Research*, (783969), 1–10.

Global Warming of 1.5 °C. (n.d.). *IPCC*. Retrieved February 21, 2022, from https://www.ipcc.ch/sr15/

Gopalakrishnan, K. (2018). Deep learning in data-driven pavement image analysis and automated distress detection: A review. *Data*, *3*(3), 28. Advance online publication. doi:10.3390/data3030028

Graves, A., Fernández, S., & Schmidhuber, J. (2005, September). Bidirectional LSTM networks for improved phoneme classification and recognition. In *International conference on artificial neural networks* (pp. 799-804). Springer. 10.1007/11550907_126

Gulati, R., & Oldroyd, J. B. (2005). The Quest for Customer Focus. *Harvard Business Review*, 92–101. PMID:15807042

Guo, S., Lucas, R. M., & Ponsonby, A. (2013). A Noval Approach for Prediction of Vitamin D Status Using Support Vector Regression. *PLoS One*, *8*(11), 1–9. doi:10.1371/journal.pone.0079970

Gürsakal, N. (2013). *Çıkarımsal İstatistik, İstatistik* (Vol. 2). Dora Basım-Yayım Dağıtım Ltd. Şti.

Gwadera, R., & Crestani, F. (2009, November). Mining and ranking streams of news stories using cross-stream sequential patterns. In *Proceedings of the 18th ACM conference on information and knowledge management* (pp. 1709-1712). 10.1145/1645953.1646210

Haneef, R., Kab, S., Hrzic, R., Fuentes, S., Fosse-Edorh, S., Cosson, E., & Gallay, A. (2021). Use of artificial intelligence for public health surveillance: A case study to develop a machine Learning-algorithm to estimate the incidence of diabetes mellitus in France. *Archives of Public Health*, *79*(1), 168. Advance online publication. doi:10.118613690-021-00687-0 PMID:34551816

Han, J., Pei, J., & Kamber, M. (2011). *Data mining: concepts and techniques*. Elsevier.

Hanspeter, W. (2001). A short history of lung cancer. *Toxicological Sciences*, *64*(1), 4–6. doi:10.1093/toxsci/64.1.4 PMID:11606795

Hardy, W., Chen, L., Hou, S., Ye, Y., & Li, X. (2016). DL4MD: A deep learning framework for intelligent malware detection. In *Proceedings of the International Conference on Data Science (ICDATA)* (p. 61). The Steering Committee of The World Congress in Computer Science, Computer Engineering and Applied Computing (WorldComp).

Hartmans, A. (2021). *Jeff Bezos Originally Wanted To Name Amazon 'Cadabra,' And 14 Other Little-Known Facts About The Early Days Of The E-Commerce Giant.* Businessinsider: https://www.businessinsider.com/jeff-bezos-amazon-history-facts-2017-4

Hashmi, A. M., Afzal, M. T., & ur Rehman, S. (2020, November). Rule Based Approach to Extract Metadata from Scientific PDF Documents. In *2020 5th International Conference on Innovative Technologies in Intelligent Systems and Industrial Applications (CITISIA)* (pp. 1-4). IEEE.

He, K., Gkioxari, G., Dollar, P., & Girshick, R. (2020). Mask R-CNN. *IEEE Transactions on Pattern Analysis and Machine Intelligence*, *42*(2), 386–397. doi:10.1109/TPAMI.2018.2844175 PMID:29994331

He, K., Zhang, X., Ren, S., & Sun, J. (2016). Deep residual learning for image recognition. *IEEE Conference on Computer Vision and Pattern Recognition, CVPR, IEEE*, 770–778.

Herath, S., Harandi, M., & Porikli, F. (2017). Going deeper into action recognition: A survey. *Image and Vision Computing*, *60*, 4–21. doi:10.1016/j.imavis.2017.01.010

Heydari, A., Shayesteh, K., & Kamalzadeh, L. (2006). Prediction of hydrate formation temperature for natural gas using artificial neural network. *Oil and Gas Business,* 1–10.

Hirsch, T., Merced, K., Narayanan, S., Imel, Z. E., & Atkins, D. C. (2017). *Designing Contestability*. Academic Press.

Holland, J. H. (1992). *Adaptation in natural and artificial systems: an introductory analysis with applications to biology, control, and artificial intelligence.* MIT Press. doi:10.7551/mitpress/1090.001.0001

Hood, A., & Kleopas, I. (2020). *Selecting the right metadata to build high-performing recommendation models with Amazon Personalize.* https://aws.amazon.com/blogs/machine-learning/selecting-the-right-metadata-to-build-high-performing-recommendation-models-with-amazon-personalize/

Huang, X., Lei, Q., Xie, T., Zhang, Y., Hu, Z., & Zhou Q. (2020). Deep Transfer Convolutional Neural Network and Extreme Learning Machine for Lung Nodule Diagnosis on CT images. *Knowledge-Based Systems, 204.*

Huang, W., & Stokes, J. W. (2016, July). MtNet: a multi-task neural network for dynamic malware classification. In *International conference on detection of intrusions and malware, and vulnerability assessment* (pp. 399-418). Springer. 10.1007/978-3-319-40667-1_20

Huang, X., Lei, Q., Xie, T., Zhang, Y., Hu, Z., & Zhou, Q. (2020). Deep transfer convolutional neural network and extreme learning machine for lung nodule diagnosis on CT images. *Knowledge-Based Systems, 204,* 106230. doi:10.1016/j.knosys.2020.106230

Hung, M. H., Pan, J. S., & Hsieh, C. H. (2014). A Fast Algorithm of Temporal Median Filter for Background Subtraction. *Journal of Information Hiding and Multimedia Signal Processing, 5*(1), 33–40.

Ide, T., Katsuki, T., Morimura, T., & Morris, R. (2017). City-Wide Traffic Flow Estimation from a Limited Number of Low-Quality Cameras. *IEEE Transactions on Intelligent Transportation Systems, 18*(4), 950–959. doi:10.1109/TITS.2016.2597160

Idika, N., & Mathur, A. P. (2007). A survey of malware detection techniques. Purdue University.

Ingleby, F. C., Woods, L. M., Atherton, I. M., Baker, M., Ellies-Brookes, L., & Belot, A. (2021). Describing Socioeconomic Variation in Life Expectancy According to An Individual's Education, Occupation and Wage in England and Wales: An Analysis of the ONS Longitudinal Study. *SSM - Population Health, 14,* 1–9. doi:10.1016/j.ssmph.2021.100815 PMID:34027013

InsideBigData. (2019). *How Amazon Used Big Data to Rule E-Commerce.* https://insidebigdata.com/2019/11/30/how-amazon-used-big-data-to-rule-e-commerce/

Islam, M. M., Yang, H. C., Poly, T. N., Jian, W. S., & Jack Li, Y. C. (2020). Deep learning algorithms for detection of diabetic retinopathy in retinal fundus photographs: A systematic review and meta-analysis. *Computer Methods and Programs in Biomedicine, 191,* 105320. doi:10.1016/j.cmpb.2020.105320 PMID:32088490

Ivanova, D., Konstantin, S., Kjartan, S., Wood, R., Vita, G., Tukker, A., & Hertwich, G. (2016). Environmental impact assessment of household consumption. *Journal of Industrial Ecology, 20*(3), 26–536. doi:10.1111/jiec.12371

Jain, S. (2017). Introduction to genetic algorithm & their application in data science. *Analytics Vidhya,* 1–31.

Jain, B., Brar, G., Malhotra, J., Rani, S., & Ahmed, S. H. (2018). A cross layer protocol for traffic management in Social Internet of Vehicles. *Future Generation Computer Systems, 82,* 707–714. doi:10.1016/j.future.2017.11.019

Jan, B., Farman, H., Khan, M., Talha, M., & Din, I. U. (2019). Designing a Smart Transportation System: An Internet of Things and Big Data Approach. *IEEE Wireless Communications, 26*(4), 73–79. doi:10.1109/MWC.2019.1800512

Janiesch, C., Zschech, P., & Heinrich, K. (2021). Machine learning and deep learning. *Electronic Markets, 31*(3), 685–695. doi:10.100712525-021-00475-2

Jankovic, R., Štrbac, N., Mihajlović, I. N., & Amelio, A. (2021). Machine learning models for ecological footprint prediction based on energy parameters. *Neural Computing & Applications*, *33*(12), 7073–7087. Advance online publication. doi:10.100700521-020-05476-4

Jetter, M., Laudage, S., & Stadelmann, D. (2019). The Intimate Link Between Income Levels and Life Expectancy: Global Evidence from 213 Years. *Social Science Quarterly*, *100*(4), 1387–1403. doi:10.1111squ.12638

Jia, G., Han, G., Li, A., & Du, J. (2018). SSL: Smart street lamp based on fog computing for smarter cities. *IEEE Transactions on Industrial Informatics*, *14*(11), 4995–5004. doi:10.1109/TII.2018.2857918

Jiang, H., Lu, Y., & Xue, J. (2016). Automatic Soccer Video Event Detection Based on a Deep Neural Network Combined CNN and RNN. In *Proceedings of IEEE 28th International Conference on Tools with Artificial Intelligence*. 10.1109/ICTAI.2016.0081

Jiang, J., Luo, L., Xu, P., & Wang, P. (2018). How Does Social Development Influence Life Expectancy? A Geographically Weighted Regression Analysis in Chine. *The Royal Society for Public Health*, *163*, 95–104.

Jiang, L., Zhang, H., & Yang, X. (2012). Research on semantic text mining based on domain ontology. In *Proc. Int. Conf. Comput. Comput. Technol. Agricult.* Berlin, Germany: Springer.

Jimeno Yepes, A., Zhong, P., & Burdick, D. (2021, September). ICDAR 2021 Competition on Scientific Literature Parsing. In *International Conference on Document Analysis and Recognition* (pp. 605-617). Springer. 10.1007/978-3-030-86337-1_40

Ji, S., Xu, W., Yang, M., & Yu, K. (2013). 3d convolutional neural networks for human action recognition. *IEEE Transactions on Pattern Analysis and Machine Intelligence*, *35*(1), 221–231. doi:10.1109/TPAMI.2012.59 PMID:22392705

Johnson, E. J. (2012). Big Data + Big Analytics = Big Opportunity: Big Data is Dominating the Strategy Discussion for Many Financial Executives. As These Market Dynamics Continue to Evolve, Expectations Will Continue to Shift About What Should Be Disclosed, When and to Whom. *Financial Executive, 28*(6).

Jothimurugan, K., Andrews, M., Lee, J., & Maggi, L. (2021). *Learning Algorithms for Regenerative Stopping Problems with Applications to Shipping Consolidation in Logistics.* arXiv preprint. arXiv:2105.02318

Kabir, M. (2008). Determinants of Life Expectancy in Developing Countries. *Journal of Developing Areas*, *41*(2), 185–204. doi:10.1353/jda.2008.0013

Kamal, M. A., Alam, M. M., Khawar, H., & Mazliham, M. S. (2019). Play and Learn Case Study on Learning Abilities through Effective Computing in Games. *MACS 2019 - 13th International Conference on Mathematics, Actuarial Science, Computer Science and Statistics, Proceedings*, 1–6. 10.1109/MACS48846.2019.9024771

Kamal, M. A., Kamal, M. K., Alam, M., & Su'ud, M. M. (2018). Context-Aware Perspective Analysis working of RFID Anti-Collision Protocols. *Journal of Independent Studies and Research - Computing, 2*(16), 19–32. doi:10.31645/jisrc/(2018).16.2.02

Kamal, M. A., Raza, H. W., Alam, M. M., & Mohd, M. (2020). Highlight the Features of AWS, GCP and Microsoft Azure that Have an Impact when Choosing a Cloud Service Provider. *International Journal of Recent Technology and Engineering*, *8*(5), 4124–4232. doi:10.35940/ijrte.D8573.018520

Karacan, I., Sennaroglu, B., & Vayvay, O. (2020). Analysis of Life Expectancy Across Countries Using a Decision Tree. *EMHJ*, *26*(2), 143–151. doi:10.26719/2020.26.2.143 PMID:32141591

Karal, Ö. (2018). Compression of ECG Data by Support Vector Regression Method. *Journal of the Faculty of Engineering and Architecture of Gazi University*, *33*(2), 743–755.

Karami, Z., & Kashef, R. (2020). Smart transportation planning: Data, models, and algorithms. *Transportation Engineering*, *2*(June), 100013. Advance online publication. doi:10.1016/j.treng.2020.100013

Karpathy, A., Toderici, G., Shetty, S., Leung, T., Sukthankar, R., & Fei-Fei, L. (2014). Large-Scale Video Classification with Convolutional Neural Networks. In *Proceedings of the 2014 IEEE Conference* (CVPR-2014). 10.1109/CVPR.2014.223

Katz, D. L. (1945). Prediction of conditions for hydrate formation in natural gases. *Transactions of the AIME*, *160*(1), 140–149. 10.2118/945140-G

Katz, D. L. V. (1959). *Handbook of natural gas engineering*. McGraw-Hill.

Kaul, V., Enslin, S., & Gross, S. A. (2020). History of artificial intelligence in medicine. *Gastrointestinal Endoscopy*, *92*(4), 807–812. doi:10.1016/j.gie.2020.06.040 PMID:32565184

Kavitha, S., Varuna, S., & Ramya, R. (2016). A Comparative Analysis on Linear Regression and Support Vector Regression. *2016 International Conference on Green Engineering and Technologies*, 1-5. 10.1109/GET.2016.7916627

Kelly, L., & Mott, T. (2015). Lung cancer: Diagnosis, treatment principles, and screening. *American Family Physician*, *91*(4), 250–256. PMID:25955626

Kenter, T., & De Rijke, M. (2015, October). Short text similarity with word embeddings. In *Proceedings of the 24th ACM international on conference on information and knowledge management* (pp. 1411-1420). ACM.

Kenton, J. D. M. W. C., & Toutanova, L. K. (2019, May). Bert: Pre-training of deep bidirectional transformers for language understanding. In *Proceedings of NAACL-HLT* (pp. 4171-4186). Academic Press.

Kermany, D. S., Goldbaum, M., Cai, W., Valentim, C. C., Liang, H., Baxter, S. L., McKeown, A., Yang, G., Wu, X., Yan, F., Dong, J., Prasadha, M. K., Pei, J., Ting, M. Y. L., Zhu, J., Li, C., Hewett, S., Dong, J., Ziyar, I., ... Zhang, K. (2018). Identifying medical diagnoses and treatable diseases by image-based deep learning. *Cell*, *172*(5), 1122–1131. doi:10.1016/j.cell.2018.02.010 PMID:29474911

Ke, W., & Chen, D. (2019). A short review on natural gas hydrate, kinetic hydrate inhibitors and inhibitor synergists. *Chinese Journal of Chemical Engineering*, *27*(9), 2049–2061. doi:10.1016/j.cjche.2018.10.010

Khamehchi, E., Shamohammadi, E., & Yousefi, S. H. (2013). Predicting the hydrate formation temperature by a new correlation and neural network. *Gas Processing*, *1*(1), 41–50. Retrieved from https://www.sid.ir/en/Journal/ViewPaper.aspx?ID=418945

Khan, S. H., Kumari, A., Chandrajit, G. D., & Amit, B. M. (2020). Thermodynamic modeling and correlations of CH_4, C_2H_6, CO_2, H_2S, and N_2 hydrates with cage occupancies. *Journal of Petroleum Exploration and Production Technology*, (0123456789). doi:10.1007/s13202-020-00998-y

Khan, M. A., Mittal, M., Goyal, L. M., & Roy, S. (2021). A deep survey on supervised learning based human detection and activity classiðcation methods. *Multimedia Tools and Applications*, *80*(18), 27867–27923. doi:10.100711042-021-10811-5

Khan, M. S., Lal, B., Sabil, K. M., & Ahmed, I. (2019). Desalination of seawater through gas hydrate process: An overview. *Journal of Advanced Research in Fluid Mechanics and Thermal Sciences*, *55*(1), 65–73.

Kido, S., Kidera, S., Hirano, Y., Mabu, S., Kamiya, T., Tanaka, N., Suzuki, Y., Yanagawa, M., & Tomiyama, N. (2022). Segmentation of Lung Nodules on CT Images Using a Nested Three-Dimensional Fully Connected Convolutional Network. *Frontiers in Artificial Intelligence*, *5*.

Kinabalu, K. (2019). *Identification of Road Surface Conditions using IoT Sensors and Machine Learning. Lecture Notes in Electrical Engineering 603 Computational Science and Technology*.

Ki, Y., Kim, E., & Kim, H. K. (2015). A novel approach to detect malware based on API call sequence analysis. *International Journal of Distributed Sensor Networks*, *11*(6), 659101. doi:10.1155/2015/659101

Kolosnjaji, B., Zarras, A., Webster, G., & Eckert, C. (2016, December). Deep learning for classification of malware system call sequences. In *Australasian joint conference on artificial intelligence* (pp. 137-149). Springer. 10.1007/978-3-319-50127-7_11

Kömeçoğlu, Y., & Akyol, S. (2021). *Turkish News Category Classification*. https://github.com/kodiks/turkish-news-classification

Kömeçoğlu, Y., & Akyol, S. (2021). *Turkish News Category Dataset (270K - Lite Version)*. https://huggingface.co/datasets/interpress_news_category_tr_lite

Kömeçoğlu, Y., Kömeçoğlu, B. B., & Yılmaz, B. (2020, August). Real-Time News Grouping: Detecting the Same-Content News on Turkish News Stream. In *International Online Conference on Intelligent Decision Science* (pp. 14-25). Springer.

Kong, Y., & Fu, Y. (2022). Human action recognition and prediction: A survey. *International Journal of Computer Vision*, *130*(5), 1366–1401. Advance online publication. doi:10.100711263-022-01594-9

Kontokosta, C. E., Hong, B., Johnson, N. E., & Starobin, D. (2018). Using Machine Learning and small area estimation to predict building-level municipal solid waste generation in cities. *Computers, Environment and Urban Systems, 70*, 151-162. . doi:10.1016/j.compenvurbsys.2018.03.004

Kourou, K., Exarchos, K. P., Papaloukas, C., Sakaloglou, P., Exarchos, T., & Fotiadis, D. I. (2021). Applied machine learning in cancer research: A systematic review for patient diagnosis, classification and prognosis. *Computational and Structural Biotechnology Journal*, *19*, 5546–5555. doi:10.1016/j.csbj.2021.10.006 PMID:34712399

Koza, J. R. (1994). Genetic programming as a means for programming computers by natural selection. *Statistics and Computing*, *4*(2), 87–112. doi:10.1007/BF00175355

Krittanawong, C., Virk, H. U. H., Bangalore, S., Wang, Z., Johnson, K. W., Pinotti, R., Zhang, H. J., Kaplin, S., Narasimhan, B., Kitai, T., Baber, U., Halperin, J. L., & Tang, W. H. W. (2020). Machine learning prediction in cardiovascular diseases: A meta-analysis. *Scientific Reports*, *10*(1), 16057. doi:10.103841598-020-72685-1 PMID:32994452

Krizhevsky, A., Sutskever, I., & Hinton, G. E. (2012). ImageNet Classification with Deep Convolutional Neural Networks. *ImageNet Classif. with Deep Convolutional Neural Networks*, 1097–1105. https://proceedings.neurips.cc/paper/2012/file/c399862d3b9d6b76c8436e924a68c45b-Paper.pdf

Kulkarni, A., Mhalgi, N., Gurnani, S., & Giri, N. (2014). Pothole Detection System using Machine Learning on Android. *International Journal of Emerging Technology and Advanced Engineering*, *4*(7), 360–364. http://www.ijetae.com/files/Volume4Issue7/IJETAE_0714_55.pdf

Kumar, A., Samadder, S. R., Kumar, N., & Singh, C. (2018, September). Estimation of the generation rate of different types of plastic wastes and possible revenue recovery from informal recycling. *Waste Management (New York, N.Y.)*, *79*, 781–790. doi:10.1016/j.wasman.2018.08.045 PMID:30343811

Kumaran, G., & Allan, J. (2004, July). Text classification and named entities for new event detection. In *Proceedings of the 27th annual international ACM SIGIR conference on research and development in information retrieval* (pp. 297-304). 10.1145/1008992.1009044

Kumaran, G., & Allan, J. (2005, October). Using names and topics for new event detection. In *Proceedings of Human Language Technology Conference and Conference on Empirical Methods in Natural Language Processing* (pp. 121-128). 10.3115/1220575.1220591

Kumari, A., Hasan, S., Majumder, K. C. B., Arora, A., & Dixit, G. (2021). Physio - chemical and mineralogical analysis of gas hydrate bearing sediments of Andaman Basin. *Marine Geophysical Research*, 1–12. doi:10.1007/s11001-020-09423-9

Kumari, A., Madhaw, M., Majumder, C. B., & Arora, A. (2021). Artificial Neural Network: A New Tool for the Prediction of Hydrate Formation Conditions. In Applications of Nature-Inspired Computing in Renewable Energy Systems (pp. 95–115). Academic Press.

Kumari, A., Khan, S. H., Misra, A. K., Majumder, C. B., & Arora, A. (2020). Hydrates of Binary Guest Mixtures: Fugacity Model Development and Experimental Validation. *Journal of Non-Equilibrium Thermodynamics*, *45*(1), 39–58. doi:10.1515/jnet-2019-0062

Kumari, A., Madhaw, M., Majumder, C. B., Arora, A., & Dixit, G. (2021). *Application of statistical learning theory for thermodynamic modeling of natural gas hydrates*. Petroleum. doi:10.1016/j.petlm.2021.10.005

Kvenvolden, K. A. (1993). *A primer on gas hydrates* (Vol. 1570). US Geological Survey.

Kwon, D., Park, S., Baek, S., Malaiya, R. K., Yoon, G., & Ryu, J. T. (2018). A study on development of the blind spot detection system for the IoT-based smart connected car. *2018 IEEE International Conference on Consumer Electronics, ICCE 2018, 2018-January*, 1–4. 10.1109/ICCE.2018.8326077

Lan, Z., Chen, M., Goodman, S., Gimpel, K., Sharma, P., & Soricut, R. (2019). *Albert: A lite bert for self-supervised learning of language representations*. arXiv preprint arXiv:1909.11942.

Lari, A. (2015). Automated Transportation Mode Detection Using Smart Phone Applications via Machine Learning: Case Study Mega City of Tehran. *Transportation Research Board 94th Annual Meeting, 6147*(May).

Larson, S. (2017, December 20). *10 biggest hacks of 2017*. Retrieved November 3, 2018, from https://money.cnn.com/2017/12/18/technology/biggest-cyberattacksof-the-year/index.html

Laugier, S., & Richon, D. (2003). Use of artificial neural networks for calculating derived thermodynamic quantities from volumetric property data. *Fluid Phase Equilibria*, *210*(2), 247–255. doi:10.1016/S0378-3812(03)00172-9

Lau, S. P., Merrett, G. V., Weddell, A. S., & White, N. M. (2015). A traffic-aware street lighting scheme for Smart Cities using autonomous networked sensors. *Computers & Electrical Engineering*, *45*, 192–207. doi:10.1016/j.compeleceng.2015.06.011

Lee, B. C. G., Mears, J., Jakeway, E., Ferriter, M., Adams, C., Yarasavage, N., . . . Weld, D. S. (2020). *The newspaper navigator dataset: extracting and analyzing visual content from 16 million historic newspaper pages in chronicling America*. doi:10.1145/3340531.3412767

Lee, H., Kim, N., & Cha, S. W. (2020). Model-Based Reinforcement Learning for Eco-Driving Control of Electric Vehicles. *IEEE Access: Practical Innovations, Open Solutions*, *8*, 202886–202896. doi:10.1109/ACCESS.2020.3036719

Lee, H., Lee, J., Kim, D. Y., Park, J., Seo, Y.-T., Zeng, H., & Moudrakovski, I. L. (2011). *Tuning clathrate hydrates for hydrogen storage. Materials For Sustainable Energy: A Collection of Peer-Reviewed Research and Review Articles from Nature Publishing Group*. World Scientific.

Lee, N., Laine, A. F., Mrquez, G., Levsky, J. M., & Gohagan, J. K. (2009). Potential of computer-aided diagnosis to improve CT lung cancer screening. *IEEE Reviews in Biomedical Engineering*, *2*, 136–146. doi:10.1109/RBME.2009.2034022 PMID:22275043

Lee, S., & Kim, I. (2018). *Multimodal Feature Learning for Video Captioning*. Hindawi Mathematical Problems in Engineering. doi:10.1155/2018/3125879

Lei, S. H. I., & Junping, D. U. (2018). Social network bursty topic discovery based on RNN and topic model. *Journal of Communication, 39*(4), 189.

Lei, Y., Tian, Y., Shan, H., Zhang, J., Wang, G., & Kalra, M. K. (2020). Shape and margin-aware lung nodule classification in low-dose CT images via soft activation mapping. *Medical Image Analysis, 60*, 101628. doi:10.1016/j.media.2019.101628 PMID:31865281

Lemon, N., & Verhoef, C. (2016). Understanding Customer Experience Throughout the Customer Journey. *Journal of Marketing,* (80), 69-96. doi:10.1509/jm.15.0420

Le, Q., & Mikolov, T. (2014, June). Distributed representations of sentences and documents. In *International conference on machine learning* (pp. 1188-1196). PMLR.

Li, M., Cui, L., Huang, S., Wei, F., Zhou, M., & Li, Z. (2019). *Tablebank: A benchmark dataset for table detection and recognition.* arXiv preprint arXiv: 1903.01949.

Li, M., Xu, Y., Cui, L., Huang, S., Wei, F., Li, Z., & Zhou, M. (2020). *DocBank: A benchmark dataset for document layout analysis.* doi:10.18653/v1/2020.coling-main.82

Liebl, B., & Burghardt, M. (2021, January). An Evaluation of DNN Architectures for Page Segmentation of Historical Newspapers. In *2020 25th International Conference on Pattern Recognition (ICPR)* (pp. 5153-5160). IEEE. 10.1109/ICPR48806.2021.9412571

Li, G., & Görges, D. (2019). Ecological adaptive cruise control for vehicles with step-gear transmission based on reinforcement learning. *IEEE Transactions on Intelligent Transportation Systems, 21*(11), 4895–4905. doi:10.1109/TITS.2019.2947756

Li, Q., & Lu, S. C. Y. (2008). Collaborative tagging applications and approaches. *IEEE MultiMedia, 15*(3), 14–21. doi:10.1109/MMUL.2008.54

Liu, W., Kim, S. W., Marczuk, K., & Ang, M. H. (2014). Vehicle motion intention reasoning using cooperative perception on urban road. *2014 17th IEEE International Conference on Intelligent Transportation Systems, ITSC 2014*, 424–430. 10.1109/ITSC.2014.6957727

Liu, A.-A., Shao, Z., Wong, Y., Li, J., Su, Y.-T., & Kankanhalli, M. (2019). LSTM-based multi-label video event detection. *Multimedia Tools and Applications, 78*(1), 677–695. doi:10.100711042-017-5532-x

Liu, L., & Lei, Y. (2018). An accurate ecological footprint analysis and prediction for Beijing based onSVM model. *Ecological Informatics, 44*, 33–42. doi:10.1016/j.ecoinf.2018.01.003

Liu, W., Jiang, L., Wu, Y., Tang, T., & Li, W. (2020). Topic detection and tracking based on event ontology. *IEEE Access: Practical Innovations, Open Solutions, 8*, 98044–98056. doi:10.1109/ACCESS.2020.2995776

Liu, X., Hou, F., Qin, H., & Hao, A. (2018). Multi-view multi-scale CNNs for lung nodule type classification from CT images. *Pattern Recognition, 77*, 262–275. doi:10.1016/j.patcog.2017.12.022

Li, Y., Shen, L., & Yu, S. (2017). HEp-2 Specimen Image Segmentation and Classification Using Very Deep Fully Convolutional Network. *IEEE Transactions on Medical Imaging, 36*(7), 1561–1572. doi:10.1109/TMI.2017.2672702 PMID:28237925

Lottemart. (2021). https://www.lotteon.com/p/display/main/lottemart?mall_no=4&chno=100195&ch_dtl_no=1000617

Louizos, C., Swersky, K., Li, Y., Welling, M., & Zemel, R. (2015). *The variational fair autoencoder.* arXiv preprint arXiv:1511.00830.

Luenendonk, M. (2019). *Uses of Big Data in Marketing*. https://www.cleverism.com/best-uses-big-data-marketing/

Lu, H., Zhao, B., Su, J., & Xie, P. (2014). Generating lightweight behavioral signature for malware detection in people-centric sensing. *Wireless Personal Communications*, *75*(3), 1591–1609. doi:10.100711277-013-1400-9

Lu, R., Xiang, L., Liu, M. R., & Yang, Q. (2012). Discovering news topics from microblogs based on hidden topics analysis and text clustering. *Pattern Recognition and Artificial Intelligence*, *25*(3), 382–387.

Lu, S., Xiao, L., & Ding, M. (2016). A Video-Based Automated Recommender (VAR) System for Garments. *Marketing Science*, *35*(3), 484–510. doi:10.1287/mksc.2016.0984

Lu, Y., Mei, Q., & Zhai, C. (2011). Investigating task performance of probabilistic topic models: An empirical study of PLSA and LDA. *Information Retrieval*, *14*(2), 178–203. doi:10.100710791-010-9141-9

Lv, Y., Duan, Y., Kang, W., Li, Z., & Wang, F.-Y. (2014). Traffic flow prediction with big data: A deep learning approach. *IEEE Transactions on Intelligent Transportation Systems*, *16*(2), 865–873. doi:10.1109/TITS.2014.2345663

Lysaght, T., Lim, H. Y., Xafis, V., & Ngiam, K. Y. (2019). AI-assisted decision-making in healthcare. *Asian Bioethics Review*, *11*(3), 299–314. doi:10.100741649-019-00096-0 PMID:33717318

M'ikanatha, N. M., Rohn, D. D., Robertson, C., Tan, C. G., Holmes, J. H., Kunselman, A. R., Polachek, C., & Lautenbach, E. (2006). Use of the internet to enhance infectious disease surveillance and outbreak investigation. *Biosecurity and Bioterrorism*, *4*(3), 293–300. doi:10.1089/bsp.2006.4.293 PMID:16999590

Machine learning can boost the value of wind energy. (2019, February 26). *DeepMind*. Retrieved February 19, 2022, from https://deepmind.com/blog/article/machine-learning-can-boost-value-wind-energy

Madakam, S., Ramaswamy, R., & Tripathi, S. (2015). Internet of Things (IoT): A Literature Review. *Journal of Computer and Communications*, *03*(05), 164–173. doi:10.4236/jcc.2015.35021

Magrelli, S., Valentini, P., Rose, C. D., Morello, R., & Buonsenso, D. (2021). Classification of Lung Disease in Children by Using Lung Ultrasound Images and Deep Convolutional Neural Network. *Frontiers in Physiology*, *12*, 12. doi:10.3389/fphys.2021.693448 PMID:34512375

Maguluri, L. P., Sorapalli, Y. S. V., Nakkala, L. K., & Tallari, V. (2018). Smart street lights using IoT. *Proceedings of the 2017 3rd International Conference on Applied and Theoretical Computing and Communication Technology, ICATccT 2017*, *3*(11), 126–131. 10.1109/ICATCCT.2017.8389119

Magumba, M. A., & Nabende, P. (2021). Evaluation of different machine learning approaches and input text representations for multilingual classification of tweets for disease surveillance in the social web. *Journal of Big Data*, *8*(1), 139. Advance online publication. doi:10.118640537-021-00528-5

Majumdar, S., Subhani, M. M., Roullier, B., Anjum, A., & Zhu, R. (2021). Congestion prediction for smart sustainable cities using IoT and machine learning approaches. *Sustainable Cities and Society*, *64*(September), 102500. doi:10.1016/j.scs.2020.102500

Makrehchi, M., Shah, S., & Liao, W. (2013, November). Stock prediction using event-based sentiment analysis. In *2013 IEEE/WIC/ACM International Joint Conferences on Web Intelligence (WI) and Intelligent Agent Technologies (IAT)* (Vol. 1, pp. 337-342). IEEE. 10.1109/WI-IAT.2013.48

Makridis, C. A., Zhao, D. Y., Bejan, C. A., & Alterovitz, G. (2021). Leveraging Machine Learning to Characterize the Role of Socio-economic Determinants on Physical Health and Well-Being Among Veterans. *Computers in Biology and Medicine*, *133*, 1–8. doi:10.1016/j.compbiomed.2021.104354 PMID:33845269

Ma, L., & Sun, B. (2020). Machine Learning and AI in Marketing – Connecting Computing Power to Human Insights. *International Journal of Research in Marketing*, 37(3), 481–504. doi:10.1016/j.ijresmar.2020.04.005

Malthouse, E. C., Haenlein, M., Skiera, B., & Zhang, E. W. (2013). Managing Customer Relationships in The Social Media Era: Introducing The Social CRM house. *Journal of Interactive Marketing*, 27(4), 270–280. doi:10.1016/j.int-mar.2013.09.008

Mao, C., Liang, H., Yu, Z., Huang, Y., & Guo, J. (2021). A Clustering Method of Case-Involved News by Combining Topic Network and Multi-Head Attention Mechanism. *Sensors (Basel)*, 21(22), 7501. doi:10.339021227501 PMID:34833580

Marquardt, D. W. (1963). An algorithm for least-squares estimation of nonlinear parameters. *Journal of the Society for Industrial and Applied Mathematics*, 11(2), 431–441. doi:10.1137/0111030

Marszalek, M., Laptev, I., & Schmid, C. (2009). Actions in context. In *Proceeding of CVPR 2009 - IEEE Conference on Computer Vision & Pattern Recognition* (pp.2929-2936). IEEE.

Marugán, A. P., Márquez, F. P. G., Perez, J. M. P., & Ruiz-Hernández, D. (2018, October). A survey of artificial neural networks in wind energy systems. *Applied Energy*, 228, 1822–1836. Advance online publication. doi:10.1016/j.apenergy.2018.07.084

März, L., Schweter, S., Poerner, N., Roth, B., & Schütze, H. (2021, September). Data Centric Domain Adaptation for Historical Text with OCR Errors. In *International Conference on Document Analysis and Recognition* (pp. 748-761). Springer. 10.1007/978-3-030-86331-9_48

Masood, A., Yang, P., Sheng, B., Li, H., Li, P., Qin, J., Lanfranchi, V., Kim, J., & Feng, D. D. (2019). Cloud-based automated clinical decision support system for detection and diagnosis of lung cancer in chest CT. *IEEE Journal of Translational Engineering in Health and Medicine*, 8, 1–13. doi:10.1109/JTEHM.2019.2955458 PMID:31929952

McCradden, M. D., Anderson, J. A., & Stephenson, E., Drysdale, E., Erdman, L., Goldenberg, A., & Zlotnik Shaul, R. (2022). A Research Ethics Framework for the Clinical Translation of Healthcare Machine Learning. *The American Journal of Bioethics*, 1–15. doi:10.1080/15265161.2021.2013977 PMID:35048782

McKinsey. (2015). *Marketing & Sales Big Data, Analytics and the Future of Marketing & Sales.* https://www.mckinsey.com

McWilliams, A., Beigi, P., Srinidhi, A., Lam, S., & MacAulay, C. E. (2015). Sex and smoking status effects on the early detection of early lung cancer in high-risk smokers using an electronic nose. *IEEE Transactions on Biomedical Engineering*, 62(8), 2044–2054. doi:10.1109/TBME.2015.2409092 PMID:25775482

Medsker, L. R., & Jain, L. C. (2001). Recurrent neural networks. *Design and Applications*, 5, 64–67.

Mehrizadeh, M. (2020). Prediction of gas hydrate formation using empirical equations and data-driven models. *Materials Today: Proceedings*. Retrieved from doi:10.1016/j.matpr.2020.06.058

Mesbah, M., Soroush, E., & Rezakazemi, M. (2017). Development of a least squares support vector machine model for prediction of natural gas hydrate formation temperature. *Chinese Journal of Chemical Engineering, 25*(9), 1238–1248. doi:10.1016/j.cjche.2016.09.007

Mesbah, M., Soroush, E., & Roham, M. (2017). *Phase equilibrium modeling of semi-clathrate hydrates of the CO 2 + H 2 / CH 4 / N 2 + TBAB aqueous solution system.* Academic Press.

Metkar, S. K., & Girigoswami, K. (2019). Diagnostic biosensors in medicine – A review. *Biocatalysis and Agricultural Biotechnology*, 17, 271–283. doi:10.1016/j.bcab.2018.11.029

Metlek, S., & Kayaalp K. (2020). Makine Öğrenmesinde, Teoriden Örnek Matlab Uygulamalarına Kadar Destek Vektör Makineleri. Ankara: İksad Yayınevi.

Mhasawade, V., Zhao, Y., & Chunara, R. (2021). Machine learning and algorithmic fairness in public and population health. *Nature Machine Intelligence*, *3*(8), 659–666. doi:10.103842256-021-00373-4

Mihaela, E. O. (2015). *The Influence of the Integrated Marketing Communication on The Consumer Buying Behavior. Procedia Economics and Finance.*

Mikolov, T., Chen, K., Corrado, G., & Dean, J. (2013). *Efficient estimation of word representations in vector space.* arXiv preprint arXiv: 1301.3781.

Mikolov, T., Chen, K., Corrado, G., & Dean, J. (2013). *Efficient estimation of word representations in vector space.* arXiv preprint arXiv:1301.3781.

Miladinov, G. (2020). Socioeconomic Development and Life Expectancy Relationship: Evidence from the EU Accession Candidate Countries. *Genus*, *76*(2), 1–20. doi:10.118641118-019-0071-0

Minchin, D. (2006). *The transport and the spread of living aquatic species.* doi:10.1007/1-4020-4504-2_5

Mirowsky, J., & Ross, C. E. (2000). Socioeconomic Status and Subjective Life Expectancy. *Social Psychology Quarterly*, *63*(2), 133–151. doi:10.2307/2695888

Mohammadi, A. H., Belandria, V., & Richon, D. (2010). Use of an artificial neural network algorithm to predict hydrate dissociation conditions for hydrogen+ water and hydrogen+ tetra-n-butyl ammonium bromide+ water systems. *Chemical Engineering Science*, *65*(14), 4302–4305. doi:10.1016/j.ces.2010.04.026

Mohammadi, A. H., Eslamimanesh, A., Richon, D., Gharagheizi, F., Yazdizadeh, M., Javanmardi, J., Hashemi, H., Zarifi, M., & Babaee, S. (2012). Gas hydrate phase equilibrium in porous media: Mathematical modeling and correlation. *Industrial & Engineering Chemistry Research*, *51*(2), 1062–1072. doi:10.1021/ie201904r

Mohammadi, A. H., Martínez-López, J. F., & Richon, D. (2010). Determining phase diagrams of tetrahydrofuran+ methane, carbon dioxide or nitrogen clathrate hydrates using an artificial neural network algorithm. *Chemical Engineering Science*, *65*(22), 6059–6063. doi:10.1016/j.ces.2010.07.013

Mohammadi, A. H., & Richon, D. (2009). Methane hydrate phase equilibrium in the presence of salt (NaCl, KCl, or CaCl2) + ethylene glycol or salt (NaCl, KCl, or CaCl2) + methanol aqueous solution: Experimental determination of dissociation condition. *The Journal of Chemical Thermodynamics*, *41*(12), 1374–1377. doi:10.1016/j.jct.2009.06.012

Mohammadi, A. H., & Richon, D. (2010). Hydrate phase equilibria for hydrogen+ water and hydrogen+ tetrahydrofuran+ water systems: Predictions of dissociation conditions using an artificial neural network algorithm. *Chemical Engineering Science*, *65*(10), 3352–3355. doi:10.1016/j.ces.2010.02.015

Mohammed, M., Khan, M. B., & Bashier, E. B. M. (2016). *Machine learning: algorithms and applications.* CRC Press. doi:10.1201/9781315371658

Mohandas, P., Dhanaraj, J. S. A., & Gao, X. Z. (2019). Artificial Neural Network based Smart and Energy Efficient Street Lighting System: A Case Study for Residential area in Hosur. *Sustainable Cities and Society*, *48*(January), 101499. Advance online publication. doi:10.1016/j.scs.2019.101499

Moradi, M. R., Nazari, K., Alavi, S., & Mohaddesi, M. (2013). Prediction of equilibrium conditions for hydrate formation in binary gaseous systems using artificial neural networks. *Energy Technology (Weinheim)*, *1*(2-3), 171–176. doi:10.1002/ente.201200056

Morgan, B. (2018). *How Amazon Has Reorganized Around Artificial Intelligence And Machine Learning.* https://www.forbes.com/sites/blakemorgan/2018/07/16/how-amazon-has-re-organized-around-artificial-intelligence-and-machine-learning/?sh=4f75f1573618

Moro, S., Rita, P., & Vala, P. (2016). Predicting Social Media Performance Metrics and Evaluation of The İmpact On Brand Building: A Data Mining Approach. *Journal of Business Research, 69*(9), 3341–3351. doi:10.1016/j.jbusres.2016.02.010

Morris, A. C., Maier, V., & Green, P. (2004). From WER and RIL to MER and WIL: improved evaluation measures for connected speech recognition. *Eighth International Conference on Spoken Language Processing.* 10.21437/Interspeech.2004-668

Motwani, T., & Mooney, R. (2012). Improving video activity recognition using object recognition and text mining. In *Proceeding of 20th European Conference on Artificial Intelligence* (pp. 600-605). Academic Press.

Muehlematter, U. J., Daniore, P., & Vokinger, K. N. (2021). Approval of artificial intelligence and machine learning-based medical devices in the USA and Europe (2015–20): A comparative analysis. *The Lancet. Digital Health, 3*(3), e195–e203. doi:10.1016/S2589-7500(20)30292-2 PMID:33478929

Munoz-Organero, M., Ruiz-Blaquez, R., & Sánchez-Fernández, L. (2018). Automatic detection of traffic lights, street crossings and urban roundabouts combining outlier detection and deep learning classification techniques based on GPS traces while driving. *Computers, Environment and Urban Systems, 68*(September), 1–8. doi:10.1016/j.compenvurbsys.2017.09.005

Muthukrishnan, R., & Maryam, J. S. (2020). Predictive Modeling Using Support Vector Regression. *International Journal of Scientific & Technology Research, 9*(2), 4863–4865.

Mykhalovskiy, E., & Weir, L. (2006). The Global Public Health Intelligence Network and Early Warning Outbreak Detection. *Canadian Journal of Public Health, 97*(1), 42–44. doi:10.1007/BF03405213 PMID:16512327

Myszczynska, M. A., Ojamies, P. N., Lacoste, A. M. B., Neil, D., Saffari, A., Mead, R., Hautbergue, G. M., Holbrook, J. D., & Ferraiuolo, L. (2020). Applications of machine learning to diagnosis and treatment of neurodegenerative diseases. *Nature Reviews. Neurology, 16*(8), 440–456. doi:10.103841582-020-0377-8 PMID:32669685

Nachev, A., & Teodosiev, T. (2018). Analysis of Employment Data Using Support Vector Machines. *International Journal of Applied Engineering Research: IJAER, 13*(18), 13525–13535.

Nahavandi, D., Alizadehsani, R., Khosravi, A., & Acharya, U. R. (2022). Application of artificial intelligence in wearable devices: Opportunities and challenges. *Computer Methods and Programs in Biomedicine, 213*, 106541. doi:10.1016/j.cmpb.2021.106541 PMID:34837860

Nataraj, L., Karthikeyan, S., Jacob, G., & Manjunath, B. S. (2011, July). Malware images: visualization and automatic classification. In *Proceedings of the 8th international symposium on visualization for cyber security* (pp. 1-7). Academic Press.

Neirotti, P., De Marco, A., Cagliano, A. C., Mangano, G., & Scorrano, F. (2014). Current trends in smart city initiatives: Some stylised facts. *Cities (London, England), 38*, 25–36. doi:10.1016/j.cities.2013.12.010

Netzer, O., Feldman, R., Goldenberg, J., & Fresko, M. (2012). Mine Your Own Business: Market structure Surveillance Through Text Mining. *Marketing Science, 31*(3), 521–543. doi:10.1287/mksc.1120.0713

Newman, N., Fletcher, R., Schulz, A., Andi, S., Robertson, C. T., & Nielsen, R. K. (2021). *Reuters Institute Digital News Report 2021.* Reuters Institute for the Study of Journalism.

Nicholas, O. (2007). *Andrews and Edward A. Fox: Recent Developments in Document Clustering. Technical Report.* Virginia Tech.

Nielsen, R., & Selva, M. (2019). *More important, but less robust? Five things everybody needs to know about the future of journalism.* Academic Press.

Nishant, R., Kennedy, M., & Corbett, J. (2020, August). Artificial intelligence for sustainability: Challenges, opportunities, and a research agenda. *International Journal of Information Management, 53*(102104), 102104. Advance online publication. doi:10.1016/j.ijinfomgt.2020.102104

OECD. (n.d.). https://data.oecd.org

Ozbayoglu, M., Kucukayan, G., & Dogdu, E. (2016). A real-time autonomous highway accident detection model based on big data processing and computational intelligence. *Proceedings - 2016 IEEE International Conference on Big Data*, 1807–1813. doi:10.1109/BigData.2016.7840798

Özdamar, K. (2013). *Paket Programlarla İstatistiksel Veri Analizi Cilt 2.* Nisan Kitabevi.

Özyer, T., Ak, D. S., & Alhajj, R. (2021). Human action recognition approaches with video datasets-A survey. *Knowledge-Based Systems, 222*, 106995. doi:10.1016/j.knosys.2021.106995

Pal, G., Rudrapaul, D., Acharjee, S., Ray, R., Chakraborty, S., & Dey, N. (2015). Video Shot Boundary Detection: A Review. *Emerging ICT for Bridging the Future, 2*, 119–127.

Park, S., & Hwang, K. (2020). *Increasing Customer Engagement and Loyalty With Personalized Coupon Recommendations Using Amazon Personalize.* https://aws.amazon.com/tr/blogs/machine-learning/increasing-customer-engagement-and-loyalty-with-personalized-coupon-recommendat ions-using-amazon-personalize/

Parmaksız, A. (2019). *Çoklu Doğrusal Regresyon Çözümlemesinde Farklı Korelasyon Yapılarında %80 Güç İçin Örneklem Büyüklüğünün Belirlenmesi.* Doktora Tezi. Hacettepe Üniversitesi Sağlık Bilimleri Enstitüsü.

Parveen, N., Zaidi, S., & Danish, M. (2017). Development of SVR-Based Model and Comparative Analysis with MLR and ANN Models for Predicting The Sorption Capacity of Cr(VI). *Process Safety and Environmental Protection, 107*, 428–437. doi:10.1016/j.psep.2017.03.007

Parveen, N., Zaidi, S., & Danish, M. (2017). Support Vector Regression Prediction and Analysis of the Copper (II) Biosorption Efficiency. *Indian Chemical Engineer, 59*(4), 295–311. doi:10.1080/00194506.2016.1270778

Pascanu, R., Stokes, J. W., Sanossian, H., Marinescu, M., & Thomas, A. (2015, April). Malware classification with recurrent networks. In *2015 IEEE International Conference on Acoustics, Speech and Signal Processing (ICASSP)* (pp. 1916-1920). IEEE. 10.1109/ICASSP.2015.7178304

Patle, A., & Chouhan, D. S. (2013). SVM Kernel Functions for Classification. *2013 International Conference on Advances in Technology and Engineering*, 1-9.

Peddoju, S. K., Upadhyay, H., Soni, J., & Prabakar, N. (2020). Natural language processing based anomalous system call sequences detection with virtual memory introspection. *International Journal of Advanced Computer Science and Applications, 11*(5). Advance online publication. doi:10.14569/IJACSA.2020.0110559

Pedregosa, F., Varoquaux, G., Gramfort, A., Michel, V., Thirion, B., Grisel, O., & Duchesnay, E. (2011). Scikit-learn: Machine learning in Python. *Journal of Machine Learning Research, 12*, 2825–2830.

Pelckmans, K., Suykens, J. A. K., Van Gestel, T., De Brabanter, J., Lukas, L., Hamers, B., & De Moor, B. (2002). LS-SVMlab: a matlab/c toolbox for least squares support vector machines. Tutorial. KULeuven-ESAT.

Pengo, T., Muñoz-Barrutía, A., & Ortiz-de-Solorzano, C. (2013). A novel automated microscopy platform for multi-resolution multispectral early detection of lung cancer cells in Bronchoalveolar lavage samples. *IEEE Systems Journal*, *8*(3), 985–994. doi:10.1109/JSYST.2013.2289152

Pennington, J., Socher, R., & Manning, C. D. (2014, October). Glove: Global vectors for word representation. In *Proceedings of the 2014 conference on empirical methods in natural language processing (EMNLP)* (pp. 1532-1543). 10.3115/v1/D14-1162

Perboli, G., De Marco, A., Perfetti, F., & Marone, M. (2014). A new taxonomy of smart city projects. *Transportation Research Procedia*, *3*(July), 470–478. doi:10.1016/j.trpro.2014.10.028

Petersen, R., Fredenslund, A., & Rasmussen, P. (1994). Artificial neural networks as a predictive tool for vapor-liquid equilibrium. *Computers & Chemical Engineering*, *18*, S63–S67. doi:10.1016/0098-1354(94)80011-1

Petkos, G., Papadopoulos, S., & Kompatsiaris, Y. (2012, June). Social event detection using multimodal clustering and integrating supervisory signals. In *Proceedings of the 2nd ACM International Conference on Multimedia Retrieval* (pp. 1-8). 10.1145/2324796.2324825

Petousis, P., Winter, A., Speier, W., Aberle, D. R., Hsu, W., & Bui, A. A. (2019). Using Sequential Decision Making to Improve Lung Cancer Screening Performance. *IEEE Access: Practical Innovations, Open Solutions*, *7*, 119403–119419. doi:10.1109/ACCESS.2019.2935763 PMID:32754420

Picot, J., Guerin, C. L., Le Van Kim, C., & Boulanger, C. M. (2012). Flow cytometry: Retrospective, fundamentals and recent instrumentation. *Cytotechnology*, *64*(2), 109–130. doi:10.100710616-011-9415-0 PMID:22271369

Potukuchi, S., & Wexler, A. S. (1997). Predicting vapor pressures using neural networks. *Atmospheric Environment*, *31*(5), 741–753. doi:10.1016/S1352-2310(96)00203-8

Pratt, H., Coenen, F., Broadbent, D. M., Harding, S. P., & Zheng, Y. (2016). Convolutional Neural Networks for Diabetic Retinopathy. *Procedia Computer Science*, *90*, 200–205. doi:10.1016/j.procs.2016.07.014

Price, W. N. II, & Cohen, I. G. (2019). Privacy in the age of medical big data. *Nature Medicine*, *25*(1), 37–43. doi:10.103841591-018-0272-7 PMID:30617331

Price, W., & Nicholson, I. (2019). Artificial intelligence in the medical system: Four roles for potential transformation. *Yale JL & Tech.*, *21*, 122.

Qayyum, A., Qadir, J., Bilal, M., & Al-Fuqaha, A. (2021). Secure and Robust Machine Learning for Healthcare: A Survey. *IEEE Reviews in Biomedical Engineering*, *14*, 156–180. doi:10.1109/RBME.2020.3013489 PMID:32746371

Qin, Z. T., Zhu, H., & Ye, J. (2021). Reinforcement Learning for Ridesharing: A Survey. *2021 IEEE International Intelligent Transportation Systems Conference (ITSC)*, 2447-2454. 10.1109/ITSC48978.2021.9564924

Raff, E., Barker, J., Sylvester, J., Brandon, R., Catanzaro, B., & Nicholas, C. K. (2018, June). Malware detection by eating a whole exe. *Workshops at the Thirty-Second AAAI Conference on Artificial Intelligence*.

Rai, P., Majumdar, G. C., DasGupta, S., & De, S. (2005). Prediction of the viscosity of clarified fruit juice using artificial neural network: A combined effect of concentration and temperature. [Elsevier.]. *Journal of Food Engineering*, *68*(4), 527–533. doi:10.1016/j.jfoodeng.2004.07.003

Ramchoun, H., Ghanou, Y., Ettaouil, M., & Janati Idrissi, M. A. (2016). *Multilayer perceptron: Architecture optimization and training*. Academic Press.

Rasouli, E., Zarifzadeh, S., & Rafsanjani, A. J. (2020). WebKey: A graph-based method for event detection in web news. *Journal of Intelligent Information Systems, 54*(3), 585–604. doi:10.100710844-019-00576-7

Raza, H. W., Kamal, M. A., Alam, M., & Su'ud, M. S. M. (2020). A Review Of Middleware Platforms In Internet Of Things: A Non – Functional Requirements Approach. *Journal of Independent Studies and Research Computing.* doi:10.31645/18

Rebai, N., Hadjadj, A., Benmounah, A., Berrouk, A. S., & Boualleg, S. M. (2019). Prediction of natural gas hydrates formation using a combination of thermodynamic and neural network modeling. *Journal of Petroleum Science and Engineering, 182*(March), 106270. doi:10.1016/j.petrol.2019.106270

Regue, R., & Recker, W. (2014, November). Proactive vehicle routing with inferred demand to solve the bikesharing rebalancing problem. *Transportation Research Part E, Logistics and Transportation Review, 72*, 192–209. doi:10.1016/j.tre.2014.10.005

Rencher, A. C., & Schaalje, G. B. (2007). *Linear Models in Statistics* (2nd ed.). Wiley-Interscience. doi:10.1002/9780470192610

Ren, S., He, K., Girshick, R., & Sun, J. (2015). Faster r-cnn: Towards real-time object detection with region proposal networks. *Advances in Neural Information Processing Systems*, 28.

Ren, X. D., Zhang, Y. K., & Xue, X. F. (2009, May). Adaptive topic tracking technique based on K-modes clustering. *Comput. Eng., 35*(9), 222–224.

Rhode, M., Burnap, P., & Jones, K. (2018). Early-stage malware prediction using recurrent neural networks. *Computers & Security, 77*, 578-594.

Rimo, T., & Walth, M. (2014). *McAfee and CSIS: Stopping Cybercrime Can Positively Impact World Economies*. McAfee.

Rivoltella, P. C. (2018). The third age of the media. *Research on Education and Media, 10*(1), 1–2. doi:10.1515/rem-2018-0001

Roohi, R., Jafari, M., Jahantab, E., Aman, M. S., Moameri, M., & Zare, S. (2020). Application of artificial neural network model for the identification of the effect of municipal waste compost and biochar on phytoremediation of contaminated soils. *Journal of Geochemical Exploration, 208*(106399), 106399. Advance online publication. doi:10.1016/j.gexplo.2019.106399

Rosa, R. L., De Silva, M. J., Silva, D. H., Ayub, M. S., Carrillo, D., Nardelli, P. H., & Rodríguez, D. Z. (2020). Event detection system based on user behavior changes in online social networks: Case of the COVID-19 pandemic. *IEEE Access: Practical Innovations, Open Solutions, 8*, 158806–158825. doi:10.1109/ACCESS.2020.3020391 PMID:34812354

Ross, C., & Guhathakurta, S. (2017). Autonomous Vehicles and Energy Impacts: A Scenario Analysis. *Energy Procedia, 143*, 47–52. doi:10.1016/j.egypro.2017.12.646

Roy, A., Siddiquee, J., Datta, A., Poddar, P., Ganguly, G., & Bhattacharjee, A. (2016). Smart traffic & parking management using IoT. *7th IEEE Annual Information Technology, Electronics and Mobile Communication Conference, IEEE IEMCON 2016.* 10.1109/IEMCON.2016.7746331

Rugani, B., & Caro, D. (2020). Impact of COVID-19 outbreak measures of lockdown on the Italian Carbon Footprint. *The Science of the Total Environment, 737*(139806), 139806. Advance online publication. doi:10.1016/j.scitotenv.2020.139806 PMID:32492608

Ryder, B., & Wortmann, F. (2017). Autonomously detecting and classifying traffic accident hotspots. *UbiComp/ISWC 2017 - Adjunct Proceedings of the 2017 ACM International Joint Conference on Pervasive and Ubiquitous Computing and Proceedings of the 2017 ACM International Symposium on Wearable Computers*, 365–370. 10.1145/3123024.3123199

Sablani, S. S., Baik, O.-D., & Marcotte, M. (2002). Neural networks for predicting thermal conductivity of bakery products. *Journal of Food Engineering*, *52*(3), 299–304. doi:10.1016/S0260-8774(01)00119-4

Saggi, G. M., & Jain, S. (2018). A Survey Towards An Integration of Big Data Analytics to Big Insights. *Information Processing & Management*, *54*(5), 758–790. doi:10.1016/j.ipm.2018.01.010

Sahoo, D., Hao, W., Ke, S., Xiongwei, W., Le, H., Achananuparp, P., . . . Hoi, S. C. H. (2019). *FoodAI: Food Image Recognition via Deep Learningfor Smart Food Logging*. Academic Press.

Sakaki, T., Okazaki, M., & Matsuo, Y. (2010, April). Earthquake shakes Twitter users: real-time event detection by social sensors. In *Proceedings of the 19th international conference on world wide web* (pp. 851-860). 10.1145/1772690.1772777

Sánchez-Corcuera, R., Nuñez-Marcos, A., Sesma-Solance, J., Bilbao-Jayo, A., Mulero, R., Zulaika, U., Azkune, G., & Almeida, A. (2019). Smart cities survey: Technologies, application domains and challenges for the cities of the future. *International Journal of Distributed Sensor Networks*, *15*(6). Advance online publication. doi:10.1177/1550147719853984

Sánchez-Martínez, S., Camara, O., Piella, G., Cikes, M., Ballester, M. A. G., Miron, M., . . . Bijnens, B. (2019). *Machine learning for clinical decision-making: challenges and opportunities*. Academic Press.

Sandler, M., Howard, A., Zhu, M., Zhmoginov, A., & Chen, L. C. (2018). Mobilenetv2: Inverted residuals and linear bottlenecks. *Proceedings of the IEEE Conference on Computer Vision and Pattern Recognition*, 4510–4520.

Sandler, M., Howard, A., Zhu, M., Zhmoginov, A., & Chen, L.-C. (2018). MobileNetV2: Inverted Residuals and Linear Bottlenecks. *The IEEE Conference on Computer Vision and Pattern Recognition (CVPR)*, 4510-4520. https://arxiv.org/abs/1801.04381

Sang, K. S., Zhou, B., Yang, P., & Yang, Z. (2018). Study of group route optimization for IoT enabled urban transportation network. *Proceedings - 2017 IEEE International Conference on Internet of Things, IEEE Green Computing and Communications, IEEE Cyber, Physical and Social Computing, IEEE Smart Data, IThings-GreenCom-CPSCom-SmartData 2017*, 888–893. 10.1109/iThings-GreenCom-CPSCom-SmartData.2017.137

Sarkodie, S. A. (2021). Environmental performance, biocapacity, carbon & ecological footprint of nations: Drivers, trends and mitigation options. *Science of The Total Environment, 751*. doi:10.1016/j.scitotenv.2020.141912

Schackart, K. E. III, & Yoon, J. Y. (2021). Machine Learning Enhances the Performance of Bioreceptor-Free Biosensors. *Sensors (Basel)*, *21*(16), 5519. Advance online publication. doi:10.339021165519 PMID:34450960

Scheltes, A., & de Almeida Correia, G. H. (2017). Exploring the use of automated vehicles as last mile connection of train trips through an agent-based simulation model: An application to Delft, Netherlands. *International Journal of Transportation Science and Technology*, *6*(1), 28–41. doi:10.1016/j.ijtst.2017.05.004

Schmitz, J. E., Zemp, R. J., & Mendes, M. J. (2006). Artificial neural networks for the solution of the phase stability problem. *Fluid Phase Equilibria*, *245*(1), 83–87. doi:10.1016/j.fluid.2006.02.013

Schuldt, C., Laptev, I., & Caputo, B. (2004). Recognizing human actions: a local SVM approach. In *Proceedings of the 17th International Conference on Pattern Recognition (Vol. 3)*. IEEE Xplore. 10.1109/ICPR.2004.1334462

Schultz, M. G., Eskin, E., Zadok, F., & Stolfo, S. J. (2000, May). Data mining methods for detection of new malicious executables. In *Proceedings 2001 IEEE Symposium on Security and Privacy. S&P 2001* (pp. 38-49). IEEE.

Schwenker, F., Kestler, H. A., & Palm, G. (2001). Three learning phases for radial-basis-function networks. *Neural Networks*, *14*(4–5), 439–458. doi:10.1016/S0893-6080(01)00027-2 PMID:11411631

Seif, M., & Kamran-pirzaman, A. (2020). Prediction of Gas and Refrigerant Hydrate Equilibrium Conditions With and Without Thermodynamic Inhibitors Using Simple Empirical Correlations. *Journal of Petroleum Science and Technology*, *10*, 61–72.

Şerban, O., Thapen, N., Maginnis, B., Hankin, C., & Foot, V. (2019). Real-time processing of social media with SENTINEL: A syndromic surveillance system incorporating deep learning for health classification. *Information Processing & Management*, *56*(3), 1166–1184. doi:10.1016/j.ipm.2018.04.011

Shao, L. (2006). Generic Feature Extraction for Image/Video Analysis. *IEEE Conference*.

Sharma, R., Singhal, D., Ghosh, R., & Dwivedi, A. (1999). Potential applications of artificial neural networks to thermodynamics: Vapor–liquid equilibrium predictions. *Computers & Chemical Engineering*, *23*(3), 385–390. doi:10.1016/S0098-1354(98)00281-6

Shaw, J. W., Horrace, W. C., & Vogel, J. (2005). The Determinants of Life Expectancy: An Analysis of the OECD Health Data. *Southern Economic Journal*, *71*(4), 768–783.

Shen, Q., & Villas-Boas, J. (2018). Behavior-based Advertising. *Management Science*, *64*(5), 2047–2064. doi:10.1287/mnsc.2016.2719

Shen, Z., Zhang, K., & Dell, M. (2020). A large dataset of historical japanese documents with complex layouts. In *Proceedings of the IEEE/CVF Conference on Computer Vision and Pattern Recognition Workshops* (pp. 548-549). 10.1109/CVPRW50498.2020.00282

Shih, H. (2018). A survey of content-aware video analysis for sports. *IEEE Trans. Circ. Syst. Vid.*, *28*(5), 1212–1231. doi:10.1109/TCSVT.2017.2655624

Shijo, P. V., & Salim, A. J. P. C. S. (2015). Integrated static and dynamic analysis for malware detection. *Procedia Computer Science*, *46*, 804–811. doi:10.1016/j.procs.2015.02.149

Shi, Y., Gao, Y., Yang, Y., Zhang, Y., & Wang, D. (2013). Multimodal sparse representation-based classification for lung needle biopsy images. *IEEE Transactions on Biomedical Engineering*, *60*(10), 2675–2685. doi:10.1109/TBME.2013.2262099 PMID:23674412

Shomanov, A. S., & Mansurova, M. E. (2021). Parallel news clustering and topic modeling approaches. *Journal of Physics: Conference Series*, *1727*(1), 012018. doi:10.1088/1742-6596/1727/1/012018

Shrestha, S., Petermann, J., Farrahi, T., Deshpande, A., & Giakos, G. C. (2015). Design, Calibration, and Testing of an Automated Near-Infrared Liquid-Crystal Polarimetric Imaging System for Discrimination of Lung Cancer Cells. *IEEE Transactions on Instrumentation and Measurement*, *64*(9), 2453–2467. doi:10.1109/TIM.2015.2415013

Shterionov, D., & Vanmassenhove, E. (2022). *The Ecological Footprint of Neural Machine Translation Systems*. arXiv preprint. arXiv:2202.02170

Siddiqui, M., Wang, M. C., & Lee, J. (2008, March). A survey of data mining techniques for malware detection using file features. In *Proceedings of the 46th annual southeast regional conference on xx* (pp. 509-510). 10.1145/1593105.1593239

Siegel, L., Miller, K. D., & Jemal, A. (2019). Cancer statistics. *CA: a Cancer Journal for Clinicians*, *69*(1), 7–34. doi:10.3322/caac.21551 PMID:30620402

Simonyan, K., & Zisserman, A. (2014). Very deep convolutional networks for large-scale image recognition. *Proceedings of ICLR*.

Simpson, J. (2017). *Finding Brand Success In The Digital World.* https://www.forbes.com/sites/forbesagencycouncil/2017/08/25/finding-brand-success-in-the-digital-world/? sh=774a012626e2

Sinehbaghizadeh, S., Javanmardi, J., Roosta, A., & Mohammadi, A. H. (2019). Estimation of the dissociation conditions and storage capacities of various sH clathrate hydrate systems using effective deterministic frameworks. *Fuel, 247,* 272–286. doi:10.1016/j.fuel.2019.01.189

Singh, A., Pang, G., Toh, M., Huang, J., Galuba, W., & Hassner, T. (2021). TextOCR: Towards large-scale end-to-end reasoning for arbitrary-shaped scene text. In *Proceedings of the IEEE/CVF Conference on Computer Vision and Pattern Recognition* (pp. 8802-8812). 10.1109/CVPR46437.2021.00869

Sloan, E. D. (1998). Physical / Chemical Properties of Gas Hydrates. *Gas Hydrates. Relevance to world margin stability and climatic change, 624*(5), 191–196.

Smith, J. B., & Colgate, M. (2007). Customer Value Creation: A Practical Framework. *Journal of Marketing Theory and Practice, 15*(1), 7–23. doi:10.2753/MTP1069-6679150101

Soni, J., & Prabakar, N. (2018). Effective machine learning approach to detect groups of fake reviewers. In *Proceedings of the 14th international conference on data science (ICDATA'18), Las Vegas, NV* (pp. 3-9). Academic Press.

Soni, J., Prabakar, N., & Upadhyay, H. (2019). *Comparative Analysis of LSTM Sequence-Sequence and Auto Encoder for real-time anomaly detection using system call sequences.* Academic Press.

Soni, J., Peddoju, S. K., Prabakar, N., & Upadhyay, H. (2021). Comparative Analysis of LSTM, One-Class SVM, and PCA to Monitor Real-Time Malware Threats Using System Call Sequences and Virtual Machine Introspection. In *International Conference on Communication, Computing and Electronics Systems* (pp. 113-127). Springer. 10.1007/978-981-33-4909-4_9

Soni, J., Prabakar, N., & Upadhyay, H. (2019, December). Behavioral Analysis of System Call Sequences Using LSTM Seq-Seq, Cosine Similarity and Jaccard Similarity for Real-Time Anomaly Detection. In *2019 International Conference on Computational Science and Computational Intelligence (CSCI)* (pp. 214-219). IEEE. 10.1109/CSCI49370.2019.00043

Soroush, E., Mesbah, M., Shokrollahi, A., Bahadori, A., & Ghazanfari, M. H. (2014). Prediction of methane uptake on different adsorbents in adsorbed natural gas technology using a rigorous model. *Energy & Fuels, 28*(10), 6299–6314. doi:10.1021/ef501550p

Soroush, E., Mesbah, M., Shokrollahi, A., Rozyn, J., Lee, M., Kashiwao, T., & Bahadori, A. (2015). Evolving a robust modeling tool for prediction of natural gas hydrate formation conditions. *Journal of Unconventional Oil and Gas Resources, 12,* 45–55.

Staykovski, T., Barrón-Cedeno, A., Da San Martino, G., & Nakov, P. (2019). Dense vs. Sparse Representations for News Stream Clustering. In Text2Story@ ECIR (pp. 47-52). Academic Press.

Sun, C.-Y., Chen, G.-J., Lin, W., & Guo, T.-M. (2003). Hydrate formation conditions of sour natural gases. *Journal of Chemical & Engineering Data, 48*(3), 600–602. doi:10.1021/je020155h

Sung, A. H., Xu, J., Chavez, P., & Mukkamala, S. (2004, December). Static analyzer of vicious executables (save). In *20th Annual Computer Security Applications Conference* (pp. 326-334). IEEE. 10.1109/CSAC.2004.37

Suoniemi, S., Meyer-Waarden, L., Munzel, A., & Straub, A. R. (2020). Big Data and Firm Performance: The Roles of Market-directed Capabilities and Business Strategy. *Information & Management, 57*(7), 103365. doi:10.1016/j.im.2020.103365

Suvarna, B., Nandipati, B. L., & Bhat, M. N. (2020). Support Vector Regression for Predicting COVID-19 Cases. *European Journal of Molecular & Clinical Medicine, 7*(3), 4882–4893.

Su, Y., Li, D., & Chen, X. (2021). Lung nodule detection based on faster R-CNN framework. *Computer Methods and Programs in Biomedicine, 200,* 105866. doi:10.1016/j.cmpb.2020.105866 PMID:33309304

Talend. (2021). *Big Data in Marketing 101: Why it's Important, Where it's Going, and How to Get Started.* https://www.talend.com/resources/big-data-marketing/

Tan, M., & Le, Q. (2019). EfficientNet: Rethinking model scaling for convolutional neural networks. *Proceedings of the 36th International Conference on Machine Learning, 97,* 6105–6114.

Tang, Y. (2013). *Deep Learning using Linear Support Vector Machines.* arXiv preprint arXiv:1306.0239

Tang, Q. (2020). Construction of Interactive Integrated Communication Marketing System in Big Data Era. *Journal of Physics: Conference Series, 1550*(3), 1550. doi:10.1088/1742-6596/1550/3/032142

Thakur, N. K., & Rajput, S. (2010). *Exploration of gas hydrates: Geophysical techniques.* Springer Science & Business Media.

The World Bank. (n.d.). https://databank.worldbank.org

Thieme, A., Belgrave, D., & Doherty, G. (2020). Machine Learning in Mental Health. *ACM Transactions on Computer-Human Interaction, 27*(5), 1–53. doi:10.1145/3398069

Timm, N. H. (2002). *Applied Multivariate Analysis.* Springer.

Tolun, S. (2008). *Destek Vektör Makineleri: Banka Başarısızlığının Tahmini Üzerine Bir Uygulama.* Doktora Tezi. İstanbul Üniversitesi Sosyal Bilimler Enstitüsü.

Torres-Barrán, A., Alonso, Á., & Dorronsoro, J. R. (2019, January). Regression tree ensembles for wind energy and solar radiation prediction. *Neurocomputing, 326-327,* 151–160. doi:10.1016/j.neucom.2017.05.104

Tran, T. K., & Sato, H. (2017, November). NLP-based approaches for malware classification from API sequences. In *2017 21st Asia Pacific Symposium on Intelligent and Evolutionary Systems (IES)* (pp. 101-105). IEEE.

Tran, S., Nghiem, T. P., Nguyen, V. T., Luong, C. M., & Burie, J.-C. (2019). Improving accuracy of lung nodule classification using deep learning with focal loss. *Journal of Healthcare Engineering, 2019,* 1–9. doi:10.1155/2019/5156416 PMID:30863524

Tripathy, A. K., Mishra, A. K., & Das, T. K. (2018). Smart lighting: Intelligent and weather adaptive lighting in street lights using IOT. *2017 International Conference on Intelligent Computing, Instrumentation and Control Technologies, ICICICT 2017,* 1236–1239. 10.1109/ICICICT1.2017.8342746

Tukymbekov, D., Saymbetov, A., Nurgaliyev, M., Kuttybay, N., Dosymbetova, G., & Svanbayev, Y. (2021). Intelligent autonomous street lighting system based on weather forecast using LSTM. *Energy, 231,* 120902. doi:10.1016/j.energy.2021.120902

Van Horn, J. D., & Toga, A. W. (2014). Human neuroimaging as a "Big Data" science. *Brain Imaging and Behavior, 8*(2), 323–331. doi:10.100711682-013-9255-y PMID:24113873

Vapnik, V. (1999). *The nature of statistical learning theory.* Springer science & business media.

Vapnik, V. N. (1999). An overview of statistical learning theory. *IEEE Transactions on Neural Networks, 10*(5), 988–999. doi:10.1109/72.788640 PMID:18252602

Vázquez-Canteli, J. R., & Nagy, Z. (2019, February). Reinforcement learning for demand response: A review of algorithms and modeling techniques. *Applied Energy, 235*(1), 1072–1089. doi:10.1016/j.apenergy.2018.11.002

Viddler. (2013). *Interactive video training and practice.* https://www.viddler.com/

Vinayakumar, R., Alazab, M., Soman, K. P., Poornachandran, P., & Venkatraman, S. (2019). Robust intelligent malware detection using deep learning. *IEEE Access: Practical Innovations, Open Solutions, 7*, 46717–46738. doi:10.1109/AC-CESS.2019.2906934

Vishwakarma, S., & Agrawal, A. (2013). A survey on activity recognition and behavior understanding in video surveillance. *The Visual Computer, 29*(10), 983–1009. doi:10.100700371-012-0752-6

Vydehi, K., Manchikanti, K., Kumari, T. S., & Shah, S. K. A. (2020). Machine Learning Techniques for Life Expectancy Prediction. *International Journal of Advanced Trends in Computer Science and Engineering, 9*(4), 4503–4507. doi:10.30534/ijatcse/2020/45942020

Wackernagel, M., & Rees, W. (1996). *Our Ecological Footprint: Reducing Human Impact on the Earth.* New Society Publishers.

Walmart. (2021). https://corporate.walmart.com/our-story/our-locations

Wang, B., & Kim, I. (2018). Short-term prediction for bike-sharing service using Machine Learning. *Transportation Research Procedia, 34*, 171–178. doi:10.1016/j.trpro.2018.11.029

Wang, L., Zhang, Y., Wang, D., Tong, X., Liu, T., Zhang, S., Huang, J., Zhang, L., Chen, L., Fan, H., & Clarke, M. (2021). Artificial Intelligence for COVID-19: A Systematic Review. *Frontiers in medicine, 8*, 704256. Advance online publication. doi:10.3389/fmed.2021.704256 PMID:34660623

Wang, W., Peng, X., Qiao, Y., & Cheng, J. (2021). *An empirical study on temporal modeling for online action detection. Complex Intell. Syst.* doi:10.100740747-021-00534-3

Wang, Y., Liu, J., Huang, Y., & Feng, X. (2016, July). Using hashtag graph-based topic model to connect semantically-related words without cooccurrence in microblogs. *IEEE Transactions on Knowledge and Data Engineering, 28*(7), 1919–1933. doi:10.1109/TKDE.2016.2531661

Wasteless. (n.d.). Retrieved February 6, 2022, from https://www.wasteless.com

Wei, Q., Hu, Y., Gelfand, G., & MacGregor, J. H. (2009). Segmentation of lung lobes in high-resolution isotropic CT images. *IEEE Transactions on Biomedical Engineering, 56*(5), 1383–1393. doi:10.1109/TBME.2009.2014074 PMID:19203878

Weisberg, S. (2005). *Applied Linear Regression.* John Wiley & Sons. doi:10.1002/0471704091

Wiencierz, C., & Röttger, U. (2018). *Big Data-Based Strategic Communication.* https://www.akademischegesellschaft.com/fileadmin/webcontent/Presse/1803_Comm_Director_CW_UR_2018_BD_based_ Strat_Comm.pdf

WorldEconomicForum. (2012). *Big Data, Big Impact: New Possibilities for International Development.* http://www3.weforum.org/docs/WEF_TC_MFS_BigDataBigImpact_ Briefing_ 2012.pdf

Wu, Y., Kirillov, A., Massa, F., Lo, W., & Girshick, R. (2019). *Detectron2.* https://github.com/facebookresearch/detectron2

Wu, C. H., Ho, J. M., & Lee, D. T. (2004). Travel-Time Prediction With Support Vector Regression. *IEEE Transactions on Intelligent Transportation Systems, 5*(4), 276–281. doi:10.1109/TITS.2004.837813

Wu, M., Wei, Y., Lam, P. T. I., Liu, F., & Li, Y. (2019, November). Is urban development ecologically sustainable? Ecological footprint analysis and prediction based on a modified artificial neural network model: A case study of Tianjin in China. *Journal of Cleaner Production*, *237*(117795), 117795. Advance online publication. doi:10.1016/j.jclepro.2019.117795

Wu, Q., Huang, C., Wang, S. Y., Chiu, W. C., & Chen, T. (2007). Robust parking space detection considering inter-space correlation. *Proceedings of the 2007 IEEE International Conference on Multimedia and Expo, ICME 2007*, 659–662. 10.1109/ICME.2007.4284736

Xia, H., & Zhan, Y. (2020). A survey on temporal action localization. *IEEE Access: Practical Innovations, Open Solutions*, *8*, 70477–70487. doi:10.1109/ACCESS.2020.2986861

Xie, Y., Zhang, J., & Xia, Y. (2019). Semi-supervised adversarial model for benign–malignant lung nodule classification on chest CT. *Medical Image Analysis*, *57*, 237–248. doi:10.1016/j.media.2019.07.004 PMID:31352126

Xu, H., Jiao, Z., Zhang, Z., Huffman, M., & Wang, Q. (2021). Prediction of methane hydrate formation conditions in salt water using machine learning algorithms. *Computers & Chemical Engineering*, *151*, 107358. doi:10.1016/j.compchemeng.2021.107358

Xu, X., Wang, C., Guo, J., Yang, L., Bai, H., Li, W., & Yi, Z. (2020). DeepLN: A framework for automatic lung nodule detection using multi-resolution CT screening images. *Knowledge-Based Systems*, *189*, 105128. doi:10.1016/j.knosys.2019.105128

Yagli, G. M., Yang, D., & Srinivasan, D. (2019, May). Automatic hourly solar forecasting using Machine Learning models. *Renewable & Sustainable Energy Reviews*, *105*, 487–498. doi:10.1016/j.rser.2019.02.006

Yang J., Javed A. & Vall-Llosera G. (2019). *Support Vector Machines on Noisy Intermediate Scale Quantum Computers*. ArXiv, abs/1909.11988.

Yang, M., & Thung, G. (2016). *Classification of Trash for Recyclability Status*. CS229 Project Report.

Yang, C. C., Shi, X., & Wei, C. P. (2009). Discovering event evolution graphs from news corpora. *IEEE Transactions on Systems, Man, and Cybernetics. Part A, Systems and Humans*, *39*(4), 850–863. doi:10.1109/TSMCA.2009.2015885

Yao, T., Mei, T., Ngo, C. W., & Li, S. (2013). Annotation for free: video tagging by mining user search behavior. In *Proceedings of 21st ACM international conference on multimedia* (pp 977-986). ACM. 10.1145/2502081.2502085

Yarveicy, H., & Ghiasi, M. M. (2017a). Modeling of gas hydrate phase equilibria: Extremely randomized trees and LSSVM approaches. *Journal of Molecular Liquids*, *243*, 533–541. doi:10.1016/j.molliq.2017.08.053

Yavuz, V., & Erdoğan-Gençyürek, M. (2019). *Advertising Applications on Internet News Sites*. Current Marketing Studies. in Image Publishing House.

Yıldırım, Y. (2018). *Destek Vektör Regresyonu ve Destek Vektör Makineleri* [Support Vector Regression and Support Vector Machines]. https://yavuz.github.io/destek-vektor-regresyonu-ve-makineleri/

Yin, X., Wu, G., Wei, J., Shen, Y., Qi, H., & Yin, B. (2021). Deep learning on traffic prediction: Methods, analysis and future directions. *IEEE Transactions on Intelligent Transportation Systems*. https://arxiv.org/pdf/2004.08555.pdf

Yuan, J., Li, H., Wang, M., Liu, R., Li, C., & Wang, B. (2020, August). An OpenCV-based Framework for Table Information Extraction. In *2020 IEEE International Conference on Knowledge Graph (ICKG)* (pp. 621-628). IEEE.

Yuan, X., Martínez, J. F., Eckert, M., & López-Santidrián, L. (2016). An improved Otsu threshold segmentation method for underwater simultaneous localization and mapping-based navigation. *Sensors (Basel)*, *16*(7), 1148. doi:10.339016071148 PMID:27455279

Yu, J., Chang, G. L., Ho, H. W., & Liu, Y. (2008). Variation based online travel time prediction using clustered neural networks. *IEEE Conference on Intelligent Transportation Systems, Proceedings, ITSC*, 85–90. 10.1109/ITSC.2008.4732594

Yukihiro, H., Yasunori, E., & Sadaaki, M. (2008). Support Vector Machine for Data with Tolerance based on Hard-Margin and Soft-Margin. *2008 IEEE International Conference on Fuzzy System*, 750-755.

Yu, V. L., & Madoff, L. C. (2004). ProMED-mail: An early warning system for emerging diseases. *Clinical Infectious Diseases*, *39*(2), 227–232. doi:10.1086/422003 PMID:15307032

Zahedi, G., Karami, Z., & Yaghoobi, H. (2009). Prediction of hydrate formation temperature by both statistical models and artificial neural network approaches. *Energy Conversion and Management*, *50*(8), 2052–2059. doi:10.1016/j.enconman.2009.04.005

Zantalis, F., Koulouras, G., Karabetsos, S., & Kandris, D. (2019). A review of machine learning and IoT in smart transportation. *Future Internet*, *11*(4), 1–23. doi:10.3390/fi11040094

ZareNezhad, B., & Aminian, A. (2012). Accurate prediction of sour gas hydrate equilibrium dissociation conditions by using an adaptive neuro fuzzy inference system. *Energy Conversion and Management*, *57*, 143–147. doi:10.1016/j.enconman.2011.12.021

Zenati, H., Foo, C. S., Lecouat, B., Manek, G., & Chandrasekhar, V. R. (2018). *Efficient gan-based anomaly detection*. arXiv preprint arXiv:1802.06222.

Zeni, M., & Weldemariam, K. (2017). Extracting information from newspaper archives in Africa. *IBM Journal of Research and Development*, *61*(6), 12–1. doi:10.1147/JRD.2017.2742706

Zhang, P. G. (2003, January). Time series forecasting using a hybrid ARIMA and neural network model. *Neurocomputing*, *50*, 159–175. doi:10.1016/S0925-2312(01)00702-0

Zhang, Q., Wang, H., Yoon, S. W., Won, D., & Srihari, K. (2019). Lung nodule diagnosis on 3D computed tomography images using deep convolutional neural networks. *Procedia Manufacturing*, *39*, 363–370. doi:10.1016/j.promfg.2020.01.375

Zhan, Y., Tan, K. H., Ji, G., & Tseng, L. C. (2018). A Big Data Framework for Facilitating Product Innovation Processes. *Business Process Management Journal*, (270), 577–595.

Zhao, Y., Wood, E. P., Mirin, N., Vedanthan, R., Cook, S. H., & Chunara, R. (2020). *Machine Learning for Integrating Social Determinants in Cardiovascular Disease Prediction Models: A Systematic Review*. Cold Spring Harbor Laboratory. doi:10.1101/2020.09.11.20192989

Zheng, H., Chen, X., & Chen, X. M. (2019). How Does On-Demand Ridesplitting Influence Vehicle Use and Purchase Willingness? A Case Study in Hangzhou, China. *IEEE Intelligent Transportation Systems Magazine*, *11*(3), 143–157. doi:10.1109/MITS.2019.2919503

Zheng, J., Lin, D., Gao, Z., Wang, S., He, M., & Fan, J. (2020). Deep learning assisted efficient AdaBoost algorithm for breast cancer detection and early diagnosis. *IEEE Access: Practical Innovations, Open Solutions*, *8*, 96946–96954. doi:10.1109/ACCESS.2020.2993536

Zheng, J., Yang, D., Zhu, Y., Gu, W., Zheng, B., Bai, C., Zhao, L., Shi, H., Hu, J., Lu, S., Shi, W., & Wang, N. (2020). Pulmonary nodule risk classification in adenocarcinoma from CT images using deep CNN with scale transfer module. *IET Image Processing*, *14*(8), 1481–1489. doi:10.1049/iet-ipr.2019.0248

Zheng, S., Guo, J., Cui, X., Veldhuis, R. N. J., Oudkerk, M., & van Ooijen, P. M. A. (2019). Automatic pulmonary nodule detection in CT scans using convolutional neural networks based on maximum intensity projection. *IEEE Transactions on Medical Imaging*, *39*(3), 797–805. doi:10.1109/TMI.2019.2935553 PMID:31425026

Zhong, X., Tang, J., & Yepes, A. J. (2019, September). Publaynet: largest dataset ever for document layout analysis. In *2019 International Conference on Document Analysis and Recognition (ICDAR)* (pp. 1015-1022). IEEE. 10.1109/ICDAR.2019.00166

Zia, B., Juan, Z., Zhou, X., Xiao, N., Wang, J., & Khan, A. (2020). Classification of malignant and benign lung nodule and prediction of image label class using multi-deep model. *International Journal of Advanced Computer Science and Applications*, *11*(3), 35–41. doi:10.14569/IJACSA.2020.0110305

Ziouzios, D., Tsiktsiris, D., Baras, N., & Dasygenis, M. (2020). A Distributed Architecture for Smart Recycling Using Machine Learning. *Future Internet*, *12*(9), 141. doi:10.3390/fi12090141

Zoph, B., Vasudevan, V., Shlens, J., & Le, Q. V. (2018). Learning transferable architectures for scalable image recognition. *Proceedings of the IEEE Conference on Computer Vision and Pattern Recognition*, 8697–8710. 10.1109/CVPR.2018.00907

About the Contributors

Vishnu S. Pendyala is with the Department of Applied Data Science at SJSU. He is the chair of IEEE Computer Society, Silicon Valley Chapter. He has over two decades of experience with software industry leaders like Cisco and Synopsys in the Silicon Valley, USA. During his recent 3-year term as an ACM Distinguished speaker and before that as a researcher and industry expert, he gave numerous (50+) invited talks. He holds MBA in Finance and PhD, MS, and BE degrees in Computer Engineering from US and Indian universities. Dr. Pendyala taught a one-week course sponsored by the Ministry of Human Resource Development (MHRD), Government of India, under the GIAN program in 2017 to faculty from all over the country and delivered the keynote in a similar program sponsored by AICTE, Government of India in 2022. Dr. Pendyala's book, "Veracity of Big Data: Machine Learning and Other Approaches to Verifying Truthfulness" made it to several libraries, including those of MIT, Stanford, CMU, and internationally. Dr. Pendyala served on the Board of Directors, Silicon Valley Engineering Council during 2018-2019. As an undergrad, he received the Ramanujan memorial gold medal at State Math Olympiad.

* * *

Serdar Akyol is a Software Engineer with experienced on Machine Learning. He works as a Machine Learning Engineer. His work focuses specifically on Natural Language Processing. He loves work and research remotely.

Ali Ayci was born in Ankara in 1977 and completed his undergraduate, graduate and doctorate studies in Business Administration. Dr. Ali Ayci, who has been working in the private sector for a while, has worked in different units of KOSGEB since 2003 and has worked in various domestic and international missions and projects. Dr. Ali Ayci is an international entrepreneurship instructor and give lectures marketing, innovation and entrepreneurship courses at universities and he has researched businesses in 23 countries, primarily in the United States, Belgium, Japan, France and Ireland, and his marketing and entrepreneurship-oriented works have been featured in many publications in Turkey and abroad. Dr. Ali Ayci has been worked as an SME Specialist at SME Development Org. of Turkey (KOSGEB) and he is involved in the preparation and implementation of national and international projects for the integration of Syrians in Turkey. As of September 2020, he has been working at Ankara Yıldırım Beyazıt University, Faculty of Business Administration. During his working life, he mentored many businesses and took part in the evaluation of many projects. As of November 25, 2021, he has been working as an Associate Professor.

Veysel Gökhan Aydin received his MS in Numerical Methods from the Ondokuz Mayıs University in 2020. He also worked as a data analyst in a research company for a while. During his MS, he worked on regression analysis and multi-criteria decision-making methods in social sciences. In 2020, he started his PhD in Numerical Methods at Ondokuz Mayıs University. He works on machine learning and artificial intelligence.

Elif Bulut completed her undergraduate education in statistic department in 2000. She received her MS in statistics in 2003 with the thesis "A review on analytic methods for regression models for longitudinal discrete responses and an application". She finished PhD in 2010 in statistics, with her study named "Model selection methods for multivariate linear partial least squares regression". She worked as an assistant in the business department and started to work as an Asst. Prof. Dr. in the business department in 2011. She is still working as an Asst. Prof. Dr. in the business department. She has publications on regression, multivariate statistics and machine learning. She is a consultant in MS and PhD programs.

Basak Buluz Komecoglu graduated from Istanbul Aydın University Mathematics-Computer and Computer Engineering Departments by completing the double major program. Then, she completed her master's degree in Gebze Technical University Computer Engineering Department with the thesis study "Graph Mining Approach in Modeling Academic Success". She has been continuing PhD at Gebze Technical University Computer Engineering Department since 2018. During her undergraduate, graduate and doctorate education, she has carried out many studies on machine learning, and now she continues her studies by concentrating on natural language processing. She worked as a lecturer at Istanbul Aydın University Anadolu Bil Vocational School for more than 6 years and also served as the Program Head of the Computer Programming (English) Program for 5 years. As of February 2020, she started to work as a research assistant at Gebze Technical University, Institute of Information Technologies.

R. S. Jadon is Professor in Dept. Computer Science & Engineering, Madhav Institute of Technology and Science Gwalior. He is having over 30 years of teaching experience in various capacities in the Institute. Dr. Jadon has done his Ph.D. in Computer Science and Engineering from IIT Delhi. He has guided 12 Ph.D. Scholars in Computer Science. He is having 80 Research publications in various International and National Journals and conferences of repute. His research interests include Artificial Intelligence and Machine Learning, video data processing, image processing, computer vision and soft computing.

Muhammad Ayoub Kamal Kaimkhani is pursuing PhD in (Information Technology), from the Malaysian Institute of Information Technology University Kuala Lumpur, Kuala Lumpur, Malaysia. He received his Master of Engineering degree in Information Technology and Bachelor of Engineering degree in Computer System Engineering from Mehran University of Engineering and Technology in 2015, 2012 respectively. He is working with IoBM as a lecturer in the computer science department. Prior to joining IoBM, he worked as a lecturer at ILMA university. He has published 9 research articles in national and international research journals including 1 HEC W category research article. His areas of research are Low-power wide area network (LPWAN), fifth-generation communication (5G), internet of things (IoT), machine to machine communication (M2M), machine learning (ML), and artificial intelligence (AI).

Poonam Khanna is a Doctorate of Philosophy in Food Science and Nutrition, working as an Associate Professor of Nutrition in the Department of Community Medicine and School of Public Health, PGIMER, Chandigarh. She is the recipient of the National Nutrition Award from the Nutrition and Natural Health Sciences Association (NNHSA) for her contributions to community nutrition (2019). She is a technical expert for the "State Technical advisory group for Anemia Mukt Haryana, Data Safety & Monitoring Board (DSMB)for pesticide control and "Strengthening the Supplementary Nutrition Programme (SNP)". Her primary research areas are food safety, maternal and child health and public health nutrition. She is actively engaged in training street food vendors, a project initiated with the Punjab government for capacity building and training of street food vendors on food safety. She monitors and supervises nutrition programs such as ICDS, Mid-Day Meal and Village Health, and Sanitation and Nutrition Committees (VHSNC) in Punjab. She has been a pioneer in nutrition and nutrition education, where she has worked to improve the nutritional status of malnourished children in rural areas of Punjab and the slums of Haryana. She is a skilled researcher and has been handling key research projects in her field practice area, to name a few Village Child Health and Nutrition Project, Community Based Management for Prevention and Control of Anemia and Community-Based Group Intervention to Promote Psychological and Nutrition WellBeing in Single Parent Children, Comprehensive National Nutrition Survey (CNNS) funded by UNICEF, IAVI, NHM, ICMR, DST, GHAI, and WCD Haryana. She is a life member of the Indian Public Health Association (IPHA), Association for Health System Analysis and Strengthening (AHSAS), Nutrition Society India (NSI), Indian Dietetic Association (IDA), World NCD Federation (WNF), and Strategic Institute of Public Health Education And Research (SIPHER) Global.

Hammad Khawar received his M.S. degree in Telecommunication and Networking from Bahria University, Karachi, Pakistan, in 2011. In 2009, he was awarded a B.S. degree in Electronic Engineering at Sir Syed University of Engineering and Technology (SSUET), Karachi, Pakistan. He has worked as a faculty member in different recognized institutes and universities of Pakistan. He is currently working as Lecturer at Baqai Institute of Information Technology (BIIT), Baqai Medical University, Pakistan. His research interests include embedded systems, wireless sensor networks, IoT, machine learning, and web development.

Yavuz Komecoglu worked as a software developer by developing web applications for corporate companies for 4 years. With his master's degree, he has worked on image processing and computer vision problems such as classification of remotely sensed hyperspectral images, object classification and object tracking with deep learning algorithms for the last 5 years and he continues his studies. Currently, he continues to develop products for the media monitoring center by working on natural language processing and image processing in the research and development team at Kodiks. While sharing the technical experiences he has learned as a blog post, he takes an active role in the Artificial Intelligence Research Initiative team, where they contribute to bringing together valuable resources in the field of artificial intelligence and deep learning in their country and producing Turkish content in this field.

Anupama Kumari is a Chemical Engineering final year PhD student at the Indian Institute of Technology Roorkee. She has submitted her PhD thesis on the topic "Studies on the Formation and Dissociation of Gas Hydrates in Porous Sediments" at the Indian Institute of Technology, Roorkee. She has worked on the project entitled "Development of Thermo Catalytic Technique for Gas Production from Hydrate Bearing Sediments" since December 2017. This project was funded by Gas Hydrate Research and Technology Centre, Oil and Natural Gas Corporation Limited. In the project, her research work was to perform experiments on the formation and dissociation of gas hydrates in porous sediments. For this, she has designed an experimental equipment, in which the dissociation of gas hydrates can be performed through Microwave or thermo-catalytic reactions. During her PhD, she performed various experiments on the formation and dissociation of gas hydrates and also performed kinetic modelling on the experimental results. She has also worked on the simulation and modelling of gas hydrates formation and dissociation. She also performed the thermodynamic modelling of gas hydrate formation to predict the phase equilibrium conditions of gas hydrates. During her PhD, one patent is granted and the second one is in review as the first inventor. She has published seven research papers in reputed journals and seven research papers at international conferences.

Savitesh Kushwaha has a Master's and M.Phil. degree in Biological Anthropology from the University of Delhi, India. He is presently working on precision nutrition in type 2 diabetes at the Postgraduate Institute of Medical Education and Research (PGIMER), Chandigarh, India. The work involves genetic analysis and dietary intervention planning using a machine learning approach. He is also working on machine learning techniques in disease prediction and screening using national-level survey datasets.

Mukund Madhaw is a self-employed person who wishes to pursue further. He is currently involved in the research work based on the gas hydrates. He studied the equilibrium conditions of gas hydrates in pure water, sea water and in the presence or absence of different inhibitors and promoters. He is currently working on the development of different thermodynamic model for the prediction of phase equilibrium data of gas hydrates. Currently, he developed the thermodynamic model for the gas hydrates using the Artificial Neural Network and Least Square Vector Machine through MATLAB. He submitted the book chapter based on Artificial Neural Network for the publication in IGI-Global and a research paper based on Least Square Vector Machine. He also compared the results obtained through these developed thermodynamic models with the results obtained by the available correlations for the prediction of phase equilibrium data of gas hydrates.

Saritha Podali is a Compliance Data Quality Analyst at Lyft, San Francisco, with a strong background in Quality Assurance for business intelligence applications, data platforms, and machine learning solutions. She holds a Master's degree in Data Analytics from San Jose State University in California, and a Bachelor's degree in Information Science & Engineering from PES Institute of Technology in India. Wearable technology for continuous health monitoring and data-driven AI applications in healthcare are her primary research interests. Biomechanics and injury management are areas that interest her personally.

Manaswini Pradhan received B.E. in Computer Science and Engineering, M.Tech in Computer Science from Utkal University, Odisha, India, and Ph.D. degree in the field of Information and Communication Technology from Fakir Mohan University, Odisha. Currently she is working as an Assistant Professor in P.G. Department of Information and Communication Technology, Fakir Mohan University, Orissa, India. She has been in the teaching profession for the last eighteen, and during this period she also has acquired research experience in the area of Artificial Neural Network, Data-mining, and other topics in the broad subject of Information & Communication Technology. She has been awarded research projects by Department of Science & Technology, Govt. of India, and UGC, New Delhi. She has a published research papers in national, & international journals, a book chapter published by Taylor &

Francis, Springer, IBI Global and presented papers in various conferences. She is involved in guiding M.Tech/M.Phil Computer Science scholars in the field of data mining, neural networks, bio-informatics, and application of ICT in healthcare management. She has had shorter stays at several Computing departments in China, USA. Her research aptitude and acumen is of very high order.

Ranjit Sahu is working as Associate Professor in the Department of Burns and Plastic Surgery, AIIMS, Bhubaneswar, Odisha, India. His research interests are in medical sciences. Apart from teaching, he has keen interest in the applications of artificial intelligence(AI) for the disease diagnosis, detection,, prediction, prevention and cure. He has published many peer reviewed articles and research papers in national and international journals of repute. His researches are of very high quality having significant scientific contribution in medical field applicable for the modern society.

Parul Saxena has obtained her Master in Computer Applications (First Division with Distinctions) from Institute of Technology and Management, Gwalior. She secured First position in MCA, 2007, from Institute of Technology and Management, Gwalior. She has been working as Assistant Professor in CSE & IT, Incharge of Dance Club at Madhav Institute of Technology and Science Gwalior (MITS), an Autonomous Institute, Madhya Pradesh, India. She possesses fourteen years teaching experience of Post Graduate and Under Graduate classes. Eight papers have been published in various international and national journals and conferences. She attended fifty workshops. Her broad area of interest includes Computer Vision & Image Processing. She is a life member of the International Association of Engineers (IAENG), Institute of Electronics and Telecommunication Engineers (IETE) and IEEE.

Jayesh Soni is a Ph.D. candidate in the Knight School of Computing and Information Sciences department at Florida International University, Miami. The primary focus of his research is to detect anomalies at the system level by leveraging Artificial Intelligence techniques. His research interests include Cyber Security, Big Data, and Parallel Processing. His research is funded by the Department Of Defense, Test Resource Management Center.

Tariq Rahim Soomro, Acting Rector, Professor of Computer Science and Dean at College of Computer Science & Information Systems, Institute of Business Management, has received BSc (Hons) and M.Sc degrees in Computer Science from the University of Sindh, Jamshoro, Pakistan, and his Ph.D. in Computer Applications from Zhejiang University, Hangzhou, China. He has more than 27 years of extensive and diverse experience as an administrator, computer programmer, researcher, and teacher. As an administrator, He served as Coordinator, Head of Department, Head of Faculty, Dean of Faculty, Head of Academic Affairs, Acting Rector and has wide experience in accreditation-related matters, including ABET, NCEAC, HEC Pakistan, and Ministry of Higher Education and Scientific Research, United Arab Emirates (UAE). He is also an IEEE Computer Society Distinguished Visitor (2021–2023). His research focuses on GIS, IDNs, Big Data, Cybersecurity, Distance Education, E-Commerce, Multimedia, UNICODE, WAP, P2P, Bioinformatics, ITIL, Cloud Computing, Green Computing, IoT, Quality of Software, Telemedicine, VoIP, Databases, Programming, and Higher Education. He has published in these areas with over 100 peer-reviewed papers. He is actively involved in community services in the research field. He is a Member Editorial Board of "Journal of Geosciences and Geomatics" and "Journal of Software Engineering" also is Member Advisory Committee "Journal of Information and Communication Technology". He also served as a Technical Program Committee Member of several international conferences and Journals. He is a Senior Member of IEEE, IEEE computer society, and IEEE Geosciences & RS Society since 2005 and IEEE Member since 1999. Member Project Management Institute (PMI) since 2007. Senior Member, International Association of Computer Science and Information Technology (IACSIT) since 2012. Life Member, Computer Society of Pakistan (CSP) since 1999. Global Member, Internet Society (ISOC) the USA since 2006 and Member ACM since 2019. He has been an active member of IEEE Karachi Section (Region 10), served as Chair GOLD Affinity Group and Member Executive Committee 2014, branch councilor. He is a member of the Task Force on Arabic Script IDNs by the Middle East Strategy Working Group (MESWG) of ICANN. He also received the ISOC Fellowship to the IETF for the 68th Internet Engineering Task Force (IETF) Meeting.

Rachana Srivastava is presently working as Program Officer at the Department of Community Medicine and School of Public Health, PGIMER, Chandigarh. She is PhD in Food and Nutrition from Punjab Agricultural University Ludhiana (2010) and was the recipient of an ICAR-Junior research fellowship (AIR-4) during her master's. She was a WoS-B fellow from the Department of Science and Technology, New Delhi, at the Department of Community Medicine and School of Public Health, PGIMER, Chandigarh (2019-2021) for the project "Development and evaluation of smartphone nutrition application for mothers of under five-year age children". She received the best poster award at IAPSMCON21 for her poster "Assessment of egg quality, food safety and hygiene practices among commercial and non-commercial poultry farms of Barwala district of Panchkula, Haryana". Her primary research areas are maternal and child nutrition, geriatric nutrition, food security, anaemia, and food safety. Her E-Goshthi and E-rasoi sessions are new ways of creating nutrition-related awareness among mothers. She has worked on several nutrition-related projects for the Indian council of medical research (ICMR) in New Delhi and the National Dairy Research Institute (NDRI) Karnal. She is a resource faculty for training CDPOs and ACDPOs at NIPCCD and house mothers and fathers at Child Protection Unit Chandigarh. She has published in several widely circulating Journals. In terms of community engagement and consultancy services, she is actively engaged with Poshan Abhiyaan and Anganwadis of Chandigarh.

Shivam Tyagi is a dynamic professional with more than eight years of industry and research experience. Currently, he is part of the Payments Team as SDE, which is revolutionizing payments CX at Amazon. Before this, he worked in Delhi Metro Rail Corporation as a Senior System Analyst, where he was leading the team of experts, working on the Networking and Telecommunication systems which help in serving millions of commuters every year. Awarded with Master degrees in VLSI Design and Software Engineering, Shivam has very diverse experience in the fields of software development, data science, network security, telecommunications and hardware design. He is an avid researcher and has been a part of research work in the fields of data science and topology network design for the MPSoCs. His work on 3D topologies for MPSoCs has been published in IEEE, T&F, and Indersince journals. Shivam has been identified as Davidson Student Scholar by San Jose State University for his exceptional research work in the field of MPSoC design for neural networks. He enjoys working on projects that involve the application of concepts from different areas as there he can utilize his knowledge and experience.

Harsh Vats has a Master's degree in Biological Anthropology from the University of Delhi, India. He is currently working on maternal and child health at University of Delhi, Delhi, India. The work involves longitudinal assessment of maternal factors on neonatal outcomes using a machine learning approach. He is also using national-level survey datasets for disease prediction and screening using machine learning techniques.

Burcu Yilmaz is an assistant professor in Institute of Information Technologies at the Gebze Technical University. She received her PhD degree in computer science from the Gebze Institute of Technology in 2010. Burcu is conducting research in data mining, machine learning, natural language processing, deep learning, graph mining, graph neural networks and social network analysis.

Index

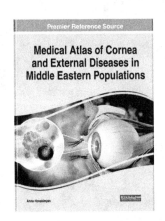
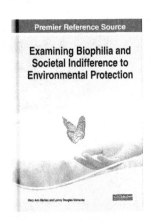
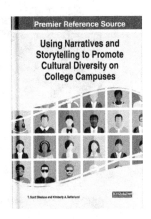

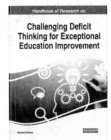

Printed in the United States
by Baker & Taylor Publisher Services